J. FENIMORE COOPER

THE WAYS OF THE HOUR

ALAN SUTTON PUBLISHING LIMITED

First published in 1850

First published in this edition in the United Kingdom in 1996
Alan Sutton Publishing Limited
Phoenix Mill • Far Thrupp • Stroud • Gloucestershire

British Library Cataloguing in Publication Data

A catalogue record for this book is available from the British Library.

ISBN 0-7509-1158-1

Cover picture: detail from Anticipation *by T. Desmarel (nineteenth century) (Bonham's, London/Bridgeman Art Library, London)*

Typeset in 10/11 Bembo.
Typesetting and origination by
Alan Sutton Publishing Limited.
Printed in Great Britain by
The Guernsey Press Company Limited,
Guernsey, Channel Islands.

BIOGRAPHICAL NOTE

JAMES FENIMORE COOPER (1789–1851) was born into a wealthy family and grew up at Otsego Hall, Cooperstown, his father's large property in New York State. After school in Albany, he spent two years at Yale before going to sea for five years, first as a foremast hand and then as a midshipman in the navy. Cooper married into a noted Westchester family, who had been loyalists during the War of Independence, and set up as a farmer on the family lands. Legend has it that Cooper wrote his first novel, *Precaution*, in 1820, to prove to his wife that he could outdo a contemporary female writer, but it seems probable that financial pressures also played a part in determining his ambition to turn novelist. Over the following thirty years Cooper produced an astonishing number and variety of works of fiction, ranging in subject from the experience of a patriotic spy in the Revolution (*The Spy*, 1821); the Leatherstocking frontier series which brought him fame; and political intrigue in early Venice (*The Bravo*, 1831). *The Ways of the Hour*, concerning criminal law, was written late in his career, in 1850, when he was working on the Putnam Author's Revised Edition of his writings. It is clearly related to his defence of the landowners' position in the Albany Anti-Rent Wars in the preceding decade. Cooper died in 1851, at Cooperstown.

Writings of James Fenimore Cooper in chronological order:

1820 *Precaution*
1821 *The Spy*
1823 *The Pioneers*
1824 *The Pilot*
1825 *Lionel Lincoln*
1826 *The Last of the Mohicans*
1827 *The Prairie*
      The Red Rover
1828 *Notions of the Americans*
1829 *The Wept of Wish-ton-Wish*
1831 *The Bravo*
1832 *The Heidenmauer*

1833 *The Headsman*
1834 *A Letter to his Countrymen*
1835 *The Monikins*
1838 *Homeward Bound*
      Home As Found
      The American Democrat
1839 *History of the Navy of the United States*
1840 *The Pathfinder*
      Mercedes of Castile
1841 *The Deerslayer*
1842 *The Two Admirals*
      The Wing-and-Wing
1843 *Wyandotté*
1844 *Afloat and Ashore*
      Miles Wallingford
1845 *Satanstoe*
1846 *The Chainbearer*
      The Redskins
1847 *The Crater*
1848 *Jack Tier*
      The Oak Openings
1849 *The Sea Lions*
1850 *The Ways of the Hour*

Allan Lloyd Smith
University of East Anglia

CHAPTER I

Mar. My lord Aumerle, is Harry Hereford armed?
Aum. Yea, at all points; and longs to enter in.

King Richard II.

In one respect, there is a visible improvement in the goodly town of Manhattan, and that is in its architecture. Of its growth, there has never been any question, while many have disputed its pretension to improvement. A vast expansion of mediocrity, though useful and imposing, rarely satisfies either the judgment or the taste; those who possess these qualities requiring a nearer approach to what is excellent, than can ever be found beneath the term just mentioned.

A town which is built of red bricks, that are faced with white marble, the whole garnished with green blinds, can never have but one outward sign — that of tawdry vulgarity. But this radical defect is slowly disappearing from the streets of Manhattan; and those who build, are getting to understand that architecture, like statuary, will not admit of strong contrasts in colours. Horace Walpole tells us of a certain old Lord Pembroke who blackened the eyes of the gods and goddesses in the celebrated gallery at Wilton, and prided himself on the achievement, as if he had been another Phidias. There have been thousands of those who have laboured in the spirit of this Earl of Pembroke in the streets of all the American towns; but travelling, hints, books, and example, are slowly effecting a change; and whole squares may now be seen in which the eye rests with satisfaction on blinds, facings, and bricks, all brought to the same pleasing, sober, architectural tint. We regard this as the first step in advance that has been made in the right direction, so far as the outward aspect of the town is concerned, and look forward with hope to the day when Manhattan shall have banished its rag-fair finery altogether, and the place will become as remarkable for the chaste simplicity of its streets, as they have hitherto been for their marked want of taste.

With this great town, mottled as it is, in people as well as in hues, with its native population collected from all parts of this vast republic, and its European representatives, amounting to scores of thousands, we shall have something to do in the succeeding pages. Our researches, however, will be bestowed more on things moral than on things physical; and we shall endeavour to carry the reader with us through scenes that, we regret to say, are far more characteristic than novel.

In one of the cross streets that communicate with Broadway, and below Canal, stands a dwelling that is obnoxious to all the charges of bad taste to which there has already been allusion, as well as to certain others that have not yet been named at all. A quarter of a century since, or within the first twenty years of its own existence, the house in question would have been regarded as decidedly patrician, though it is now lost amid the thousands of similar abodes that have arisen since its own construction. There it stands, with its red bricks, periodically painted redder; its marble facings, making a livery of red turned up with white; its green blinds, its high stoop, its half-buried and low basement, and all its neatness and comfort, notwithstanding its flagrant architectural sins. Into this building we now propose to enter at the very early hour of eight in the morning.

The principal floor was divided, as usual, between a dining and a drawing-room, with large communicating doors. This was the stereotyped construction of all Manhattanese dwellings of any pretension, a quarter of a century since; and that of Mr Thomas Dunscomb, the owner and occupant of the house in question, had been built in rigid conformity with the fashion of its day. 'Squire Dunscomb, as this gentleman was termed in all the adjacent country counties, where he was well known as a reliable and sound legal adviser; Mr Thomas Dunscomb, as he was styled by various single ladies, who wondered he never married; or Tom Dunscomb, as he was familiarly called by a herd of unyoked youths, all of whom were turned of sixty, was a capital fellow in each of his many characters. As a lawyer, he was as near the top of the bar as a man can be, who never had any pretensions to be an orator, and whose longest effort seldom exceeded half an hour. Should the plan of placing eloquence in hobbles reach our own bar, his habit of condensing, his trick of getting *multum in parvo*, may yet bring him to the very summit; for he will have an immense advantage over those who, resembling a country buck at a town ball, need the whole field to cut their flourishes in. As a man of the world, he was well-bred, though a little cynical, very agreeable, most especially with the ladies, and quite familiar with all the better habits of the best-toned circles of the place. As a boon companion, Tom Dunscomb was an immense favourite, being particularly warm-hearted, and always ready for any extra eating or drinking. In addition to these leading qualities, Dunscomb was known to be rich, having inherited a very tolerable estate, as well as having added much to his means by a large and lucrative practice. If to these circumstances we add that of a very prepossessing personal appearance, in which age was very green, the reader has all that is necessary for an introduction to one of our principal characters.

Though a bachelor, Mr Dunscomb did not live alone. He had a nephew and a niece in his family, the orphan children of a sister, who had now been dead many years. They bore the name of Wilmeter, which, in the family parlance, was almost always pronounced Wilmington. It was Jack Wilmington, and Sally Wilmington, at school, at home, and with all their intimates; though Mr John Wilmeter and Miss Sarah Wilmeter were often spoken of in their little out-door world; it being rather an affectation of the times to prove, in this manner, that one retains some knowledge of the spelling-book. We shall write the name as it is written by the parties themselves, forewarning the reader that if he desire to pronounce it by the same family standard, he must take the unauthorised spelling as a guide. We own ourselves to a strong predilection for old familiar sounds, as well as old familiar faces.

At half-past 8 a.m., of a fine morning, late in May, when the roses were beginning to show their tints amid the verdure of the leaves in Mr Dunscomb's yard, the three individuals just mentioned were at the breakfast-table of what it is the fashion of New York to term a dining-room. The windows were open, and a soft and fragrant air filled the apartment. We have said that Mr Dunscomb was affluent, and he chose to enjoy his means, not à la Manhattan, in idle competition with the nouveaux riches, but in a more quiet and rational way. His father had occupied lots, 'running through,' as it is termed; building his house on one street and his stables on the other; leaving himself a space in the rear of the former, that was prodigious for a town so squeezed into parallelograms of twenty-five feet by a hundred. This open space was of the usual breadth, but it actually measured a hundred and fifty feet in length, an area that would have almost justified its being termed a 'park,' in the nomenclature of the town. This yard Sarah had caused to be well garnished with shrubbery, and, for its dimensions, it was really a sort of oasis in that wilderness of bricks.

The family was not alone that morning. A certain Michael Millington was a guest of Jack's, and seemingly quite at home in the little circle. The business of eating and drinking was pretty well through with, though each of the four cups had its remains of tea or coffee, and Sarah sat stirring hers idly, while her soft eyes were turned with interest on the countenances of the two young men. The last had a sheet of writing-paper lying between them, and their heads were close together, as both studied that which was written on it in pencil. As for Mr Dunscomb himself, he was fairly surrounded by documents of one sort and another. Two or three of the morning papers, glanced at but not read, lay opened on the floor; on each side of his plate was a brief, or some lease or release; while a copy of the new and much talked of code was in his hand. As we say in our American English, Mr Dunscomb was 'emphatically' a common-law lawyer; and, as our transatlantic brethren would remark in their sometime cockney dialect, he was not at all 'agreeable' to this great innovation on 'the perfection of human reason.' He muttered occasionally as he read, and now and then he laid down the book, and seemed to muse. All this, however, was quite lost on Sarah, whose soft blue eyes still rested on the interested countenances of the two young men. At length Jack seized the paper, and wrote a line or two hurriedly, with his pencil.

'There, Mike,' he said, in a tone of self-gratulation, 'I think *that* will do!'

'It has one merit of a good toast,' answered the friend, a little doubtingly; 'it is sententious.'

'As all toasts ought to be. If we are to have this dinner, and the speeches, and all the usual publications afterwards, I choose that we should appear with some little credit. Pray, sir,' raising his eyes to his uncle, and his voice to correspond, 'what do you think of it now?'

'Just as I always have, Jack. It will never do at all. Justice would halt miserably under such a system of practice. Some of the forms of pleadings are infernal, if pleadings they can be called at all. I detest even the names they give their proceedings – complaints and answers!'

'They are certainly not as formidable to the ear,' returned Jack, a little saucily, 'as rebutters and sur-rebutters. But I was not thinking of the code, sir; I was asking your opinion of my new toast.'

'Even a fee could not extract an opinion, unless I heard it read.'

'Well, sir, here it is: "The Constitution of the United States, the palladium of our civil and religious liberties." Now, I do not think I can much better that, Uncle Tom!'

'I'm very sorry to hear you say so, Jack.'

'Why so, sir? I'm sure it is good American sentiment; and what is more, it has a flavour of the old English principles that you so much admire, about it, too. Why do you dislike it, sir?'

'For several reasons – it would be commonplace, which a toast should never be, were it true; but there happens not to be a word of truth in your sentiment, sonorous as it may sound in your ears.'

'Not true! Does not the constitution guarantee to the citizen religious liberty?'

'Not a bit of it.'

'You amaze me, sir! Why, here, just listen to its language, if you please.'

Hereupon Jack opened a book, and read the clause on which he relied to confute one of the ablest constitutional lawyers and clearest heads in America. Not that Mr Dunscomb was what is called an 'expounder,' great or small; but he never made a mistake on the subject in hand, and had often caused the best of the 'expounders' to retrace their steps. He was an original thinker, but of the safest and most useful sort; one who distinguished between the *institutions* of England and America, while he submitted to the fair application of minor principles that are so common to both. As for his nephew, he knew no more of the great instrument he held in his hand, than he had gleaned from ill-digested newspaper remarks, vapid speeches in Congress, and the erroneous notions that float about the country, coming from 'nobody knows whom,' and leading literally to nothing. The ignorance that prevails on such subjects is really astounding, when one remembers the great number of battles that are annually fought over this much-neglected compact.

'Ay, here is the clause – just please to hear it, sir,' continued Jack: – '"Congress shall make no law respecting an establishment of religion, or prohibiting the free exercise thereof; or abridging the freedom of speech, or of the press; or the right of the people peaceably to assemble, and to petition the government for a redress of grievances." There, I think that will go far towards justifying the whole toast, Mike!'

This was said a little triumphantly, and not a little confidently. The only answer Mr Dunscomb condescended to make, was an expressive 'Umph!' As for Michael Millington, he was a little timid about expressing an opinion, and that for two reasons; he had often experienced Mr Dunscomb's superior wisdom, and he knew that Sarah heard all that passed.

'I wish your uncle would lay aside that code for a minute, Jack, and let us know what he thinks of our authorities,' said Michael, in an under tone.

'Come, Uncle Tom,' cried the more hardy nephew; 'come out of your reserve, and face the constitution of your country. Even Sarah can see that, for once, *we* are right, and that my toast is of proof.'

'It is a very good proof-*sheet*, Jack, not only of your own mind, but of half the minds in the country. Ranker nonsense cannot be uttered, however, than to say that the Constitution of the United States is the palladium of anything in which civil or religious liberty is concerned.'

'You do not dispute the fidelity of my quotation, sir?'

'By no means. The clause you read is a very useless exhibition of certain facts that existed just as distinctly before it was framed, as they do to-day. Congress had no power to make an established religion, or abridge the freedom of speech, or that of the press, or the right of the people to petition, before that amendment was introduced, and consequently the clause itself is supererogatory. You take nothing by your motion, Jack.'

'I do not understand you, sir. To me, it seems that I have the best of it.'

'Congress has no power but what has been conceded to it directly, or by necessary connection. Now, there happens to be nothing said about granting any such authority to Congress, and consequently the prohibition is not necessary. But, admitting that Congress did really possess the power to establish a religion previously to the adoption of this amendment, the constitution would not prove a palladium to religious liberty, unless it prohibited everybody else from meddling with the opinions of the citizen. Any State of this Union that pleases, may establish a religion, and compel its citizens to support it.'

'Why, sir, our own state constitution has a provision similar to this, to prevent it.'

'Very true; but our own state constitution, can be altered in this behalf, without asking permission of any one but our own people. I think that even Sarah will understand that the United States is no palladium of religious liberty, if it cannot prevent a state from establishing Mohamedanism, as soon as a few forms can be complied with.'

Sarah coloured, glanced timidly at Michael Millington, but made no reply. She did not understand much of what she had just heard, though rather an intelligent girl, but had hoped that Jack and his friend were nearer right than was likely to turn out to be the case. Jack, himself, being a young limb of the law, comprehended what his uncle meant, and had the grace to colour, too, at the manner in which he had manifested his ignorance of the great national compact. With a view to relieve himself from his dilemma, he cried, with a ready dexterity, –

'Well, since this won't do, I must try the jury. "The trial by jury, the palladium of our liberties." How do you like that, sir?'

'Worse than the other, boy. God protect the country that has no better shield against wrong, than that which a jury can hold before it.'

Jack looked at Michael, and Michael looked at Jack; while Sarah looked at both in turn.

'You surely will not deny, sir, that the trial by jury is one of the most precious of the gifts received from our ancestors?' said the first, a little categorically, Sarah brightening up at this question, as if she fancied that her brother had now got on solid ground.

'Your question cannot be answered in a breath, Jack,' returned the uncle. 'The trial by jury *was* undoubtedly a most precious boon bestowed on a people among whom there existed an hereditary ruling power, on the abuses of which it was often a most salutary check.'

'Well, sir, is it not the same check here; assuring to the citizens independent justice?'

'Who compose the ruling power in America, Jack?'

'The people, to be sure, sir.'

'And who the jurors?'

'The people, too, I suppose,' answered the nephew, hesitating a little before he replied.

'Well, let us suppose a citizen has a conflict of rights with the public, which is the government, who will compose the tribunal that is to decide the question?'

'A jury, to be sure, sir. The trial by jury is guaranteed by the constitution to us all.'

'Ay,' said Mr Dunscomb, smiling, 'much as are our religious and political liberties. But according to your own admission, this is very much like making one of the parties a judge in his own case. A. insists that he has a right to certain lands, for instance, which the public claims for itself. In such a case, part of the public compose the tribunal.'

'But is it not true, Mr Dunscomb,' put in Millington, 'that the popular prejudice is usually against government, in all cases with private citizens?'

Sarah's face looked brighter now than ever, for she felt sure that Mike, as her brother familiarly called his friend, had asked a most apposite question.

'Certainly; you are right as to particular sets of cases, but wrong as to others. In a commercial town like this, the feeling is against government in all cases connected with the collection of the revenue, I admit; and you will see that the fact makes against the trial by jury in another form, since a judge ought to be strictly impartial; above all prejudice whatever.'

'But, uncle, a judge and a jury are surely very different things,' cried Sarah, secretly impelled to come to Michael's rescue, though she scarce knew anything of the merits of the subject.

'Quite right, my dear,' the uncle answered, nodding his head kindly, casting a glance at his niece that caused her to blush under the consciousness of being fully understood in her motives, if not in her remark. 'Most profoundly right; a judge and a juror ought to be very different things. What I most complain of is the fact that the jurors are fast becoming judges. Nay, by George! they are getting to be legislators, making the law as well as interpreting it. How often does it happen, now-a-days, that the court tell the jury that such is the law, and the jury comes in with a verdict which tells the court that such is *not* the law? This is an every-day occurrence, in the actual state of public opinion.'

'But the court will order a new trial, if the verdict is against law and evidence,' said Michael, determined that Sarah should be sustained.

'Ay, and another jury will be quite likely to sustain the old one. No – no – the trial by jury is no more a palladium of our liberties than the Constitution of the United States.'

'Who, or what is, then, sir?' demanded Jack.

'God! Yes, the Deity, in his Divine Providence; if anything is to save us. It may not be his pleasure to let us perish, for it would seem that some great plan for the advancement of civilization is going on, and it may be a part of it to make us important agents. All things regarded, I am much inclined to believe such is the fact. But, did the result depend on us, miserable instruments in the Almighty hands as we are, woeful would be the end!'

'You do not look at things *couleur de rose*, uncle Tom,' Sarah smilingly observed.

'Because I am not a young lady of twenty, who is well satisfied with herself and her advantages. There is but one character for which I have a greater contempt than that of a senseless grumbler, who regards all things *à tort et à travers*, and who cries, there is nothing good in the world.'

'And what is the exception, sir?'

'The man who is puffed up with conceit, and fancies all around him perfection, when so much of it is the reverse; who ever shouts "liberty," in the midst of the direst oppression.'

'But direst oppression is certainly no term to be applied to anything in New York!'

'You think not? What would you say to a state of society in which the law is available to one class of citizens only, in the way of compulsion, and not at all in the way of protection?'

'I do not understand you, sir; here, it is our boast that all are protected alike.'

'Ay, so far as *boasting* goes, we are beyond reproach. But what are the facts? Here is a man that owes money. The law is appealed to, to compel payment. Verdict is rendered, and execution issued. The sheriff enters his house, and sells his very furniture to extort the amount of the debt from him.'

'That is his misfortune, sir. Such things must happen to all debtors who cannot, or will not, pay.'

'If this were true I should have nothing to say. Imagine this very debtor to be also a creditor; to have debts due to him, of many times the sums that he owes, but which the law will *not* aid him in collecting. For him, the law is all oppression – no protection.'

'But surely, Uncle Tom, nothing of the sort exists here!'

'Surely, Miss Sarah Wilmeter, such things *do* exist here in practice, whatever may be the theory on the subject; what is more, they exist under the influence of facts that are directly connected with the working of the institutions. My case is not suppositious at all, but real. Several landlords have quite recently felt all the rigours of the law as debtors, when it was a dead letter to them, in their character of creditors. This has actually happened, and that more than once; and it might happen a hundred times, were the landlords more in debt. In the latter case it would be an every-day occurrence.'

'What, sir,' exclaimed Michael Millington; 'the law enforce when it will not protect?'

'That it does, young man, in many interests that I could point out to you. But here is as flagrant a case of unmitigated tyranny as can be cited against any country in Christendom. A citizen is sold out of house and home, under process of law, for debt; and when he asks for the use of the same process of law to collect his undeniable dues, it is, in effect, denied him. And this among the people who boast that their independence is derived from a spirit that would not be taxed! A people who are hourly shouting hosannas in honour of their justice!'

'It cannot be, Uncle Tom, that this is done, in terms,' cried the astounded nephew.

'If, by terms, you mean professions of justice, and liberty, and equal rights, they are fair enough; in all those particulars we are irreproachable. As "*professors*" no people can talk more volubly or nearer to the point – I allude only to facts.'

'But these facts may be explained – qualified – are not as flagrant as they seem under your statement?'

'In what manner?'

'Why, sir, this is but a *temporary* evil, perhaps.'

'It has lasted, not days, nor weeks, nor months, but years. What is more, it is an evil that has not occurred in a corner, where it might be overlooked; but it exists within ten miles of your capital, in plain sight of your legislators, and owes its impunity solely to their profound deference to votes. In a word, it is a part of the political system under which we live; and that far more so than any disposition to tyranny that might happen to manifest itself in an individual king.'

'Do not the tenants who refuse to pay, fancy that their landlords have no right to their estates, and does not the whole difficulty arise from misapprehension?' asked Michael, a little timidly.

'What would that have to do with the service of process, if it were true? When a sheriff's officer comes among these men, they take his authority from him, and send him away empty. Rights are to be determined only by the law, since they are derived from the law; and he who meets the law at the threshold, and denies it entrance, can never seriously pretend that he resists because the other party has no claims. No, no, young gentleman – this is all a fetch. The evil is of years' standing; it is of the character of the direst oppression, and of oppression of the worst sort, that of many oppressing a few; cases in which the sufferer is cut off from sympathy, as you can see by the apathy of the community, which is singing hosannas to its own perfection, while this great wrong is committed under its very nose. Had a landlord oppressed his tenants, their clamour would have made itself heard throughout the land. The worst feature in the case is that which connects the whole thing so very obviously with the ordinary working of the institutions. If it were merely human covetousness struggling against the institutions, the last might prove the strongest; but it is cupidity, of the basest and most transparent nature, *using* the institutions themselves to effect its purpose.'

'I am surprised that something was not done by the last convention to meet the evil!' said Jack, who was much struck with the enormity of the wrong placed before his eyes in its simplest form, as it had been by his direct-minded and clear-headed kinsman.

'That is because you do not know what a convention has got to be. Its object is to push principles into impracticable extremes, under the silly pretension of progress, and not to abate evils. I made a suggestion myself, to certain members of that convention, which, in my poor judgment, would have effectually cured this disease; but no member had the courage to propose it. Doubtless, it would have been useless had it been otherwise.'

'It was worth the trial, if such were likely to be its result. What was your plan, sir?'

'Simply to disfranchise any district in which the law could not be enforced by means of combinations of its people. On application to the highest court of the state, an order might be granted that no polls should be held in one, or more, towns, or counties, in which combinations existed of a force sufficient to prevent the laws from being put in force. Nothing could be more just than to say that men who will not obey the law shall not have a voice in making it; and to me it really seems that some such provision would be the best possible expedient to check this growing evil. It would be choking the enemy with his own food.'

'Why was it not done, sir?'

'Simply because our sages were speculating on votes, and not on principles. They will talk to you like so many books touching the vices of all foreign systems, but are ready to die in defence of the perfection of their own.'

'Why was it necessary to make a new constitution the other day,' asked Sarah, innocently, 'if the old one was so very excellent?'

'Sure enough – the answer might puzzle wiser heads than yours, child. Perfection requires a great deal of tinkering, in this country. We scarcely adopt one plan that shall secure everybody's rights and liberties, than another is broached to secure some newly-discovered rights and liberties. With the dire example before them of the manner in which the elective franchise is abused in this anti-rent movement, the sages of the land have just given to the mass the election of judges; as beautiful a scheme for making the bench coalesce with the jury-box as human ingenuity could invent!'

As all present knew that Mr Dunscomb was bitterly opposed to the new constitution, no one was surprised at this last assertion. It did create wonder, however, in the minds of all three of the ingenuous young persons, when the fact – an undeniable and most crushing one it is too, so far as any high pretension to true liberty is concerned – was plainly laid before them, that citizens were to be found in New York *against* whom the law was rigidly enforced, while it was powerless in their behalf. We have never known this aspect of the case presented to any mind, that it did not evidently produce a deep impression *for the moment*; but, alas! 'what is everybody's business is nobody's business,' and few care for the violation of a principle when the wrong does not affect themselves. These young folk were, like all around them, unconscious even that they dwelt in a community in which so atrocious a wrong was daily done, and, for the moment, were startled when the truth was placed before their eyes. The young men, near friends, and by certain signs likely to be even more closely united, were much addicted to speculating on the course of events, as they conceived them to be tending in other countries. Michael Millington, in particular, was a good deal of a general politician, having delivered several orations, in which he had laid some stress on the greater happiness of the people of this much-favoured land over those of all other countries, and especially on the subject of equal rights. He was too young yet to have learned the wholesome truth, that equality of rights in practice exists nowhere; the ingenuity and selfishness of man finding the means to pervert to narrow purposes the most cautious laws that have ever been adopted in furtherance of a principle that would seem to be so just. Nor did he know that the Bible contains all the wisdom and justice, transmitted as Divine precepts, that are necessary to secure to every man all that it is desirable to possess here below.

The conversation was terminated by the entrance of a fourth colloquist, in the person of Edward McBrain, M.D., who was not only the family physician, but the bosom friend of the lawyer. The two liked each other on the principle of loving their opposites. One was a bachelor, the other was about to marry his third wife; one was a little of a cynic, the other much of a philanthropist; one distrustful of human nature, the other too confiding; one cautious to excess, the other absolutely impetuous, whenever anything strongly interested his feelings. They were alike in being Manhattanese by birth, somewhat a novelty in a New Yorker; in being equally graduates of Columbia, and classmates; in a real love of their fellow-creatures; in goodness of heart and in integrity. Had either been wanting in these last great essentials, the other could not have endured him.

CHAPTER II

O change! – stupendous change!
There lies the soulless clod;
The sun eternal breaks –
The new immortal wakes –
Wakes with his God.

MRS SOUTHEY.

As Dr McBrain entered the room, the two young men and Sarah, after saluting him like very familiar acquaintances, passed out into what the niece called her 'garden.' Here she immediately set her scissors at work in clipping roses, violets, and other early flowers, to make bouquets for her companions. That of Michael was much the largest and most tasteful; but this her brother did not remark, as he was in a brown study, reflecting on the singularity of the circumstance that the Constitution of the United States should not be the 'palladium of his political and religious liberties.' Jack saw, for the first time in his life, that a true knowledge of the constitution was not to be found floating about in society, and that 'there was more in the nature of the great national compact than was dreamt of in his philosophy.'

'Well, Ned,' said the lawyer, holding out his hand kindly, but not rising from his chair, 'what has brought you here so early? Has old Martha spoilt your tea?'

'Not at all; I have paid this visit, as it might be, professionally.'

'Professionally! I never was better in my life; and set you down as a false prophet, or no doctor, if you like that better, for the gout has not even given a premonitory hint, this spring; and I hope, now I have given up Sauterne altogether, and take but four glasses of Madeira at dinner——'

'Two too many.'

'I'll engage to drink nothing but sherry, Ned, if you'll consent to four, and that without any of those forbidding looks.'

'Agreed; sherry has less acidity, and consequently less gout than Madeira. But my business here this morning, though professional, does not relate to my craft, but to your own.'

'To the law? Now I take another look at you, I do see trouble in your physiognomy: am I not to draw the marriage settlements, after all?'

'There are to be none. The new law gives a woman the entire control of all her property, they tell me, and I suppose she will not expect the control of mine.'

'Umph! Yes; she ought to be satisfied with things as they are, for she will remain mistress of all her cups and saucers, even, – ay, and of her houses and lands, in the bargain. Hang me, if I would ever marry, when the contract is so one-sided.'

'You never did, when the contract was t'other-sided. For my part, Tom, I'm disposed to leave a woman mistress of her own. The experiment is worth the trial, if it be only to see the use she will make of her money.'

'You are always experimenting among the women, and are about to try a third wife. Thank Heaven, I've got on sixty years, quite comfortably, without even one.'

'You have only half-lived your life. No old bachelor – meaning a man after forty – knows anything of real happiness. It is necessary to be married, in order to be truly happy.'

'I wonder you did not add, "two or three times." But you may make this new contract with greater confidence than either of the others. I suppose you have seen this new divorce project that is, or has been, before the legislature?'

'Divorce! I trust no such foolish law will pass. This calling marriage a "contract," too, is what I never liked. It is something far more than a "contract," in my view of the matter.'

'Still, that is what the law considers it to be. Get out of this new scrape, Ned, if you can with any honour, and remain an independent freeman for the rest of your days. I dare say the widow could soon find some other amorous youth to place her affections on. It matters not much whom a woman loves, provided she love. Of this, I'm certain, from seeing the sort of animals so many *do* love.'

'Nonsense; a bachelor talking of love, or matrimony, usually makes a zany of himself. It is *terra incognita* to you, my boy, and the less you say about it the better. You are the only human being, Tom, I ever met with who has not, some time or other, been in love. I really believe you never knew what the passion is.'

'I fell in love, early in life, with a certain my lord Coke, and have remained true to my first attachment. Besides, I saw I had an intimate friend who would do all the marrying that was necessary for two, or even for three; so I determined from the first to remain single. A man has only to be firm, and he may set Cupid at defiance. It is not so with women, I do believe; it is part of their nature to love, else would no woman admire you at your time of life.'

'I don't know that – I am by no means sure of that. Each time I had the misfortune to become a widower, I was just as determined to pass the remainder of my days in reflecting on the worth of her I had lost, as you can be to remain a bachelor; but somehow or other, I don't pretend to account for it, not a year passed before I have found inducements to enter into new engagements. It is a blessed thing, is matrimony, and I am resolved not to continue single an hour longer than is necessary.'

Dunscomb laughed out at the earnest manner in which his friend spoke, though conversations, like this we have been relating, were of frequent occurrence between them.

'The same old sixpence, Ned! A Benedict as a boy, a Benedict as a man, and a Benedict as a dotard——'

'Dotard! My good fellow, let me tell you——'

'Poh! I don't desire to hear it. But as you came on business connected with the law, and that business is not a marriage settlement, what is it? Does old Kingsborough maintain his right to the Harlem lot?'

'No, he has given the claim up, at last. My business, Tom, is of a very different nature. What are we coming to, and what is to be the end of it all?'

As the doctor looked far more than he expressed, Dunscomb was struck with his manner. The Siamese twins scarce understand each other's impulses and wishes better than these two men comprehended each other's feelings; and Tom saw at once that Ned was now very much in earnest.

'Coming to!' repeated Dunscomb. 'Do you mean the new code, or the "Woman-hold-the-Purse Law," as I call it? I don't believe you look far enough ahead to foresee all the damnable consequences of an elective judiciary.'

'It is not that – this, or that – I do not mean codes, constitutions or pin-money. What is the *country* coming to, Tom Dunscomb? – that is the question I ask.'

'Well, and has the country nothing to do with constitutions, codes, and elective judges? I can tell you, Master Ned McBrain, M.D., that if the patient is to be saved at all, it must be by means of the judiciary; and I do not like the advice that has just been called in.'

'You are a croaker. They tell me the new judges are reasonably good.'

'"Reasonably" is an expressive word. The new judges are *old* judges, in part, and in so much they do pretty well, by chance. Some of the new judges are excellent – but one of the very best men on the whole bench was run against one of the worst men who could have been put in his place. At the next heat, I fear the bad fellow will get the track. If you do not mean what I have mentioned, what do you mean?'

'I mean the increase of crime – the murders, arsons, robberies, and other abominations that seem to take root among us, like so many exotics transplanted to a genial soil.'

'"Exotics" and "genial" be hanged! Men are alike everywhere. No one but a fool ever supposed that a republic is to stand or fall by its virtue.'

'Yet the common opinion is that such must be the final test of our institutions.'

'Jack has just been talking nonsense on this subject, and now *you* must come to aid him. But what has your business with me, this morning, to do with the general depreciation in morals?'

'A great deal, as you will allow, when you come to hear my story.'

Dr McBrain then proceeded forthwith to deliver himself of the matter which weighed so heavily on his mind. He was the owner of a small place in an adjoining county, where it was his custom to pass as much time, during the pleasant months, as a very extensive practice in town would allow. This was not much, it is true, though the worthy physician so contrived matters, that his visits to Timbully, as the place was called, if not long, were tolerably numerous. A kind-hearted, as well as a reasonably-affluent man, he never denied his professional services to his country neighbours, who eagerly asked his advice whenever there was need of it. This portion of the doctor's practice flourished on two accounts, – one being his known skill, and the other his known generosity. In a word, Dr McBrain never received any compensation for his advice from any in the immediate neighbourhood of his country residence. This rendered him exceedingly popular; and he might have been sent to Albany, but for a little cold water that was thrown on the project by a shrewd patriot, who suggested that while the physician was attending to affairs of state, he could not be administering to the ailings of his Timbully neighbours. This may have checked the doctor's advancement, but it did not impair his popularity.

Now it happened that the bridegroom-expectant had been out to Timbully, a distance of less than fifteen miles from his house in Bleecker Street, with a view to order matters for the reception of the bride, it being the intention of the couple that were soon to be united, to pass a few days there immediately after the ceremony was performed. It was while at his place, attending to this most important duty, that an express came from the county town, requiring his presence before the coroner, where he was expected to give his evidence as a medical man. It seems that a house had been burned, and its owners, an aged couple, had been burnt in it. The remains of the bodies had been found, and an inquest was about to be held on them. This was pretty much all that the messenger could tell, though he rather thought that it was suspected the house had been set on fire, and the old people consequently murdered.

As a matter of course, Dr McBrain obeyed the summons. A county town in America is often little more than a hamlet, though in New York they are usually places of some greater pretensions. The state has now near a dozen incorporated cities with their mayors and aldermen, and, with one exception, we believe these are all county towns. Then come the incorporated villages, in which New York is fast getting to be rich, places containing from one to six or seven thousand souls, and which as a rule are steadily growing into respectable provincial towns. The largest of these usually contain 'the county buildings,' as it is the custom to express it. But in the older counties, immediately around the great commercial capital of the entire republic, these large villages do not always exist; or, when they do exist, are not sufficiently central to meet the transcendental justice of democratic equality – a quality that is sometimes of as exacting pretension as of real imbecility; as witness the remarks of Mr Dunscomb in our opening chapter.

The county buildings of —— happen to stand in a small village, or what is considered a small village, in the lower part of the state. As the events of this tale are so recent, and the localities so familiar to many persons, we choose to call this village 'Biberry,' and the county 'Dukes.' Such was once the name of a New York county, though the appellation has been dropped, and this not from any particular distaste for the strawberry leaves; 'Kings,' 'Queens,' and 'Duchess' having been wisely retained – wisely, as names should be as rarely changed as public convenience will allow.

Dr McBrain found the village of Biberry in a high state of excitement; one, indeed, of so intense a nature as to be far from favourable to the judicial inquiry that was then going on in the court-house. The old couple who were the sufferers in this affair had been much respected by all who knew them; he as a common-place, well-meaning man of no particular capacity, and she as a managing, discreet, pious woman, whose greatest failing was a neatness that was carried somewhat too near to ferocity. Nevertheless, Mrs Goodwin was generally even more respected than her husband, for she had the most mind, transacted most of the business of the family, and was habitually kind and attentive to every one who entered her dwelling; provided, always, that they wiped their feet on her mats, of which it was necessary to pass no less than six before the little parlour was reached, and did not spit on her carpet, or did not want any of her money. This popularity added greatly to the excitement; men, and women also, commonly feeling a stronger desire to investigate wrongs done to those they esteem than to investigate wrongs done to those concerning whom they are indifferent.

Dr McBrian found the charred remains of this unfortunate couple laid on a table in the court-house, the coroner in attendance, and a jury empanelled. Much of the evidence concerning the discovery of the fire had been gone through with, and was of a very simple character. Some one who was stirring earlier than common had seen the house in a bright blaze, had given the alarm, and had preceded the crowd from the village, on the road to the burning dwelling. The Goodwins had resided in a neat, retired cottage, at the distance of near two miles from Biberry, though in sight from the village; and by the time the first man from the latter reached the spot the roof had fallen in, and the materials were mostly consumed. A dozen or more of the nearest neighbours were collected around the ruins, and some articles of household furniture had been saved; but, on the whole, it was regarded as one of the most sudden and destructive fires ever known in that part of the country. When the engine arrived from the village, it played briskly on the fire, and was the means of soon reducing all within the outer walls, which were of stone, to a pile of blackened and smouldering wood. It was owing to this circumstance that any portion of the remains of the late owners of the house had been found, as was done in the manner thus described, in his testimony, by Peter Bacon, the person who had first given the alarm in Biberry.

'As soon as ever I seed it was Peter Goodwin's house that made the light,' continued this intelligent witness, in the course of his examination, 'I guv' the alarm, and started off on the run, to see what I could do. By the time I got to the top of Brudler's Hill I was fairly out of breath, I can tell you, Mr Coroner and Gentlemen of the Jury, and so I was obliged to pull up a bit. This guv' the fire a so much better sweep, and when I reached the spot, there was little chance for doing much good. We got out a chest of drawers; and the young woman who boarded with the Goodwins was helped down out of the window, and most of her clothes, I b'lieve, was saved, so far as I know.'

'Stop,' interrupted the coroner; 'there was a young woman in the house, you say.'

'Yes; what I call a young woman, or a gal like; though other some calls her a young woman. Waal, she was got out; and her clothes was got out; but nobody could get out the old folks. As soon as the ingyne come up we turned on the water, and that put out the fire about the quickest. Arter that we went to diggin', and soon found what folks call the remains, though to my notion there is little enough on 'em that is left.'

'You dug out the remains,' said the coroner, writing; 'in what state did you find them?'

'In what I call a pretty poor state; much as you see 'em there, on the table.'

'What has become of the young *lady* you have mentioned?' inquired the coroner, who as a public functionary, deemed it prudent to put all of the sex into the same general category.

'I can't tell you, 'squire; I never see'd her arter she was got out of the window.'

'Do you mean that she was the hired girl of the family, – or had the old lady no help?'

'I kinder think she was a boarder, like; one that paid her keepin',' answered the witness, who was not a person to draw very nice distinctions, as the reader will have no difficulty in conceiving, from his dialect. 'It seems to me I heer'n tell of another help in the Goodwin family – a sorter Jarman, or Irish lady.'

'Was any such woman seen about the house this morning, when the ruins were searched?'

'Not as I'ner. We turned over the brands and sticks, until we come across the old folks; then everybody seemed to think the work was pretty much done.'

'In what state, or situation, were these remains found?'

'Burnt to a crisp, just as you see 'em, 'squire, as I said afore; a pretty poor state for human beings to be in.'

'But where were they lying, and were they near each other?'

'Close together. Their heads, if a body can call them black lookin' skulls heads at all, almost touched, if they didn't quite touch, each other; their feet lay further apart.'

'Do you think you could place the skeletons in the same manner, as respects each other, as they were when you first saw them? But let me first inquire, if any other person is present, who saw these remains before they had been removed?'

Several men, and one or two women, who were in attendance to be examined, now came forward, and stated that they had seen the remains in the condition in which they had been originally found. Selecting the most intelligent of the party, after questioning them all round, the coroner desired that the skeletons might be laid, as near as might be, in the same relative positions as those in which they had been found. There was a difference of opinion among the witnesses, as to several of the minor particulars, though all admitted that the bodies, or what remained of them, had been found quite close together; their heads touching, and their feet some little distance apart. In this manner, then, were the skeletons now disposed; the arrangement being completed just as Dr McBrain entered the court-room. The coroner immediately directed the witnesses to stand aside, while the physician made an examination of the crisped bones.

'This looks like foul play!' exclaimed the doctor, almost as soon as his examination commenced. 'The skulls of both these persons have been fractured; and, if this be anything near the positions in which the skeletons were found, as it would seem, by the same blow.'

He then pointed out to the coroner and jury, a small fracture in the frontal bone of each skull, and so nearly in a line as to render his conjecture highly probable. This discovery gave an entirely new colouring to the whole occurrence, and every one present began to speculate on the probability of arson and murder being connected with the unfortunate affair. The Goodwins were known to have lived at their ease, and the good woman, in particular, had the reputation of being a little miserly. As everything like order vanished temporarily from the court-room, and tongues were going in all directions, many things were related that were really of a suspicious character, especially by the women.

The coroner adjourned the investigation for the convenience of irregular conversation, in order to obtain useful clues to the succeeding inquiries.

'You say that old Mrs Goodwin had a good deal of specie?' inquired that functionary of a certain Mrs Pope, a widow woman, who had been free with her communications, and who very well might know more than the rest of the neighbours, from a very active propensity she had ever manifested, to look into the affairs of all around her. 'Did I understand you, that you had seen this money yourself?'

'Yes, sir; often and often. She kept it in a stocking of the old gentleman's, that was nothing but darns; so darny, like, that nobody could wear it. Mrs Goodwin wasn't a woman to put away anything that was of use. A clusser body wasn't to be found, anywhere near Biberry.'

'And some of this money was gold, I think I heard you say. A stocking pretty well filled with gold and silver.'

'The foot was cramming full, when I saw it, and that wasn't three months since. I can't say there was any great matter in the leg. Yes, there was gold in it, too. She showed me the stocking the last time I saw it, on purpose to ask me what might be the valie of a piece of gold that was almost as big as half-a-dollar.'

'Should you know that piece of gold, were you to see it again?'

'That I should. I didn't know its name, or its valie, for I never seed so big a piece afore; but I told Mrs Goodwin I thought it must be ra'al Californy. Them's about now, they tell me, and I hope poor folks will come in for their share. Old as I am – that is, not so very old neither – but such as I am, I never had a piece of gold in my life.'

'You cannot tell, then, the name of this particular coin?'

'I couldn't; if I was to have it for the telling, I couldn't. It wasn't a five dollar piece; that I know – for the old lady had a good many of *them*, and this was much larger, and yellower, too; better gold, I conclude.'

The coroner was accustomed to garrulous, sight-seeing females, and knew how to humour them.

'Where did Mrs Goodwin keep her specie?' he inquired. 'If you saw her put the stocking away, you must know its usual place of deposit.'

'In her chest of drawers,' answered the woman eagerly. 'That very chest of drawers which was got out of the house, as sound as the day it went into it, and has been brought down into the village for safe keeping.'

All this was so, and measures were taken to push the investigation further, and in that direction. Three or four young men, willing volunteers in such a cause, brought the bureau into the court-room, and the coroner directed that each of the drawers should be publicly opened in the presence of the jurors. The widow was first sworn, however, and testified regularly to the matter of the stocking, the money, and the place of usual deposit.

'Ah! you'll not find it there,' observed Mrs Pope, as the village cabinet-maker applied a key, the wards of which happened to fit those of the locks in question. 'She kept her money in the lowest drawer of all. I've seen her take the stocking out, first and last, at least a dozen times.'

The lower drawer was opened, accordingly. It contained female apparel, and a goodly store of such articles as were suited to the wants of a respectable woman in the fourth or fifth of the gradations into which all society so naturally, and unavoidably, divides itself. But there was no stocking full of darns, no silver, no gold. Mrs Pope's busy and nimble fingers were thrust hastily into an inner corner of the drawer, and a silk dress was unceremoniously opened, that having been the precise receptacle of the treasure as she had seen it last bestowed.

'It's gone!' exclaimed the woman. – 'Somebody must have taken it!'

A great deal was now thought to be established. The broken skulls, and the missing money, went near to establish a case of murder and robbery, in addition to the high crime of arson. Men who had worn solemn and grave countenances all that morning, now looked excited and earnest. The desire for a requiting justice was general and active, and the dead became doubly dear by means of their wrongs.

All this time, Dr McBrain had been attending exclusively to the part of the subject that most referred to his own profession. Of the fractures in the two skulls he was well assured, though the appearance of the remains was such as almost to baffle investigation. Of another important fact he was less certain. While all he heard prepared him to meet with the skeletons of a man and his wife, so far as he could judge, in the imperfect state in which they were laid before him, the bones were those of two females.

'Did you know this Mr Goodwin, Mr Coroner?' inquired the physician, breaking into the more regular examination with very little ceremony; 'or was he well known to any here?'

The coroner had no very accurate knowledge of the deceased, though every one of the jurors had been well acquainted with him. Several had known him all their lives.

'Was he a man of ordinary size?' asked the doctor.

'Very small. Not taller than his wife, who might be set down as quite a tall old lady.'

It often happens in Europe, especially in England, that the man and his wife are so nearly of a height, as to leave very little sensible difference in their statures; but it is a rare occurrence in this country. In America, the female is usually delicate, and of a comparatively small frame, while the average height of man is something beyond that of the European standard. It was a little out of the common way, therefore, to meet with a couple so nearly of a size, as these remains would make Goodwin and his wife to have been.

'These skeletons are very nearly of the same length,' resumed the doctor, after measuring them for the fifth time. 'The man could not have been much, if any, taller than his wife.'

'He was not,' answered a juror. 'Old Peter Goodwin could not have been more than five feet five, and Dorothy was all of that, I should think. When they came to meeting together, they looked much of a muchness.'

Now, there is nothing on which a prudent and regular physician is more cautious than in committing himself on unknown and uncertain ground. He has his theories, and his standard of opinions, usually well settled in his mind, and he is ever on the alert to protect and bolster them; seldom making any admission that may contravene either. He is apt to denounce the water cure, however surprising may have been its effects; and there is commonly but one of the 'opathies' to which he is in the least disposed to defer, and that is the particular 'opathy' on which he has moulded his practice. As for Dr McBrain, he belonged strictly to the allopathic school, and might be termed almost an ultra in his adherence to its laws, while the number of the new schools that were springing up around him, taught him caution, as well as great prudence, in the expression of his opinions. Give him a patient, and he went to work boldly, and with the decision and nerve of a physician accustomed to practice in an exaggerated climate; but place him before the public, as a theoretical man, and he was timid and wary. His friend Dunscomb had observed this peculiarity thirty years before the commencement of our tale, and had quite recently told him, 'You are bold in the only thing in which I am timid, Ned, and that is in making up to the women. If Mrs Updyke were a new-fangled theory, now, instead of an old-fashioned widow, as she is, hang me if I think you would have ever had the spirit to propose.' This peculiarity of temperament, and, perhaps, we might add of character, rendered Dr McBrain, now, very averse to saying, in the face of so much probability, and the statements of so many witnesses, that the multilated and charred skeletons that lay on the court-house table were those of two females, and not those of a man and his wife. It was certainly possible he might be mistaken; for the conflagration had made sad work of these poor emblems of mortality; but science has a clear eye, and the doctor was a skilful and practised anatomist. In his own mind, there were very few doubts on the subject.

As soon as the thoughtful physician found time to turn his attention on the countenances of those who composed the crowd in the court-room, he observed that nearly all eyes were bent on the person of one particular female, who sat apart, and was seemingly labouring under a shock of some sort or other, that materially affected her nerves. McBrain saw, at a glance, that this person belonged to a class every way superior to that of even the highest of those who pressed around the table. The face was concealed in a handkerchief, but the form was not only youthful but highly attractive. Small, delicate hands and feet could be seen; such hands and feet as we are all accustomed to see in an American girl who has been delicately brought up. Her dress was simple, and of studied modesty; but there was an air about *that*, which a little surprised the kind-hearted individual who was now so closely observing her.

The doctor had little difficulty in learning from those near him that this 'young woman,' so all in the crowd styled *her*, though it was their practice to term most girls, however humble their condition, 'ladies,' had been residing with the Goodwins for a few weeks, in the character of a boarder, as some asserted, while others affirmed it was as a *friend*. At all events, there was a mystery about her; and most of the girls of Biberry had called her proud, because she did not join in their frivolities, flirtations, and visits. It was true, no one had ever thought of discharging the duties of social life by calling on *her*, or in making the advances usual to well-bred people; but this makes little difference where there is a secret consciousness of inferiority, and of an inferiority that is felt while it is denied. Such things are of every-day occurrence, in country-life in particular, while American town-life is far from being exempt from the weakness. In older countries the laws of society are better respected.

It was now plain that the blight of suspicion had fallen on this unknown, and seemingly friendless girl. If the fire had been communicated intentionally, who so likely to be guilty as she? if the money was gone who had so many means of securing it as herself? These were questions that passed from one to another, until distrust gathered so much head that the coroner deemed it expedient to adjourn the inquest, while the proof might be collected, and offered in proper form.

Dr McBrain was, by nature, kind-hearted; then he could not easily get over that stubborn scientific fact, of both the skeletons having belonged to females. It is true that, admitting this to be the case, it threw very little light on the matter, and in no degree lessened any grounds of suspicion that might properly rest on the 'young woman;' but it separated him from the throng, and placed his mind in a sort of middle condition, in which he fancied it might be prudent, as well as charitable, to doubt. Perceiving that the crowd was dispersing, though not without much animated discussion in under-tones, and that the subject of all this conversation still remained in her solitary corner, apparently unconscious of what was going on, the worthy doctor approached the immovable figure, and spoke.

'You have come here as a witness, I presume,' he said, in a gentle tone; 'if so, your attendance just now will no longer be necessary, the coroner having adjourned the inquest until to-morrow afternoon.'

At the first sound of his voice the solitary female removed a fine cambric handkerchief from her face, and permitted her new companion to look upon it. We shall say nothing, here, touching that countenance or any other personal peculiarity, as a sufficiently minute description will be given in the next chapter, through the communications made by Dr McBrain to Dunscomb. Thanking her informant for his information, and exchanging a few brief sentences on the melancholy business which had brought both there, the young woman arose, made a slight but very graceful inclination of her body, and withdrew.

Dr McBrain's purpose was made up on the spot. He saw very plainly that a fierce current of suspicion was setting against this pleasing, and, as it seemed to him, friendless young creature; and he determined at once to hasten back to town and get his friend to go out to Biberry, without a moment's delay, that he might appear there that very afternoon in the character of counsel to the helpless.

CHAPTER III

I am informed thoroughly of the cause.
Which is the merchant here, and which the Jew?
Merchant of Venice.

Such was the substance of the communication that Doctor McBrain now made to his friend, Tom Dunscomb. The latter had listened with an interest he did not care to betray, and when the other was done he gaily cried –

'I'll tell the widow Updyke of you, Ned!'

'She knows the whole story already, and is very anxious lest you should have left town to go to the Rockland circuit, where she has been told you have an important case to try.'

'The cause goes over on account of the opposite counsel's being in the court of appeals. Ah's me! I have no pleasure in managing a cause since this Code of Procedure has innovated on all our comfortable and venerable modes of doing business. I believe I shall close up my affairs and retire as soon as I can bring all my old cases to a termination.'

'If you *can* bring those old cases to a termination, you will be the first lawyer who ever did.'

'Yes, it is true, Ned,' answered Dunscomb, coolly taking a pinch of snuff, 'you doctors *have* the advantage of us in this behalf; *your cases* certainly do not last for ever.'

'Enough of this, Tom – you will go to Biberry, I take it for granted.'

'You have forgotten the fee. Under the new code, compensation is a matter of previous agreement.'

'You shall have a pleasant excursion, over goods roads, in the month of May, in an easy carriage, and drawn by a pair of as spirited horses as ever trotted on the Third Avenue.'

'The animals you have just purchased in honour of Mrs Updyke, that is – Mrs McBrain that is to be,' touching the bell, and adding to the very respectable black who immediately answered the summons, 'Tell Master Jack and Miss Sarah I wish to see them. So, Ned, you have let the widow know all about it, and she does not pout or look distrustful; that is a good symptom, at least.'

'I would not marry a jealous woman, if I never had a wife!'

'Then you will never marry at all. Why, Dr McBrain, it is in the nature of woman to be distrustful – to be jealous – to fancy things that are merely figments of the brain.'

'You know nothing about them, and would be wisest to be silent; but here are the young people already, to ask your pleasure.'

'Sarah, my dear,' resumed the uncle, in a kind and affectionate tone of voice, one that the old bachelor almost universally held towards that particular relative, 'I must give you a little trouble. Go into my room, child, and put up, in my smallest travelling bag, a clean shirt, a handkerchief or two, three or four collars, and a change all round, for a short expedition into the country.'

'Country! Do you quit us to-day, sir?'

'Within an hour, at latest,' looking at his watch. 'If we leave the door at ten, we can reach Biberry before the inquest reassembles. You told those capital beasts of yours, Ned, to come here?'

'I told Stephen to give them a hint to that effect. You may rely on their punctuality.'

'Jack, you had better be of our party. I go on some legal business of importance, and it may be well for you to go along, in order to pick up an idea or two.'

'And why not Michael, also, sir? He has as much need of ideas as I have myself.'

A pretty general laugh succeeded, though Sarah, who was just quitting the room, did not join in it. She rather looked grave, as well as a little anxiously towards the last-named neophyte of the law.

'Shall we want any books, sir?' demanded the nephew.

'Why, yes – we will take the Code of Procedure. One can no more move without *that*, just now, than he can travel in some countries without a passport. Yes, put up the code, Jack, and we'll pick it to pieces as we trot along.'

'There is little need of that, sir, if what they say be true. I hear, from all quarters, that it is doing that for itself, on a gallop.'

'Shame on thee, lad – I have half a mind to banish thee to Philadelphia! But put up the code; thy joke can't be worse than that joke. As for Michael, he can accompany us if he wish it; but you must both be ready by ten. At ten, precisely, we quit my door, in the chariot of Phoebus, eh, Ned?'

'Call it what you please, so you do but go. Be active, young gentlemen, for we have no time to throw away. The jury meet again at two, and we have several hours of road before us. I will run round and look at my slate, and be here by the time you are ready.'

On this suggestion everybody was set in active motion. John went for his books, and to fill a small rubber bag for himself; Michael did the same, and Sarah was busy in her uncle's room. As for Dunscomb, he made the necessary disposition of some papers, wrote two or three notes, and held himself at the command of his friend. This affair was just the sort of professional business in which he liked to be engaged. Not that he had any sympathy with crime, for he was strongly averse to all communion with rogues; but it appeared to him, by the representations of the doctor, to be a mission of mercy. A solitary, young, unfriended female, accused, or suspected, of a most heinous crime, and looking around for a protector and an adviser, was an object too interesting for a man of his temperament to overlook, under the appeal that had been made. Still he was not the dupe of his feelings. All his coolness, sagacity, knowledge of human nature, and professional attainments, were just as active in him as they ever had been in his life. Two things he understood well: that we are much too often deceived by outward signs, mistaking character by means of a fair exterior and studied words, and that neither youth, beauty, sex, nor personal graces were infallible preventives of the worst offences, on the one hand; and that, on the other, men nurture distrust and suspicion, often until it grows too large to be concealed, by means of their own propensity to feed the imagination and to exaggerate. Against these two weaknesses he was now resolved to arm himself; and when the whole party drove from the door, our counsellor was as clear-headed and impartial, according to his own notion of the matter, as if he were a judge.

By this time the young men had obtained a general notion of the business they were on, and the very first subject that was started, on quitting the door, was in a question put by John Wilmeter, in continuation of a discussion that had been commenced between himself and his friend.

'Mike and I have a little difference of opinion, on a point connected with this matter, which I could wish you to settle for us, as an arbiter. On the supposition that you find reason to believe that this young woman has really committed these horrible crimes, what would be your duty in the case – to continue to befriend her, and advise her, and use your experience and talents in order to shield her against the penalties of the law, or to abandon her at once?'

'In plain English, Jack, you and your brother student wish to know whether I am to act as a palladium, or as a runagate, in this affair. As neophytes in your craft, it may be well to suggest to you, in the first place, that I have not yet been fee'd. I never knew a lawyer's conscience trouble him about questions in casuistry, until he had received something down.'

'But you can suppose that something paid, in this case, sir, and then answer our question.'

'This is just the case in which I can suppose nothing of the sort. Had McBrain given me to understand I was to meet a client, with a well-lined purse, who was accused of arson and murder, I would have seen him married to two women, at the same time, before I would have budged. It's the want of a fee that takes me out of town, this morning.'

'And the same want, I trust, sir, will stimulate you to solve our difficulty.'

The uncle laughed, and nodded his head, much as if he would say, 'Pretty well for *you*;' then he gave a thought to the point in professional ethics that had started up between his two students.

'This is a very old question with the profession, gentlemen,' Dunscomb answered, a little more gravely. 'You will find men who maintain that the lawyer has, morally, a right to do whatever his client would do; that he puts himself in the place of the man he defends, and is expected to do everything precisely as if he were the accused party himself. I rather think that some vague notion, quite as loose as this, prevails pretty generally among what one may call the minor moralists of the profession.'

'I confess, sir, that I have been given to understand that some such rule *ought* to govern our conduct,' said Michael Millington, who had been in Dunscomb's office only for the last six months.

'Then you have been very loosely and badly instructed in the duties of an advocate, Mr Michael. A more pernicious doctrine was never broached, or one better suited to make men scoundrels. Let a young man begin practice with such notions, and two or three thieves for clients will prepare him to commit petit larceny; and a case or two of perjury would render him an exquisite at an affidavit. No, my boys, here is your rule in this matter: an advocate has a *right* to do whatever his client has a *right* to do – not what his client *would* do.'

'Surely, sir, an advocate is justified in telling his client to plead not guilty, though guilty; and in aiding him to persuade a jury to acquit him, though satisfied himself he ought to be convicted!'

'You have got hold of the great point in the case, Jack, and one on which something may be said on both sides. The law is so indulgent as to permit an accused who has formally pleaded "guilty," thus making a distinct admission of his crime, to withdraw that plea and put in another of "not guilty." Now, had the same person made a similar admission *out* of court, and under circumstances that put threats or promises out of the question, the law would have accepted *that* admission as the best possible evidence of his guilt. It is evident, therefore, that an understanding exists, to which the justice of the country is a party, that a man, though guilty, shall get himself out of the scrape, if he can do so by legal means. No more importance is attached to the "not guilty" than to the "not at home" to a visitor; it being understood, by general convention, that neither means anything. Some persons are so squeamish as to cause their servants to say "they are engaged," by way of not telling a lie; but a lie consists in the intentional deception, and "not in" and "not guilty" mean no more, in the one case, than "you can't see my master," and in the other, than "I'll run the chances of a trial."'

'After all, sir, this is going pretty near the wind, in the way of morals.'

'It certainly is. The Christian man who has committed a crime ought not to attempt to deny it to his country, as he certainly cannot to his God. Yet, nine hundred and ninety-nine in a thousand of the most strait-laced Christians in the community would so deny their guilt, if arraigned. We must not tax poor human nature too heavily, though I think the common law contains many things, originating in a jealousy of hereditary power, that it is great folly for us to preserve. But, while we are thus settling principles we forget facts. You have told me nothing of your client, Ned.'

'What would you wish to know.'

'You called her young, I remember; what may be her precise age?'

'That is more than I know; somewhere between sixteen and five-and-twenty.'

'Five-and-twenty! Is she as old as that?'

'I rather think not; but I have been thinking much of her this morning, and I really do not remember to have seen another human being who is so difficult to describe.'

'She has eyes, of course?'

'Two, and very expressive they are; though, sworn, I could not tell their colour.'

'And hair?'

'In very great profusion; so much of it, and so very fine and shining, that it was the first thing about her person which I observed. But I have not the least notion of its colour.'

'Was it red?'

'No; nor yellow, nor golden, nor black, nor brown, – and yet a little of all blended together, I should say.'

'Ned, I'll tell the Widow Updyke of thee, thou rogue.'

'Tell her, in welcome. She has asked me all these questions herself, this very morning.'

'Oh, she has, has she? Umph! Woman never changes her nature. You cannot say anything about the eyes beyond the fact of their being very expressive?'

'And pleasing; more than that, even − engaging. Winning, is a better term.'

'Ned, you dog, you have never told the widow one-half!'

'Every syllable. I even went farther, and declared I had never beheld a countenance that, in so short an interview, made so deep an impression on me. If I were not to see this young woman again I should never forget the expression of her face; so spirited, so sad, so gentle, so feminine, and so very intelligent. It seemed to me to be what I should call an illuminated countenance.'

'Handsome?'

'Not unusually so, among our sweet American girls, except through the expression. That was really wonderful; though, you will remember, I saw her under very peculiar circumstances.'

'Oh, exceedingly peculiar. Dear old soul! what a thump she has given him! How were her mouth and her teeth? − complexion, stature, figure, and smile?'

'I can tell you little of all these. Her teeth are fine; for she gave me a faint smile, such as a lady is apt to give a man in quitting him, and I saw just enough of the teeth to know that they are exceedingly fine. You smile, young gentlemen, but *you* may have a care for your hearts, in good truth; for if this strange girl interests either of you one-half as much as she has interested me, she will be either Mrs John Wilmeter, or Mrs Michael Millington, within a twelvemonth.'

Michael looked very sure that she would never fill the last situation, which was already bespoke for Miss Sarah Wilmeter; and as for Jack, he laughed outright.

'We'll tell Mrs Updyke of him, when we get back, and break off that affair, at least,' cried the uncle, winking at the nephew, but in a way his friend should see him; 'then there will be one marriage the less in the world.'

'But is she a lady, doctor?' demanded John, after a short pause. 'My wife must have some trifling claims in that way, I can assure you.'

'As for family, education, association, and fortune, I can say nothing, − I know nothing. Yet will I take upon myself to say she *is* a lady, − and that in the strict signification of the term.'

'You are not serious now, Ned!' exclaimed the counsellor, quickly. 'Not a *bony fide*, as some of our gentlemen have it? You cannot mean *exactly* what you say.'

'I do though; and that literally.'

'And she suspected of arson and murder! Where are her connections and friends, – those who made her a lady? Why is she there alone, and, as you say, unfriended?'

'So it seemed to me. You might as well ask me why she is there at all. I know nothing of all this. I heard plenty of reasons in the street, why she ought to be distrusted, – nay, convicted; for the feeling against her had got to be intense, before I left Biberry; but no one could tell me whence she came, or why she was there.'

'Did you learn her name?'

'Yes; that was in every mouth, and I could not help hearing it. She was called Mary Monson by the people of Biberry – but I much doubt if that be her real name.'

'So your angel in disguise will have to be tried under an "alias!" That is not much in her favour, Ned. I shall ask no more questions, but wait patiently to see and judge for myself.'

The young men put a few more interrogatories, which were civilly answered, and then the subject was dropped. Well it has been said that 'God made the country; man made the town.' No one feels this more than he who has been shut up between walls of brick and stone for many months, on his first escape into the open, unfettered fields and winding pleasant roads. Thus was it now with Dunscomb. He had not been out of town since the previous summer, and great was his delight at smelling the fragrance of the orchards, and feasting his eyes on their beauties. All the other charms of the season came in aid of these, and when the carriage drove into the long, broad, and we might almost say single street of Biberry, Dunscomb in particular was in a most tranquil and pleasant state of mind. He had come out to assist a friendless woman, cheerfully and without a thought of the sacrifice, either as to time or money, though in reflecting on all the circumstances he began to have his doubts of the wisdom of the step he had taken. Nevertheless, he preserved his native calmness of manner and coolness of head.

Biberry was found to be in a state of high excitement. There were at least a dozen physicians collected there, all from the county, and five or six reporters had come from town. Rumours of all sorts were afloat, and Mary Monson was a name in every person's mouth. She had not been arrested, however, it having been deemed premature for that: but she was vigilantly watched, and two large trunks of which she was the mistress, as well as an oilskin-covered box of some size, if not absolutely seized, were so placed that their owner had no access to them. This state of things, however, did not seem to give the suspected girl any uneasiness; she was content with what a carpet-bag contained, and with which she said she was comfortable. It was a question with the wiseacres whether she knew that she was suspected or not.

Had Dunscomb yielded to McBrain's solicitations, he would have gone at once to the house in which Mary Monson was now lodged, but he preferred adopting a different course. He thought it the most prudent to be a looker-on, until after the next examination, which was now close at hand. Wary by long habit, and cool by temperament, he was disposed to observe the state of things before he committed himself. The presence of the reporters annoyed him; not that he stood in any dread of the low tyranny that is so apt to characterize this class of men, for no member of the bar had held them, and the puny efforts of many among them to build up and take away professional character, in greater contempt than he had done; but he disliked to have his name mixed up with a cause of this magnitude, unless he had made up his mind to go through with it. In this temper, then, no communication was held with Mary Monson, until they met, at the hour appointed for the inquest, in the court-house.

The room was crowded, at least twice as many having collected on this occasion as had got together on the sudden call of the previous examination. Dunscomb observed that the coroner looked grave, like a man who felt he had important business on his hands, while a stern expectation was the expression common to nearly all the others present. He was an utter stranger himself, even by sight, to every being present, his own party and two or three of the reporters excepted. These last no sooner observed him, however, than out came their little note-books, and the gold pens were at work scribbling something. It was probably a sentence to say, 'we observed among the crowd Thomas Dunscomb, Esq., the well-known counsel *from the city*;' but Dunscomb cared very little for such vulgarisms, and continued passive.

As soon as the inquest was organised, the coroner directed a physician of the neighbourhood to be put on the stand. It had gone forth that a 'city doctor' had intimated that neither of the skeletons was that of Peter Goodwin, and there was a common wish to confront him with a high country authority. It was while the medical man now in request was sent for, that McBrain pointed out to Dunscomb the person of Mary Monson. She sat in a corner different from that she had occupied the day before, seemingly for the same purpose or that of being alone. Alone she was not strictly, however, a respectable-looking female of middle age being at her side. This was a Mrs Jones, the wife of a clergyman, who had charitably offered the suspected young stranger a home under her own roof pending the investigation. It was thought generally that Mary Monson had but very vague notions of the distrust that rested on her, it being a part of the plan of those who were exercising all their wits to detect the criminal, that she was first to learn this fact in open court, and under circumstances likely to elicit some proofs of guilt. When Dunscomb learned this artifice, he saw how ungenerous and unmanly it was, readily imagined a dozen signs of weakness that a female might exhibit in such a strait that had no real connection with crime, and felt a strong disposition to seek an interview and put the suspected party on her guard. It was too late for this, however, just then; and he contented himself for the moment with studying such signs of character and consciousness as his native sagacity and long experience enabled him to detect.

Although nothing could be more simple or unpretending than the attire of Mary Monson, it was clearly that of a lady. Everything about her denoted that station, or origin; though everything about her, as Dunscomb fancied, also denoted a desire to bring herself down, as nearly as possible, to the level of those around her, most probably that she might not attract particular attention. Our lawyer did not exactly like this slight proof of management, and wished it were not so apparent. He could see the hands, feet, figure, hair, and general air of the female he was so strangely called on to make the subject of his investigations, but he could not yet see her face. The last was again covered with a cambric handkerchief, the hand which held it being ungloved. It was a pretty little American hand, white, well-proportioned, and delicate. It was clear that neither its proportions nor its colour had been changed by uses unsuited to its owner's sex or years. But it had no ring in this age of bejewelled fingers. It was the left hand, moreover, and the fourth finger, like all the rest, had no ornament or sign of matrimony. He inferred from this that the stranger was unmarried; one of the last things that a wife usually lays aside being her wedding-ring. The foot corresponded with the hand, and was decidedly the smallest, best-formed, and best-decorated foot in Biberry. John Wilmeter thought it the prettiest he had ever seen. It was not studiously exhibited, however, but rested naturally and gracefully in its proper place. The figure generally, so far as a capacious shawl would allow of its being seen, was pleasing, graceful, and a little remarkable for accuracy of proportions, as well as of attire.

Once or twice Mrs Jones spoke to her companion; and it was when answering some question thus put, that Dunscomb first got a glimpse of his intended client's face. The handkerchief was partly removed, and remained so long enough to enable him to make a few brief observations. It was then that he felt the perfect justice of his friend's description. It was an indescribable countenance, in all things but its effect; which was quite as marked on the lawyer, as it had been on the physician. But the arrival of Dr Coe put an end to these observations, and drew all eyes on that individual, who was immediately sworn. The customary preliminary questions were put to this witness, respecting his profession, length of practice, residence, &c., when the examination turned more on the matter immediately under investigation.

'You see those objects on the table, doctor?' said the coroner. 'What do you say they are?'

'*Ossa hominum*; human bones, much defaced and charred by heat.'

'Do you find any proof about them of violence committed, beyond the damage done by fire?'

'Certainly. There is the *os frontis* of each fractured by a blow; a common blow, as I should judge.'

'What do you mean, sir, by a common blow? An accidental, or an intentional blow?'

'By common blow, I mean that one blow did the damage to both *cranys*.'

'*Crany?* – how do you spell that word, doctor? Common folks get put out by foreign tongues.'

'Cranys, in the plural, sir. We say cran*ium* for *one* skull, and cranys for two.'

'I wonder what he would say for numskull?' whispered John to Michael.

'Yes, sir; I understand you, now. I trust the reporters will get it right.'

'Oh! they never make any mistakes, especially in legal proceedings,' quietly remarked Mr Dunscomb to the doctor. 'In matters of law and the constitution, they are of proof! Talk of letters on the constitution! What are equal to those that come to us, *hibernally*, as one may say, from Washington?'

'Hibernially would be the better word,' answered McBrain, in the same under tone.

'You ought to know; your grandfather was an Irishman, Ned. But listen to this examination.'

'And now, Dr Coe, have the goodness to look at these skeletons,' resumed the coroner, 'and tell us whether they belong to man, woman, or child. Whether they are the remains of adults, or of children.'

'Of adults, certainly. On that point, sir, I conceive there can be no doubt.'

'And as to the sex?'

'I should think that is equally clear. I have no doubt that one are the remains of Peter Goodwin, and the other those of his wife. Science can distinguish between the sexes, in ordinary cases, I allow; but this is a case in which science is at fault, for want of facts; and taking all the known circumstances into consideration, I have no hesitation in saying that, according to my best judgment, those are the remains of the missing man and woman – man and wife.'

'Am I to understand that you recognise the particular skeletons by any outward visible proofs?'

'Yes; there is the stature. Both of the deceased were well known to me; and I should say that, making the usual allowance for the absence of the *musculi*, the *pellis*, and other known substances——'

'Doctor, would it be just as agreeable to you to use the common dialect?' demanded a shrewd-looking farmer, one of the jury, who appeared equally amused and vexed at this display of learning.

'Certainly, sir – certainly, Mr Blore; *musculi* means muscles, and *pellis* is the skin. Abstract the muscles and skin, and the other intermediate substances, from the bones, and the apparent stature would be reduced as a matter of course. Making those allowances, I see in those skeletons the remains of Peter and Dorothy Goodwin. Of the fact, I entertain no manner of doubt.'

As Dr Coe was very sincere in what he said, he expressed himself somewhat earnestly. A great many eyes were turned triumphantly towards the stranger who had presumed to intimate that the bones of both the remains were those of women, when everybody in and about Biberry knew Peter Goodwin so well, and knew that his wife, if anything, was the taller of the two. No one in all that crowd doubted as to the fact, except McBrain and his friend; and the last doubted altogether on the faith of the doctor's science. He had never known him mistaken, though often examined in court, and was aware that the bar considered him one of the safest and surest witnesses they could employ in all cases of controverted facts.

Dr Coe's examination proceeded.

'Have you a direct knowledge of any of the circumstances connected with this fire?' demanded the coroner.

'A little, perhaps. I was called to visit a patient about midnight, and was obliged to pass directly before the door of Goodwin's house. The jury knows that it stood on a retired road, and that one would not be likely to meet with any person travelling it so early in the morning. I did pass, however, two men, who were walking very fast, and in the direction of Goodwin's. I could not see their faces, nor did I know them by their figures and movements. As I see everybody, and know almost everybody hereabouts, I concluded they were strangers. About four, I was on my return along the same road, and as my sulky rose to the top of Windy Hill, I got a view of Goodwin's house. The flames were just streaming out of the east end of the roof, and the little wing on that end of the building, in which the old folks slept, was in a bright blaze. The other end was not much injured; and I saw at an upper window the figure of a female – she resembled, as well as I could judge by that light, and at that distance, the young lady now present, and who is said to have occupied the chamber under the roof, in the old house, for some time past; though I can't say I have ever seen her there, unless I saw her then under the circumstances mentioned. The old people could not have been as ailing this spring as was common with them, as I do not remember to have been stopped by them once. They never were in the habit of sending for the doctor, but seldom let me go past the door without calling me in.'

'Did you see any one beside the figure of the female at the window?'

'Yes. There were two men beneath that window, and they appeared to me to be speaking to, or holding some sort of communication with the female. I saw gestures, and I saw one or two articles thrown out of the window. My view was only for a minute; and when I reached the house, a considerable crowd had collected, and I had no opportunity to observe particularly in a scene of such confusion.'

'Was the female still at the upper window when you reached the house?'

'No. I saw the lady now present standing near the burning building, and held by a man – Peter Davidson, I think it was – who told me she wanted to rush into the house to look for the old folks.'

'Did you see any efforts of that sort in her.'

'Certainly. She struggled to get away from Peter, and acted like a person who wished to rush into the burning building.'

'Were the struggles natural – or might they not have been affected?'

'They might. If it was acting, it was *good* acting. I have seen as good, however, in my life.'

The doctor had a meaning manner, that said more than his words. He spoke very low – so low as not to be audible to those who sat in the farther parts of the room; which will explain the perfect indifference to his testimony that was manifested by the subject of his remarks. An impression, however, was made on the jury, which was composed of men much disposed to push distrust to demonstration.

The coroner now thought it time to spring the principal mine, which had been carefully prepared during the recess in the investigation; and he ordered 'Mary Monson' to be called – a witness who had been regularly summoned to attend among the crowd of persons that had received similar notices.

CHAPTER IV

My deed's upon my head! I crave the law,
The penalty and forfeit of my bond.

Shylock.

The eyes of Dunscomb were fastened intently on the female stranger as she advanced to the place occupied by the witnesses. Her features denoted agitation, certainly; but he saw no traces of guilt. It seemed so improbable, moreover, that a young woman of her years and appearance should be guilty of so dark an offence, and that for money, too, that all the chances were in favour of her innocence. Still, there were suspicious circumstances, out of all question, connected with her situation; and he was too much experienced in the strange and unaccountable ways of crime not to be slow to form his conclusions.

The face of Mary Monson was now fully exposed; it being customary to cause female witnesses to remove their hats, in order that the jurors may observe their countenances. And what a countenance it was! Feminine, open, with scarce a trace of the ordinary passions about it, and illuminated from within as we have already intimated. The girl might have been twenty, though she afterwards stated her age to be a little more than twenty-one – perhaps the most interesting period of a female's existence. The features were not particularly regular, and an artist might have discovered various drawbacks on her beauty, if not positive defects; but no earthly being could have quarrelled with the expression. That was a mixture of intelligence, softness, spirit, and feminine innocence that did not fail to produce an impression on a crowd which had almost settled down into a firm conviction of her guilt. Some even doubted, and most of those present thought it very strange.

The reporters began to write, casting their eyes eagerly towards this witness; and Dunscomb, who sat near them, soon discovered that there were material discrepancies in their descriptions. These, however, were amicably settled by comparing notes; and when the accounts of that day's examination appeared in the journals of the time, they were sufficiently consistent with each other; much more so, indeed, than with the truth in its severer aspects. There was no wish to mislead, probably; but the whole system has the capital defect of making a trade of news. The history of passing events comes to us sufficiently clouded and obscured by the most vulgar and least praiseworthy of all our lesser infirmities, even when left to take what may be termed its natural course; but as soon as the money-getting principle is applied to it, facts become articles for the market, and go up and down, much as do other commodities, in the regular prices-current.

Mary Monson trembled a little when sworn; but she had evidently braced her nerves for the trial. Women are very capable of self-command, even in situations as foreign to their habits as this, if they have time to compose themselves, and to come forward under the influence of resolutions deliberately formed. Such was probably the state of mind of this solitary and seemingly unfriended young woman; for, though pale as death, she was apparently composed. We say unfriended, – Mrs Jones herself having given all her friends to understand that she had invited the stranger to her house under a sense of general duty, and not on account of any private or particular interest she felt in her affairs. She was as much a stranger to her as to every one else in the village.

'Will you be so good as to tell us your name, place of ordinary residence, and usual occupation?' asked the coroner, in a dry, cold manner, though not until he had offered the witness a seat, in compliment to her sex.

If the face of Mary Monson was pale the instant before, it now flushed to scarlet. The tint that appears in the August evening sky, when heat-lightning illuminates the horizon is scarce more bright than that which chased the previous pallid hue from her cheeks. Dunscomb understood her dilemma, and interposed. She was equally unwilling to tell her real name, and to give a false one, under the solemn responsibility of an oath. There is, probably, less of deliberate, calculated false-swearing than of any other offence against justice, few having the nerve or the moral obtuseness that is necessary to perjury. We do not mean by this that all which legal witnesses say is true, or the half of it; for ignorance, dull imaginations working out solutions of half-comprehended propositions, and the strong propensity we all feel to see things as we have expected to find them, in a measure disqualifies fully half of those on whom the law has devolved a most important duty, to discharge it with due intelligence and impartiality.

'As a member of the bar, I interfere in behalf of the witness,' said Dunscomb, rising. 'She is evidently unacquainted with her true position here, and consequently with her rights. Jack, get a glass of water for the young lady;' and never did Jack obey a request of his uncle with greater alacrity. 'A witness cannot, with propriety, be treated as a criminal, or one suspected, without being apprised that the law does not require of those thus circumstanced answers affecting themselves.'

Dunscomb had listened more to his feelings than to his legal knowledge in offering this objection, inasmuch as no very searching question had as yet been put to Mary Monson. This the coroner saw, and he did not fail to let it be understood that he was aware of the weakness of the objection.

'Coroners are not governed by precisely the same rules as ordinary committing magistrates,' he quietly observed, 'though we equally respect the rules of evidence. No witness is obliged to answer a question before an inquest, that will criminate himself, any more than at the Oyer and Terminer. If the lady will say she does not wish to tell her real name, *because it may criminate her*, I shall not press the question myself, or allow it to be pressed by others.'

'Very true, sir; but the law requires, in these preliminary proceedings, no more than such accuracy as is convenient in making out the records. I conceive that in this particular case the question might be varied by asking, "You are known by the name of Mary Monson, I believe?"'

'What great harm can it be to this young female to give her real name, Mr Dunscomb, as I understand you are that distinguished counsellor, if she be perfectly innocent of the death of the Goodwins?'

'A perfectly innocent person may have good reasons for wishing to conceal her name. These reasons obtain additional force when we look around us, and see a committee of reporters, who stand ready to transmit all that passes to the press; – but, it might better serve the ends of justice to allow me to confer with the witness in private.'

'With all my heart, sir. Take her into one of the jury rooms, and I will put another physician on the stand. When you are through with your consultation, Mr Dunscomb, we shall be ready to proceed with your client.'

Dunscomb offered his arm to the girl, and led her through the crowd, while a third medical man was sworn. This witness corroborated all of Dr Coe's opinions, treating the supposition that both the skeletons were those of women with very little respect. It must be admitted that the suspected stranger lost a great deal of ground in the course of that half-hour. In the first place, the discussion about the name was received very much as an admission of guilt; for Dunscomb's argument that persons who were innocent might have many reasons for concealing their names, did not carry much weight with the good people of Biberry. Then any doubts which might have been raised by McBrain's suggestion concerning the nature of the skeletons, were effectually removed by the corroborating testimony of Dr Short, who so fully sustained Dr Coe. So much are the Americans accustomed to refer the decision of nearly all questions to numbers, it scarcely exaggerates the truth to say that, on the stand, the opinion of half-a-dozen country surveyors touching a problem in geometry, would be very apt to overshadow that of a professor from West Point, or old Yale. Majorities are the *primum mobile* of the common mind, and he who can get the greatest number on his side is very apt to be considered right, and to reap the benefits of being so.

A fourth and a fifth medical man were examined, and they concurred in the opinions of Dr Coe and his neighbours. All gave it as the result of their inquiries, that they believed the two skulls had been broken with the same instrument, and that the blow, if it did not cause immediate death, must have had the effect to destroy consciousness. As regards the sex, the answers were given in a tone somewhat supercilious.

'Science is a very good thing in its place,' observed one of these last witnesses; 'but science is subject to known facts. We all know that Peter Goodwin and his wife lived in that house; we all know that Dorothy Goodwin was a large woman, and that Peter Goodwin was a small man, – that they were about of a height, in fact, – and that these skeletons very accurately represent their respective statures. We also know that the house is burnt, that the old couple are missing, that these bones were found in a wing in which they slept, and that no other bones have been found there. Now, to my judgment, these facts carry as much weight, ay, even more weight, than any scientific reasoning in the premises. I conclude, therefore, that these are the remains of Peter and Dorothy Goodwin – have no doubt that they are, indeed.'

'Am I permitted to ask this witness a question, Mr Coroner?' demanded Dr McBrain.

'With all my heart, sir. The jury wishes to ascertain all they can, and our sole object is justice. Our inquests are not very rigid as to forms, and you are welcome to examine the witness as much as you please.'

'You knew Goodwin?' asked McBrain, directly of the witness.

'I did, sir; quite well.'

'Had he all his teeth, as you remember?'

'I think he had.'

'On the supposition that his front upper teeth were all gone, and that the skeleton you suppose to be his *had* all the front upper teeth, would you still regard the facts you have mentioned as better, or even as good proof, as the evidence of science, which tells us that the man who has lost his teeth cannot possess them?'

'I scarcely call that a scientific fact at all, sir. Any one may judge of that circumstance, as well as a physician. If it were as you say, I should consider the presence of the teeth pretty good proof that the skeleton was that of some other person, unless the teeth were the work of a dentist.'

'Then why not put any other equally sure anatomical fact in opposition to what is generally supposed, in connection with the wing, the presence of the man, and all the other circumstances you have mentioned?'

'If there were any other *sure* anatomical fact, so I would. But, in the condition in which those remains are, I do not think the best anatomist could say that he can distinguish whether they belonged to a man or to a woman.'

'I confess that the case has its difficulties,' McBrain quietly answered. 'Still I incline to my first opinion. I trust, Mr Coroner, that the skeletons will be carefully preserved, so long as there may be any reason to continue these legal inquiries?'

'Certainly, sir. A box is made for that purpose, and they will be carefully deposited in it, as soon as the inquest adjourns for the day. It is no unusual thing, gentlemen, for doctors to disagree.'

This was said with a smile, and had the effect to keep the peace. McBrain, however, had all the modesty of knowledge, and was never disposed to show off his superior attainments in the faces of those who might be supposed to know less than himself. Nor was he, by any means, certain of his fact; though greatly inclined to believe that both the skeletons were those of females. The heat had been so powerful as to derange, in some measure, if not entirely to deface, his proofs; and he was not a man to press a fact, in a case of this magnitude, without sufficient justification. All he now wanted, was to reserve a point that might have a material influence hereafter in coming to a correct conclusion.

It was fully an hour before Dunscomb returned, bringing Mary Monson on his arm. John followed the latter closely, for, though not admitted to the room in which this long private conference had been held, he had not ceased to pace the gallery in front of its door during the whole time. Dunscomb looked very grave, and, as McBrain thought, and he was very expert in interpreting the language of his friend's countenance, disappointed. The girl herself had evidently been weeping, and that violently. There was a paleness of the face, and a tremor in the frame, too, that caused the observant physician to suppose that, for the first time, she had been made to comprehend that she was the object of such dire distrust. No sooner were the two in their old seats, than the coroner prepared to renew the suspended examination.

'Witness,' repeated that functionary with marked formality, 'what is your name?'

The answer was given in a tremulous voice, but with sufficient readiness, as if previously prepared.

'I am known, in and around Biberry, by the name of Mary Monson.'

The coroner paused, passed a hand over his brow, mused a moment, and abandoned a half-formed determination he had made to push this particular inquiry as far as he could. To state the truth, he was a little afraid of Mr Thomas Dunscomb, whose reputation at the bar was of too high a character to have escaped his notice. On the whole, therefore, he decided to accept the name of Mary Monson, reserving the right of the state to inquire further hereafter.

'Where do you reside?'

'At present, in this place; lately, in the family of Peter Goodwin, whose remains are supposed to be in this room.'

'How long had you resided in that family?'

'Nine weeks, to a day. I arrived in the morning, and the fire occurred at night.'

'Relate all that you know concerning that fire, if you please, Miss: I call you Miss, supposing you to be unmarried?'

Mary Monson merely made a slight inclination of her head, as one acknowledges that a remark is heard and understood. This did not more than half satisfy the coroner, his wife, for reasons of her own, having particularly desired him to ask the 'Monson girl,' when she was put on the stand, whether she was or was not married. But it was too late, just then, to ascertain this interesting fact, and the examination proceeded.

'Relate all that you know concerning the fire, if you please, ma'am.'

'I know very little. I was awakened by a bright light; arose, and dressed myself as well as I could, and was about to descend the stairs, when I found I was too late. I then went to a window, and intended to throw my bed out and let myself down on it, when two men appeared, and raised a ladder by which I got safely out.'

'Were any of your effects saved?'

'All, I believe. The same two persons entered my room, and passed my trunks, box, and carpet-bag, writing-desk, and other articles out of the room, as well as most of its furniture. It was the part of the building last on fire, and it was safe entering the room I occupied for near half an hour after I escaped.'

'How long had you known the Goodwins?'

'From the time when I first came to live in their house.'

'Did you pass the evening of the night of the fire in their company?'

'I did not. Very little of my time was passed in their company, unless it was at meals.'

This answer caused a little stir among the audience, of whom much the larger portion thought it contained an admission to be noted. Why should not a young woman who lived in a house so much apart from a general neighbourhood, not pass most of her time in the company of those with whom she dwelt? 'If they were good enough to live with, I should think they might be good enough to associate with,' whispered one of the most active female talkers of Biberry, but in a tone so loud as to be heard by all near her.

This was merely yielding to a national and increasing susceptibility to personal claims; it being commonly thought aristocratic to refuse to associate with everybody, when the person subject to remark has any apparent advantages to render such association desirable. All others may do as they please.

'You did not, then, make one of the family regularly, but were there for some particular purpose of your own?' resumed the coroner.

'I think, sir, on reflection, that you will see this examination is taking a very irregular course,' interposed Dunscomb. 'It is more like an investigation for a commitment than an inquest.'

'The law allows the freest modes of inquiry in all such cases, Mr Dunscomb. Recollect, sir, there have been arson and murder – two of the highest crimes known to the books.'

'I do not forget it; and recognise not only all your rights, sir, but your duties. Nevertheless, this young lady has rights, too, and is to be treated distinctly in one of two characters; as a witness, or as a party accused. If in the latter, I shall at once advise her to answer no more questions in this state of the case. My duty, as her counsel, requires me to say as much.'

'She has, then, regularly retained you, Mr Dunscomb?' the coroner asked, with interest.

'That, sir, is a matter between her and myself. I appear here as counsel, and shall claim the rights of one. I know that you can carry on this inquest without my interference, if you see fit; but no one can exclude the citizen from the benefit of advice. Even the new code, as extravagant and high-flying an invention as ever came from the misguided ingenuity of man, will allow of this.'

'There is no wish, Mr Dunscomb, to put any obstacles in your way. Let every man do his whole duty. Your client can certainly refuse to answer any questions she may please, on the ground that the answer may tend to criminate herself; and so may any one else.'

'I beg your pardon, sir; the law is still more indulgent in these preliminary proceedings. A party who knows himself to be suspected, has a right to evade questions that may militate against his interests; else would the boasted protection which the law so far throws around every one that he need not be his own accuser, become a mere pretence.'

'I shall endeavour to put my questions in such a way as to give her the benefit of all her rights. Miss Monson, it is said that you have been seen, since the fire, to have some gold in your possession; have you any objection to let that gold be seen by the jury?'

'None in the world, sir. I have a few gold pieces – here they are in my purse. They do not amount to much, either in numbers or value. You are at liberty to examine them as much as you please.'

Dunscomb had betrayed a little uneasiness at this question; but the calm, steady manner in which the young woman answered, and the coolness with which she put her purse into the coroner's hand, re-assured, or rather surprised him. He remained silent, therefore, interposing no objection to the examination.

'Here are seven half-eagles, two quarter-eagles, and a strange coin that I do not remember ever to have seen before,' said the coroner. 'What do you call this piece, Mr Dunscomb?'

'I cannot tell you, sir; I do not remember ever to have seen the coin before, myself.'

'It is an Italian coin, of the value of about twenty dollars, they tell me,' answered Mary, quietly. 'I think it is called after the reigning sovereign, whoever he may be. I got it, in exchange for some of our own money, from an emigrant from Europe, and kept it as a thing a little out of the common way.'

The simplicity, distinctness, not to say nerve, with which this was said, placed Dunscomb still more at his ease, and he now freely let the inquiry take its course. All this did not prevent his being astonished that one so young, and seemingly so friendless, should manifest so much coolness and self-possession under circumstances so very trying. Such was the fact, however, and he was fain to await further developments, in order better to comprehend the character of his client.

'Is Mrs Pope present?' inquired the coroner. 'The lady who told us yesterday she had seen the specie of the late Mrs Goodwin during the life-time of the latter?'

It was almost superfluous to ask if any particular person were present, as nearly all Biberry were in, or about, the court-house. Up started the widow, therefore, at this appeal, and coming forward with alacrity, she was immediately sworn, which she had not been the previous day, and went on the stand as a regular witness.

'Your name?' observed the coroner.

'Abigail Pope – folks write "relict of John Pope, deceased," in all my law papers.'

'Very well, Mrs Pope; the simple name will suffice for the present purposes. Do you reside in this neighbourhood?'

'In Biberry. I was born, brought up, married, became a widow, and still dwell, all within half-a-mile of this spot. My maiden name was Dickson.'

Absurd and forward as these answers may seem to most persons, they had an effect on the investigation that was then going on in Biberry. Most of the audience saw and felt the difference between the frank statements of the present witness, and the reserve manifested by the last.

'Now, why couldn't that Mary Monson answer all these questions just as well as Abigail Pope?' said one female talker to a knot of listeners. 'She has a glib enough tongue in her head, if she only sees fit to use it! I'll engage no one can answer more readily, when she wishes to let a thing out. There's a dreadful history behind the curtain, in my judgment, about that same young woman, could a body only get at it.'

'Mr Sanford *will* get at it, before he has done with her, I'll engage,' answered a friend. 'I have heard it said he is the most investigating coroner in the state, when he sets about a case in good earnest. He'll be very apt to make the most of this, for we never have had anything one-half so exciting in Biberry as these murders! I have long thought we were rather out of the way of the rest of the world, until now; but our time has come, and we sha'n't very soon hear the last of it!'

'It's all in the papers, already!' exclaimed a third. 'Biberry looks as grand as York, or Albany, in the columns of every paper from town this morning! I declare it did me good to see our little place holding up its head among the great of the earth, as it might be——'

What else, in the way of local patriotism, may have escaped this individual cannot now be known, the coroner drawing off her auditors by the question next put to the widow.

'Did you ever see any gold coins in the possession of the late Mrs Goodwin?' asked that functionary.

'Several times – I don't know but I might say often. Five or six times, at least. I used to sew for the old lady, and you know how it is when a body works, in that way, in a family – its next thing, I do suppose, to being a doctor, so far as secrets go.'

'Should you know any of that coin were you to see it again, Mrs Pope?'

'I think I might. There's one piece in partic'lar that I suppose I should know anywhere. It's a wonderful-looking piece of money, and true Californy, I conclude.'

'Did any of Mrs Goodwin's gold coins bear a resemblance to this?' showing a half-eagle.

'Yes, sir – that's a five-dollar piece – I've had one of them myself in the course of my life.'

'Mrs Goodwin had coins similar to this, I then understand you to say?'

'She had as many as fifty, I should think. Altogether, she told me she had as much as four hundred dollars in that stocking! I remember the sum, for it sounded like a great deal for anybody to have, who wasn't a bank, like. It quite put me in mind of the *place ers*.'

'Was there any coin like this?' showing the widow the Italian piece.

'That's the piece! I'd know it among a thousand! I had it in my hands as much as five minutes, trying to read the Latin on it, and make it out into English. All the rest was American gold, the old lady told me; but this piece, she said, was foreign.'

This statement produced a great sensation in the court-room. Although Mrs Pope was flippant, a gossip, and a little notorious for meddling with her neighbour's concerns, no one suspected her of fabricating such a story, under oath. The piece of gold passed from juror to juror; and each man among them felt satisfied that he would know the coin again after an interval of a few weeks. Dunscomb probably put less faith in this bit of testimony than any other person present; and he was curious to note its effect on his client. To his great surprise she betrayed no uneasiness; her countenance maintaining a calm that he now began to apprehend denoted a practised art; and he manifested a desire to examine the piece of gold for himself. It was put in his hand, and he glanced at its face a little eagerly. It was an unusual coin; but it had no defect or mark that might enable one to distinguish between it and any other piece of a similar impression. The coroner interpreted the meaning of his eye, and suspended the examination of the widow to question Mary Monson herself.

'Your client sees the state of the question, Mr Dunscomb,' he said; 'and you will look to her rights. Mine authorize me, as I understand them, to inquire of her concerning a few facts in relation to this piece of money.'

'I will answer your questions, sir, without any hesitation,' the accused replied, with a degree of steadiness that Dunscomb deemed astonishing.

'How long has this piece of gold been in your possession, if you please, miss?'

'About a twelvemonth. I began to collect the gold I have very nearly a-year since.'

'Has it been in your possession, uninterruptedly, all that time?'

'So far as I know, sir, it has. A portion of the time, and a large portion of it, it has not been kept in my purse; but I should think no one could have meddled with it when it has been elsewhere.'

'Have you anything to remark on the testimony just given?'

'It is strictly true. Poor Mrs Goodwin certainly had the store of gold mentioned by Mrs Pope, for she once showed it to me. I rather think she was fond of such things; and had a pleasure in counting her hoards and showing them to other persons. I looked over her coins, and finding she was fond of those that are a little uncommon, I gave her one or two of those that I happened to own. No doubt Mrs Pope saw the counterpart of this piece, but surely not the piece itself.'

'I understand you to say, then, that Mrs Goodwin had a gold coin similar to this, which gold coin came from yourself. What did Mrs Goodwin allow you in the exchange?'

'Sir?'

'How much did you estimate the value of that Italian piece at, and in what money did Mrs Goodwin pay you for it? It is necessary to be particular in these cases.'

'She returned me nothing for the coin, sir. It was a present from me to her, and, of course, not to be paid for.'

This answer met with but little favour. It did not appear to the people of Biberry at all probable that an unknown, and seemingly friendless young woman, who had been content to dwell two months in the 'garret-room' of the 'old Goodwin house,' faring none of the best, certainly, and neglecting so many superior tenements and tables that were to be met with on every side of her, would be very likely to give away a piece of gold of that unusual size. It is true, we are living in a marvellous age, so far as this metal is concerned; but the Californian gold had not then arrived in any great quantity, and the people of the country are little accustomed to see anything but silver and paper, which causes them to attach an unwonted value to the more precious metal. Even the coroner took this view of the matter; and Dunscomb saw that the explanation just made by his client was thought to prove too much.

'Are you in the habit, miss, of giving away pieces of gold?' asked one of the jurors.

'That question is improper,' interposed Mr Dunscomb. 'No one can have a right to put it.'

The coroner sustained this objection, and no answer was given. As Mrs Pope had suggested that others, besides herself, had seen Mrs Goodwin's stocking, four more witnesses were examined to this one point. They were all females, who had been admitted by the deceased, in the indulgence of her passion, to feast their eyes with a sight of her treasure. Only one, however, of these four professed to have any recollection of the particular coin that had now become, as it might be, the pivoting point in the inquiry; and her recollections were by no means as clear as those of the widow. She *thought* she had seen such a piece of gold in Mrs Goodwin's possession, though she admitted she was not allowed to touch any of the money, which was merely held up, piece by piece, before her admiring eyes, in the hands of its proper owner. It was in this stage of the inquiry that Dunscomb remarked to the coroner, that 'it was not at all surprising a woman who was so fond of exposing her treasure should be robbed and murdered!' This remark, however, failed of its intended effect, in consequence of the manner in which suspicion had become riveted, as it might be, through the testimony of Mrs Pope, on the stranger who had so mysteriously come to lodge with the Goodwins. The general impression now appeared to be that the whole matter had been previously arranged, and that the stranger had come to dwell in the house expressly to obtain facilities for the commission of the crime.

A witness who was related to the deceased, who was absent from home, but had been told, by means of the wires, to return, and who had intimated an intention to comply, was still wanting; and the inquest was again adjourned for an hour, in order to allow of the arrival of a stage from town. During this interval Dunscomb ascertained how strongly the current was setting against his client. A hundred little circumstances were cited, in confirmation of suspicions that had now gained a firm footing, and which were so nearly general as to include almost every person of any consequence in the place. What appeared strangest to Dunscomb, was the composure of the young girl who was so likely to be formally accused of crimes so heinous. He had told her of the nature of the distrust that was attached to her situation, and she received his statement with a degree of emotion that, at first, had alarmed him. But an unaccountable calmness soon succeeded this burst of feeling, and he had found it necessary to draw confidence in the innocence of his client, from that strangely illuminated countenance, to study which was almost certain to subdue a man by its power. While thus gazing at the stranger, he could not believe her guilty; but, while reflecting on all the facts of the case, he saw how difficult it might be to persuade others to entertain the same opinion. Nor were there circumstances wanting to shake his own faith in expression, sex, years, and all the other probabilities. Mary Monson had declined entering at all into any account of her previous life; evaded giving her real name even to him; carefully abstained from all allusions that might furnish any clue to her former place of abode, or to any fact that would tend to betray her secret.

At the appointed hour the stage arrived, bringing the expected witness. His testimony went merely to corroborate the accounts concerning the little hoard of gold that his kinswoman had undeniably possessed, and to the circumstance that she always kept it in a particular drawer of her bureau. The bureau had been saved, for it did not stand in the sleeping-room of the deceased, but had formed a principal embellishment of her little parlour, and the money was not in it. What was more, each drawer was carefully locked, but no keys were to be found. As these were articles not likely to be melted under any heat to which they might have been exposed, a careful but fruitless search had been made for them among the ruins. They were nowhere to be seen.

About nine o'clock in the evening, the jury brought in the result of their inquest. It was a verdict of murder in the first degree, committed, in the opinion of the jurors, by a female who was known by the name of Mary Monson. With the accusation of arson, the coroner's inquest, as a matter of course, had no connection. A writ was immediately issued, and the accused arrested.

CHAPTER V

'It was the English,' Kasper cried,
    'Who put the French to rout;
But what they killed each other for,
    I could not well make out.
But everybody said,' quoth he,
    'That 'twas a famous victory.'

SOUTHEY.

The following day, after an early breakfast, Dunscomb and his friend the doctor were on their way back to town. The former had clients and courts, and the latter patients, who were not to be neglected, to say nothing of the claims of Sarah and Mrs Updyke. John and Michael remained at Biberry; the first being detained there by divers commissions connected with the comforts and treatment of Mary Monson, but still more by his own inclinations; and the last remaining, somewhat against his wishes, as a companion to the brother of her who so strongly drew him back to New York.

As the commitment was for offences so serious, crimes as grave as any known to the law, bail would not have been accepted, could any have been found. We ought not to speak with too much confidence, however, on this last point; for Dr McBrain, a man of very handsome estate, the result of a liberal profession steadily and intelligently pursued, was more than half disposed to offer himself for one of the sureties, and to go and find a second among his friends. Nothing, indeed, prevented his doing so, but Dunscomb's repeated assurances that no bondsmen would be received. Even charming young women, when they stand charged with murder and arson, must submit to be incarcerated, until their innocence is established in due form of law; or, what is the same thing in effect, until the caprice, impulses, ignorance, or corruption of a jury acquits them.

The friends did not entirely agree in their manner of viewing this affair. The doctor was firmly impressed with the conviction of Mary Monson's innocence; while Dunscomb, more experienced in the ways of crime and the infirmities of the human heart, had his misgivings. So many grounds of suspicion had occurred, or been laid open to his observation, during the hour of private communication, that it was not easy for one who had seen so much of the worst side of human nature, to cast them off under the mere influence of a graceful form, winning manner, and bright countenance. Then, the secondary facts, well established, and, in one important particular, admitted by the party accused, were not of a character to be overlooked. It often happens, and Dunscomb well knew it, that innocence appears under a repulsive exterior, while guilt conceals itself in forms and aspects so fair, as to deceive all but the wary and experienced.

'I hope that the comfort of Miss Monson has been properly attended to, since she must be confined for a few days,' said McBrain, while he took a last look at the little gaol, as the carriage passed the brow of a hill. 'Justice can ask no more than security.'

'It is a blot on the character of the times, and on this country in particular,' answered Dunscomb, coldly, 'that so little attention is paid to the gaols. We are crammed with false philanthropy in connection with convicted rogues, who ought to be made to feel the penalties of their offences; while we are not even just in regard to those who are only accused, many of whom are really innocent. But for my interference, this delicate and friendless girl would, in all probability, have been immured in a common dungeon.'

'What! before her guilt is established?'

'Relatively, her treatment after conviction, would be far more humane than previously to that event. Comfortable, well-furnished, but secure apartments, ought to be provided for the accused in every county in the state, as acts of simple justice, before another word of mawkish humanity is uttered on the subject of the treatment of recognised criminals. It is wonderful what a disposition there is among men to run into octaves, in everything they do, forgetting that your true melody is to be found only in the simpler and more natural notes. There is as much of the *falsetto*, now-a-days, in philanthropy, as in music.'

'And this poor girl is thrust into a dungeon?'

'No; it is not quite as bad as that. The gaol has one decent apartment, that was fitted up for the comfort of a prize-fighter, who was confined in it not long since; and as the room is sufficiently secure, I have persuaded the gaoler's wife to put Mary Monson in it. Apart from loss of air and exercise, and the happiness of knowing herself respected and beloved, the girl will not be very badly off there. I dare say the room is quite as good as that she occupied under the roof of those unfortunate Goodwins.'

'How strange, that a female of her appearance should have been the inmate of such a place! She does not seem to want money, either. You saw the gold she had in her purse?'

'Ay; it were better had that gold not been there, or not seen. I sincerely wish it had been nothing but silver.'

'You surely do not agree with that silly woman, the Widow Pope, as they call her, in believing that she has got the money of those persons who have been murdered?'

'On that subject I choose to suspend my opinion – I may, or I may not; as matters shall turn up. She has money; and in sufficient quantity to buy herself out of jeopardy. At least, she offered me a fee of a hundred dollars, in good city paper.'

'Which you did not take, Tom?'

'Why not? It is my trade, and I live by it. Why not take her fee, if you please, sir? Does the Widow Updyke teach you such doctrines? Will you drive about town for nothing? Why not take her fee, Master Ned?'

'Why not, sure enough! That girl has bewitched me, I believe; and that is the solution.'

'I'll tell you what, Ned, unless there is a stop put to this folly, I'll make Mrs Updyke acquainted with the whole matter, and put an end to nuptials No. 3. Jack is head and ears in love already; and here you are flying off at a tangent from all your engagements and professions, to fall at the feet of an unknown girl of twenty, who appears before you, on a first interview, in the amiable light of one accused of the highest crimes.'

'And of which I no more believe her guilty than I believe you to be guilty of them.'

'Umph! "Time will show;" which is the English, I suppose, of the *nous verrons*, that is flying about in the newspapers. Yes, she has money to buy three or four journals, to get up a "sympathy" in her behalf, when her acquittal would be almost certain, if her trial were not a legal impossibility. I am not sure it is not her safest course, in the actual state of the facts.'

'Would you think, Dunscomb, of advising any one who looked up to you for counsel to take such a course?'

'Certainly not – and you know it well enough, McBrain; but that does not lessen or increase the chances of the expedient. The journals have greatly weakened their own power by the manner in which they have abused it; but enough still remains to hoodwink, not to say to overshadow, justice. The law is very explicit and far-sighted as to the consequences of allowing any one to influence the public mind in matters of its own administration; but in a country like this, in which the virtue and intelligence of the people are said to be the *primum mobile* in everything, there is no one to enforce the ordinances that the wisdom of our ancestors has bequeathed to us. Any editor of a newspaper who publishes a sentence reflecting on the character or rights of a party to a pending suit, is guilty, at common law, of what the books call a "libel on the courts of justice," and can be punished for it as for any other misdemeanour; yet you can see for yourself how little such a provision, healthful and most wise – nay essential as it is to justice – is looked down by the mania which exists, of putting everything into print. When one remembers that very little of what he reads is true, it is fearful to reflect that a system, of which the whole merit depends on its power to extract facts, and to do justice on their warranty, should be completely overshadowed by another contrivance which, when stripped of its pretension, and regarded in its real colours, is nothing more than one of the ten thousand schemes to make money that surround us with a little higher pretension than common to virtue.'

'"Completely overshadowed" are strong words, Dunscomb!'

'Perhaps they are, and they may need a little qualifying. Overshadowed often – much too often, however, is not a particle stronger than I am justified in using. Every one who thinks at all sees and feels the truth of this; but here is the weak side of a popular government. The laws are enforced by means of public virtue, – and public virtue, like private virtue, is very frail. We all are willing enough to admit the last, as regards our neighbours at least, while there seems to exist in most minds a species of idolatrous veneration for the common sentiment, as sheer a quality of straw, as any image of a lover drawn by the most heated imagination of sixteen.'

'You surely do not disregard public opinion, Tom, or set it down as unworthy of all respect!'

'By no means; if you mean that opinion which is the result of deliberate judgment, and has a direct connection with our religion, morals, and manners. That is a public opinion to which we all ought to defer, when it is fairly made up, and has been distinctly and independently pronounced; most especially when it comes from high quarters, and not from low. But the country is full of simulated public opinion, in the first place, and it is not always easy to tell the false from the true. Yes, the country is full of what I shall call an artificial public opinion, that has been got up to effect a purpose, and to that no wise man will defer, if he can help it. Now, look at our scheme of administering justice. Twelve men taken out of the bosom of the community, by a species of lottery, are set apart to pronounce on your fortune or mine – nay, to utter the fearful words of "guilty" or "not guilty." All the accessories of this plan, as they exist here, make against its success. In the first place jurors are paid, and that just enough to induce the humblest on the list to serve, and not enough to induce the educated and intelligent. It is a day-labourer's wages, and the day-labourer will be most likely to profit by it. Men who are content to toil for seventy-five cents a day are very willing to serve on juries for a dollar; while those whose qualifications enable them to obtain enough to pay their fines, disregard the penalty and stay away.'

'Why is not an evil as flagrant as this remedied? I should think the whole bar would protest against it.'

'With what result? Who cares for the bar? Legislators alone can change this system, and men very different from those who are now sent must go to the legislature, before one is found, honest enough, or bold enough, to get up and tell the people they are not all fit to be trusted. No, no; this is not the way of the hour. We have a cycle in opinion to make, and it may be that when the round is fairly made, men may come back to their senses, and perceive the necessity of fencing in justice by some of the useful provisions that we are now so liberally throwing away. To tell you the truth, Ned, the state is submitting to the influence of two of the silliest motives that can govern men – ultra conservatism, and ultra progress; the one holding back, often, to preserve that which is not worth keeping; and the other "going ahead," as it is termed, merely for the sake of boasting of their onward tendencies. Neither course is in the least suited to the actual wants of society, and each is pernicious in its way.'

'It is thought, however, that when opinion thus struggles with opinion, a healthful compromise is made, in which society finds its advantage.'

'The cant of mediocrity, depend on it, Ned. In the first place, there is no compromise about it; one side or the other gains the victory; and as success is sustained by numbers, the conquerors push their advantages to the utmost. They think of their own grosser interests, their passions and prejudices, rather than of any "healthful compromise," as you term it. What compromise is there in this infernal code?' – Dunscomb was an ultra himself, in opposition to a system that has a good deal of that which is useful, diluted by more that is not quite so good – 'or what in this matter of the election of judges by the people? As respects the last, for instance, had the tenure of office been made "good behaviour," there would have been something like a compromise; but, no – the conquerors took all; and what is worse, the conquerors were actually a minority of the voters, so easy is it to cow even numbers by political chicanery. In this respect, democracy is no more infallible, than any other form of government.'

'I confess, I do not see how this is shown, since the polls were free to every citizen.'

'The result fairly proves it. Less than half of the known number of the electors voted for the change. Now, it is absurd to suppose that men who really and affirmatively wished a new constitution would stay away from the polls.'

'More so, than to suppose that they who did not wish it, would stay away, too?'

'More so; and for this reason. Thousands fancied it useless to stem the current of what they fancied a popular movement, and were passive in the matter. Any man, of an extensive acquaintance, may easily count a hundred such idlers. Then a good many stood on their legal rights, and refused to vote, because the manner of producing the change was a palpable violation of a previous contract; the old constitution pointing out the manner in which the instrument could be altered, which was not the mode adopted. Then tens of thousands voted for the new constitution who did not know anything about it. They loved change, and voted for change's sake; and, possibly, with some vague notion that they were to be benefited by making the institutions as popular as possible.'

'And is not this the truth? Will not the mass be all the better off by exercising as much power as they can?'

'No; and for the simple reason that masses cannot, in the nature of things, exercise more than a very limited power. You yourself, for instance, one of the mass, cannot exercise this very power of choosing a judge as it ought to be exercised, and of course are liable to do more harm than good.'

'The deuce I cannot! Why is not my vote as good as your own? or that of any other man?'

'For the simple reason that you are ignorant of the whole matter. Ask yourself the question, and answer it like an honest man: would you – *could* you, with the knowledge you possess, lay your finger on any man in this community, and say, "I make you a judge?"'

'Yes; my finger would be laid on you in a minute.'

'Ah, Ned, that will do as a friend; but how would it do as a judicious selection of a judge you do not know? You are ignorant of the law, and must necessarily be ignorant of the qualifications of any particular person to be an interpreter of it. What is true of you, is equally true of a vast majority of those who are now the electors of our judges.'

'I am not a little surprised, Tom, to hear *you* talk in this way; for you profess to be a democrat!'

'To the extent of giving the people all power in the last resort – all power that they can intelligently and usefully use; but not to the extent of permitting them to make the laws, to execute the laws, and to interpret the laws. All that the people want is, sufficient power to secure their liberties, which is simply such a state of things as shall secure what is right between man and man. Now, it is the want of this all-important security, in a practical point of view, of which I complain. Rely on it, Ned, the people gain nothing by exercising an authority that they do not know how to turn to good account. It were far better for them, and for the state, to confine themselves to the choice of general agents of whose characters they may know something, and then confide all other powers to servants appointed by those named by these agents, holding all alike to a rigid responsibility. As for the judges, they will soon take decided party characters; and men will as blindly accuse, and as blindly defend them, as they now do their other leading partisans. What between the bench and the jury-box, we shall shortly enjoy a legal pandemonium.'

'Yet there are those who think the trial by jury is the palladium of our liberties.'

Dunscomb laughed outright, for he recollected his conversation with the young men, which we have already related. Then, suppressing his risible propensity, he continued gravely:–

'Yes, one or two papers, well fee'd by this young woman's spare cash, might do her more good than any service I can render her. I dare say the accounts now published, or soon to be published, will leave a strong bias against her.'

'Why not fee a reporter as well as a lawyer, eh, Tom? There is no great difference as I can see.'

'Yes you can, and will, too, as soon as you look into the matter. A lawyer is paid for a known and authorized assistance, and the public recognises in him one engaged in the interests of his client, and accepts his statements and efforts accordingly. But the conductor of a public journal sets up a claim to strict impartiality, in his very profession, and should tell nothing but what he believes to be true, neither inventing nor suppressing. In his facts he is merely the publisher of a record; in his reasoning, a judge; not an advocate.'

The Doctor now laughed, in his turn, and well he might: few men being so ignorant as not to understand how far removed from all this are most of those who control the public journals.

'After all, it is a tremendous power to confide to irresponsible men!' he exclaimed.

'That it is, and there is nothing among us that so completely demonstrates how far, very far, the public mind is in the rear of the facts of the country, than the blind, reckless manner in which the press is permitted to tyrannise over the community, in the midst of all our hosannas to the Goddess of Liberty. Because, forsooth, what is termed a free press is useful, and has been useful in curbing an irresponsible, hereditary power, in other lands, we are just stupid enough to think it is of equal importance here, where no such power exists, and where all that remains to be done is to strictly maintain the equal rights of all classes of citizens. Did we understand ourselves, and our own real wants, not a paper should be printed in the state that did not make a deposit to meet the legal penalties it might incur by the abuse of its trust. This is or was done in France, the country of all others that best respects equality of rights in theory if not in practice.'

'You surely would not place restrictions on the press!'

'I would though, and very severe restrictions, as salutary checks on the immense power it wields. I would, for instance, forbid the publication of any statement whatever, touching parties in the courts, whether in civil or criminal cases, pending the actions, that the public mind might not be tainted by design. Give the right to publish, and it will be, and is abused, and that most flagrantly, to meet the wishes of corruption. I tell you, Ned, as soon as you make a trade of news you create a stock market that will have its rise and fall, under the impulses of fear, falsehood, and favour, just like your money transactions. It is a perversion of the nature of things to make of news more than a simple statement of what has actually occurred.'

'It is surely natural to lie!'

'That is it, and this is the very reason we should not throw extraordinary protection around a thousand tongues which speak by means of types, that we do not give to the natural member. The lie that is told by the press is ten thousand times a lie, in comparison with that which issues from the mouth of man.'

'By George! Tom, if I had your views, I would see that some of this strange young woman's money should be used in sustaining her by means of the agents you mention?'

'That would never do. This is one of the cases in which "want of principle" has an ascendancy over "principle." The upright man cannot consent to use improper instruments, while the dishonest fellows seize on them with avidity. So much the greater, therefore, is the necessity for the law's watching the interests of the first with the utmost jealousy. But, unfortunately, we run away with the sound, and overlook the sense of things.'

We have related this conversation at a length which a certain class of our readers will probably find tedious, but it is necessary to a right comprehension of various features in the picture we are about to draw. At the Stag's Head the friends stopped to let the horses blow, and, while the animals were cooling themselves under the care of Stephen Hoof, McBrain's coachman, the gentlemen took a short walk in the hamlet. At several points, as they moved along, they overheard the subject of the murders alluded to, and saw divers newspapers, in the hands of sundry individuals, who were eagerly perusing accounts of the same events; sometimes by themselves, but oftener to groups of attentive listeners. The travellers were now so near town as to be completely within its moral, not to say physical, atmosphere – being little more than a suburb of New York.

On their return to the inn, the Doctor stopped under the shed to look at his horses, before Stephen checked them up again, previously to a fresh start. Stephen was neither an Irishman nor a black; but a regular, old-fashioned, Manhattanese coachman; a class apart, and of whom, in the confusion of tongues that pervades that modern Babel, a few still remain, like monuments of the past, scattered along the Appian Way.

'How do your horses stand the heat, Stephen?' the doctor kindly inquired, always speaking of the beasts as if they were the property of the coachman, and not of himself. 'Pill looks as if he had been well warmed this morning.'

'Yes, sir, he takes it somewhat hotter than Poleus, in the spring of the year, as a gineral thing. Pill vill vork famously, if a body vill only give him his feed in vhat I calls a genteel vay; but them 'ere country taverns has nothing nice about 'em, not even a clean manger; and a town horse that is accustomed to a sweet stable and proper company, won't stand up to the rack as he should do, in one of their holes. Now, Poleus I calls a gineral feeder; it makes no matter vith him vhether he is at home, or out on a farm – he finishes his oats; but it isn't so vith Pill, sir – his stomach is delicate, and the horse that don't get his proper food vill sweat, summer or vinter.'

'I sometimes think, Stephen, it might be better to take them both off their oats for a few days, and let blood, perhaps; they say that the fleam is as good for a horse as the lancet is for a man.'

'Don't think on't, sir, I beg of you! I'm sure they has doctor-stuff in their names, not to crowd 'em down vith any more, jist as varm veather is a settin' in. Oats is physic enough for a horse, and vhen the creaturs vants anything more, sir, jist leave 'em to me. I knows as peculiar a drench as ever vas poured down a vheeler's throat, vithout troublin' that academy in Barclay Street, vhere so many gentlemen goes two or three times a veek, and vhere they do say, so many goes in as never comes out whole.'

'Well, Stephen, I'll not interfere with your treatment, for I confess to very little knowledge of the diseases of horses. What have you got in the paper there, that I see you have been reading?'

'Vhy, sir,' answered Stephen, scratching his head, 'it's all about our affair, up yonder.'

'Our affair! Oh! you mean the inquest, and the murder. Well, what does the paper say about it, Hoof?'

'It says it's a most "thrilling a'count," sir, and an "awful tragedy;" and it vonders vhat young vomen is a coming to, next. I am pretty much of the same vay of thinking, sir, myself.'

'You are in the habit of thinking very much as the newspapers do, are you not, Stephen?' asked Dunscomb.

'Vell, 'Squire Dunscomb, you've hit it! There is an onaccountable resemblance, like, in our thoughts. I hardly ever set down to read a paper, that, afore I've got half vay through it, I find it thinking just as I do! It puzzles me to know how them that writes for these papers finds out a body's thoughts so vell!'

'They have a way of doing it; but it is too long a story to go over now. So this paper has something to say about our young woman, has it, Stephen? and it mentions the Biberry business?'

'A good deal, 'squire, and vhat I calls good sense, too. Vhy, gentlemen, vhat shall ve all come to, if young gals of fifteen can knock us in the head, matched, like, or in pairs, killing a whole team at one blow, and then set fire to the stables, and burn us up to our anatomies?'

'Fifteen! Does your account say that Miss Monson is only fifteen?'

'"She appears to be of the tender age of fifteen, and is of extr'ornary personal attractions." Them's the werry vords, sir; but perhaps you'd like to read it yourselves, gentlemen?'

As Stephen made this remark, he very civilly offered the journal to Dunscomb, who took it; but was not disposed to drop the conversation just then to read it, though his eye did glance at the article, as he continued the subject. This was a habit with him; his clerks often saying, he could carry the chains of arguments of two subjects in his mind at the same moment. His present object was, to ascertain from this man what might be the popular feeling in regard to his client, at the place they had just left, and the scene of the events themselves.

'What is thought and said, at Biberry, among those with whom you talked, Stephen, concerning this matter?'

'That it's a most awful ewent, 'squire! One of the werry vorst that has happened in these werry vicked times, sir. I heard one gentleman go over all the murders that has taken place about York during these last ten years, and a perdigious sight on 'em there vas; so many, that I began to vonder I vasn't one of the wictims myself; but he counted 'em off on his fingers, and made this out to be one of the werry vorst of 'em all, sir. He did, indeed, sir.'

'Was he a reporter, Stephen? one of the persons who are sent out by the papers to collect news?'

'I believe he vas, sir. Quite a gentleman; and vith something to say to all he met. He often came out to the stables, and had a long conwersation vith as poor a feller as I be.'

'Pray, what could he have to say to you, Stephen?' demanded the doctor, a little gravely.

'Oh! lots of things, sir. He began by praising the horses, and asking their names. I give him *my* names, sir, not *yourn*; for I thought he might get it into print, somehow, that Dr McBrain calls his coach-horses after his physic, Pill and Poleus' — 'Bolus,' was the real appellation that the owner had been pleased to give this beast; but as Stephen fancied the word had some connection with 'pole-horse,' he chose to pronounce it as written — 'Yes, I didn't vish *your* names to get into the papers, sir; and so I told him "Pill" vas called "Marygoold," and "Poleus," "Dandelion." He promised an article about 'em, sir; and I give him the ages, blood, sires, and dams of both the beauties. He told me he thought the names delightful; and I'm in hopes, sir, you'll give up *yourn*, arter all, and take to *mine*, altogether.'

'We shall see. And he promised an article, did he?'

'Yes, sir, quite woluntary. I know'd that the horse couldn't be outdone, and told him as much as that; for I thought, as the subject vas up, it might be as vell to do 'm all the credit I could. Perhaps, vhen they gets to be too old for vork, you might vish to part vith 'em, sir, and then a good newspaper character could do 'em no great harm.'

Stephen was a particularly honest fellow, as to things in general: but he had the infirmity which seems to be so general among men, that of a propensity to cheat in a transfer of horseflesh. Dunscomb was amused at this exhibition of character, of which he had seen so much in his day, and felt disposed to follow it up.

'I believe you had some difficulty in choosing one of the horses, Stephen' — McBrain commissioned his coachman to do all the bargaining of this sort, and had never lost a cent by his confidence — 'Pill, I think it was, that didn't bring as good a character as he might have done?"

'Beg your pardon, 'squire, 'twasn't he, but Marygoold. Vhy, the thing vas this; a gentleman of the church had bought Marygoold to go in a buggy; but soon vanted to part vith him, 'cause of his shyin' in single harness, vich frightened his vife, *as he said*. Now, all the difficulty vas in this one thing: not that I cared at all about the creatur's shyin', vhich vas no great matter in double harness, you know, sir, and a body could soon coax him out of the notion on it, by judgematical drivin'; but the difficulty vas here — if the owner of a horse owned so much ag'in his character, there must be a great deal behind, that a feller must find out as vell as he could. I've know'd a foundered animal put off under a character for shyin'.'

'And the owner a clergyman, Stephen?'

'Perhaps not, sir. But it makes no great matter in tradin' horses; church and the vorld is much of a muchness.'

'Did that reporting gentleman ask any questions concerning the owner, as well as concerning the horses?'

'Vhy, yes, sir; vhen he vas done vith the animals, he did make a few obserwations about the doctor. He vanted to know if he vas married yet, and vhen it vas to happen; and how much I thought he might be vorth, and how much Mrs Updyke vas counted for; and if there was children; and vich house the family vas to live in; and vhere he should keep the slate arter the veddin' had come off; and how much the doctor's practice vas vorth; and vhether he vas vhig or locy; and, most of all, he vanted to know why he and you, sir, should go to Biberry about this murder.'

'What did you tell him, Stephen, in reference to the last?'

'Vhat could I, sir? I don't know myself. I've druv' the doctor often and often to see them that has died soon arter our visit; but I never druv' him afore to wisit the dead. That gentleman seemed to think he vas much mistaken about the skeletons; but it's all in the paper, sir.'

On hearing this, Dunscomb quickly turned to the columns of the journal again, and was soon reading their contents aloud to his friend; in the meantime, Stephen set Marygoold and Dandelion in motion once more.

The account was much as Dunscomb expected to find it; so written as to do no possible good, while it might do a great deal of harm. The intention was to feed a morbid feeling in the vulgar for exaggerated accounts of the shocking — the motive being gain. Anything that would sell, was grist for this mill; and the more marvellous and terrible the history of the event could be made, the greater was the success likely to be. The allusions to Mary Monson were managed with a good deal of address; for, while there was a seeming respect for her rights, the reader was left to infer that her guilt was not only beyond a question, but of the darkest dye. It was while reading and commenting on these articles, that the carriage entered Broadway, and soon set Dunscomb down at his own door. There the doctor left it; choosing to walk as far as Mrs Updyke's, rather than give Stephen more materials for the reporter.

CHAPTER VI

Then none was for a party;
    Then all were for the state;
Then the great man help'd the poor,
    And the poor man lov'd the great;
Then lands were fairly portion'd;
    Then spoils were fairly sold;
The Romans were like brothers
    In the brave days of old.

                                                    MACAULAY.

It has been said that John Wilmeter was left by his uncle at Biberry, to look after the welfare of their strange client. John, or Jack, as he was commonly called by his familiars, including his pretty sister, was in the main a very good fellow, though far from being free from the infirmities to which the male portion of the human family are subject, when under the age of thirty. He was frank, manly, generous, disposed to think for himself, and what is somewhat unusual with his countrymen, of a temperament that led him to make up his mind suddenly, and was not to be easily swayed by the notions that might be momentarily floating about in the neighbourhood. Perhaps a little of a spirit of opposition to the feeling that was so rapidly gaining head in Biberry, inclined him to take a warmer interest in the singular female who stood charged with such enormous crimes, than he might otherwise have done.

The instructions left by Mr Dunscomb with his nephew, also gave the latter some uneasiness. In the first place, they had been very ample and thoughtful on the subject of the prisoner's comforts, which had been seen to in a way that is by no means common in a gaol. Money had been used pretty freely in effecting this object, it is true; but out of the large towns, money passes for much less on such occasions, in America, than in most other countries. The people are generally kind-hearted, and considerate for the wants of others; and fair words will usually do quite as much as dollars. Dunscomb, however, had made a very judicious application of both, and beyond the confinement and the fearful nature of the charges brought against her, Mary Monson had very little to complain of in her situation.

The part of his instructions which gave John Wilmeter most uneasiness, which really vexed him, related to the prisoner's innocence or guilt. The uncle distrusted; the nephew was all confidence. While the first had looked at the circumstances coolly, and was, if anything, leaning to the opinion that there might be truth in the charges; the last beheld in Mary Monson an attractive young person of the other sex, whose innocent countenance was the pledge of an innocent soul. To John, it was preposterous to entertain a charge of this nature against one so singularly gifted.

'I should as soon think of accusing Sarah of such dark offences, as of accusing this young lady!' exclaimed John to his friend Michael Millington, while the two were taking their breakfast next day. 'It is preposterous – wicked – monstrous, to suppose that a young, educated female, would, or could, commit such crimes! Why, Mike, she understands French and Italian, and Spanish; and I think it quite likely that she can also read German, if, indeed, she cannot speak it!'

'How do you know this? – Has she been making a display of her knowledge?'

'Not in the least – it all came out as naturally as possible. She asked for some of her own books to read, and when they were brought to her, I found that she had selected works in all four of these languages. I was quite ashamed of my own ignorance, I can assure you; which amounts to no more than a smattering of French, in the face of her Spanish, Italian, and German!'

'Poh! I shouldn't have minded it in the least,' Michael very coolly replied, his mouth being half full of beefsteak. 'The girls lead us in such things, of course. No man dreams of keeping up with a young lady who has got into the living languages. Miss Wilmeter might teach us both, and laugh at our ignorance in the bargain.'

'Sarah! Ay, she is a good enough girl in her *way* – but no more to be compared——'

Jack Wilmeter stopped short, for Millington dropped his knife, with not a little clatter, on his plate, and was gazing at his friend in a sort of fierce astonishment.

'You don't dream of comparing your sister to this unknown and suspected stranger!' at length Michael got out, speaking very much like one whose head has been held under water until his breath was nearly exhausted. 'You ought to recollect, John, that virtue should never be brought unnecessarily in contact with vice.'

'Mike, and do you, too, believe in the guilt of Mary Monson?'

'I believe that she is committed under a verdict given by an inquest, and think it best to suspend my opinion as to the main fact, in waiting for further evidence. Remember, Jack, how often your uncle has told us that, after all, good witnesses were the *gist* of the law. Let us wait and see what a trial may bring forth.'

Young Wilmeter covered his face with his hands, bowed his head to the table, and ate not another morsel that morning. His good sense admonished him of the prudence of the advice just given; while feelings, impetuous, and excited almost to fierceness, impelled him to go forth and war on all who denied the innocence of the accused. To own the truth, John Wilmeter was fast becoming entangled in the meshes of love.

And, sooth to say, notwithstanding the extreme awkwardness of her situation, the angry feeling that was so fast rising up against her in Biberry and its vicinity, and the general mystery that concealed her real name, character and history, there was that about Mary Monson, in her countenance, other personal advantages, and most of all in her manner and voice, that might well catch the fancy of a youth of warm feelings, and through his fancy, sooner or later, touch his heart. As yet, John was only under the influence of the new-born sentiment, and had he now been removed from Biberry, it is probable that the feelings and interest which had been so suddenly and powerfully awakened in him would have passed away altogether, or remained in shadow on his memory, as a melancholy and yet pleasant record of hours past, under circumstances in which men live fast, if they do not always live well. Little did the uncle think of the great danger to which he exposed his nephew when he placed him, like a sentinel in law, on duty near the portal of his immured client. But the experienced Dunscomb was anxious to bring John into active life, and to place him in situations that might lead him to think and execute for himself; and it had been much his practice, of late, to put the young man forward whenever circumstances would admit of it. Although the counsellor was more than at his ease in fortune, and John and Sarah each possessed very respectable means, that placed them altogether above dependence, he was exceedingly anxious that his nephew should succeed to his own business, as the surest mode of securing his happiness and respectability in a community where the number of the idle is relatively so small as to render the pursuits of a class that is by no means without its uses, where it can be made to serve the tastes and manners of a country difficult of attainment. He had the same desire in behalf of his niece, or that she should become the wife of a man who had something to do; and the circumstance that Millington, though of highly reputable connections, was almost entirely without fortune, was no objection in his eyes to the union that Sarah was so obviously inclined to form. The two young men had been left on the ground, therefore, to take care of the interests of a client whom Dunscomb was compelled to admit was one that interested him more than any other in whose services he had ever been employed, strongly as he was disposed to fear that appearances might be deceitful.

Our young men were not idle. In addition to doing all that was in their power to contribute to the personal comforts of Miss Monson, they were active and intelligent in obtaining, and making notes of, all the facts that had been drawn out by the coroner's inquest, or which could be gleaned in the neighbourhood. These facts, or rumours, John classed into the 'proved,' the 'reported,' the 'probable' and the 'improbable;' accompanying each division with such annotations as made a very useful sort of brief for any one who wished to push the inquiries further.

'There, Millington,' he said, when they reached the gaol, on their return from a walk as far as the ruins of the house which had been burnt, and after they had dined, 'there; I think we have done tolerably well for one day, and are in a fair way to give uncle Tom a pretty full account of this miserable business. The more I see and learn of it, the more I am convinced of the perfect innocence of the accused. I trust it strikes you in the same way, Mike?'

But Mike was by no means as sanguine as his friend. He smiled faintly at this question, and endeavoured to evade a direct answer. He saw how lively were the hopes of John, and how deeply his feelings were getting to be interested in the matter, while his own judgment, influenced, perhaps, by Mr Dunscomb's example, greatly inclined him to the worst foreboding of the result. Still he had an honest satisfaction in saying anything that might contribute to the gratification of Sarah's brother, and a good opportunity now offering, he did not let it escape him.

'There is one thing, Jack, that seems to have been strangely overlooked,' he said, 'and out of which some advantage may come, if it be thoroughly sifted. You may remember it was stated by some of the witnesses, that there was a German woman in the family of the Goodwins, the day that preceded the fire – one employed in housework?'

'Now you mention it, I do! Sure enough; what has become of that woman?'

'While you were drawing your diagram of the ruins, and projecting your plan of the out-buildings, garden, fields and so on, I stepped across to the nearest house, and had a chat with the ladies. You may remember I told you it was to get a drink of milk; but I saw petticoats, and thought something might be learned from woman's propensity to talk?'

'I know you left me, but was too busy, just then, to see on what errand, or whither you went.'

'It was to the old stone farm-house that stands only fifty rods from the ruins. The family in possession is named Burton, and a more talkative set I never encountered in petticoats.'

'How many had you to deal with, Mike?' John inquired, running his eyes over his notes as he asked the question, in a way that showed how little he anticipated from this interview with the Burtons. 'If more than one of the garrulous set, I pity you, for I had a specimen of them yesterday morning myself, in a passing interview.'

'There were three talkers, and one silent body. As is usual, I thought that the silent member of the house knew more than the speaker, if she had been inclined to let out her knowledge.'

'Ay, that is the way we have of judging of one another; but it is as often false as true. As many persons are silent because they have nothing to say, as because they are reflecting; and of those who *look* very wise, about one-half, as near as I can judge, *look* so as a sort of apology for being very silly.'

'I can't say how it was with Mrs Burton, the silent member of the family, in this case; but I do know that her three worthy sisters-in-law are to be classed among the foolish virgins.'

'Had they no oil to trim their lamps withal?'

'It had all been used to render their tongues limber. Never did three damsels pour out words in so full a rivulet as I was honoured with for the first five minutes. By the end of that time I was enabled to put a question or two; after which they were better satisfied to let me interrogate, while they were content to answer.'

'Did you learn anything, Mike, to reward you for all this trouble?' again glancing at his notes.

'I think I did. With a good deal of difficulty in *eliminating* the surplussage, if I may coin a word for the occasion, I got these facts: — It would seem that the German woman was a newly-arrived immigrant, who had strolled into the country, and offered to work for her food, &c. Mrs Goodwin usually attended to all her own domestic matters; but she had an attack of the rheumatism that predisposed her to receive this offer, and that so much the more willingly, because the "help" was not to be paid. It appears that the deceased female was an odd mixture of miserly propensities with a love of display. She hoarded all she could lay her hands on, and took a somewhat uncommon pleasure in showing her hoards to her neighbours. In consequence of this last weakness, the whole neighbourhood knew not only of her gold, for she turned every coin into that metal before it was consigned to her stocking, but of the amount to a dollar, and the place where she kept it. In this all agreed, even to the silent matron.'

'And what has become of this German woman?' asked John, closing his notes with sudden interest. 'Why was she not examined before the inquest? and where is she now?'

'No one knows. She has been missing ever since the fire, and a few fancy that she may, after all, be the person who has done the whole mischief. It does wear a strange look, that no trace can be heard of her!'

'This must be looked into closely, Mike. It is unaccountably strange that more was not said of her before the coroner. Yet, I fear one thing, too. Dr McBrain is a man of the highest attainments as an anatomist, and you will remember that he inclines to the opinion that both the skeletons belonged to females. Now, it may turn out that this German woman's remains have been found; which will put her guilt out of the question.'

'Surely, Jack, you would not be sorry to have it turn out that any human being should be innocent of such crimes!'

'By no means; though it really does seem to me more probable that an unknown straggler should be the guilty one in this case, than an educated young female, who has every claim in the way of attainments to be termed a lady. Besides, Michael, these German immigrants have brought more than their share of crime among us. Look at the reports of murders and robberies for the last ten years, and you will find that an undue proportion of them have been committed by this class of immigrants. To me nothing appears more probable than this affair's being traced up to that very woman.'

'I own you are right in saying what you do of the Germans. But it should be remembered that some of their states are said to have adopted the policy of sending their rogues to America. If *England* were to attempt that now I fancy Jonathan would hardly stand it!'

'He ought not to stand it for an hour, from any nation on earth. If there ever was a good cause for war, this is one. Yes, yes; that German immigrant must be looked up, and examined.'

Michael Millington smiled faintly at John Wilmeter's disposition to believe the worst of the High Dutch; touching the frailties of whom, however, neither of the two had exaggerated anything. Far more than their share of the grave crimes of this country have, within the period named, been certainly committed by immigrants from Germany; whether the cause be in the reason given, or in national character. This is not according to ancient opinion, but we believe it to be strictly according to fact. The Irish are clannish, turbulent, and much disposed to knock each other on the head; but it is not to rob, or to pilfer, but to quarrel. The Englishman will pick your pocket, or commit burglary, when inclined to roguery, and frequently he has a way of his own of extorting, in the way of vails. The Frenchmen may well boast of their freedom from wrongs done to persons or property in this country; no class of immigrants furnishing to the prisons, comparatively, fewer criminals. The natives, out of all proportion, are freest from crime, if the blacks be excepted, and when we compare the number of the convicted with the number of the people. Still, such results ought not to be taken as furnishing absolute rules by which to judge of large bodies of men; since unsettled lives on the one hand, and the charities of life on the other, may cause disproportions that would not otherwise exist.

'If one of these skeletons be that of the German woman, and Dr McBrain should prove to be right,' said John Wilmeter, earnestly, 'what has become of the remains of Mr Goodwin? There was a husband as well as a wife, in that family.'

'Very true,' answered Millington; 'and I learned something concerning him, too. It seems that the old fellow drank intensely, at times, when he and his wife made the house too hot to hold them. All the Burtons agreed in giving this account of the good couple. The failing was not generally known, and had not yet gone so far as to affect the old man's general character, though it would seem to have been known to the immediate neighbours.'

'And not one word of all this, is to be found in any of the reports in the papers from town! Not a particle of testimony on the point before the inquest! Why, Mike, this single fact may furnish a clue to the whole catastrophe.'

'In what way?' Millington very quietly inquired.

'Those bones are the bones of females; old Goodwin has robbed the house, set fire to it, murdered his wife and the German woman in a drunken frolic, and run away. Here is a history for Uncle Tom, that will delight him; for if he do not feel quite certain of Mary Monson's innocence now, he would be delighted to learn its truth!'

'You make much out of a very little, Jack, and imagine far more than you can prove. Why should old Goodwin set fire to his own house – for I understand the property was his – steal his own money – for, though married women did then hold a separate estate in a bed-quilt, or a gridiron, the law could not touch the previous accumulations of a *femme covert* – and murder a poor foreigner, who could neither give nor take away anything that the building contained? Then he is to burn his own house, and make himself a vagrant in his old age – and that among strangers! I learn he was born in that very house, and has passed his days in it. Such a man would not be very likely to destroy it.'

'Why not, to conceal a murder? Crime must be concealed, or it is punished.'

'Sometimes,' returned Michael, drily. – 'This Mary Monson will be hanged, out of all question, should the case go against her, for she understands French, and Italian, and German, you say; either of which tongues would be sufficient to hang her; but had old Mrs Goodwin murdered *her*, philanthropy would have been up and stirring, and no rope would be stretched.'

'Millington, you have a way of talking, at times, that is quite shocking! I do wish you could correct it. What use is there in bringing a young lady like Miss Monson down to the level of a common criminal?'

'She will be brought down as low as that, depend on it, if guilty. There is no hope for one who bears about her person, in air, manner, speech, and deportment, the unequivocal signs of a lady. Our sympathies are all kept for those who are less set apart from the common herd. Sympathy goes by majorities as well as other matters.'

'You think her, at all events, a lady?' said John, quickly. 'How, then, can you suppose it possible that she has been guilty of the crimes of which she stands accused?'

'Simply, because my old-fashioned father has given me old-fashioned notions of the meaning of terms. So thin-skinned have people become lately that even language must be perverted to gratify their conceit. The terms "gentleman" and "lady" have as defined meanings as any two words we possess – signifying persons of cultivated minds, and of certain refinements in tastes and manners. Morals have nothing to do with either, necessarily, as a "gentleman" or "lady" may be very wicked; nay, often are. It is true there are particular acts, partaking of meannesses, rather than anything decidedly criminal, that, by a convention, a gentleman or lady may not commit; but there are a hundred others, that are far worse, which are not prohibited. It is unlady-like to *talk* scandal; but it is not deemed always unlady-like to give grounds to scandal. Here is a bishop who has lately been defining a gentleman, and, as usually happens with such men, unless they were originally on a level with their dioceses, he describes a "Christian," rather than a "gentleman." This notion of making converts by means of enlisting our vanity and self-love in the cause, is but a weak one, at the best.'

'Certainly, Mike; I agree with you in the main. As large classes of polished people do exist, who have loose enough notions of morals, there ought to be terms to designate them, as a class, as well as to give any other name, when we have the thing. Use has applied those of "gentlemen" and "ladies," and I can see no sufficient reason for changing them.'

'It comes wholly from the longings of human vanity. As a certain distinction is attached to the term, everybody is covetous of obtaining it, and all sorts of reasoning is resorted to, to drag them into the categories. It would be the same, if it were a ground of distinction to have but one ear. But this distinction will be very likely to make things go hard with our client, Jack, if the jury say "guilty."'

'The jury never can – never *will* render such a verdict! I do not think the grand jury will even return a bill. Why should they? The testimony wouldn't convict an old state-prison-bird.'

Michael Millington smiled, a little sadly, perhaps – for John Wilmeter was Sarah's only brother – but he made no reply, perceiving that an old negro, named Sip, or Scipio, who lived about the gaol by a sort of sufferance, and who had now been a voluntary adherent of a place that was usually so unpleasant to men of his class for many years, was approaching, as if he were the bearer of a message. Sip was an old-school black, grey-headed, and had seen more than his three-score years and ten. No wonder, then, that his dialect partook, in a considerable degree, of the peculiarities that were once so marked in a Manhattan 'nigger.' Unlike his brethren of the present day, he was courtesy itself to all 'gentlemen,' while his respect for 'common folks' was a good deal more equivocal. But chiefly did the old man despise 'yaller fellers;' these he regarded as a mongrel race, who could neither aspire to the pure complexion of the Circassian stock, nor lay claim to the glistening dye of Africa.

'Mrs Gott, she want to see masser,' said Scipio, bowing to John, grinning – for a negro seldom loses his teeth – and turning civilly to Millington, with a respectful inclination of a head that was as white as snow. 'Yes, sah; she want to see masser, soon as conben'ent; and soon as he can come.'

Now Mrs Gott was the wife of the sheriff, and, alas for the dignity of the office! the sheriff was the keeper of the county gaol. This is one of the fruits born on the wide-spreading branches of the tree of democracy. Formerly, a New York sheriff bore a strong resemblance to his English namesake. He was one of the county gentry, and executed the duties of his office with an air and a manner; appeared in court with a sword, and carried with his name a weight and an authority that now are nearly wanting. Such men would scarcely become gaolers. But that universal root of all evil, the love of money, made the discovery that there was profit to be had in feeding the prisoners, and a lower class of men aspired to the offices, and obtained them; since which time, more than half of the sheriffs of New York have been their own gaolers.

'Do you know *why* Mrs Gott wishes to see me, Scipio?' demanded Wilmeter.

'I b'lieve, sah, dat 'e young woman, as murders ole Masser Goodwin and he wife, ask her to send for masser.'

This was plain enough, and it caused Jack a severe pang; for it showed how conclusively and unsparingly the popular mind had made up its opinion touching Mary Monson's guilt. There was no time to be lost, however; and the young man hastened towards the building to which the gaol was attached, both standing quite near the court-house. In the door of what was her dwelling, for the time being, stood Mrs Gott, the wife of the high sheriff of the county, and the only person in all Biberry who, as it appeared to John, entertained his own opinions of the innocence of the accused. But Mrs Gott was by nature a kind-hearted woman; and, though so flagrantly out of place in her united characters, was just such a person as ought to have the charge of the female department of a prison. Owing to the constant changes of the democratic principle of rotation in office, one of the most impudent of all the devices of a covetous envy, this woman had not many months before come out of the bosom of society, and had not seen enough of the ways of her brief and novel situation to have lost any of those qualities of her sex, such as extreme kindness, gentleness of disposition, and feminine feelings, that are anything but uncommon among the women of America. In many particulars she would have answered the imaginative bishop's descriptions of a 'lady;' but she would have been sadly deficient in some of the requisites that the opinions of the world have attached to the character. In these last particulars, Mary Monson, as compared with this worthy matron, was like a being of another race; though, as respects the first, we shall refer the reader to the events to be hereafter related, that he may decide the question according to his own judgment.

'Mary Monson has sent for you, Mr Wilmeter,' the good Mrs Gott commenced, in a low confidential sort of tone, as if she imagined that she and John were the especial guardians of this unknown and seemingly ill-fated young woman's fortunes. 'She is wonderfully resigned and patient – a great deal more patient than I should be, if I was obliged to live in this gaol – that is, on the other side of the strong doors; but she told me, an hour ago, that she is not sure, after all, her imprisonment is not the very best thing that could happen to her!'

'That was a strange remark,' returned John. 'Did she make it under a show of feeling, as if penitence, or any other strong emotion, induced her to utter it?'

'With as sweet a smile, as composed a manner, and as gentle and soft a voice as a body ever sees, or listens to! What a wonderfully soft and musical voice she has, Mr Wilmeter!'

'She has, indeed. I was greatly struck with it the moment I heard her speak. How much like a lady, Mrs Gott, she uses it – and how correct and well-pronounced are her words!'

Although Mrs Gott and John Wilmeter had very different ideas, at the bottom, of the requisites to form a lady, and the pronunciation of the good woman was by no means faultless, she cordially assented to the truth of the young man's eulogy. Indeed, Mary Monson, for the hour, was her great theme; and though still a young woman herself, and good-looking withal, she really seemed never to tire of uttering her praises.

'She has been educated, Mr Wilmeter, far above any female hereabout, unless it may be some of the ——s and ——s,' the good woman continued. 'Those families, you know, are our upper crust – not upper ten thousand, as the newspapers call it, but upper hundred, and their ladies may know as much as Mary; but beyond *them*, no female hereabouts can hold a candle to her! Her books have been brought in, and I looked them over – there isn't more than one in three that I can read at all. What is more, they don't seem to be all in one tongue, the foreign books, but in three or four!'

'She certainly has a knowledge of several of the living languages, and an accurate knowledge, too. I know a little of such things myself, but my friend Millington is quite strong in both the living and dead languages, and he says that what she knows she knows well.'

'That is comforting – for a young lady that can speak so many different tongues would hardly think of robbing and murdering two old people in their beds. Well, sir, perhaps you had better go to the door and see her, though I could stay here and talk about her all day. Pray, Mr Wilmeter, which of the languages is really dead?'

John smiled, but civilly enlightened the sheriff's lady on this point, and then, preceded by her, he went to the important door which separated the dwelling of the family from the rooms of the gaol. Once opened, an imperfect communication is obtained with the interior of the last, by means of a grating in an inner door. The gaol of Duke's county is a recent construction, and is built on a plan that is coming much into favour, though still wanting in the highest proof of civilization, by sufficiently separating criminals, and in treating the accused with a proper degree of consideration until the verdict of a jury has pronounced them guilty.

The construction of this gaol was very simple. A strong, low, oblong building had been erected on a foundation so filled in with stones as to render digging nearly impossible. The floors were of large massive stones, that ran across the whole building, a distance of some thirty feet, or if there were joints, they were under the partition walls, rendering them as secure as if solid. The cells were not large, certainly, but of sufficient size to admit of light and air. The ceilings were of the same enormous flat stones as the floors, well secured by a load of stones and beams to brace them, and the partitions were of solid masonry. There the prisoner is encased in stone, and nothing can be more hopeless than an attempt to get out of one of these cells, provided the gaoler gives even ordinary attention to their condition. Above and around them are erected the outer walls of the gaol. The last comprise an ordinary stone house, with roof, windows, and the other customary appliances of a human abode. As these walls stand several feet without those of the real prison, and are somewhat higher, the latter are an *imperium in imperio*; a house within a house. The space between the walls of the two buildings forms a gallery extending around all the cells. Iron grated gates divide the several parts of this gallery into so many compartments, and in the gaol of Biberry care has been had so to arrange these subdivisions that those within any one compartment may be concealed from those in all of the others, but the two that immediately join it. The breezes are admitted by means of the external windows, while the height of the ceiling in the galleries, and the space above the tops of the cells, contribute largely to comfort and health in this important particular. As the doors of the cells stand opposite to the windows, the entire gaol can be, and usually is, made airy and light.

Stoves in the galleries preserve the temperature, and effectually remove all disagreeable moisture. In a word, the place is as neat, convenient, and decent as the gaol of convicts need ever to be; but the proper sort of distinction is not attended to between them and those who are merely accused. Our civilization in this respect is defective. While the land is filled with senseless cries against an aristocracy which, if it exist at all, exists in the singular predicament of being far less favoured than the democracy, involving a contradiction in terms; against a feudality that consists in men's having bargained to pay their debts in chickens, no one complaining in behalf of those who have entered into contracts to do the same in wheat; and against *rent*, while *usury* is not only smiled on, but encouraged, and efforts are made to legalise extortion; the public mind is quiet on the subject of the treatment of those whom the policy of government demands should be kept in security until their guilt or innocence be established. What reparation, under such circumstances, can be made to him to whom the gates are finally opened, for having been incarcerated on charges that are groundless? The gaols of the Christian world were first constructed by an irresponsible power, and to confine the weak. We imitate the vices of the system with a cool indifference, and shout 'feudality' over a bantam, or a pound of butter, that are paid under contracted covenants for rent!

CHAPTER VII

'Sir, this is the house; please it you that I call?'
Taming of the Shrew.

The grated window which John Wilmeter now approached commanded nearly an entire view of the gallery that communicated with the cell of Mary Monson. It also commanded a partial view of the cell itself. As he looked through the grates he saw how neat and comfortable the last had been made by means of Mrs Gott's care, aided, doubtless, by some of the prisoner's money – that gold which was, in fact, the strongest and only very material circumstance against her. Mrs Gott had put a carpet in the cell, and divers pieces of furniture that were useful, as well as two or three that were intended to be ornamental, rendering the otherwise gloomy little apartment tolerably cheerful. The gallery, much to John's surprise, had been furnished, also. Pieces of new carpeting were laid on the flags, chairs and table had been provided, and among other articles of this nature was a very respectable looking-glass. Everything appeared new, and as if just sent from the different shops where the various articles were sold. Wilmeter fancied that not less than a hundred dollars had been expended in furnishing that gallery. The effect was surprising; taking away from the place its chilling, gaol-like air, and giving to it what it had never possessed before, one of household comfort.

Mary Monson was walking to and fro in this gallery with slow, thoughtful steps, her head a little bowed, and her hands hanging before her with the fingers interlocked. So completely was she lost in thought that John's footstep, or presence at the grate, was not observed, and he had an opportunity to watch her for near a minute, unseen himself. The occupation was not exactly excusable; but, under all the circumstances, young Wilmeter felt as if it might be permitted. It was his duty to ascertain all he fairly might concerning his client.

It has already been said that this strange girl, extraordinary by her situation as a person accused of crimes so heinous, and perhaps still more so by her manner of bearing up against the terrors and mortifications of her condition, as well as by the mystery which so completely veiled her past life, was not a beauty, in the common acceptation of the term. Nevertheless, not one female in ten thousand would sooner ensnare the heart of a youth, by means of her personal attractions alone. It was not regularity of features, nor brilliancy of complexion, nor lustre of the eyes, nor any of the more ordinary charms, that gave her this power, but an indescribable union of feminine traits, in which intellectual gifts, spirit, tenderness, and modesty, were so singularly blended, as to leave it questionable which had the advantage. Her eyes were of a very gentle and mild expression when in a state of rest; excited, they were capable of opening windows to the inmost soul. Her form was faultless; being the true medium between vigorous health and womanly delicacy; which in this country implies much less of the robust and solid than one meets with in the other hemisphere.

It is not easy to tell how we acquire those in-and-in habits, which get to be a sort of second nature, and almost bestow on us new instincts. It is by these secret sympathies, these tastes that pervade the moral, as the nerves form a natural telegraph through the physical, system, that one *feels* rather than *sees*, when he is in the company of persons in his own class in life. Dress will not afford an infallible test on such an occasion, though the daw is instantly seen not to be the peacock; neither will *address*, for the distinctive qualities lie much deeper than the surface. But so it is; a gentleman can hardly be brought into the company of man or woman, without his at once perceiving whether he or she belong to his own social caste or not. What is more, if a man of the world, he detects almost instinctively the *degrees* of caste, as well as the greater subdivisions, and knows whether his strange companions have seen much or little; whether their gentility is merely the result of the great accident, with its customary advantages, or has been smoothed over by a liberal intercourse with the better classes of a general society. Most of all may a travelled person be known – and that more especially in a provincial country, like our own – from one that has not travelled; though the company kept in other lands necessarily draws an obvious distinction between the last. Now John Wilmeter, always mingling with the best society of his own country, had also been abroad, and had obtained that 'second sight' which so insensibly, but certainly, increases the vision of all Americans who enjoy the advantage of acquiring it. What is more, though his years and the plans of his uncle for his future welfare had prevented his staying in Europe long enough to receive all the benefit such a tour can bestow, he had remained long enough to pass beyond the study of merely physical things; and had made certain acquisitions in other matters, more essential to tastes if not to character. When an American returns from an excursion into the Old World, with 'I come back better satisfied than ever with my own country,' it is an infallible sign that he did not stay long enough abroad; and when he returns only to find fault, it is equally proof that he has stayed too long. There is a happy medium which teaches something near the truth, and that would tell us that there are a thousand things to be amended and improved at home, while there are almost as many enjoyed, that the oldest and most polished people on earth might envy. John Wilmeter had not reached the point that enabled him to make the nicest distinctions, but he was sufficiently advanced to have detected what he conceived to be signs that this singular young creature, unknown, unsupported by any who appeared to take an interest in her, besides himself and the accidental acquaintances formed under the most painful circumstances, had been abroad; perhaps, had been educated there. The regulated tones of one of the sweetest voices he had ever heard, the distinctness and precision of her utterance, as far as possible removed from mouthing and stiffness, but markedly quiet and even, with a total absence of all the affectations of boarding-school grammar, were so many proofs of even a European education, as he fancied; and before that week was terminated John had fully made up his mind that Mary Monson – though an American by birth, about which there could be no dispute – had been well taught in some of the schools of the Old World.

This was a conclusion not reached immediately. He had to be favoured with several interviews, and to worm himself gradually into the confidence of his uncle's client, ere he could be permitted to see enough of the subject of his studies to form an opinion so abstruse and ingenious.

When Mary Monson caught a glimpse of John Wilmeter's head at her grate – where he stood respectfully uncovered, as in a lady's presence – a slight flush passed over her face; but expecting him, as she did, she could not well be surprised.

'This bears some resemblance, Mr Wilmeter, to an interview in a convent,' she then said, with a slight smile, but with perfect composure of manner. 'I am the novice – and novice am I indeed to scenes like this – you, the excluded friend, who is compelled to pay his visit through a grate! I must apologize for all the trouble I am giving you.'

'Do not name it – I cannot be better employed than in your behalf. I am rejoiced that you sustain yourself so well against what must be a most unheard-of calamity, for one like yourself, and cannot but admire the admirable equanimity with which you bear your cruel fortune.'

'Equanimity!' repeated Mary with emphasis, and a slight display of intense feeling, powerfully controlled; 'if it be so, Mr Wilmeter, it must be from the sense of security that I feel. Yes; for the first time in months, I do feel myself safe – secure.'

'Safe! – Secure! – What, in a gaol?'

'Certainly; gaols are intended for places of security, are they not?' answered Mary, smiling, but faintly and with a gleam of sadness on her face. 'This may appear wonderful to you, but I do tell no more than sober truth, in repeating that, for the first time in months, I have now a sense of security. I am what you call in the hands of the law, and one there must be safe from everything but what the law can do to her. Of that I have no serious apprehensions, and I feel happy.'

'Happy!'

'Yes; by comparison, happy. I tell you this the more willingly, for I plainly see you feel a generous interest in my welfare – an interest which exceeds that of the counsel in his client——'

'A thousand times exceeds it, Miss Monson! Nay – is not to be named with it!'

'I thank you, Mr Wilmeter – from my heart I thank you,' returned the prisoner, a slight flush passing over her features, while her eyes were cast towards the floor. 'I believe you are one of strong feelings and quick impulses, and am grateful that these have been in my favour, under circumstances that might well have excused you for thinking the worst. From the hints of this kind woman, Mrs Gott, I am afraid that the opinion of Biberry is less consoling?'

'You must know how it is in country villages, Miss Monson, – every one has something to say, and every one bring all things down to the level of his own knowledge and understanding.'

Mary Monson smiled again; this time more naturally, and without any painful expression to lessen the bright influence that lighting up of her features gave to a countenance so remarkable for its appearance of illumination from within.

'Is not such the case in towns as well as in villages, Mr Wilmeter?' she asked.

'Perhaps it is; but I mean that the circle of knowledge is more confined in a place like this than in a large town, and that the people here could not well go beyond it.'

'Biberry is so near New York that I should think, taking class against class, no great difference can be found in their inhabitants. That which the good folk of Biberry think of my case, I am afraid will be thought of it by those of your own town.'

'*My* own town? – and are you not really from New York, Miss Monson?'

'In no manner,' answered Mary, once more smiling; this time, however, because she understood how modestly and readily her companion was opening a door by which she might let a secret she had declined to reveal to his uncle, escape. 'I am not what you call a Manhattanese in either descent, birth, or residence; in no sense whatever.'

'But, surely, you have never been educated in the country? You must belong to some large town – your manners show that – I mean that you——'

'Do not belong to Biberry. In that you are quite right, sir. I had never seen Biberry two months since; but, as for New York, I have not passed a month there in my whole life. The longest visit I ever paid you was one of ten days, when I landed coming from Havre, about eighteen months since.'

'From Havre! Surely you are an American, Miss Monson – our own countrywoman?'

'Your own countrywoman, Mr Wilmeter, by birth, descent, and feelings. But an American female may visit Europe.'

'Certainly; and be educated there, as I had already suspected was your case.'

'In part it was, and in part it was not.' Here Mary paused, looked a little arch, seemed to hesitate, and to have some doubts whether she ought to proceed or not, but finally added – 'You have been abroad, yourself.'

'I have. I was nearly three years in Europe, and have not been home yet quite a twelvemonth.'

'You went into the east, I believe, after passing a few months in the Pyrenees?' continued the prisoner, carelessly.

'You are quite right; we travelled as far as Jerusalem. The journey has got to be so common, that it is no longer dangerous. Even ladies make it, now, without any apprehension.'

'I am aware of that, having made it myself——'

'You, Miss Monson! You been at Jerusalem!'

'Why not, Mr Wilmeter? You say, yourself, that females constantly make the journey; why not I, as well as another?'

'I scarce know, myself; but it is so strange — all about you is so very extraordinary——'

'You think it extraordinary that one of my sex, who has been partly educated in Europe, and who has travelled in the Holy Land, should be shut up in this gaol in Biberry — is it not so?'

'That is one view of the matter, I will confess; but it was scarcely less strange that such a person should be dwelling in a garret-room of a cottage like that of these unfortunate Goodwins.'

'That touches on my secret, sir; and no more need be said. You may judge how important I consider that secret, when I know its preservation subjects me to the most cruel distrust; and that, too, in the minds of those with whom I would so gladly stand fair. Your excellent uncle, for instance, and — yourself.'

'I should be much flattered, could I think the last — I who have scarcely the claim of an acquaintance.'

'You forget the situation in which your respectable and most worthy uncle has left you here, Mr Wilmeter; which, of itself, gives you higher claims to my thanks and confidence than any that mere acquaintance could bestow. Besides, we are not' — another arch, but scarcely perceptible smile, again illuminated that remarkable countenance — 'the absolute strangers to each other that you seem to think us.'

'Not strangers? You amaze me! If I have ever had the honour—'

'Honour!' interrupted Mary, a little bitterly. 'It is truly a great honour to know one in my situation!'

'I esteem it an honour, and no one has a right to call in question my sincerity. If we have ever met before, I will frankly own that I am ignorant of both the time and place.'

'This does not surprise me, in the least. The time is long, for persons as young as ourselves, and the place was far away. Ah! those were happy days for me, and most gladly would I return to them! But we have talked enough on this subject. I have declined telling my tale to your most excellent and very respectable uncle; you will, therefore, the more easily excuse me, if I decline telling it to you.'

'Who am not "most excellent and very respectable," to recommend me.'

'Who are too near my own age, to make you a proper confidant, were there no other objection. The character that I learned of you, when we met before, Mr Wilmeter, was, however, one of which you have no reason to be ashamed.'

This was said gently, but earnestly; was accompanied by a most winning smile, and was instantly succeeded by a slight blush. John Wilmeter rubbed his forehead, sooth to say, in a somewhat stupid manner, as if expecting to brighten his powers of recollection by friction.

A sudden change was given to the conversation, however, by the fair prisoner herself, who quietly resumed –

'We will defer this part of the subject to another time. I did not presume to send for you, Mr Wilmeter, without an object, having your uncle's authority for giving you all this trouble——'

'And my own earnest request to be permitted to serve you in any way I could.'

'I have not forgotten that offer, nor shall I ever. The man who is willing to serve a woman, whom all around her frown on, has a fair claim to be remembered. Good Mrs Gott and yourself are the only two friends I have in Biberry. Even your companion, Mr Millington, is a little disposed to judge me harshly.'

John started; the movement was so natural, that his honest countenance would have betrayed him, had he been disposed to deny the imputation.

'That Millington has fallen into the popular notion about here, I must allow, Miss Monson; but he is an excellent fellow at the bottom and will hear reason. Prejudices that are beyond reason are detestable, and I generally avoid those whose characters manifest this weakness; but Mike will always listen to what he calls "law and facts," and so we get along very well together.'

'It is fortunate; since you are about to be so nearly connected——'

'Connected! Is it possible that *you* know this circumstance?'

'You will find, in the end, Mr Wilmeter,' returned the prisoner, smiling – this time naturally, as one manifests satisfaction without pain of any sort – 'that I know more of your private affairs than you had supposed. But let me come to business, if you please, sir; I have great occasion here for a maid-servant. Do you not think that Miss Wilmeter might send me one from town.'

'A servant! I know the very woman that will suit you. A perfect jewel, in her way!'

'That is a very housekeeper sort of a character,' rejoined Mary, absolutely laughing, in spite of her prison walls, and all the terrible charges that had brought her within them; 'just such a character as I might have expected from Dr McBrain's intended, Mrs Updyke——'

'And you know it, too! Why will you not tell us more, since you tell us so much!'

'In good time, I suppose all will come out. Well, I endeavour to submit to my fate; or to the will of God!' There was no longer anything merry, in voice, face, or manner, but a simple, natural pathos was singularly mixed in the tones with which these few words were uttered. Then rousing herself, she gravely resumed the subject which had induced her to send for John.

'You will pardon me, if I say that I would prefer a woman chosen and recommended by your sister, Mr Wilmeter, than one chosen and recommended by yourself,' said Mary. 'When I shall have occasion for a footman, I will take your advice. It is very important that I should engage a respectable, discreet woman; and I will venture to write a line, myself, to Miss Wilmeter, if you will be so kind as to send it. I know this is not the duty of a counsel, but you see my situation. Mrs Gott has offered to procure a girl for me, it is true; but the prejudice is so strong against me in Biberry, that I doubt if the proper sort of person could be obtained. At any rate, I should be receiving a spy into my little household, instead of a domestic, in whom I could place confidence.'

'Sarah would join me in recommending Marie, who has been with herself more than two years, and only left her to take care of her father in his last illness. Another, equally excellent, has been taken in her place; and now, that she wishes to return to my sister's service, there is no opening for her. Mike Millington is dying to return to town, and will gladly go over this evening. By breakfast-time to-morrow, the woman might be here, if——'

'She will consent to serve a mistress in my cruel situation. I feel the full weight of the objection, and know how difficult it will be to get a female, who values her character as a servant, to enter on such an engagement. You called this woman Marie; by that, I take it she is a foreigner?'

'A Swiss – her parents emigrated; but I knew her in the service of an American family abroad, and got her for Sarah. She is the best creature in the world – if she can be persuaded to come.'

'Had she been an American, I should have despaired of succeeding unless her feelings could have been touched; but, as she is a foreigner, perhaps money will procure her services. Should Miss Wilmeter approve of your selection, sir, I will entreat her to go as high as fifty dollars a month, rather than not get the sort of person I want. You can imagine how much importance I attach to success. To escape remarks and gossiping, the person engaged can join me as a companion, or friend, and not as a servant.'

'I will get Mike off in half an hour, and Sarah will at least make an effort. Yes, Marie Moulin, or Mary Mill, as the girls call her, is just the thing!'

'Marie Moulin! Is that the name of the woman? She who was in the service of the Barringers, at Paris? Do you mean *that* person – five-and-thirty, slightly pock-marked, with light blue eyes, and yellowish hair – more like a German, than her French name would give reason to expect?'

'The very same; and you knew her, *too!* Why not bring all your friends around you at once, Miss Monson, and not remain here an hour longer than is necessary.'

Mary was too intent on the subject of engaging the woman in question to answer this last appeal. Earnestly did she resume her instructions, therefore, and with an eagerness of manner young Wilmeter had never before observed in her.

'If Marie Moulin be the person meant,' she said, 'I will spare no pains to obtain her services. Her attentions to poor Mrs Barringer, in her last illness, were admirable; and we all loved her, I may say. Beg your sister to tell her, Mr Wilmeter, that an old acquaintance, in distress, implores her assistance. That will bring Marie sooner than money, Swiss though she be.'

'If you would write her a line, enclosing your real name, for we are persuaded it is not Monson, it might have more effect than all our solicitations in behalf of one that is unknown.'

The prisoner turned slowly from the grate, and walked up and down her gallery for a minute or two, as if pondering on this proposal. Once she smiled, and it almost gave a lustre to her remarkable countenance; then a cloud passed over her face, and once more she appeared sad.

'No,' she said, stopping near the grate again, in one of her turns. 'I will not do it – it will be risking too much. I can do nothing just now, that will tell more of me than your sister can state.'

'Should Marie Moulin know you, she must recognise you when you meet.'

'It will be wiser to proceed a little in the dark. I confide all to your powers of negotiation, and shall remain as tranquil as possible until to-morrow morning. There is still another little affair that I must trouble you with, Mr Wilmeter. My gold is sequestered, as you know, and I am reduced to an insufficient amount of twos and threes. Might I ask the favour of you to obtain smaller notes for this, without mentioning in whose behalf it is done?'

While speaking, Mary handed through the grate a hundred dollar note of one of the New York Banks, with a manner so natural and unpretending as at once to convince John Wilmeter, ever so willing to be persuaded into anything in her favour, that she was accustomed to the use of money in considerable sums; or, what might be considered so, for the wants and habits of a female. Luckily he had nearly money enough in his wallet to change the note, making up a small balance that was needed by drawing five half-eagles from his purse. The prisoner held the last in the open palm of one of the most beautiful little hands the eyes of man ever rested on.

'This metal has been my bane, in more ways than one, Mr Wilmeter,' she said, looking mournfully at the coin. 'Of one of its evil influences on my fate I may not speak now, if ever; but you will understand me when I say, that I fear that gold piece of Italian money is the principal cause of my being where I am.'

'No doubt it has been considered one of the most material of the facts against you, Miss Monson; though it is by no means conclusive, as evidence, even with the most bitter and prejudiced.'

'I hope not. Now, Mr Wilmeter, I will detain you no longer; but beg you to do my commission with your sister, as you would do it for her with me. I would write, but my hand is so peculiar it were better that I did not.'

Mary Monson now dismissed the young man, with a manner of one very familiar with the tone of good society, a term that it is much the fashion to ridicule just now, but which conveys a meaning that it were better the scoffers understood. This she did, however, after again apologising for the trouble she was giving, and thanking him earnestly for the interest he took in her affairs. We believe in animal magnetism, and cannot pretend to say what is the secret cause of the powerful sympathy that is so often suddenly awakened between persons of different sexes, and in some instances between those who are of the same sex; but Mary Monson, by that species of instinct that teaches the female where she has awakened an interest livelier than common, and possibly where she has not, was certainly already aware that John Wilmeter did not regard her with the same cool indifference he would have felt towards an ordinary client of his uncle's. In thanking him, therefore, her own manner manifested a little of the reflected feeling that such a state of things is pretty certain to produce. She coloured, and slightly hesitated once, as if she paused to choose her terms with more than usual care; but, in the main, acquitted herself well. The parting betrayed interest, perhaps feeling, on both sides; but nothing very manifest escaped either of our young people.

Never had John Wilmeter been at a greater loss to interpret facts, than he was on quitting the grate. The prisoner was truly the most incomprehensible being he had ever met with. Notwithstanding the fearful nature of the charges against her – charges that might well have given great uneasiness to the firmest man – she actually seemed in love with her prison. It is true, that worthy Mrs Gott had taken from the place many of its ordinary, repulsive features; but it was still a gaol, and the sun could be seen only through grates, and massive walls separated her that was within, from the world without. As the young man was predisposed to regard everything connected with this extraordinary young woman *couleur de rose*, however, he saw nothing but the surest signs of innocence in several circumstances that might have increased the distrust of his cooler-headed uncle; but most persons would have regarded the gentle tranquillity that now seemed to soothe a spirit that had evidently been much troubled of late, as a sign that her hand could never have committed the atrocities with which she was charged.

'Is she not a sweet young thing, Mr Wilmeter?' exclaimed kind Mrs Gott, while locking the doors after John, on his retiring from the grate. 'I consider it an honour to Biberry gaol, to have such a prisoner within its walls!'

'I believe that you and I stand alone in our favourable opinion of Miss Monson,' John answered; 'so far, at least, as Biberry is concerned. The excitement against her seems to be at the highest pitch; and I much doubt whether a fair trial can be had in the county.'

'The newspapers won't mend the matter, sir. The papers from town, this morning, are full of the affair, and they all appear to lean the same way. But it's a long road that has no turning, Mr Wilmeter.'

'Very true, and nothing wheels about with a quicker step than the sort of public opinion that is got up under a cry, and runs itself out of breath, at the start. I expect to see Mary Monson the most approved and most extolled woman in this county, yet!'

Mrs Gott hoped with all her heart that it might be so, though *she* had, certainly, misgivings that the young man did not feel. Half an hour after John Wilmeter had left the gaol, his friend, Michael Millington, was on the road to town, carrying a letter to Sarah, with a most earnest request that she would use all her influence with Marie Moulin to engage in the unusual service asked of her, for a few weeks, if no longer a period. This letter reached its destination in due time, and greatly did the sister marvel over its warmth, as well as over the nature of the request.

'I never knew John to write so earnestly!' exclaimed Sarah, when she and Michael had talked over the matter a few moments. 'Were he actually in love, I could not expect him to be more pressing.'

'I will not swear that he is not,' returned the friend, laughing. 'He sees everything with eyes so different from mine, that I scarce know what to make of him. I have never known John so deeply interested in any human being, as he is at this moment in this strange creature!'

'Creature! You men do not often call young ladies *creatures*; and my brother affirms that this Mary Monson is a lady.'

'Certainly she is, so far as exterior, manner, education, and, I suppose, tastes are concerned. Nevertheless, there is too much reason to think she is, in some way unknown to us, connected with crime.'

'I have read accounts of persons of these attainments, who have been leagued together, and have carried on a great system of plundering for years, with prodigious success. That, however, was in older countries, where the necessities of a crowded population drive men into extremes. We are hardly sufficiently advanced, or civilized as they call it, for such bold villany.

'A suspicion of that nature has crossed my mind,' returned Millington, looking askance over his shoulder, as if he apprehended that his friend might hear him. 'It will not do, however, to remotely hint to John anything of the sort. His mind is beyond the influence of testimony.'

Sarah scarce knew what to make of the affair, though sisterly regard disposed her to do all she could to oblige her brother. Marie Moulin, however, was not easily persuaded into consenting to serve a mistress who was in prison. She held up her hands, turned up her eyes, uttered fifty exclamations, and declared, over and over again *'c'est impossible*;' and wondered how a female in such a situation could suppose any respectable domestic would serve her, as it would be very sure to prevent her ever getting a good place afterwards. This last objection struck Sarah as quite reasonable, and had not her brother been so very urgent with her, would of itself have induced her to abandon all attempt at persuasion. Marie, however, finally yielded to a feeling of intense curiosity, when no bribe in money could have bought her. John had said the prisoner knew her – had known her in Europe – and she was soon dying with the desire to know who, of all her many acquaintances in the old world, could be the particular individual who had got herself into this formidable difficulty. It was impossible to resist this feeling, so truly feminine, which was a good deal stimulated by a secret wish in Sarah, also, to learn who this mysterious person might be; and who did not fail to urge Marie, with all her rhetoric, to consent to go and, at least, see the person who had so strong a wish to engage her services. The Swiss had not so much difficulty in complying, provided she was permitted to reserve her final decision until she had met the prisoner, when she might gratify her curiosity, and return to town prepared to enlighten Miss Wilmeter, and all her other friends, on a subject that had got to be intensely interesting.

It was not late, next morning, when Marie Moulin, attended by John Wilmeter, presented herself to Mrs Gott, as an applicant for admission to the gallery of Mary Monson. The young man did not show himself on this occasion; though he was near enough to hear the grating of the hinges when the prison-door opened.

'C'est bien vous donc, Marie!' said the prisoner, in a quick but pleased salutation.

'Mademoiselle!' exclaimed the Swiss. The kisses of women succeeded. The door closed, and John Wilmeter learned no more, on that occasion.

CHAPTER VIII

And can you by no drift of conference
Get from him, why he puts on this confusion—

Hamlet.

There is something imaginative, if not very picturesque, in the manner in which the lawyers of Manhattan occupy the buildings of Nassau Street, a thoroughfare which connects Wall Street with the Tombs. There they throng, resembling the remains of so many monuments along the Appian way, with a '*siste, viator*' of their own, to arrest the footsteps of the wayfarer. We must now transfer the scene to a building in this street, which stands about half-way between Maiden Lane and John Street, having its front plastered over with little tin signs, like a debtor marked by writs, or what are now called 'complaints.' Among these signs, which afforded some such pleasant reading as an almanac, was one that bore this simple and reasonably intelligent inscription:

'Thomas Dunscomb, 2nd floor, in front.'

'It is somewhat singular that terms as simple as those of first-floor, second floor, &c., should not signify the same things in the language of the mother-country, and that of this land of progress and liberty. Certain it is, nevertheless, that in American parlance, more especially in that of Manhattan, a first-floor is never up one pair of stairs, as in London, unless indeed the flight is that by which the wearied foot-passenger climbs the high stoop to gain an entrance into the building. In other words, an English first-floor corresponds with an American second; and, taking that as the point of departure, the same difference exists throughout. Tom Dunscomb's office (or offices would be the better term) occupied quite half of the second story of a large double house, that had once been the habitation of some private family of note, but which had long been abandoned to the occupation of these ministers of the law. Into those offices it has now become our duty to accompany one who seemed a little strange in that den of the profession, at the very moment he was perfectly at home.

'Lawyer Dunscomb in?' demanded this person, who had a decided rustic mien, though his dress had a sort of legal dye on it, speaking to one of the five or six clerks who raised their heads on the stranger's entrance.

'In, but engaged in a consultation, I believe,' answered one who, being paid for his services, was the working clerk of the office; most of the others being students who get no remuneration for their time, and who very rarely deserve it.

'I'll wait till he is through,' returned the stranger, helping himself coolly to a vacant chair, and taking his seat in the midst of dangers that might have alarmed one less familiar with the snares, and quirks, and quiddities of the law. The several clerks, after taking a good look each at their guest, cast their eyes down on their books or foolscap, and seemed to be engrossed with their respective occupations. Most of the young men, members of respectable families in town, set the stranger down for a rustic client; but the working clerk saw at once, by a certain self-possessed and shrewd manner, that the stranger was a country practitioner.

In the course of the next half-hour, Daniel Lord and George Wood came out of the *sanctum*, attended as far as the door by Dunscomb himself. Exchanging 'good morning' with his professional friends, the last caught a glimpse of his patient visitor, whom he immediately saluted by the somewhat brief and familiar name of Timms, inviting him instantly, and with earnestness, to come within the limits of the privileged. Mr Timms complied, entering the *sanctum* with the air of one who had been there before, and appearing to be in no manner overcome by the honour he enjoyed. And now, as a faithful chronicler of events, it is here become our painful, not to say revolting duty, to record an act on the part of the man who was known throughout Duke's county as 'Squire Timms, which it will never do to overlook, since it has got to be perfectly distinctive and characteristic of late years, not of an individual, but of large classes who throng the bar, the desk, the steamboats, the taverns, the streets. A thousand paragraphs have been written on the subject of American spitting, and not one line, as we can remember, on the subject of an equally common and still grosser offence against the minor morals of the country, if decency in manners may be thus termed. Our meaning will be explained more fully in the narrative of the stranger's immediate movements on entering the *sanctum*.

'Take a seat, Mr Timms,' said Dunscomb, motioning to a chair, while he resumed his own well-cushioned seat, and deliberately proceeded to light a cigar, not without pressing several with a species of intelligent tenderness, between his thumb and finger. 'Take a seat, sir; and take a cigar.'

Here occurred the great tour de force in manners of 'Squire Timms. Considerately turning his person quartering towards his host, and seizing himself by the nose, much as if he had a quarrel with that member of his face, he blowed a blast that sounded sonorously, and which fulfilled all that it promised. Now a better mannered man than Dunscomb it would not be easy to find. He was not particularly distinguished for elegance of deportment, but he was perfectly well-bred. Nevertheless, he did not flinch before this broad hint from vulgarity, but stood it unmoved. To own the truth, so large has been the inroad from the base of society, within the last five-and-twenty years, on the habits of those who once exclusively dwelt together, that he had got hardened even to *this* innovation. The fact is not to be concealed, and, as we intend never to touch upon the subject again, we shall say distinctly that Mr Timms blowed his nose with his fingers, and that, in so doing, he did not innovate one-half as much, to-day, on the usages of the Upper Ten thousand, as he would have done had he blowed his nose with his thumb only, a quarter of a century since.

Dunscomb bore this infliction philosophically; and well he might, for there was no remedy. Waiting for Timms to use his handkerchief, which was produced somewhat tardily for such an operation, he quietly opened the subject of their interview.

'So the grand jury has actually found a bill for murder and arson, my nephew writes me,' Dunscomb observed, looking inquiringly at his companion, as if really anxious for further intelligence.

'Unanimously, they tell me, Mr Dunscomb,' answered Timms. 'I understand that only one man hesitated, and he was brought round before they came into court. That piece of money damns our case in old Duke's.'

'Money saves more cases than it damns, Timms; and no one knows it better than yourself.'

'Very true, sir. Money may defy even the new code. Give me five hundred dollars, and change the proceedings to a civil action, and I'll carry anything in my own county that you'll put on the calendar, barring some twenty or thirty jurors I could name. There *are* about thirty men in the county that I can do nothing with – for that matter, whom I dare not approach.'

'How the deuce is it, Timms, that you manage your causes with so much success? for I remember you have given me a good deal of trouble in suits in which law and fact were both clearly enough on my side.'

'I suppose those must have been causes in which we "horse-shedded" and "pillowed" a good deal.'

'Horse-shedded and pillowed! Those are legal terms of which I have no knowledge!'

'They are country phrases, sir, and country customs, too, for that matter. A man might practise a long life in town and know nothing about them. The Halls of Justice are not immaculate; but they can tell us nothing of horse-shedding and pillowing. They do business in a way of which we in the country are just as ignorant as you are of our mode.'

'Have the goodness, Timms, just to explain the meaning of your terms, which are quite new to me. I will not swear they are not in the Code of Practice, but they are in neither Blackstone nor Kent.'

'Horse-shedding, 'Squire Dunscomb, explains itself. In the country, most of the jurors, witnesses, &c., have more or less to do with the horse-sheds, if it's only to see that their beasts are fed. Well, we keep proper talkers there, and it must be a knotty case indeed into which an ingenious hand cannot thrust a doubt or an argument. To be frank with you, I've known three pretty difficult suits summed up under a horse-shed in one day; and twice as many opened.'

'But how is this done? – do you present your arguments directly, as in court?'

'Lord bless you, no. In court, unless the jury happen to be unusually excellent, counsel have to pay some little regard to the testimony and the law; but, in horse-shedding, one has no need of either. A skilful horse-shedder, for instance, will talk a party to pieces, and not say a word about the case. That's the perfection of the business. It's against the law you know, Mr Dunscomb, to talk of a case before a juror – an indictable offence – but one may make a case of a party's general character, of his means, his miserly qualities, or his aristocracy; and it will be hard to get hold of the talker for any of them qualities. Aristocracy, of late years, is a capital argument, and will suit almost any state of facts, or any action you can bring. Only persuade the jury that the plaintiff or defendant fancies himself better than they are, and the verdict is certain. I got a thousand dollars in the Springer case, solely on that ground. Aristocracy did it! It is doing to do us a great deal of harm in this murder and arson indictment.'

'But Mary Monson is no aristocrat – she is a stranger, and unknown. What privileges does she enjoy to render her obnoxious to the charge of aristocracy?'

'More than will do her any good. Her aristocracy does her almost as much harm in old Duke's as the piece of gold. I always consider a cause as half lost when there is any aristocracy in it.'

'Aristocracy means exclusive political privileges in the hands of a few; and it means nothing else. Now, what exclusive political privileges does this unfortunate young woman enjoy? She is accused of two of the highest crimes known to the laws; is indicted, imprisoned, and will be tried.'

'Yes, and by her *peers*,' said Timms, taking out a very respectable-looking box, and helping himself liberally to a pinch of cut tobacco. 'It's wonderful 'Squire Dunscomb, how much breadth the *peerage* possesses in this country! I saw a trial, a year or two since, in which one of the highest intellects of the land was one of the parties, and in which a juror asked the judge to explain the meaning of the word "bereaved." *That* citizen had his rights referred to his peers, with a vengeance!'

'Yes; the venerable maxim of the common law is, occasionally, a little caricatured among us. This is owing to our adhering to antiquated opinions after the facts in which they had their origin have ceased to exist. But, by your manner of treating the subject, Timms, I infer that you give up the aristocracy.'

'Not at all. Our client will have more risks to run on account of *that*, than on account of any other weak spot in her case. I think we might get along with the piece of gold, as a life is in question; but it is not quite so easy to see how we are to get along with the aristocracy.'

'And this in the face of her imprisonment, solitary condition, friendless state, and utter dependence on strangers for her future fate? I see no one feature of aristocracy to reproach her with.'

'But I see a great many, and so does the neighbourhood. It is already getting to be the talk of half the county. In short, all are talking about it, but they who know better. You'll see, 'Squire Dunscomb, there are two sorts of aristocracy in the eyes of most people; *your* sort, and *my* sort. *Your* sort is a state of society that gives privileges and power to a few, and keeps it there. That is what I call old-fashioned aristocracy, about which nobody cares anything in this country. We have no such aristocrats, I allow, and consequently they don't signify a straw.'

'Yet they are the only true aristocrats, after all. But what, or who are yours.'

'Well now, 'squire, *you* are a sort of aristocrat yourself, in a certain way. I don't know how it is – I'm admitted to the bar as well as you – have just as many rights——'

'More, Timms, if leading jurors by the nose, and horse-shedding, can be accounted rights.'

'Well, more, in some respects, may be. Notwithstanding all this, there is a difference between us – a difference in our ways, in our language, in our ideas, our manner of thinking and acting, that sets you up above me in a way I should not like in any other man. As you did so much for me when a boy, sir, and carried me through to the bar on your shoulders, as it might be, I shall always look up to you; though I must say that I do not always like even *your* superiority.'

'I should be sorry, Timms, if I ever so far forget my own great defects, as to parade unfeelingly any little advantages I may happen to possess over you, or over any other man, in consequence of the accidents of birth and education.'

'You do not parade them unfeelingly, sir; you do not *parade* them at all. Still, they will show themselves; and they are just the things I do not like to look at. Now, what is true of me, is true of all my neighbours. We call anything aristocracy that is a touch above us, let it be what it may. I sometimes think 'Squire Dunscomb is a sort of an aristocrat in the law! Now, as for our client, she has a hundred ways with her that are not the ways of Duke's, unless you go among the tip-toppers.'

'The Upper Ten——'

'Pshaw! I know better than that myself, 'squire. Their Upper Ten should be upper one, or two, to be common sense. Rude and untaught as

I was until you took me by the hand, sir, I can tell the difference between
those who wear kids, and ride in their coaches, and those who are fit for
either. Our client has none of this, sir; and that it is which surprises me.
She has no Union Place, or Fifth Avenue, about her; but is the true coin.
There is one thing in particular that I'm afraid may do her harm.'

'It is the true coin which usually passes with the least trouble from
hand to hand. But what is this particular source of uneasiness?'

'Why, the client has a lady-friend——'

A little exclamation from Dunscomb caused the speaker to pause,
while the counsellor removed the cigar from his mouth, knocked off its
ashes, and appeared to ponder for a moment, touching the best manner
of treating a somewhat delicate subject. At length, native frankness
overcame all scruples, and he spoke plainly, or as the familiar instructor
might be expected to address a very green pupil.

'If you love me, Timms, never repeat that diabolical phrase again,'
said Dunscomb, looking quite serious, however much there might have
been of affectation in his aspect. 'It is even worse than Hurlgate, which
I have told you fifty times I cannot endure. "Lady-friend" is infernally
vulgar, and I *will* not stand it. You may blow your nose with your
fingers, if it give you especial satisfaction, and you may blow out against
aristocracy as much as you please; but you shall not talk to me about
"lady-friends" or "Hurlgate." I am no dandy, but a respectable elderly
gentleman, who professes to speak English, and who wishes to be
addressed in his own language. Heaven knows what the country is
coming to! There is Webster, to begin with, cramming a Yankee dialect
down our throats for good English; then comes all the cant of the day,
flourishing finical phrases, and new significations to good old homely
words, and changing the very nature of mankind by means of terms.
Last of all, is this infernal Code, in which the ideas are as bad as
possible, and the terms still worse. But whom do you mean by your
"lady-friend?"'

'The French lady that has been with our client, now, for a fortnight.
Depend on it, *she* will do us no good when we are on. She is too
aristocratic altogether.'

Dunscomb laughed outright. Then he passed a hand across his brow,
and seemed to muse.

'All this is very serious,' he at length replied, 'and is really no laughing
matter. A pretty pass are we coming to, if the administration of the law is
to be influenced by such things as these! The doctrine is openly held that
the rich shall not, ought not to embellish their amusements at a cost that
the poor cannot compass; and here we have a member of the bar telling
us a prisoner shall not have justice because she has a foreign maid-
servant!'

'A servant! Call her anything but that, 'squire, if you wish for success! A prisoner accused of capital crimes, with a servant, would be certain to be condemned. Even the court would hardly stand *that*.'

'Timms, you are a shrewd, sagacious fellow, and are apt to laugh in your sleeve at follies of this nature, as I well know from long acquaintance; and here you insist on one of the greatest of all the absurdities.'

'Things are changed in Ameriky, Mr Dunscomb. The people are beginning to govern; and when they can't do it legally, they do it without law. Don't you see what the papers say about having operas and playhouses at the people's prices, and the right to hiss? There's Constitution for you! I wonder what Kent and Blackstone would say to *that*?'

'Sure enough. They would find some novel features in a liberty which says a man shall not set the price on the seats in his own theatre, and that the hissing may be done by an audience in the *streets*. The facts are, Timms, that all these abuses about O.P.'s, and controlling other persons' concerns under the pretence that the public has rights where, as a public, it has no rights at all, come from the reaction of a half-way liberty in other countries. Here, where the people are really free, having all the power, and where no political right is hereditary, the people ought, at least, to respect their own ordinances.'

'Do you not consider a theatre a public place, 'Squire Dunscomb?'

'In one sense it is, certainly; but not in the sense that bears on this pretended power over it. The very circumstance that the audience pay for their seats, makes it, in law as in fact, a matter of covenant. As for this newfangled absurdity about its being a duty to furnish low-priced seats for the poor, where they may sit and look at pretty women because they cannot see them elsewhere, it is scarcely worth an argument. If the rich should demand that the wives and daughters of the poor should be paraded in the pits and galleries, for *their* patrician eyes to feast on, a pretty clamour there would be! If the state requires cheap theatres, and cheap women, let the state pay for them, as it does for its other wants; but, if these amusements are to be the object of private peculations, let private wisdom control them. I have no respect for one-sided liberty, let it cant as much as it may.'

'Well, I don't know, sir; I have read some of these articles, and they seemed to me——'

'What – convincing?'

'Perhaps not just that, 'squire; but very *agreeable*. I'm not rich enough to pay for a high place at an opera or a theatre; and it is pleasant to fancy that a poor feller can get one of the best seats at half-price. Now, in England, they tell me, the public won't stand prices they don't like.'

'Individuals of the public may refuse to purchase, and there their rights cease. An opera, in particular, is a very expensive amusement; and in all countries where the rates of admission are low, the governments contribute to the expenditures. This is done from policy, to keep the people quiet, and possibly to help civilize them; but, if we are not far beyond the necessity of any such expedients, our institutions are nothing but a sublime mystification.'

'It is wonderful, 'squire, how many persons see the loose side of democracy, who have no notion of the tight! But, all this time, our client is in gaol at Biberry, and must be tried next week. Has nothing been done, 'squire, to choke off the newspapers, who have something to say about her almost every day. It's quite time the other side should be heard.'

'It is very extraordinary that the persons who control these papers should be so indifferent to the rights of others as to allow such paragraphs to find a place in their columns.'

'Indifferent! What do they care, so long as the journal sells? In our case, however, I rather suspect that a certain reporter has taken offence; and when men of that class get offended, look out for news of the colour of their anger. Isn't it wonderful, 'Squire Dunscomb, that the people don't see and feel that they are sustaining low tyrants, in two-thirds of their silly clamour about the liberty of the press?'

'Many do see it; and I think this engine has lost a great deal of its influence within the last few years. As respects proceedings in the courts, there never will be any true liberty in the country, until the newspapers are bound hand and foot.'

'You are right enough in one thing, 'squire, and that is in the ground the press has lost. It has pretty much used itself up in Duke's; and I would pillow and horse-shed a cause through against it, the best day it ever saw!'

'By the way, Timms, you have not explained the pillowing process to me.'

'I should think the word itself would do that, sir. You know how it is in the country. Half a dozen beds are put in the same room, and two in a bed. Waal, imagine three or four jurors in one of these rooms, and two chaps along with 'em, with instructions how to talk. The conversation is the most innocent and nat'ral in the world; not a word too much or too little; but it sticks like a bur. The juror is a plain, simple-minded countryman, and swallows all that his room-mates say, and goes into the box next day in a beautiful frame of mind to listen to reason and evidence! No, no; give me two or three of these pillow-counsellors, and I'll undo all that the journals can do, in a single conversation. You'll remember, 'squire, that we get the last word by this system: and if the first blow is half the battle in war, the last word is another half in the law. Oh! it's a beautiful business, is this trial by jury.'

'All this is very wrong, Timms. For a long time I have known that you have exercised an extraordinary influence over the jurors of Duke's; but this is the first occasion on which you have been frank enough to reveal the process.'

'Because this is the first occasion on which we have ever had a capital case together. In the present state of public opinion in Duke's, I much question whether we can get a jury empanelled in this trial at all.'

'The Supreme Court will then send us to town, by way of mending the matter. *A propos*, Timms——'

'One word if you please, 'squire; what does *à propos* really mean? I hear it almost every day, but never yet knew the meaning.'

'It has shades of difference in its signification – as I just used it, it means "speaking of *that*."'

'And it is right to say *à propos* to such a thing?'

'It is better to say *à propos of*, as the French do. In old English it was always *to*; but in our later mode of speaking, we say "of."'

'Thank you, sir. You know how I glean my knowledge in driblets; and out in the country not always from the highest authorities. Plain and uncouth as I know I appear to you, and to Miss Sarah, I have an ambition to be a gentleman. Now, I have observation enough to see that it is these little matters, after all, and not riches and fine clothes, that make gentlemen and ladies.'

'I am glad you have so much discrimination, Timms; but, you must permit me to remark, that you will never make a gentleman until you learn to let your nose alone.'

'Thank you, sir – I am thankful for even the smallest hints on manners. It's a pity that so handsome and so agreeable a young lady should be hanged, Mr Dunscomb!'

'Timms, you are as shrewd a fellow, in your own way, as I know. Your law does not amount to any great matter, nor do you take hold of the strong points of a case very often; but you perform wonders with the weaker. In the way of an opinion on facts, I know few men more to be relied on. Tell me, then, frankly, what do you think of the guilt or innocence of Mary Monson?'

Timms screwed up his mouth, passed a hand over his brow, and did not answer for near a minute.

'Perhaps it is right, after all, that we should understand each other on this subject,' he then said. 'We are associated as counsel, and I feel it a great honour to be so associated, 'Squire Dunscomb, I give you my word; and it is proper that we should be as free with each other as brothers. In the first place, then, I never saw such a client before, as this same lady – for lady I suppose we must call her until she is convicted——'

'Convicted! – You cannot think there is much danger of *that*, Timms?'

'We never know, sir; we never know. I have lost cases of which I was sure, and gained them of which I had no hopes – cases which I certainly ought not to have gained – ag'in all law and the facts.'

'Ay, that came of the horse-shed, and the sleeping of two in a bed.'

'Perhaps it did, 'squire,' returned Timms, laughing very freely, though without making any noise; 'perhaps it did. When the smallpox is about, there is no telling who may take it. As for this case, 'Squire Dunscomb, it is my opinion we shall have to run for disagreements. If we can get the juries to disagree once or twice, and can get a change of *venue*, with a couple of charges, the deuce is in it if a man of your experience don't corner them so tightly, they'll give the matter up, rather than have any more trouble about it. After all, the state can't gain much by hanging a young woman that nobody knows, even if she be a little aristocratical. We must get her to change her dress altogether, and some of her ways too; which, in her circumstances, I call downright hanging ways; and the sooner she is rid of them, the better.'

'I see that you do not think us very strong on the merits, Timms, which is as much as admitting the guilt of our client. I was a good deal inclined to suspect the worst myself; but two or three more interviews, and what my nephew Jack Wilmeter tells me, have produced a change. I am now strongly inclined to believe her innocent. She has some great and secret cause of apprehension, I will allow; but I do not think these unfortunate Goodwins have anything to do with it.'

'Waal, one never knows. The verdict, if "not guilty," will be just as good as if she was innocent as a child a year old. I see how the work is to be done. All the law, and the summing up, will fall to your share; while the out-door work will be mine. We *may* carry her through; though I'm of opinion that, if we do, it will be more by means of bottom than by means of foot. There is one thing that is very essential, sir – the money must hold out.'

'Do you want a refresher so soon, Timms? Jack tells me that she has given you two hundred and fifty dollars already?'

'I acknowledge it, sir; and a very respectable fee it is; *you* ought to have a thousand, 'squire.'

'I have not received a cent, nor do I mean to touch any of her money. My feelings are in the case, and I am willing to work for nothing.'

Timms give his old master a quick but scrutinizing glance. Dunscomb was youthful, in all respects, for his time of life; and many a man has loved, and married, and become the parent of a flourishing family, who had seen all the days he had seen. That glance was to inquire if it were possible that the uncle and nephew were likely to be rivals, and to obtain as much knowledge as could be readily gleaned in a quick, jealous look. But the counsellor was calm as usual, and no tinge of colour, no sigh, no gentleness of expression, betrayed the existence of the master passion. It was reported among the bachelor's intimates that formerly, when he was about five-and-twenty, he had had an affair of the heart, which had taken such deep hold that even the lady's marriage with another man had not destroyed its impression. That marriage was said not to have been happy, and was succeeded by a second, that was still less so; though the parties were affluent, educated, and possessed all the means that are commonly supposed to produce felicity. A single child was the issue of the first marriage, and its birth had shortly preceded the separation that followed. Three years later the father died, leaving the whole of a very ample fortune to this child, coupled with the strange request that Dunscomb, once the betrothed of her mother, should be the trustee and guardian of the daughter. This extraordinary demand had not been complied with, and Dunscomb had not seen any of the parties from the time he broke with his mistress. The heiress married young, died within the year, and left another heiress; but no further allusion to our counsellor was made in any of the later wills and settlements. Once, indeed, he had been professionally consulted concerning the devises in favour of the granddaughter – a certain Mildred Millington – who was a second-cousin to Michael of that name, and as rich as he was poor. For some years a sort of vague expectation prevailed that these two young Millingtons might marry; but a feud existed in the family, and little or no intercourse was permitted. The early removal of the young lady to a distant school prevented such a result; and Michael, in due time, fell within the influence of Sarah Wilmeter's gentleness, beauty, and affection.

Timms came to the conclusion that his old master was not in love.

'It is very convenient to be rich, 'squire,' this singular being remarked; 'and I dare say it may be very pleasant to practise for nothing, when a man has his pocket full of money. I am poor, and have particular satisfaction in a good warm fee. By the way, sir, my part of the business requires plenty of money. I do not think I can even commence operations with less than five hundred dollars.'

Dunscomb leaned back, stretched forth an arm, drew his cheque-book from its niche, and filled a cheque for the sum just mentioned. This he quietly handed to Timms, without asking for any receipt; for, while he knew that his old student and fellow-practitioner was no more to be trusted in matters of practice than was an eel in the hand, he knew that he was scrupulously honest in matters of account. There was not a man in the state to whom Dunscomb would sooner confide the care of uncounted gold, or the administration of an estate, or the payment of a legacy, than this very individual; who, he also well knew, would not scruple to set all the provisions of the law at naught, in order to obtain a verdict, when his feelings were really in the case.

'There, Timms,' said the senior counsel, glancing at his draft before he handed it to the other, in order to see that it was correct; 'there is what you ask for. Five hundred for expenses, and half as much as a fee.'

'Thank you, sir. I hope this is not gratuitous, as well as the services?'

'It is not. There is no want of funds, and I am put in possession of sufficient money to carry us through with credit; but it is as a trustee, and not as a fee. This, indeed, is the most extraordinary part of the whole affair, – to find a delicate, educated, accomplished lady, with her pockets well lined, in such a situation!'

'Why, 'squire,' said Timms, passing his hand down his chin, and trying to look simple and disinterested; 'I am afraid clients like ours are often flush. I have been employed about the Tombs a good deal in my time, and I have gin'rally found that the richest clients were the biggest rogues.'

Dunscomb gave his companion a long and contemplative look. He saw that Timms did not entertain quite as favourable an opinion of Mary Monson as he did himself, or rather that he was fast getting to entertain; for his own distrust originally was scarcely less than that of this hackneyed dealer with human vices. A long, close, and stringent examination of all of Timms's facts succeeded – facts that had been gleaned by collecting statements on the spot. Then a consultation followed, from which it might be a little premature, just now, to raise the veil.

CHAPTER IX

—— Her speech is nothing,
Yet the unshaped use of it doth move
The hearers to collection. They aim at it,
And botch the words up fit to their own thoughts.

Hamlet.

The reader is not to be surprised at the intimacy which existed between Thomas Dunscomb and the half-educated semi-rude being who was associated with him as counsel in the important cause that was now soon to be tried. Such intimacies are by no means uncommon in the course of events; men often overlooking great dissimilarities in principles, as well as in personal qualities, in managing their associations, so far as they are connected with the affairs of this world. The circumstance that Timms had studied in our counsellor's office would, as a matter of course, produce certain relations between them in after-life; but the student had made himself useful to his former master on a great variety of occasions, and was frequently employed by him whenever there was a cause depending in the courts of Duke's, the county in which the unpolished, half-educated, but hard-working and successful county practitioner had established himself. It may be questioned if Dunscomb really knew all the agencies set in motion by his coadjutor in difficult cases; but, whether he did or not, it is quite certain that many of them were of a character not to see the light. It is very much the fashion of our good republic to turn up its nose at all other lands, a habit no doubt inherited from our great ancestors the English; and one of its standing themes of reproach, are the legal corruptions and abuses known to exist in France, Spain, Italy, &c.; all over the world, in short, except among ourselves. So far as the judges are concerned, there is a surprising adherence to duty, when bribes alone are concerned, no class of men on earth being probably less obnoxious to just imputations of this character than the innumerable corps of judicial officers; unpaid, poor, hard-worked, and we might almost add unhonoured, as they are. That cases in which bribes are taken do occur, we make no doubt; it would be assuming too much in favour of human nature to infer the contrary; but, under the system of publicity that prevails, it would not be easy for this crime to extend very far without its being exposed. It is greatly to the credit of the vast judicial corps of the States, that bribery is an offence which does not appear to be even suspected at all; or, if there be exceptions to the rule, they exist in but few and isolated cases. Here, however, our eulogies on American justice must cease. All that Timms has intimated, and Dunscomb has asserted, concerning the juries is true; and the evil is one that each day increases. The tendency of everything belonging to the government is to throw power directly into the hands of the people, who, in nearly all cases, use it as men might be supposed to do who are perfectly irresponsible, have only a remote, and half the time an invisible interest in its exercise; who do not feel or understand the consequences of their own deeds, and have a pleasure in asserting a seeming independence, and of appearing to think and act for themselves. Under such a regime it is self-apparent that principles and law must suffer; and so the result proves daily, if not hourly. The institution of the jury, one of very questionable utility in its best aspects in a country of really popular institutions, becomes nearly intolerable, unless the courts exercise a strong and salutary influence on the discharge of its duties. This influence, unhappily, has been gradually lessening among us for the last half century, until it has reached a point where nothing is more common than to find the judge charging the law one way, and the jury determining it another. In most cases, it is true, there is a remedy for this abuse of power, but it is costly, and ever attended with that delay in hope 'which maketh the heart sick.' Any one, of even the dullest apprehension, must, on a little reflection, perceive that a condition of things in which the *ends* of justice are defeated, or so procrastinated as to produce the results of defeat, is one of the least desirable of all those in which men can be placed under the social compact; to say nothing of its corrupting and demoralizing effects on the public mind.

All this Dunscomb saw more vividly, perhaps, than most others of the profession, for men gradually get to be so accustomed to abuses as not only to tolerate them, but to come to consider them as evils inseparable from human frailty. It was certain, however, that while our worthy counsellor so far submitted to the force of things as frequently to close his eyes to Timms's manoeuvres, a weakness of which nearly every one is guilty who has much to do with the management of men and things, he was never known to do aught himself that was unworthy of his high standing and well-merited reputation at the bar. There is nothing unusual in this convenient compromise between direct and indirect relations with that which is wrong.

It had early been found necessary to employ local counsel in Mary Monson's case, and Timms was recommended by his old master as one every way suited to the particular offices needed. Most of the duties to be performed were strictly legal; though it is not to be concealed that some soon presented themselves that would not bear the light. John Wilmeter communicated to Timms the particular state of the testimony, as he and Michael Millington had been enabled to get at it; and among other things he stated his conviction that the occupants of the farm nearest to the late dwelling of the Goodwins were likely to prove some of the most dangerous of the witnesses against their client. This family consisted of a sister-in-law, the Mrs Burton already mentioned, three unmarried sisters, and a brother, who was the husband of the person first named. On this hint Timms immediately put himself in communication with these neighbours, concealing from them, as well as from all others but good Mrs Gott, that he was retained in the case at all.

Timms was soon struck with the hints and half-revealed statements of the persons of this household; more especially with those of the female portion of it. The man appeared to him to have observed less than his wife and sisters; but even he had much to relate, though, as Timms fancied, more that he had gleaned from those around him than from his own observations. The sisters, however, had a good deal to say; while the wife, though silent and guarded, seemed to this observer, as well as to young Millington, to know the most. When pressed to tell all, Mrs Burton looked melancholy and reluctant, frequently returning to the subject of her own accord when it had been casually dropped, but never speaking explicitly, though often invited so to do. It was not the cue of the counsel for the defence to drag out unfavourable evidence; and Timms employed certain confidential agents, whom he often used in the management of his causes, to sift this testimony as well as it could be done without the constraining power of the law. The result was not very satisfactory in any sense, more appearing to be suppressed than was related. It was feared that the legal officers of the State would meet with better success.

The investigations of the junior counsel did not end here. He saw that the public sentiment was setting in a current so strongly against Mary Monson, that he soon determined to counteract it, as well as might be by producing a reaction. This is a very common, not to say a very powerful agent, in the management of all interests that are subject to popular opinion in a democracy. Even the applicant for public favour is none the worse for beginning his advances by 'a little aversion,' provided he can contrive to make the premeditated change in his favour take the aspect of a reaction. It may not be so easy to account for this caprice of the common mind, as it is certain that it exists. Perhaps we like to yield to a seeming generosity, have a pleasure in appearing to pardon, find a consolation for our own secret consciousness of errors in thus extending favour to the errors of others, and have more satisfaction in preferring those who are fallible than in exalting the truly upright and immaculate, if, indeed, any such there be. Let the cause be what it may, we think the facts to be beyond dispute; and so thought Timms also, for he no sooner resolved to counteract one public opinion by means of another, than he set about the task with coolness and intelligence – in short, with a mixture of all the good and bad qualities of the man.

The first of his measures was to counteract, as much as he could, the effects of certain paragraphs that had appeared in some of the New York journals. A man of Timms's native shrewdness had no difficulty in comprehending the more vulgar moral machinery of a daily press. Notwithstanding its "we's," and its pretension to represent public opinion, and to protect the common interests, he thoroughly understood it was merely one mode of advancing the particular views, sustaining the personal schemes, and not unfrequently of gratifying the low malignity of a single individual; the press in America differing from that of nearly all other countries in the fact that it is not controlled by associations, and does not reflect the decisions of many minds, or contend for principles that, by their very character, have a tendency to elevate the thoughts. There are some immaterial exceptions as relates to the latter characteristic, perhaps, principally growing out of the great extra-constitutional question of slavery, that has quite unnecessarily been drawn into the discussions of the times through the excited warmth of zealots; but, as a rule, the exciting political questions that elsewhere compose the great theme of the newspapers, enlarging their views, and elevating their articles, may be regarded as settled among ourselves. In the particular case with which Timms was now required to deal, there was neither favour nor malice to counteract. The injustice, and a most cruel injustice it was, was merely in catering to a morbid desire for the marvellous in the vulgar, which might thus be turned to profit.

Among the reporters there exists the same diversity of qualities as among other men, beyond a question; but the tendency of the use of all power is to abuse; and Timms was perfectly aware that these men had far more pride in the influence they wielded, than conscience in its exercise. A ten or a twenty dollar note, judiciously applied, would do a great deal with this 'Palladium of our Liberties,' – there being at least a dozen of these important safeguards interested in the coming trial – our associate counsel very well knew; and Dunscomb suspected that some such application of the great persuader had been made, in consequence of one or two judicious and well-turned paragraphs that appeared soon after the consultation. But Timms's management of the press was mainly directed to that of the county newspapers. There were three of these; and as they had better characters than most of the Manhattanese journals, so were they more confided in. It is true, that the Whig readers never heeded in the least anything that was said in 'The Duke's County Democrat;' but the friends of the last took their revenge in discrediting all that appeared in the columns of the 'Biberry Whig.' In this respect, the two great parties of the country were on a par; each manifesting a faith that, in a better cause, might suffice to move mountains; and, on the other hand, an unbelief that drove them into the dangerous folly of disregarding their foes. As Mary Monson had nothing to do with politics, it was not difficult to get suitable paragraphs inserted in the hostile columns, which was also done within eight-and-forty hours after the return of the junior counsel to his own abode.

Timms, however, was far from trusting to the newspapers alone. He felt that it might be well enough to set 'fire to fight fire;' but his main reliance was on the services that could be rendered by a timely and judicious use of 'the little member.' *Talkers* was what he wanted; and well did he know where to find them, and how to get them at work. A few he paid in a direct, business-like way; taking no vouchers for the sums bestowed, the reader may be assured; but entering each item carefully in a little memorandum-book kept for his own private information. These strictly confidential agents went to work with experienced discretion but great industry, and soon had some ten or fifteen fluent female friends actively engaged in circulating 'They says,' in their respective neighbourhoods.

Timms had reflected a great deal on the character of the defence it might be most prudent to get up and enlarge on. Insanity had been worn out by too much use of late; and he scarce gave that plea a second thought. This particular means of defence had been discussed between him and Dunscomb, it is true; but each of the counsel felt a strong repugnance against resorting to it; the one on account of his indisposition to rely on anything but the truth; the other, to use his own mode of expressing himself on the occasion in question, because he 'believed that jurors could no longer be humbugged with that plea. There have been all sorts of madmen and madwomen——'

'Gentlemen and lady murderers' – put in Dunscomb, drily.

'I ask your pardon, 'squire; but, since you give me the use of my nose, I will offend as little as possible with the tongue – though, I rather conclude' – a form of expression much in favour with Timms – 'that should our verdict be "guilty," you will be disposed to allow there may be one lady criminal in the world.'

'She is a most extraordinary creature, Timms; bothers me more than any client I ever had!'

'Indeed! Waal, I had set her down as just the contrary – for to me she seems to be as unconcerned as if the wise four-and-twenty had not presented her to justice in the name of the people.'

'It is not in that sense that I am bothered – no client ever gave counsel less trouble than Mary Monson in that respect. To me, Timms, she does not appear to have any concern in reference to the result.'

'Supreme innocence, or a well-practised experience. I have defended many a person whom I knew to be guilty, and two or three whom I believed to be innocent; but never before had as cool a client as this!'

And very true was this. Even the announcement of the presentment by the grand jury appeared to give Mary Monson no great alarm. Perhaps she anticipated it from the first, and had prepared herself for the event, by an exercise of a firmness little common to her sex until the moment of extreme trial, when their courage would seem to rise with the occasion. On her companion, whom Timms had so elegantly styled her 'Lady-friend,' certainly as thoroughly vulgar an expression as was ever drawn into the service of the heroics in gentility, warm-hearted and faithful Marie Moulin, the intelligence produced far more effect. It will be remembered that Wilmeter overheard the single cry of 'Mademoiselle' when this Swiss was first admitted to the gaol; after which an impenetrable veil closed around their proceedings. The utmost good feeling and confidence were apparent in the intercourse between the young mistress and her maid; if, indeed, Marie might thus be termed, after the manner in which she was treated. So far from being kept at the distance which it is usual to observe towards an attendant, the Swiss was admitted to Mary Monson's table; and to the eyes of indifferent observers she might very well pass for what Timms had so elegantly called a 'Lady-friend.' But Jack Wilmeter knew too much of the world to be so easily

misled. It is true, that when he paid his short visits to the gaol, Marie
Moulin sat sewing at the prisoner' side, and occasionally she even
hummed low, national airs while he was present; but knowing the
original condition of the maid-servant, our young man was not to be
persuaded that his uncle's client was her peer, any more than were the
jurors who, agreeably to that profound mystification of the common law,
are thus considered and termed. Had not Jack Wilmeter known the real
position of Marie Moulin, her 'Mademoiselle' would have let him deeper
into the secrets of the two than it is probable either ever imagined. This
word, in common with those of 'Monsieur' and 'Madame,' are used, by
French servants, differently from what they are used in general society.
Unaccompanied by the names, the domestics of France commonly and
exclusively apply them to the heads of families, or those they more
immediately serve. Thus it was far more probable that Marie Moulin,
meeting a mere general acquaintance in the prisoner, would have called
her 'Mademoiselle Marie,' or 'Mademoiselle Monson,' or whatever might
be the name by which she had known the young lady, than by the
general and still more respectful appellation of 'Mademoiselle.' On this
peculiarity of deportment Jack Wilmeter speculated profoundly; for a
young man who is just beginning to submit to the passion of love is very
apt to fancy a thousand things that he would never dream of seeing in his
cooler moments. Still, John had fancied himself bound in the spells of
another, until this extraordinary client of his uncle's so unexpectedly
crossed his path. Such is the human heart.

Good and kind-hearted Mrs Gott allowed the prisoner most of the
privileges that at all comported with her duty. Increased precautions were
taken for the security of the accused, as soon as the presentment of the
grand jury was made, by a direct order from the court; but, these
attended to, it was in the power of her whom Timms might have called
the 'lady sheriff,' to grant a great many little indulgencies, which were
quite cheerfully accorded, and, to all appearances, as gratefully accepted.

John Wilmeter was permitted to pay two regular visits at the grate each
day, and as many more as his ingenuity could invent plausible excuses for
making. On all occasions Mrs Gott opened the outer door with the
greatest good will; and, like a true woman as she is, she had the tact to
keep as far aloof from the barred window where the parties met, as the
dimensions of the outer room would allow. Marie Moulin was equally
considerate, generally plying her needle at such times, in the depth of the
cell, with twice the industry manifested on other occasions. Nevertheless,
nothing passed between the young people that called for this delicate
reserve. The conversation, it is true, turned as little as possible on the
strange and awkward predicament of one of the colloquists, or the
employment that kept the young man at Biberry. Nor did it turn at all on

love. There is a premonitory state in these attacks of the heart, during which skilful observers may discover the symptoms of approaching disease, but which do not yet betray the actual existence of the epidemic. On the part of Jack himself, it is true that these symptoms were getting to be not only somewhat apparent, but they were evidently fast becoming more and more distinct; while, on the part of the lady, any one disposed to be critical might have seen that her colour deepened, and there were signs of daily increasing interest in them, as the hours for these interviews approached. She was interested in her young legal adviser; and interest, with women, is the usual precursor of the master-passion. Woe betide the man who cannot interest, but who only amuses!

Although so little to the point was said in the short dialogues between Wilmeter and Mary Monson, there were dialogues held with the good Mrs Gott, by each of the parties respectively, in which less reserve was observed; and the heart was permitted to have more influence over the movements of the tongue. The first of these conversations that we deem it necessary to relate, that took place after the presentment, was one that immediately succeeded an interview at the barred window, and which occurred three days subsequently to the consultation in town, and two after Timms's machinery was actively at work in the county.

'Well, how do you find her spirits to-day, Mr Wilmington?' asked Mrs Gott, kindly, and catching the conventional sound of the young man's name, from having heard it so often in the mouth of Michael Millington. 'It is an awful state for any human being to be in, and she a young, delicate woman; to be tried for murder, and for setting fire to a house, and all so soon!'

'The most extraordinary part of this very extraordinary business, Mrs Gott,' Jack replied, 'is the perfect indifference of Miss Monson to her fearful jeopardy! To me, she seems much more anxious to be closely immured in gaol, than to escape from a trial that one would think, of itself, might prove more than so delicate a young lady could bear up against.'

'Very true, Mr Wilmington; and she never seems to think of it at all! You see what she has done, sir?'

'Done! – Nothing in particular, I hope?'

'I don't know what *you* call particular; but to me it does seem to be remarkably particular. Didn't you hear a piano, and another musical instrument, as you approached the gaol?'

'I did, certainly, and wondered who could produce such admirable music in Biberry.'

'Biberry has a great many musical ladies, I can tell you, Mr Wilmington,' returned Mrs Gott, a little coldly, though her good-nature instantly returned, and shone out in one of her most friendly smiles; 'and those, too, that have been to town, and heard all the great performers from Europe, of whom there have been so many of late years. I have heard good judges say that Duke's county is not much behind the Island of Manhattan with the piano in particular.'

'I remember, when at Rome, to have heard an Englishman say that some young ladies from Lincolnshire were astonishing the Romans with their Italian accent, in singing Italian operas,' answered Jack, smiling. 'There is no end, my dear Mrs Gott, to provincial perfection in all parts of the world.'

'I believe I understand you, but I am not at all offended at your meaning. We are not very sensitive about the gaols. One thing I will admit, however, — Mary Monson's harp is the first, I rather think, that was ever heard in Biberry. Gott tells me' — this was the familiar manner in which the good woman spoke of the *high* sheriff of Duke's, as the journals affectedly call that functionary — 'that he once met some German girls strolling about the county, playing and singing for money, and who had just such an instrument, but not one half as elegant; and it has brought to my mind a suspicion that Mary Monson may be one of these travelling musicians.'

'What! to stroll about the country and play and sing in the streets of villages?'

'No, not that; I see well enough she cannot be of *that* sort. But there are all descriptions of musicians, as well as all descriptions of doctors and lawyers, Mr Wilmington. Why may not Mary Monson be one of these foreigners who get so rich by singing and playing? She has just as much money as she wants, and spends it freely too. This I know, from seeing the manner in which she uses it. For my part I wish she had less music and less money just now, for they are doing her no great good in Biberry!'

'Why not? Can any human being find fault with melody and a liberal spirit?'

'Folks will find fault with anything, Mr Wilmington, when they have nothing better to do. You know how it is with our villagers here as well as I do. Most people think Mary Monson guilty, and a few do not. Those that think her guilty say it is insolent in her to be singing and playing in the very gaol in which she is confined, and talk loud against her for that very reason.'

· 'Would they deprive her of a consolation as innocent as that she obtains from her harp and her piano, in addition to her other sufferings! Your Biberry folk must be particularly hard-hearted, Mrs Gott.'

'Biberry people are like York people, and American people, and English people, and all other people, I fancy, if the truth was known, Mr Wilmington. What they don't like they disapprove of, that's all. Now, was I one of them that believe Mary Monson did actually murder the

Goodwins, and plunder their drawers, and set fire to their house, it would go ag'in *my* feelings too to hear her music, well as she plays, and sweet as she draws out the sounds from those wires. Some of our folks take the introduction of the harp into the gaol particularly hard!'

'Why that instrument more than another? It was the one on which David played.'

'They say it *was* David's favourite, and ought only to be struck to religious words and sounds.'

'It is a little surprising that your excessively conscientious people so often forget that charity is the chief of all the Christian graces.'

'They think that the love of God comes first, and that they ought never to lose sight of His honour and glory. But I agree with you, Mr Wilmington; "feel for your fellow-creatures" is my rule, and I am certain I am then feeling for my Maker. Yes, many of the neighbours insist that a harp is unsuited to a gaol, and they tell me that the instrument on which Mary Monson plays is a real antique.'

'Antique! What, a harp made in remote ages?'

'No, I don't mean that exactly,' returned Mrs Gott, colouring a little; 'but a harp made so much like those used by the Psalmist that one could not tell them apart.'

'I dare say David had many varieties of stringed instruments, from the lute up; but harps are very common, Mrs Gott, so common that we hear them now in the streets, and on board the steamboats even. There is nothing new in them, even in this country.'

'Yes, sir, in the streets and on board the boats; but the public will tolerate things done for *them* that they won't tolerate in individuals. I suppose you know *that*, Mr Wilmington?'

'We soon learn as much in this country; but the gaols are made for the public, and the harps ought to be privileged in them as well as in other public places.'

'I don't know how it is – I'm not very good at reasoning – but somehow or another the neighbours don't like that Mary Monson should play on the harp, or even on the piano, situated as she is. I do wish, Mr Wilmington, you could give her a hint on the subject?'

'Shall I tell her that the music is unpleasant to *you*?'

'As far from that as possible! I delight in it; but the neighbours do not. Then she never shows herself at the grate to folks outside, like all the other prisoners. The public wants to see and to converse with her.'

'You surely could not expect a young and educated female to be making a spectacle of herself, for the gratification of the eyes of all the vulgar and curious in and about Biberry!'

'Hush, Mr Wilmington, you are most too young to take care of such a cause. 'Squire Timms, now, is a man who understands Duke's county, and he would tell you it is not wise to talk of the vulgar hereabouts; at least not until the verdict is in. Besides, most people would think that folks have a right to look at a prisoner in the common gaol. I know they act as if they thought so.'

'It is hard enough to be accused and confined, without subjecting the party to any additional degradation. No man has a right to ask to look at Miss Monson, but those she sees fit to receive, and the officials of the law. It would be an outrage to tolerate mere idle curiosity.'

'Well, if you think so, Mr Wilmington, do not let everybody know it. Several of the clergy have either been here, or have sent to offer their visits, if acceptable.'

'And what has been the answer?' demanded Jack, a little eagerly.

'Mary Monson has received all these offers as if she had been a queen! politely, but coldly; once or twice, or when the Methodist and the Baptist came, and they commonly come first, I thought she seemed hurt. Her colour went and came like lightning. Now, she was pale as death, — next, as bright as a rose — what a colour she has at times, Mr Wilmington! Duke's is rather celebrated for rosy faces; but it would be hard to find her equal when she is not thinking.'

'Of what, my good Mrs Gott?'

'Why, most of the neighbours say, of the Goodwins. For my part, as I do not believe she ever hurt a hair of the head of the old man and old woman, I can imagine that she has disagreeable things to think of that are in no wise connected with *them*.'

'She certainly has disagreeable things to make her cheeks pale that *are* connected with that unfortunate couple. But, I ought to know all. To what else do the neighbours object?'

'To the foreign tongues — they think when a grand jury has found a bill, the accused ought to talk nothing but plain English, so that all near her can understand what she says.'

'In a word, it is not thought sufficient to be accused of such a crime as murder, but all other visitations must follow, to render the charge as horrible as may be!'

'That is not the way they look at it. The public fancies that in a public matter they have a right to know all about a thing.'

'And when there is a failure in the proof, they imagine, invent, and assert.'

''Tis the ways of the land. I suppose all nations have their ways, and follow them.'

'One thing surprises me a little in this matter,' Jack rejoined, after musing a moment; 'it is this. In most cases in which women have any connection with the law, the leaning in this country, and more particularly of late, has been in their favour.'

'Well,' Mrs Gott quietly but quickly interrupted, 'and ought it not to be so?'

'It ought not, unless the merits are with them. Justice is intended to do that which is equitable; and it is not fair to assume that women are always right, and men always wrong. I know my uncle thinks that not only the decisions of late years, but the laws, have lost sight of the wisdom of the past, and are gradually placing the women above the men, making *her* instead of *him* the head of the family.'

'Well, Mr Wilmington, and isn't that quite right?' demanded Mrs Gott, with a good-natured nod.

'My uncle thinks it very wrong, and that by a mistaken gallantry the peace of families is undermined, and their discipline destroyed; as, in punishment, by a false philanthropy rogues are petted at the expense of honest folk. Such are the opinions of Mr Thomas Dunscomb, at least.'

'Ay, Mr Thomas Dunscomb is an old bachelor; and bachelors' wives, and bachelors' children, as we well know, are always admirably managed. It is a pity they are not more numerous,' retorted the indomitably good-humoured wife of the sheriff. 'But, you see that, in this case of Mary Monson, the feeling is against, rather than in favour of a woman. That may be owing to the fact that one of the persons murdered was a lady also.'

'Dr McBrain says that both were females – or lady-murdered – as I suppose we must call them; as doubtless you have heard, Mrs Gott. Perhaps he is believed, and the fact may make doubly against the accused.'

'He is *not* believed. Everybody hereabouts *knows*, that one of the skeletons was that of Peter Goodwin. They say that the District Attorney means to show *that*, beyond all dispute. They tell me that it is a law, in a case of this sort, first to show there has been a murder; second, to show who did it.'

'This is something like the course of proceeding, I believe; though I never sat on a trial for this offence. It is of no great moment what the District Attorney does, so that he do not prove that Miss Monson is guilty; and this, my kind-hearted Mrs Gott, you and I do not believe he *can* do.'

'In that we are agreed, sir. I no more think that Mary Monson did these things, than I think I did them myself.'

Jack expressed his thanks in a most grateful look, and there the interview terminated.

CHAPTER X

In peace, Love tunes the shepherd's reed;
In war, he mounts the warrior's steed;
In halls, in gay attire is seen;
In hamlets, dances on the green.
Love rules the court, the camp, the grove,
And men below, and saints above;
For love is heaven, and heaven is love.

SCOTT.

'It is the ways of the land,' said good Mrs Gott, in one of her remarks in the conversation just related. Other usages prevail, in connection with other interests; and the time is come when we must refer to one of them. In a word, Dr McBrain and Mrs Updyke were about to be united in the bands of matrimony. As yet we have said very little of the intended bride; but the incidents of our tale render it now necessary to bring her more prominently on the stage, and to give some account of herself and family.

Anna Wade was the only child of very respectable and somewhat affluent parents. At nineteen she married a lawyer of suitable years, and became Mrs Updyke. This union lasted but eight years, when the wife was left a widow with two children; a son and a daughter. In the course of time these children grew up, the mother devoting herself to their care, education, and well-being. In all this there was nothing remarkable, widowed mothers doing as much daily, with a self-devotion that allies them to the angels. Frank Updyke, the son, had finished his education, and was daily expected to arrive from a tour of three years in Europe. Anna, her mother's namesake, was at the sweet age of nineteen, and the very counterpart of what the elder Anna had been at the same period in life. The intended bride was far from being unattractive, though fully five-and-forty. In the eyes of Dr McBrain, she was even charming; although she did not exactly answer those celebrated conditions of female influence that have been handed down to us in the familiar toast of a voluptuous English prince. Though forty, Mrs Updyke was neither 'fat' nor 'fair;' being a brunette of a well-preserved and still agreeable person.

It was perhaps a little singular, after having escaped the temptations of a widowhood of twenty years, that this lady should think of marrying at a time of life when most females abandon the expectation of changing their condition. But Mrs Updyke was a person of a very warm heart; and she foresaw the day when she was to be left alone in the world. Her son was much inclined to be a rover; and, in his letters, he talked of still longer journeys and of more protracted absences from home. He inherited an independency from his father, and had now been his own master for several years. Anna was much courted by the circle to which she belonged; and young, affluent, pretty to the very verge of beauty, gentle, quiet, and singularly warm-hearted, it was scarcely within the bounds of possibility that she could escape an early marriage in a state of society like that of Manhatten. These were the reasons Mrs Updyke gave to her female confidants, when she deemed it well to explain the motives of her present purpose. Without intending to deceive, there was not a word of truth in these explanations. In point of fact, Mrs Updyke, well as she had loved the husband of her youth, preserved *les beaux restes* of a very warm and affectionate heart; and McBrain, a well-preserved, good-looking man, about a dozen years older than herself, had found the means to awaken its sympathies to such a degree, as once more to place the comely widow completely within the category of Cupid. It is very possible for a woman of forty to love, and to love with all her heart; though the world seldom takes as much interest in her weaknesses, if weakness it is, than in those of younger and fairer subjects of the passion. To own the truth, Mrs Updyke was profoundly in love, while her betrothed met her inclination with an answering sympathy that, to say the least, was fully equal to any tender sentiment he had succeeded in awakening.

All this was to Tom Dunscomb what he called 'nuts.' Three times had he seen his old friend in this pleasant state of feeling, and three times was he chosen to be an attendant at the altar; once in the recognised character of a groomsman, and on the other two occasions in that of a chosen friend. Whether the lawyer had himself completely escaped the darts of the little god, no one could say, so completely had he succeeded in veiling this portion of his life from observation; but, whether he had or not, he made those who did submit to the passion the theme of his untiring merriment.

Children usually regard these tardy inclinations of their parents with surprise, if not with downright distaste. Some little surprise the pretty Anna Updyke may have felt, when she was told by a venerable great-aunt that her mother was about to be married; but of distaste there was none. She had a strong regard for her new step-father that was to be; and thought it the most natural thing in the world to love. Sooth to say, Anna Updyke had not been out two years – the American girls are brought out so young! – without having sundry suitors. Manhattan is the easiest place in the world for a pretty girl, with a good fortune, to get offers. Pretty girls with good fortunes are usually in request everywhere; but it requires the precise state of society that exists in the 'Great *Commercial* Emporium,' to give a young woman the highest chance in the old lottery. There where one-half of the world came from other worlds some half dozen years since; where a good old Manhattan name is regarded as upstart among a crowd that scarcely knows whence it was itself derived, and whither it is destined, and where few have any real position in society, and fewer still know what the true meaning of the term is, money and beauty are the constant objects of pursuit. Anna Updyke formed no exception. She had declined, in the gentlest manner possible, no less than six direct offers, coming from those who were determined to lose nothing by diffidence; had thrown cold water on more than twice that number of little flames that were just beginning to burn; and had thrown into the fire some fifteen or sixteen anonymous effusions, in prose and verse that came from adventurers who could admire from a distance, at the Opera and in the streets, but who had no present means of getting any nearer than these indirect attempts at communication. We say 'thrown into the fire;' for Anna was too prudent, and had too much self-respect, to retain such documents, coming as they did, from so many 'Little Unknowns.' The anonymous effusions were consequently burnt – with one exception. The exception was in the case of a sonnet in which her hair – and very beautiful it is – was the theme. From some of the little free-masonry of the intercourses of the sexes, Anna fancied these lines had been written by Jack Wilmeter, one of the most constant of her visitors, as well as one of her admitted favourites. Between Jack and Anna there had been divers passages of gallantry, which had been very kindly viewed by McBrain and the mother. The parties themselves did not understand their own feelings; for matters had not gone far, when Mary Monson so strangely appeared on the stage, and drew Jack off, on the trail of wonder and mystery, if not on that of real passion. As Sarah Wilmeter was the most intimate friend of Anna Updyke, it is not extraordinary that this singular fancy of the brother's should be the subject of conversation between the two young women, each of whom probably felt more interest in his movements than any other persons on earth. The dialogue we are about to relate took place in Anna's own room the morning of the day which preceded that of the wedding, and followed, naturally enough, as the sequence of certain remarks which had been made on the approaching event.

'If *my* mother were living, and *must* be married,' said Sarah Wilmeter, 'I should be very well content to have *such* a man as Dr McBrain for a step-father. I have known him all my life, and he is, and ever has been, so intimate with Uncle Tom, that I almost think him a near relation.'

'And I have known him as long as I can remember,' Anna steadily rejoined, 'and have not only a great respect, but a warm regard for him. Should I ever marry myself, I do not believe I should have one-half the attachment for my father-in-law as I am sure I shall feel for my step-father.'

'How do you know there will be any father-in-law in the case? I am sure John has no parent.'

'John!' returned Anna, faintly – 'What is John to me?'

'Thank you, my dear – he is something, at least, to *me*.'

'To be sure – a brother naturally is – but Jack is no brother of mine, you will please to remember.'

Sarah cast a quick inquiring look at her friend; but the eyes of Anna were thrown downward on the carpet, while the bloom on her cheek spread to her temples. Her friend saw that, in truth, Jack was no *brother* of *hers*.

'What I mean is this,' – continued Sarah, following a thread that ran through her own mind, rather than anything that had been already expressed – 'Jack is making himself a very silly fellow just now.'

Anna now raised her eyes; her lip quivered a little, and the bloom deserted even her cheek. Still, she made no reply. Women can listen acutely at such moments; but it commonly exceeds their powers to speak. The friends understood each other, as Sarah well knew, and she continued her remarks precisely as if the other had answered them.

'Michael Millington brings strange accounts of Jack's behaviour at Biberry! He says that he seems to do nothing, think of nothing, talk of nothing, but of the hardship of this Mary Monson's case.'

'I'm sure it *is* cruel enough to awaken the pity of a rock,' said Anna Updyke, in a low tone; 'a woman, and she a lady, accused of such terrible crimes – murder and arson!'

'What is arson, child? – and how do *you* know anything about it?'

Again Anna coloured, her feelings being all sensitiveness on this subject; which had caused her far more pain than she had experienced from any other event in her brief life. It was, however, necessary to answer.

'Arson is setting fire to an inhabited house,' she said, after a moment's reflection; 'and I know it from having been told its signification by Mr Dunscomb.'

'Did uncle Tom say anything of this Mary Monson, and of Jack's singular behaviour?'

'He spoke of his client as a very extraordinary person, and of her accomplishments, and readiness, and beauty. Altogether, he does not seem to know what to make of her.'

'And what did he say about Jack? – You need have no reserve with me, Anna; I am his sister.'

'I know that very well, dear Sarah – but Jack's name was not mentioned, I believe – certainly not at the particular time, and in the conversation to which I now refer.'

'But at some *other* time, my dear, and in some *other* conversation.'

'He did once say something about your brother's being very attentive to the interests of the person he calls his Duke's county client – nothing more, I do assure you. It is the duty of young lawyers to be very attentive to the interests of their clients, I should think.'

'Assuredly – and that most especially when the client is a young lady with a pocket full of money. But Jack is above want, and can afford to act right at all times and on all occasions. I wish he had never seen this strange creature.'

Anna Updyke sat silent for some little time, playing with the hem of her pocket-handkerchief. Then she said, timidly, speaking as if she wished an answer, even while she dreaded it –

'Does not Marie Moulin know something about her?'

'A great deal, if she would only tell it. But Marie, too, has gone over to the enemy, since she has seen this siren. Not a word can I get out of her, though I have written three letters, beyond the fact that she knows *Mademoiselle*, and that she cannot believe her guilty.'

'The last, surely, is very important. If really innocent, how hard has been the treatment she has received! It is not surprising that your brother feels so deep an interest in her. He is very warm-hearted and generous, Sarah; and it is just like him to devote his time and talents to the service of the oppressed.'

It was Sarah's turn to be silent and thoughtful. She made no answer, for she well understood that an impulse very different from that mentioned by her friend was, just then, influencing her brother's conduct.

We have related this conversation as the briefest mode of making the reader acquainted with the true state of things in and about the neat dwelling of Mrs Updyke, in Eighth-street. Much, however, remains to be told; as the morning of the very day which succeeded that on which the foregoing dialogue was held, was the one named for the wedding of the mistress of the house.

At the very early hour of six, the party met at the church door, one of the most gothic structures in the new quarter of the town; and five minutes sufficed to make the two one. Anna sobbed as she saw her mother passing away from her, as it then appeared to her; and the bride herself was a little overcome. As for McBrain, as his friend Dunscomb expressed it, in a description given to a brother bachelor, who met him at dinner –

'He stood fire like a veteran! You're not going to frighten a fellow who has held forth the ring three times. You will remember that Ned has previously killed two wives, besides all the other folk he has slain; and I make no doubt the fellow's confidence was a good deal increased by the knowledge he possesses that none of us are immortal – as husbands and wives, at least.'

But Tom Dunscomb's pleasantries had no influence on his friend's happiness. Odd as it may appear to some, this connection was one of a warm and very sincere attachment. Neither of the parties had reached the period of life when nature begins to yield to the pressure of time; and there was the reasonable prospect before them of their contributing largely to each other's future happiness. The bride was dressed with great simplicity, but with a proper care; and she really justified the passion that McBrain insisted, in his conversations with Dunscomb, that he felt for her. Youthful, for her time of life, modest in demeanour and aspect, still attractive in person, the 'Widow Updyke' became Mrs McBrain, with as charming an air of womanly feeling as might have been exhibited by one of less than half her age. Covered with blushes, she was handed by the bridegroom into his own carriage, which stood at the church-door, and the two proceeded to Timbully.

As for Anna Updyke, she went to pass a week in the country with Sarah Dunscomb; even a daughter being a little *de trop* in a honeymoon. Rattletrap was the singular name Tom Dunscomb had given to his country-house. It was a small villa-like residence on the banks of the Hudson, and within the island of Manhattan. Concealed in a wood, it was a famous place for a bachelor to hide his oddities in. Here Dunscomb concentrated all his out-of-the-way purchases, including ploughs that were never used, all sorts of farming utensils that were condemned to the same idleness, and such contrivances in the arts of fishing and shooting as struck his fancy, though the lawyer never handled a rod or levelled a fowling piece. But Tom Dunscomb, though he professed to despise love, had fancies of his own. It gave him a certain degree of pleasure to *seem* to have these several tastes; and he threw away a good deal of money in purchasing these characteristic ornaments for Rattletrap. When Jack Wilmeter ventured one day to ask his uncle what pleasure he could find in collecting so many costly and perfectly useless articles, implements that had not the smallest apparent connection with his ordinary pursuits and profession, he got the following answer:–

'You are wrong, Jack, in supposing that these traps are useless. A lawyer has occasion for a vast deal of knowledge that he will never get out of his books. One should have the elements of all the sciences, and of most of the arts, in his mind, to make a thoroughly good advocate; for their application will become necessary on a thousand occasions, when Blackstone and Kent can be of no service. No, no; I prize my professions highly, and look upon Rattletrap as my Inn of Court.'

Jack Wilmeter had come over from Biberry to attend the wedding, and had now accompanied the party into the country, as it was called; though the place of Dunscomb was so near town, that it was not difficult, when the wind was at the southward, to hear the firebell on the City Hall. The meeting between John Wilmeter and Anna Updyke had been fortunately a little relieved by the peculiar circumstances in which the latter was placed. The feeling she betrayed, the pallor of her cheek, and the nervousness of her deportment, might all, naturally enough, be imputed to the emotions of a daughter, who saw her own mother standing at the altar by the side of one who was not her natural father. Let this be as it might, Anna had the advantage of the inferences which those around her made on these facts. The young people met first in the church, where there was no opportunity for any exchange of language or looks. Sarah took her friend away with her alone, on the road to Rattletrap, immediately after the ceremony, in order to allow Anna's spirits and manner to become composed, without being subjected to unpleasant observation. Dunscomb and his nephew drove out in a light vehicle of the latter's; and Michael Millington appeared later at the villa, bringing with him to dinner, Timms, who came on business connected with the approaching trial.

There never had been any love-making, in the direct meaning of the term, between John Wilmeter and Anna Updyke. They had known each other so long and so intimately, that both regarded the feeling of kindness that each knew subsisted, as a mere fraternal sort of affection. 'Jack is Sarah's brother,' thought Anna, when she permitted herself to reason on the subject at all; 'and it is natural that I should have more friendship for him than for any other young man.' 'Anna is Sarah's most intimate friend,' thought Jack, 'and that is the long and short of my attachment for *her*. Take away Sarah, and Anna would be nothing to me; though she is so pretty, and clever, and gentle, and lady-like. I must like those Sarah likes, or it might make us both unhappy.' This was the reasoning of nineteen, and when Anna Updyke was just budding into young womanhood; at a later day, habit had got to be so much in the ascendant, that neither of the young people *thought* much on the subject at all. The preference was strong in each – so strong, indeed, as to hover over the confines of passion, and quite near to its vortex; though the long accustomed feeling prevented either from entering into its analysis. The attachments that grow up with our daily associations, and get to be so interwoven with our most familiar thoughts, seldom carry away those who submit to them, in the whirlwind of passion; which are much more apt to attend sudden and impulsive love. Cases do certainly occur in which the parties have long known each other, and have lived on for years in a dull appreciation of mutual merit – sometimes with prejudices and alienation active between them; when suddenly all is changed, and the scene that was lately so tranquil and tame becomes tumultuous and glowing, and life assumes a new charm, as the profound emotions of passion chase away its dulness; substituting hope, and fears, and lively wishes, and soul-felt impressions in its stead. This is not usual in the course of the most wayward of all our impulses; but it does occasionally happen, brightening existence with a glow that might well be termed divine, were the colours bestowed derived from a love of the Creator, in lieu of that of one of his creatures. In these sudden awakenings of dormant feelings, some chord of mutual sympathy, some deep-rooted affinity is aroused, carrying away their possessors in a torrent of the feelings. Occasionally, wherever the affinity is active, the impulse natural and strongly sympathetic, these sudden and seemingly wayward attachments are the most indelible, colouring the whole of the remainder of life; but oftener do they take the character of mere impulse, rather than that of deeper sentiment, and disappear, as they were first seen, in some sudden glow of the horizon of the affections.

In this brief analysis of some of the workings of the heart, we may find a clue to the actual frame of mind in which John Wilmeter returned from Biberry, where he had now been, like a sentinel on post, for several weeks, in vigilant watchfulness over the interests of Mary Monson. During all that time, however, he had not once been admitted within the legal limits of the prison; holding his brief, but rather numerous conferences with his client, at the little grate in the massive door that separated the gaol from the dwelling of the sheriff. Kind-hearted Mrs Gott would have admitted him to the gallery, whenever he chose to ask that favour; but this act of courtesy had been forbidden by Mary Monson herself. Timms she did receive, and she conferred with him in private on more than one occasion, manifesting great earnestness in the consultations that preceded the approaching trial. But John Wilmeter she would receive only at the grate, like a nun in a well-regulated convent. Even this coyness contributed to feed the fire that had been so suddenly lighted in the young man's heart, on which the strangeness of the prisoner's situation, her personal attractions, her manners, and all the other known peculiarities of person, history, education and deportment, had united to produce a most lively impression, however fleeting it was to prove in the end.

Had there been any direct communications on the subject of the attachment that had so long, so slowly, but so surely been taking root in the hearts of John and Anna, any reciprocity in open confidence, this unlooked-for impulse in a new direction could not have overtaken the young man. He did not know how profound was the interest that Anna took in him; nor, for that matter, was she aware of it herself, until Michael Millington brought the unpleasant tidings of the manner in which his friend seemed to be entranced with his uncle's client at Biberry. Then, indeed, Anna was made to feel that surest attendant of the liveliest love, a pang of jealousy; and, for the first time in her young and innocent life, she became aware of the real nature of her sentiments in behalf of John Wilmeter. On the other hand, drawn aside from the ordinary course of his affections by sudden, impulsive, and exciting novelties, John was first submitting to the influence of the charms of the fair stranger, as has been more than once intimated in our opening pages, as the newly-fallen snow melts under the rays of a noon-day sun.

Such, then, was the state of matters in this little circle, when the wedding took place, and John Wilmeter joined the family-party. Although Dunscomb did all he could to make the dinner gay, Rattletrap had seldom entertained a more silent company than that which sat down at its little round table on this occasion. John thought of Biberry and Mary Monson; Sarah's imagination was quite busy in wondering why Michael Millington stayed away so long; and Anna was on the point of bursting into tears half-a-dozen times, under the depression produced by the joint events of her mother's marriage, and John Wilmeter's obvious change of deportment towards her.

'What the deuce has kept Michael Millington and that fellow Timms, from joining us at dinner?' said the master of the house, as the fruit was placed upon the table; and, closing one eye, he looked with the other through the ruby rays of a glass of well-cooled Madeira – his favourite wine. 'Both promised to be punctual; yet here are they both sadly out of time. They knew the dinner was to come off at four.'

'As is one, sir, so are both,' answered John. 'You will remember they were to come together?'

'True – and Millington is rather a punctual man – especially in visiting at Rattletrap' – here Sarah blushed a little; but the engagement in her case being announced, there was no occasion for any particular confusion. 'We shall have to take Michael with us into Duke's next week, Miss Wilmeter; the case being too grave to neglect bringing up all our forces.'

'Is Jack, too, to take a part in the trial, uncle Tom?' demanded the niece, with a little interest in the answer.

'Jack, too – everybody, in short. When the life of a fine young woman is concerned, it behoves her counsel to be active and diligent. I have never before had a cause into which my feelings have so completely entered – no, never.'

'Do not counsel always enter, heart and hand, into their clients' interests, and make themselves, as it might be, as you gentlemen of the bar sometimes term these things, a "part and parcel" of their concerns?'

This question was put by Sarah, but it caused Anna to raise her eyes from the fruit she was pretending to eat, and to listen intently to the reply. Perhaps she fancied that the answer might explain the absorbed manner in which John had engaged in the service of the accused.

'As far from it as possible, in many cases,' returned the uncle; 'though there certainly are others in which one engages with all his feelings. But every day lessens my interest in the law, and all that belongs to it.'

'Why should that be so, sir? – I have heard you called a devotee of the profession.'

'That's because I have no wife. Let a man live a bachelor, and ten to one he gets some nickname or other. On the other hand, let him marry two or three times, like Ned McBrain – beg your pardon, Nanny, for speaking disrespectfully of your papa – but let a fellow just get his third wife, and they tack "family" to his appellation at once. He's an excellent *family* lawyer, or a capital *family* physician, or a supremely pious – no, I don't know that they've got so far as the parsons, for *they* are all *family* fellows.'

'You have a spite against matrimony, Uncle Tom.'

'Well, if I have, it stops with me, as a *family* complaint. *You* are free from it, my dear; and I'm half inclined to think Jack will marry before he is a year older. But here are the tardies at last.'

Although the uncle made no allusion to the person his nephew was to marry, everybody but himself thought of Mary Monson at once. Anna turned pale as death; Sarah looked thoughtful, and even sad; and John became as red as scarlet. But the entrance of Michael Millington and Timms caused the conversation to turn on another subject, as a matter of course.

'We expected you to dinner, gentlemen,' Dunscomb drily remarked, as he pushed the bottle to his guests.

'Business before eating is my maxim, 'Squire Dunscomb,' Timms replied. 'Mr Millington and I have been very busy in the office, from the moment Dr McBrain and his lady——'

'Wife – say "wife," Timms, if you please. Or, "Mrs McBrain," if you like that better.'

'Well, sir, I used the word I did out of compliment to the other ladies present. They love to be honoured and signalized in our language when we speak of them, sir, I believe.'

'Poh! poh! Timms; take my advice, and let all these small matters alone. It takes a life to master them, and one must begin from the cradle. When all is ended, they are scarce worth the trouble they give. Speak good, plain, direct, and manly English, I have always told you, and you'll get along well enough; but make no attempts to be fine. "Dr McBrain and *lady*" is next thing "to going through Hurlgate," or meeting a "lady-friend." You'll never get the right sort of a wife until you drop all such absurdities.'

'I'll tell you how it is, 'squire: so far as law goes, or even morals, and I don't know but I may say general government politics, I look upon you as the best adviser I can consult. But when it comes to matrimony I can't see how you should know any more about it than I do myself. I *do* intend to get married one of these days, which is more, I fancy, than you ever had in view.'

'No; my great concern has been to escape matrimony; but a man may get a very tolerable notion of the sex while manoeuvring among them with that intention. I am not certain that he who has had two or three handsomely managed escapes, doesn't learn as much as he who has had two or three wives – I mean of useful information. What do you think of all this, Millington?'

'That I wish for no escapes, when my choice has been free and fortunate.'

'And you, Jack?'

'Sir!' answered the nephew, starting, as if aroused from a brown study. 'Did you speak to me, Uncle Tom?'

'*He*'ll not be of much use to us next week, Timms,' said the counsellor, coolly, filling his own and his neighbour's glass, as he spoke, with iced Madeira – 'These capital cases demand the utmost vigilance; more especially when popular prejudice sets in against them.'

'Should the jury find Mary Monson to be guilty, what would be the sentence of the court?' demanded Sarah, smiling, even while she seemed much interested. – 'I believe that is right, Mike – the court "sentences," and the jury "convicts." If there be any mistake, you must answer for it.'

'I am afraid to speak of laws or constitutions in the presence of your uncle, since the rebuke Jack and I got in that affair of the toast,' returned Sarah's betrothed, arching his eye-brows.

'By the way, Jack, did that dinner ever come off?' demanded the uncle, suddenly; 'I looked for your toasts in the journals, but do not remember ever to have seen them.'

'You could not have seen any of mine, sir; for I went to Biberry that very morning, and only left there last evening.' – Anna's countenance resembled a lily, just as it begins to droop – 'I believe, however, the whole affair fell through, as no one seems to know, just now, who are and who are not the friends of liberty. It is the people to-day; the Pope next day; some prince to-morrow; and, by the end of the week, we may have a Massaniello or a Robespierre uppermost. The times seem sadly out of joint, just now, and the world is fast getting to be upside-down.'

'It's all owing to this infernal code, Timms, which is enough to revolutionize human nature itself!' cried Dunscomb, with an animation that produced a laugh in the young folk (Anna excepted), and a simper in the person addressed. 'Ever since this thing has come into operation among us, I never know when a case is to be heard, the decision had, or the principles that are to come uppermost. Well, we must try and get some good out of it, if we can, in this capital case.'

'Which is drawing very near, 'squire; and I have some facts to communicate in that affair which it may be well to compare with the law, without much more delay.'

'Let us finish this bottle – if the boys help us, it will not be much more than a glass apiece.'

'I don't think the 'squire will ever be up*held* at the polls by the Temperance people.' said Timms, filling his glass to the brim; for, to own the truth, it was seldom that he got such wine.

'As *you* are expecting to be held *up* by them, my fine fellow. I've heard of your management, Master Timms, and am told you aspire as high as the State Senate. Well; there is room for better, but much worse men have been sent there. Now, let us go to what I call the "Rattletrap Office."'

CHAPTER XI

The strawberry grows underneath the nettle;
And wholesome berries thrive and ripen best,
Neighbour'd by fruit of baser quality.

King Henry V.

There stood a very pretty pavilion in one of the groves of Rattletrap, overhanging the water, with the rock of the river-shore for its foundation. It had two small apartments, in one of which Dunscomb had caused a book-case, a table, a rocking-chair, and a lounge to be placed. The other was furnished more like an ordinary summer-house, and was at all times accessible to the inmates of the family. The sanctum, or office, was kept locked; and here its owner often brought his papers, and passed whole days, during the warm months, when it is the usage to be out of town, in preparing his cases. To this spot, then, the counsellor now held his way, attended by Timms, having ordered a servant to bring a light and some cigars; smoking being one of the regular occupations of the office. In a few minutes, each of the two men of the law had a cigar in his mouth, and was seated at a little window that commanded a fine view of the Hudson, its fleet of sloops, steamers, tow-boats and colliers, and its high, rocky western shore, which has obtained the not inappropriate name of the Palisades.

The cigars, the glass, and the pleasant scenery, teeming as was the last with movement and life, appeared, for the moment, to drive from the minds of the two men of the law the business on which they had met. It was a proof of the effect of habit that a person like Dunscomb, who was really a good man, and one who loved his fellow-creatures, could just then forget that a human life was, in some measure, dependent on the decisions of this very interview, and permit his thoughts to wander from

so important an interest. So it was, however; and the first topic that arose
in this consultation had no reference whatever to Mary Monson, or her
approaching trial, though it soon led the colloquists round to her
situation, as it might be without their intending it.

'This is a charming retreat, 'Squire Dunscomb,' commenced Timms,
settling himself with some method in a very commodious armchair; 'and
one that I should often frequent, did I own it.'

'I hope you will live to be master of one quite as pleasant, Timms,
some time or other. They tell me your practice, now, is one of the best in
Duke's; some two or three thousand a year, I dare say, if the truth were
known.'

'It's as good as anybody's on our circuit, unless you count the bigwigs
from York. I won't name the sum, even to as old a friend as yourself,
'squire; for the man who lets the world peep into his purse will soon find
it footing him up, like a sum in arithmetic. You've gentlemen in town,
however, who sometimes get more for a single case than I can 'arn in a
twelvemonth.'

'Still, considering your beginning, and late appearance at the bar,
Timms, you are doing pretty well. Do you lead in many trials at the
circuit?'

'That depends pretty much on age, you know, 'squire. Gen'rally older
lawyers are put into all my causes; but I have carried one or two through,
on my own shoulders, and that by main strength too.'

'It must have been by your facts, rather than by your law. The verdicts
turned altogether on testimony, did they not?'

'Pretty much – and *that's* the sort of case *I* like. A man can prepare his
evidence beforehand, and make some calculations where it will land him;
but, as for the law, I do not see that studying it as hard as I will, makes me
much the wiser. A case is no sooner settled one way, by a judge in New
York, than it is settled in another, in Pensylvany or Virginny.'

'And that, too, when courts were identical, and had a character! Now,
we have eight Supreme Courts, and they are beginning to settle the law
in eight different ways. Have you studied the code pretty closely,
Timms?'

'Not I, sir. They tell me things will come round under it in time, and I
try to be patient. There's one thing about it that I *do* like. It has taken all
the Latin out of the law, which is a great help to us poor scholars.'

'It has that advantage, I confess; and before it is done, it will take all the
law out of the Latin. They tell me it was proposed to call the old process
of "*ne exeat*" a writ of "no go."'

'Well, to my mind, the last would be the best term of the two.'

'Ay, to *your* mind, it might, Timms. How do you like the fee-bills, and
the new mode of obtaining your compensation?'

'Capital! The more they change them matters, the deeper we'll dig into 'em, 'squire! I never knew reform help the great body of the community – all it favours is individdles.'

'There is more truth in that, Timms, than you are probably aware of yourself. Reform, fully half the time, does no more than shift the pack-saddle from one set of shoulders to another. Nor do I believe much is gained by endeavouring to make law cheap. It were better for the community that it should be dear; though cases do occur in which its charges might amount to a denial of justice. It is to be regretted that the world oftener decides under the influence of exceptions, rather than under that of the rule. Besides, it is no easy matter to check the gains of a thousand or two of hungry attorneys.'

'There you're right, 'squire, if you never hit the nail on the head before! But the new scheme is working well for *us*, and, in one sense, it may work well for the people. The compensation is the first thing thought of now; and when that is the case, the client stops to think. It isn't every person that holds as large and as open a purse as our lady at Biberry!'

'Ay, she continues to fee you, does she, Timms? Pray, how much has she given you altogether?'

'Not enough to build a new wing to the Astor Library, nor to set up a parson in a gothic temple; still, enough to engage me, heart and hand, in her service. First and last, my receipts have been a thousand dollars, besides money for the outlays.'

'Which have amounted to——'

'More than as much more. This is a matter of life and death, you know, sir; and, prices rise accordingly. All I have received has been handed to me either in gold or in good current paper. The first troubled me a good deal; for I was not certain some more pieces might not be recognized, though they were all eagles and half-eagles.'

'Has any such recognition occurred?' demanded Dunscomb, with interest.

'To be frank with you, 'Squire Dunscomb, I sent the money to town at once, and set it afloat in the great current in Wall Street, where it could do neither good nor harm on the trial. It would have been very green in me to pay out the precise coin among the people of Duke's. No one could say what might have been the consequences.'

'It is not very easy for me to foretell the consequences of the substitutes which, it seems, you *did* use. A fee to a counsel I can understand; but what the deuce you have done, legally, with a thousand dollars out-of-doors, exceeds my penetration. I trust you have not been attempting to purchase jurors, Timms?'

'Not I, sir. I know the penalties too well to venture on such a defence. Besides, it is too soon to attempt that game. Jurors may be bought; sometimes *are* bought, I have heard say' – here Timms screwed up his face into a most significant mimicry of disapprobation – 'but *I* have done nothing of the sort in the "State *v.* Mary Monson." It is too soon to operate, even should the testimony drive us to *that*, in the long run.'

'I forbid all illegal measures, Timms. You know my rule of trying causes is never to overstep the limits of the law.'

'Yes, sir; I understand your principle, which will answer, provided both sides stick to it. But, let a man act as close to what is called honesty as he please, what certainty has he that his adversary will observe the same rule? This is the great difficulty I find in getting along in the world, 'squire; opposition upsets all a man's best intentions. Now, in politics, sir, there is no man in the country better disposed to uphold respectable candidates and just principles than I am myself; but the other side squeeze us up so tight, that before the election comes off, I'm ready to vote for the devil, rather than get the worst of it.'

'Ay, that's the wicked man's excuse all over the world, Timms. In voting for the gentleman you have just mentioned, you will remember you are sustaining the enemy of your race, whatever may be his particular relation to his party. But in this affair at Biberry, you will please to remember it is not an election, nor is the devil a candidate. What success have you had with the testimony?'

'There's an abstract of it, sir; and a pretty mess it is! So far as I can see, we shall have to rest entirely on the witnesses of the State; for I can get nothing out of the accused.'

'Does she still insist on her silence, in respect of the past?'

'As close as if she had been born dumb. I have told her in the strongest language that her life depends on her appearing before the jury with a plain tale and a good character; but she will help me to neither. I never had such a client before——'

'Open-handed, you mean, I suppose, Timms?'

'In that partic'lar, 'Squire Dunscomb, she is just what the profession likes – liberal, and pays down. Of course, I am so much the more anxious to do all I can in her case; but she will not let me serve her.'

'There must be some strong reason for all this reserve, Timms. – Have you questioned the Swiss maid that my niece sent to her. We know *her*, and it would seem that she knows Mary Monson. Here is so obvious a way of coming at the past, I trust you have spoken to her?'

'She will not let me say a word to the maid. There they live together, chatter with one another from morning to night, in French, that nobody understands; but will see no one but me, and me only in public, as it might be.'

'In public! – You have not asked for *private* interviews, eh! Timms? Remember your views upon the county, and the great danger there is of the electors' finding you out.'

'I well know, 'Squire Dunscomb, that your opinion of me is not very flattering in some partic'lars; while in others, I think you place me pretty well up the ladder. As for old Duke's, I believe I stand as well in that county as any man in it, now the Revolutionary patriots are nearly gone. So long as any of *them,* lasted, we modern fellows had no chance; and the way in which relics were brought to light was wonderful! If Washington only had an army one-tenth as strong as these patriots make it out to be, he would have driven the British from the country years sooner than it was actually done. Luckily, my grandfather *did* serve a short tour of duty in that war; and my own father was a captain of militia in 1814, lying out on Harlem Heights and Harlem Common, most of the fall; when and where he caught the rheumatism. This was no bad capital to start upon; and, though you treat it lightly, 'squire, I'm a favourite in the county – I *am!*'

'Nobody doubts it, Timms; or can doubt it, if he knew the history of these matters. Let me see – I believe I first heard of you as a Temperance Lecturer?'

'Excuse me; I began with the Common Schools, on which I lectured with some success one whole season. *Then* came the Temperance cause, out of which, I will own, not a little capital was made.'

'And do you stop there, Timms; or do you ride some other hobby into power?'

'It's my way, Mr Dunscomb, to try all sorts of med'cines. Some folks that wunt touch rhubarb will swallow salts; and all palates must be satisfied. Free Sile and Emancipation Doctrines are coming greatly into favour; but they are ticklish things, that cut like a two-edged sword, and I do not fancy meddling with them. There are about as many opposed to meddling with slavery in the free States as there are in favour of it. I wish I knew your sentiments, 'Squire Dunscomb, on this subject. I've always found your doctrines touching the Constitution to be sound, and such as would stand examination.'

'The constitutional part of the question is very simple, and presents no difficulties whatever,' returned the counsellor, squinting through the ruby of his glass with an old bachelor sort of delight, 'except for those who have special ends to obtain.'

'Has, or has not, Congress a legal right to enact laws preventing the admission of slaves into California?'

'Congress has the legal right to govern any of its territories despotically; of course, to admit or to receive what it may please within their limits. The resident of a territory is not a citizen, and has no *legal* claim to be so considered. California, as a conquered territory, may be thus governed by the laws of nations, unless the treaty of cession places some restrictions on the authority of the conqueror. A great deal of absurdity is afloat among those who should know better, touching the powers of government in this country. You, yourself, are one of those fellows, Timms, who get things upside down, and fancy the Constitution is to be looked into for everything.'

'And is it not, 'squire? – that is, in the way of theory – in practice, I know it is a very different matter. Are we not to look into the Constitution for all the powers of the Government?'

'Of the *Government*, perhaps, in one sense; – but not for those of the *nation*. Whence come the powers to make war and peace, to form treaties and alliances, maintain armies and navies, coin money, &c.?'

'You'll find them all in the Constitution, as I read it, sir.'

'There is just your mistake; and connected with it are most of the errors that are floating about in our political world. The *country* gets its legal right to do all these things from the laws of nations; the Constitution merely saying *who* shall be its agents in the exercise of these powers. Thus *war* is rendered legal by the custom of nations, and the Constitution says Congress shall declare war. It also says Congress shall pass all laws that become necessary to carry out this power. It follows, Congress may pass any law that has a legitimate aim to secure a conquest. Nor is this all the functionaries of the Government can do, on general principles, in the absence of any special provisions by a direct law. The latter merely supersedes or directs the power of the former. The Constitution guarantees nothing to the territories. They are strictly subject, and may be governed absolutely. The only protection of their people is in the sympathy and habits of the people of the States. We give them political liberty, not as of legal necessity, but as a boon to which they are entitled in good-fellowship, – or as the father provides for his children.'

'Then you think Congress has power to exclude slavery from California?'

'I can't imagine a greater legal absurdity than to deny it. I see no use in any legislation on the subject, as a matter of practice, since California will shortly decide on this interest for itself; but, as a right in theory, it strikes me to be madness to deny that the Government of the United States has full power over all its territories, both on general principles and under the Constitution.'

'And in the Deestrict – you hold to the same power in the Deestrict?'

'Beyond a question. Congress can abolish domestic servitude or slavery in the District of Columbia, whenever it shall see fit. The *right* is as clear as the sun at noon-day.'

'If these are your opinions, 'squire, I'll go for Free Sile and Abolition in the Deestrict. They have a popular cry, and take wonderfully well in Duke's, and will build me up considerable. I like to be right; but, most of all, I like to be strong.'

'If you adopt such a course, you will espouse trouble without any dower, and that will be worse than McBrain's three wives; and, what is more, in the instance of the District, you will be guilty of an act of oppression. You will remember that the possession of a legal power to do a particular thing, does not infer a moral right to exercise it. As respects your Free Soil, it may be well to put down a foot; and, so far as votes legally used can be thrown, to prevent the further extension of slavery. In this respect you are right enough, and will be sustained by an overwhelming majority of the nation; but, when it comes to the District, the question has several sides to it.'

'You said yourself, 'squire, that Congress has all power to legislate for the Deestrict?'

'No doubt it has – but the possession of a power does not necessarily imply its use. We have power, as a nation to make war on little Portugal, and crush her; but it would be very wicked to do so. When a member of Congress votes on any question that strictly applies to the District, he should reason precisely as if his Constituents all lived in the District itself. You will understand, Timms, that liberty is closely connected with practice, and is not a mere creature of phrases and professions. What more intolerable tyranny could exist, than to have a man elected by New Yorkers legislating for the District on strictly New York policy; or, if you will, on New York prejudices? If the people of the District wish to get rid of the institution of domestic slavery, there are ways for ascertaining the fact; and once assured of that, Congress ought to give the required relief. But in framing such a law, great care should be taken not to violate the comity of the Union. The comity of nations is, in practice, a portion of their laws, and is respected as such; how much more, then, ought we to respect this comity in managing the relations between the several States of this Union!'

'Yes, the *sovereign* States of the Union,' laying emphasis on the word we have italicized.

'Pshaw – they are no more sovereign than you and I are sovereign.'

'Not sovereign, sir!' exclaimed Timms, actually jumping to his feet in astonishment; 'why this is against the National Faith – contrary to all the theories.'

'Something so, I must confess; yet very good common sense. If there be any sovereignty left in the States, it is the very minimum, and a thing of show, rather than of substance. If you will look at the Constitution, you will find that the equal representation of the States in the Senate is the only right of a sovereign character that is left to the members of the Union, separate and apart from their confederated communities.'

Timms rubbed his brows, and seemed to be in some mental trouble. The doctrine of the 'Sovereign States' is so very common, so familiar in men's mouths, that no one dreams of disputing it. Nevertheless, Dunscomb had a great reputation in his set, as a constitutional lawyer; and the 'expounders' were very apt to steal his demonstrations, without giving him credit for them. As before the nation, a school-boy would have carried equal weight; but the direct, vigorous, common-sense arguments that he brought to the discussions, as well as the originality of his views, ever commanded the profound respect of the intelligent. Timms had cut out for himself a path by which he intended to ascend in the scale of society; and had industriously, if not very profoundly, considered all the agitating questions of the day, in the relations they might be supposed to bear to his especial interests. He had almost determined to come out an abolitionist; for he saw that the prejudices of the hour were daily inclining the electors of the northern States, more and more, to oppose the further extension of domestic slavery, so far as surface was concerned, which was in effect preparing the way for the final destruction of the institution altogether. For Mr Dunscomb, however, this wily limb of the law, and skilful manager of men, had the most profound respect; and he was very glad to draw him out still further on a subject that was getting to be of such intense interest to himself, as well as to the nation at large; for, out of all doubt, it is *the* question, not only of the 'Hour,' but for years to come.

'Well, sir, this surprises me more and more. The States not sovereign! – Why, they *gave* all the power it possesses to the Federal Government!'

'Very true; and it is precisely for *that* reason they are not sovereign – that which is given away is no longer possessed. All the great powers of sovereignty are directly bestowed on the Union, which alone possesses them.'

'I will grant you that, 'squire; but enough is retained to hang either of us. The deuce is in it if that be not a sovereign power.'

'It does not follow from the instance cited. Send a squadron abroad, and its officers can hang; but they are not sovereign, for the simple reason that there is a recognised authority over them, which can increase, sustain, or take away altogether, any such and all other power. Thus is it with the States. By a particular clause, the Constitution can be amended, including all the interests involved, with a single exception. This is an instance in which the exception does strictly prove the rule. All interests but the one excepted can be dealt with, by a species of legislation that is higher than common. The Union can constitutionally abolish domestic slavery altogether——'

'It can! – It would be the making of any political man's fortune to be able to show *that*!'

'Nothing is easier than to show it, in the way of theory, Timms; though nothing would be harder to achieve, in the way of practice. The

Constitution can be legally amended so as to effect this end, provided majorities in three-fourths of the States can be obtained; though every living soul in the remaining States were opposed to it. That this is the just construction of the great fundamental law, as it has been solemnly adopted, no discreet man can doubt; though, on the other hand, no discreet person would think of attempting such a measure, as the vote necessary to success cannot be obtained. To talk of the sovereignty of a community over this particular interest, for instance, when all the authority on the subject can be taken from it in direct opposition to the wishes of every man, woman, and child it contains, is an absurdity. The sovereignty, as respects slavery, is in the Union, and not in the several States; and therein you can see the fallacy of contending that Congress has nothing to do with the interest, when Congress can take the initiative in altering this or any other clause of the great national compact.'

'But, the Deestrict – the Deestrict, 'Squire Dunscomb – what can and ought to be done there?'

'I believe in my soul, Timms, you have an aim on a seat in Congress! Why stop short of the Presidency? Men as little likely as yourself to be elevated to that high office have been placed in the executive chair; and why not you as well as another?'

'It is an office "neither to be sought nor declined," said an eminent statesman,' answered Timms, with a seriousness that amused his companion; who saw, by his manner, that his old pupil held himself in reserve for the accidents of political life. 'But, sir, I am very anxious to get right on the subject of the Deestrict' – Timms pronounced this word as we have spelt it – 'and I know that if any man can set me right, it is yourself.'

'As respects the District, Mr Timms, here is my faith. It is a territory provided for in the Constitution for a national purpose, and must be regarded as strictly national property, held exclusively for objects that call all classes of citizens within its borders. Now, two great principles, in my view, should control all legislation for this little community. As I have said already, it would be tyranny to make the notions and policy of New York or Vermont bear on the legislation of the District, but every member is bound to act strictly as a representative of the people of the spot for whom the law is intended. If I were in Congress, I would at any time, on a respectable application, vote to refer the question of abolition to the people of the District; if they said ay, I would say ay; if no, no. Beyond this I would never go; nor do I think the man who wishes to push matters beyond this, sufficiently respects the general principles of representative government, or knows how to respect the spirit of the national compact. On the supposition that the District ask relief from the institution of slavery, great care should be observed in granting the necessary legislation. Although the man in South Carolina has no more right to insist that the District should maintain the "peculiar institution," because his particular State maintains it, than the Vermontese to insist on carrying his Green Mountain notions into the District laws; yet has the Carolinian rights in this territory that must ever be respected, let the general policy adopted be what it may. Every American has an implied right to visit the District on terms of equality. Now, there would be no equality if a law were passed excluding the domestics from any portion of the country. In the Slave States, slaves exclusively perform the functions of domestics; and sweeping abolition might very easily introduce regulations that would be unjust towards the slave-holders. As respects the northern man, the existence of slavery in or out of the District is purely a speculative question; but it is not so with the southern. This should never be forgotten; and I always feel disgust when I hear a northern man swagger and make a parade of his morality on this subject.'

'But the southern men swagger and make a parade of their chivalry, 'squire, on the other hand!'

'Quite true; but, with them, there is a strong provocation. It is a matter of life and death to the south; and the comity of which I spoke requires great moderation on our part. As for the threats of dissolution, of which we have had so many, like the cry of "wolf," they have worn themselves out, and are treated with indifference.'

'The threat is still used, Mr Dunscomb!'

'Beyond a doubt, Timms; but of one thing you may rest well assured – if ever there be a separation between the Free and the Slave States of this Union, the wedge will be driven home by northern hands; not by indirection, but coolly, steadily, and with a thorough northern determination to open the seam. There will be no fuss about chivalry, but the thing will be done. I regard the measure as very unlikely to happen, the Mississippi and its tributaries binding the States together, to say nothing of ancestry, history, and moral ties, in a way to render a rupture very difficult to effect; but, should it come at all, rely on it, it will come directly from the north. I am sorry to say there is an impatience of the threats and expedients that have so much disfigured southern policy, that have set many at the north to "calculating the value;" and thousands may now be found where, ten years since, it would not have been easy to meet with one, who deem separation better than union with slavery. Still, the general feeling of the north is passive; and I trust it will so continue.'

'Look at the laws for the recovery of fugitives, 'squire, and the manner in which they are administered.'

'Bad enough, I grant you, and full of a want of good faith. Go to the bottom of this subject, Timms, or let it alone altogether. Some men will tell you that slavery is a sin, and contrary to revealed religion. This I hold to be quite untrue. At all events, if it be a sin, it is a sin to give the son the rich inheritance of the father, instead of dividing it among the poor; to eat a dinner while a hungrier man than yourself is within sound of your voice; or, indeed, to do anything that is necessary and agreeable, when the act may be still more necessary to, or confer greater pleasure on, another. I believe in a Providence; and I make little doubt that African slavery is an important feature in God's Laws, instead of being disobedience to them. – But enough of this, Timms – you will court popularity, which is your Archimedean lever, and forget all I tell you. Is Mary Monson in greater favour now than when I last saw you?'

'The question is not easily answered, sir. She pays well, and money is a powerful screw!'

'I do not inquire what you do with her money,' said Dunscomb, with the evasion of a man who knew that it would not do to probe every weak spot in morals, any more than it would do to inflame the diseases of the body; 'but, I own, I should like to know if our client has any suspicions of its uses?'

Timms now cast a furtive glance behind him, and edged his chair nearer to his companion, in a confidential way, as if he would trust *him* with a private opinion that he should keep religiously from all others.

'Not only does she know all about it,' he answered, with a knowing inclination of the head, 'but she enters into the affair, heart and hand. To my great surprise, she has even made two or three suggestions that were capital in their way! Capital! yes, sir; quite capital! If you were not so stiff in your practice, 'squire, I should delight to tell you all about it. She's sharp, you may depend on it! She's wonderfully sharp!'

'What! – That refined, lady-like, accomplished young woman!'

'She has an accomplishment or two you've never dreamed of, 'squire. I'd pit her ag'in the sharpest practitioner in Duke's, and she'd come out ahead. I thought I knew something of preparing a cause; but she has given hints that will be worth more to me than all her fees!'

'You do not mean that she shows *experience* in such practices?'

'Perhaps not. It seems more like mother-wit, I acknowledge; but it's mother-wit of the brightest sort. She understands them reporters by instinct as it might be. What is more, she backs all her suggestions with gold, or current bank-notes.'

'And where can she get so much money?'

'That is more than I can tell you,' returned Timms, opening some papers belonging to the case, and laying them a little formally before the senior counsel to invite his particular attention. 'I've never thought it advisable to ask the question.'

'Timms, you do not, *cannot* think Mary Monson guilty?'

'I never go beyond the necessary facts of a case; and my opinion is of no consequence whatever. We are employed to defend her; and the counsel for the State are not about to get a verdict without some working for it. That's my conscience in these matters, 'Squire Dunscomb.'

Dunscomb asked no more questions. He turned gloomily to the papers, shoved his glass aside, as if it gave him pleasure no longer, and began to read. For near four hours he and Timms were earnestly engaged in preparing a brief, and in otherwise getting the cause ready for trial.

CHAPTER XII

> *Hel.* O, that my prayers could such affection move!
> *Her.* The more I hate, the more he follows me.
> *Hel.* The more I love the more he hateth me.
> *Her.* His folly, Helena, is no fault of mine.
>
> *Midsummer Night's Dream.*

While Dunscomb and Timms were thus employed, the younger members of the party very naturally sought modes of entertainment that were more in conformity with their tastes and years. John Wilmeter had been invited to be present at the consultation; but his old feelings were revived, and he found a pleasure in being with Anna that induced him to disregard the request. His sister and his friend were now betrothed, and they had glided off along one of the pretty paths of the Rattletrap woods, in a way that is so very common to persons in their situation. This left Jack alone with Anna. The latter was timid, shy even; while the former was thoughtful. Still, it was not easy to separate; and they too, almost unconsciously to themselves, were soon walking in that pleasant wood, following one of its broadest and most frequented paths, however.

John, naturally enough, imputed the thoughtfulness of his companion to the event of the morning; and he spoke kindly to her, and with a gentle delicacy on the subject, that more than once compelled the warm-hearted girl to struggle against her tears. After he had said enough on this topic, the young man followed the current of his own thoughts, and spoke of her he had left in the gaol of Biberry.

'Her case is most extraordinary,' continued John, 'and it has excited our liveliest sympathy. By ours, I mean the disinterested and intelligent; for the vulgar prejudice is strong against her. Sarah, or even yourself, Anna' – his companion looked more like herself, at this implied compliment, than she had done before that day – 'could not seem less likely to be guilty of anything wrong than this Miss Monson; yet she stands indicted, and is to be tried for murder and arson! To me it seems monstrous to suspect such a person of crimes so heinous.'

Anna remained silent half a minute, for she had sufficient good sense to know that appearances, unless connected with facts, ought to have no great weight in forming an opinion of guilt or innocence. As Jack evidently expected an answer, however, his companion made an effort to speak.

'Does she say nothing of her friends, nor express a wish to have them informed of her situation?' Anna succeeded in asking.

'Not a syllable. I could not speak to her on the subject, you know——'

'Why not?' demanded Anna, quickly.

'Why not? – You've no notion, Anna, of the kind of person this Miss Monson is. You cannot talk to *her* as you would to an every-day sort of young lady; and, now she is in such distress, one is naturally more cautious about saying anything to add to her sorrow.'

'Yes, I can understand *that*,' returned the generous-minded girl; 'and I think you are very right to remember all this on every occasion. Still, it is so natural for a female to lean on her friends, in every great emergency, I cannot but wonder that your client——'

'Don't call her my *client*, Anna, I beg of you. I hate the word as applied to this lady. If I serve her in any degree it is solely as a friend. The same feeling prevails with Uncle Tom; for I understand he has not received a cent of Miss Monson's money, though she is liberal of it to profuseness. Timms is actually getting rich on it.'

'Is it usual for you gentlemen of the bar to give their services gratuitously to those who can pay for them?'

'As far from it as possible,' returned Jack, laughing. 'We look to the main chance like so many merchants or brokers, and seldom open our mouths without shutting our hearts. But this is a case altogether out of the common rule, and Mr Dunscomb works for love and not for money.'

Had Anna cared less for John Wilmeter, she might have said something clever about the nephew's being in the same category as the uncle; but her feelings were too deeply interested to suffer her even to think what would seem to her profane. After a moment's pause, therefore, she quietly said –

'I believe you have intimated that Mr Timms is not quite so disinterested?'

'Not he. Miss Monson has given him fees amounting to a thousand dollars, by his own admission; and the fellow has had the conscience to take the money. I have remonstrated about his fleecing a friendless woman in this extravagant manner; but he laughs in my face for my pains. Timms has good points, but honesty is not one of them. He says no woman can be friendless who has a pretty face and a pocket full of money.'

'You can hardly call a person unfriended who has so much money at command, John,' Anna answered with timidity; but not without manifest interest in the subject. 'A thousand dollars sounds like a large sum to me!'

'It is a good deal of money for a fee; though much more is sometimes given. I dare say Miss Monson would have gladly given the same to Uncle Tom, if he would have taken it. Timms told me that she proposed offering as much to him; but he persuaded her to wait until the trial was over.'

'And where does all this money come from, John?'

'I'm sure I do not know – I am not at all in Miss Monson's confidence; on her pecuniary affairs, at least. She *does* honour me so much as to consult me about her trial occasionally, it is true; but to me she has never alluded to money, except to ask me to obtain change for large notes. I do not see anything so very wonderful in a lady's having money. You, who are a sort of heiress yourself, ought to know that.'

'I do not get money in thousands, I can assure you, Jack; nor do I think that I have it to get. I believe my whole income would not much more than meet the expenditure of this strange woman——'

'Do not call her *woman*, Anna; it pains me to hear you speak of her in such terms.'

'I beg her pardon and yours, Jack; but I meant no disrespect. We are all women.'

'I know it is foolish to feel nervous on such a subject; but I cannot help it. One connects so many ideas of vulgarity and crime, with prisons, and indictments, and trials, that we are apt to suppose all who are accused to belong to the commoner classes. Such is not the fact with Miss Monson, I can assure you. Not even Sarah – nay, not even *yourself*, my dear Anna, can pretend to more decided marks of refinement and education. I do not know a more distinguished young woman——'

'There, Jack; now *you* call her a woman yourself,' interrupted Anna, a little archly; secretly delighted at the compliment she had just heard.

'*Young* woman – anybody can say *that*, you know, without implying anything common or vulgar; and *woman*, too, sometimes. I do not know how it was; but I did not exactly like the word as you happened to use it. I believe close and long watching is making me nervous; and I am not quite as much myself as usual.'

Anna gave a very soft sigh, and that seemed to afford her relief, though it was scarcely audible; then she continued the subject.

'How old is this extraordinary young lady?' she demanded, scarce speaking loud enough to be heard.

'Old! How can I tell? She is very youthful in appearance; but, from the circumstance of her having so much money at command, I take it for granted she is of age. The law now gives to every woman the full command of all her property, even though married, after she becomes of age.'

'Which I trust you find a very proper attention to the rights of our sex!'

'I care very little about it; though uncle Tom says it is of a piece with all our late New York legislation.'

'Mr Dunscomb, like most elderly persons, has little taste for change.'

'It is not that. He thinks that minds of an ordinary stamp are running away with the conceit that they are on the road of progress; and that most of our recent improvements, as they are called, are marked by empiricism. This "tea-cup law," as he terms it, will set the women above their husbands, and create two sets of interest where there ought to be but one.'

'Yes; I am aware such is his opinion. He remarked, the day he brought home my mother's settlement for the signatures, that it was the most ticklish part of his profession to prepare such papers. I remember one of his observations, which struck me as being very just.'

'Which you mean to repeat to me, Anna?'

'Certainly, John, if you wish to hear it,' returned a gentle voice, coming from one unaccustomed to refuse any of the reasonable requests of this particular applicant. 'The remark of Mr Dunscomb was this: – He said that most family misunderstandings grew out of money; and he thought it unwise to set it up as a bone of contention between man and wife. Where there was so close a union in all other matters, he thought there might safely be a community of interests in this respect. He saw no sufficient reason for altering the old law, which had the great merit of having been tried.'

'He could hardly persuade rich fathers, and vigilant guardians, who have the interests of heiresses to look after, to subscribe to all his notions. They say that it is better to make a provision against imprudence and misfortune, by settling a woman's fortune on herself, in a country where speculation tempts so many to their ruin.'

'I do not object to anything that may have an eye to an evil day, provided it be done openly and honestly. But the income should be common property, and like all that belongs to a family, should pass under the control of its head.'

'It is very liberal in you to say and think this, Anna!'

'It is what every woman, who has a true woman's heart, could wish, and would do. For myself, I would marry no man whom I did not respect and look up to in most things; and surely, if I gave him my heart and my hand, I could wish to give him as much control over my means as circumstances would at all allow. It might be prudent to provide against misfortune by means of settlements; but this much done, I feel certain it would afford me the greatest delight to commit all that I could to a husband's keeping.'

'Suppose that husband were a spendthrift, and wasted your estate?'

'He could waste but the income, were there a settlement; and I would rather share the consequences of his imprudence with him, than sit aloof in selfish enjoyment of that in which he did not partake.'

All this sounded very well in John's ears; and he knew Anna Updyke too well to suppose she did not fully mean all that she said. He wondered what might be Mary Monson's views on this subject.

'It is possible for the husband to partake of the wife's wealth, even when he does not command it,' the young man resumed, anxious to hear what more Anna might have to say.

'What! as a dependant on her bounty? No woman who respects herself could wish to see her husband so degraded; nay, no female, who has a true woman's heart, would ever consent to place the man to whom she has given her hand, in so false a position. It is for the woman to be dependent on the man, and not the man on the woman. I agree fully with Mr Dunscomb, when he says that "silken knots are too delicate to be rudely undone by dollars." The family in which the head has to ask the wife for the money that is to support it, must soon go wrong; as it is placing the weaker vessel uppermost.'

'You would make a capital wife, Anna, if these are really your opinions!'

Anna blushed, and almost repented of her generous warmth; but, being perfectly sincere, she would not deny her sentiments.

'They ought to be the opinion of every wife,' she answered. 'I could not endure to see the man to whom I could wish on all occasions to look up, soliciting the means on which we both subsisted. It would be my delight, if I had money and he had none, to pour all into his lap, and then come and ask of him as much as was necessary to my comfort.'

'If he had the soul of a man he would not wait to be asked, but would endeavour to anticipate your smallest wants. I believe you are right, and that happiness is best secured by confidence.'

'And in not reversing the laws of nature. Why do women vow to obey and honour their husbands, if they are to retain them as dependants? I declare, John Wilmeter, I should almost despise the man who could consent to live with me on any terms but those in which nature, the church, and reason, unite in telling us he ought to be the superior.'

'Well, Anna, this is good, old-fashioned, womanly sentiment; and I will confess it delights me to hear it from *you*. I am the better pleased, because, as Uncle Tom is always complaining, the weakness of the hour is to place your sex above ours, and to reverse all the ancient rules in this respect. Let a woman, now-a-days, run away from her husband and carry off the children, it is ten to one but some crotchety judge, who thinks more of a character built up on gossip than of deferring properly to that which the laws of God and the wisdom of man have decreed, refuse to issue a writ of *habeas corpus* to restore the issue to the parent.'

'I do not know, John,' Anna hesitatingly rejoined with a true woman's instinct, 'it *would* be so hard to rob a mother of her children!'

'It might be *hard*, but in such a case it would be *just*. I like that word "rob," for it suits both parties. To me it seems that the father is the party robbed, when the wife not only steals away from her duty to her husband, but deprives him of his children too.'

'It is wrong, and I have heard Mr Dunscomb express great indignation at what he called the "soft-soapiness" of certain judges in cases of this nature. Still, John, the world is apt to think a woman would not abandon the most sacred of her duties without a cause. That feeling must be at the bottom of what you call the decision, I believe, of these judges.'

'If there be such a cause as would justify a woman in deserting her husband, and in stealing his children -- for it is robbery after all, and robbery of the worst sort, since it involves breaches of faith of the most heinous nature - let that cause be shown that justice may pronounce between the parties. Besides, it is not true that women will not sometimes forget their duties without sufficient cause. There are capricious, and uncertain, and egotistical women, who follow their own wayward inclinations, as well as selfish men. Some women love power intensely, and are never satisfied with simply filling the place that was intended for them by nature. It is hard for such to submit to their husbands, or, indeed, to submit to any one.'

'It must be a strange female,' answered Anna, gently, 'who cannot suffer the control of the man of her choice after quitting father and mother for his sake.'

'Different women have different sources of pride that make their husbands very uncomfortable, even when they remain with them, and affect to discharge their duties. One will pride herself on family, and take every occasion to let her beloved partner know how much better she is connected than he may happen to be; another is conceited, and fancies herself cleverer than her lord and master, and would fain have him take *her* advice on all occasions; while a third may have the most money, and delight in letting it be known that it is *her* pocket that sustains the household.'

'I did not know, John, that you thought so much of these things,' said Anna, laughing, 'though I think you are very right in your opinions. Pray, which of the three evils that you have mentioned would you conceive the greatest?'

'The second. I might stand family pride, though it is disgusting when it is not ridiculous. Then the money might be got along with for its own sake, provided the purse were in my hand; but I really do not think I could live with a woman who fancied she knew the most.'

'But, in many things, women ought to, and *do* know the most.'

'Oh! as to accomplishments, and small talk, and making preserves, and dancing, and even poetry and religion – yes, I will throw in religion – I could wish my wife to be clever – very clever – as clever as you are yourself, Anna' – The fair listener coloured, though her eyes brightened at this unintended but very direct compliment – 'Yes, yes; all that would do well enough. But when it came to the affairs of men, out-of-door concerns, or politics, or law, or anything, indeed, that called for a masculine education and understanding, I could not endure a woman who fancied she knew the most.'

'I should think few wives would dream of troubling their husbands with their opinions touching the law!'

'I don't know that. You've no notion, Anna, to what a pass conceit can carry a person; – you, who are so diffident and shy, and always so ready to yield to those who ought to know best. I've met with women who, not content with arraying their own charms in their own way, must fancy they can teach us how to put on our clothes, tell us how to turn over a wristband, or settle a shirt-collar!'

'This is not conceit, John, but good taste,' cried Anna, now laughing outright, and appearing herself again. 'It is merely female tact teaching male awkwardness how to adorn itself. But, surely, no woman, John, would bother herself about law, let her love of domination be as strong as it might.'

'I'm not so sure of that. The only really complaisant thing I ever saw about this Mary Monson,' – a cloud again passed athwart the bright countenance of Anna – 'was a sort of strange predilection for law. Even Timms has remarked it, and commented on it too.'

'The poor woman——'

'Do not use that word in speaking of her, if you please, Anna.'

'Well, lady – if you like that better——'

'No – say young lady – or Miss Monson – or Mary, which has the most agreeable sound of all.'

'Yet, I think I have been told that none of you believe she has been indicted by her real name.'

'Very true; but it makes no difference. Call her by that she has assumed; but do not call her by an alias as wretched as that of "poor woman."'

'I meant no slight, I do assure you, John; for I feel almost as much interest in Miss Monson as you do yourself. It is not surprising, however, that one in her situation should feel an interest in the law.'

'It is not this sort of interest that I mean. It has seemed to me, once or twice, that she dealt with the difficulties of her own case as if she took a pleasure in meeting them – had a species of professional pleasure in conquering them. Timms will not let me into his secrets, and I am glad of it, for I fancy all of them would not bear the light; but he tells me, honestly, that some of Miss Monson's suggestions have been quite admirable!'

'Perhaps she has been,' – Anna checked herself with the consciousness that what she was about to utter might appear to be, and what was of still greater importance in her own eyes, might really be, ungenerous.

'Perhaps what? Finish the sentence, I beg of you.'

Anna shook her head.

'You intended to say that perhaps Miss Monson had some *experience* in the law, and that it gave her a certain satisfaction to contend with its difficulties, in consequence of previous training. Am I not right?'

Anna would not answer in terms; but she gave a little nod in assent, colouring scarlet.

'I knew it; and I will be frank enough to own that Timms thinks the same thing. He has hinted as much as that; but the thing is impossible. You have only to look at her, to see that such a thing is impossible.'

Anna Updyke thought that almost anything of the sort might be possible to a female who was in the circumstances of the accused; this, however, she would not say, lest it might wound John's feelings, for which she had all the tenderness of warm affection, and a woman's self-denial. Had the case been reversed, it is by no means probable that her impulsive companion would have manifested the same forbearance on her account. John would have contended for victory, and pressed his adversary with all the arguments, facts and reasons he could muster, on such an occasion. Not so with the gentler and more thoughtful young woman who was now walking quietly, and a little sadly, at his side, instinct with all the gentleness, self-denial, and warm-hearted affection of her sex.

'No, it is worse than an absurdity' – resumed John – 'it is cruel, to imagine anything of the sort of Miss ——. By the way, Anna, do you know that a very singular thing occurred last evening, before I drove over to town, to be present at the wedding? You know Marie Mill?'

'Certainly – Marie Moulin, you should say.'

'Well, in answering one of her mistress's questions, she said "oui, *Madame*."'

'What would you have had her say? – "*non*, Madame?"'

'But why Madame at all? – Why not Mademoiselle?'

'It would be very vulgar to say "Yes, Miss," in English.'

'To be sure it would; but it is very different in French. One *can* say – *must* say Mademoiselle to a young unmarried female in that language; though it be vulgar to say Miss, without the name, in English. French, you know, Anna, is a much more precise language than our own; and those who speak it, do not take the liberties with it that we take with the English. *Madame* always infers a married woman; unless, indeed, it be with a woman a hundred years old.'

'No French woman is ever *that*, John – but it *is* odd that Marie Moulin, who so well understands the usages of her own little world, should have said *Madame* to a *démoiselle*. Have I not heard, nevertheless, that Marie's first salutation, when she was admitted to the gaol, was a simple exclamation of "Mademoiselle"?'

'That is very true; for I heard it myself. What is more, that exclamation was almost as remarkable as this; French servants always adding the name under such circumstances, unless they are addressing their own particular mistresses. Madame, and Mademoiselle, are appropriated to those they serve; while it is Mademoiselle this, or Madame that, to every one else.'

'And now she calls her *Mademoiselle* or *Madame*! It only proves that too much importance is not to be attached to Marie Moulin's sayings and doings.'

'I'm not so sure of that. Marie has been three years in this country, as we all know. Now the young person that she left a *Mademoiselle* might very well have become a *Madame* in that interval of time. When they met, the domestic may have used the old and familiar term in her surprise; or she may not have known of the lady's marriage. Afterwards, when there had been leisure for explanations between them, she gave her mistress her proper appellation.'

'Does she habitually say Madame now, in speaking to this singular being?'

'Habitually she is silent. Usually she remains in the cell, when any one is with Miss – or Mrs Monson, perhaps I ought to say' – John used this last term with a strong expression of spite, which gave his companion a suppressed but infinite delight – 'but when any one is with the mistress, call her what you will, the maid commonly remains in the dungeon or cell. Owing to this, I have never been in the way of hearing the last address the first, except on the two occasions named. I confess I begin to think——'

'What, John?'

'Why, that our *Miss* Monson may turn out to be a married woman, after all.'

'She is very young, is she not? Almost too young to be a wife?'

'Not at all! What do you call too young? She is between twenty and twenty-two or three. She may even be twenty-five or six.'

Anna sighed, though almost imperceptibly to herself; for these were ages that well suited her companion, though the youngest exceeded her own by a twelvemonth. Little more, however, was said on the subject at that interview.

It is one of the singular effects of the passion of love, more especially with the generous-minded and just of the female sex, that a lively interest is often awakened in behalf of a successful or favoured rival. Such was now the fact as regards the feeling that Anna Updyke began to entertain towards Mary Monson. The critical condition of the lady would of itself excite interest where it failed to produce distrust; but the circumstance that John Wilmeter saw so much to admire in this unknown female, if he did not actually love her, gave her an importance in the eyes of Anna that at once elevated her into an object of the highest interest. She was seized with the liveliest desire to see the accused, and began seriously to reflect on the possibility of effecting such an end. No vulgar curiosity was mingled with this new-born purpose; but, in addition to the motives that were connected with John's state of mind, there was a benevolent and truly feminine wish, on the part of Anna, to be of service to one of her own sex, so cruelly placed and cut off, as it would seem, from all communication with those who should be her natural protectors and advisers.

Anna Updyke gathered, through that which had fallen from Wilmeter and his sister, that the intercourse between the former and his interesting client had been of the most reserved character; therein showing a discretion and self-respect on the part of the prisoner, that spoke well for her education and delicacy. How such a woman came to be in the extraordinary position in which she was placed was of course as much a mystery to her as to all others; though, like every one else who knew aught of the case, she indulged in conjectures of her own on the subject. Being of a particularly natural and frank disposition, without a particle of any ungenerous or detracting quality, and filled with woman's kindness in her very soul, this noble-minded young woman began now to feel far more than an idle curiosity in behalf of her who had so lately caused herself so much pain, not to say bitterness of anguish. All was forgotten in pity for the miserable condition of the unconscious offender; unconscious, for Anna was sufficiently clear-sighted and just to see and to admit that, if John had been led astray by the charms and sufferings of this stranger, the fact could not rightfully be imputed to the last, as a fault. Every statement of John's went to confirm this act of justice to the stranger.

Then the unaccountable silence of Marie Moulin doubled the mystery and greatly increased the interest of the whole affair. This woman had gone to Biberry pledged to communicate to Sarah all she knew or might learn touching the accused; and well did Anna know that her friend would make her the repository of her own information on this as well as on other subjects; but a most unaccountable silence governed the course of the domestic, as well as that of her strange mistress. It really seemed that, in passing the principal door of the gaol, Marie Moulin had buried herself in a convent, where all communication with the outer world was forbidden. Three several letters from Sarah had John handed in at the grate, certain that they must have reached the hands of the Swiss, but no answer had been received. All attempts to speak to Marie were quietly, but most ingeniously evaded, by the tact and readiness of the prisoner; and the hope of obtaining information from that source was abandoned by Sarah, who was too proud to solicit a servant for that which the last was reluctant to communicate. With Anna the feeling was different. She had no curiosity on the subject, separated from a most generous and womanly concern in the prisoner's forlorn state; and she thought far less of Marie Moulin's disrespect and forgetfulness of her word, than of Mary Monson's desolation and approaching trial.

CHAPTER XIII

Was it for this we sent out
Liberty's cry from our shore?
Was it for this that her shout
Thrill'd to the world's very core.
                    MOORE'S *National Airs.*

The third day after the interviews just related, the whole party left Rattletrap for Timbully, where their arrival was expected by the bride and bridegroom, if such terms can be applied to a woman of forty-five and a man of sixty. The Duke's county circuit and oyer and terminer were about to be held, and it was believed that Mary Monson was to be tried. By this time so lively an interest prevailed among the ladies of the McBrain and Dunscomb connections in behalf of the accused, that they had all come to a determination to be present in court. Curiosity was not so much at the bottom of this movement as womanly kindness and sympathy. There seemed a bitterness of misery in the condition of Mary Monson that appealed directly to the heart, and that silent but eloquent appeal was answered, as has just been stated, generously and with warmth by the whole party from town. With Anna Updyke the feeling went materially farther than with any of her friends. Strange as it may seem, her interest in John increased that which she felt for his mysterious client; and her feelings became enlisted in the stranger's behalf so much the more in consequence of this triangular sort of passion.

The morning of the day on which the party crossed the country from Rattletrap to Timbully, Timms arrived at the latter place. He was expected, and was soon after closeted with the senior counsel in the pending and most important cause.

'Does the District Attorney intend to move for the trial?' demanded Dunscomb, the instant the two were alone.

'He tells me he does, sir; and that early in the week, too. It is my opinion we should go for postponement. We are hardly ready, while the State is too much so.'

'I do not comprehend this, Timms. The law-officers of the public would hardly undertake to run down a victim, and she a solitary and unprotected woman!'

'That's not it. The law-officers of the State don't care a straw whether Mary Monson is found guilty or is acquitted. That is, they care nothing about it *at present*. The case may be different when they are warmed up by a trial and opposition. Our danger comes from Jesse Davis, who is a nephew of Peter Goodwin, his next of kin and heir, and who thinks a great deal of money was hoarded by the old people; much more than the stocking ever held or could hold, and who has taken it into his wise head that the prisoner has laid hands on this treasure, and is carrying on her defence with his cash. This has roused him completely, and he has retained two of the sharpest counsel on our circuit, who are beginning to work as if the bargain has been clenched in the hard metal. Williams has given me a great deal of trouble already. I know him; he will not work without pay; but pay him liberally, and he is up to anything.'

'Ay, you are diamond cut diamond, Timms – outsiders in the profession. You understand that I work only in the open court, and will know nothing of this out-door management.'

'We do not mean to let you know anything about it, 'squire,' returned Timms, drily. 'Each man to his own manner of getting along. I ought to tell you, however, it has got out that you are working without a fee, while I am paid in the most liberal manner.'

'I am sorry for that. There is no great harm in the thing itself; but I dislike the parade of seeming to be unusually generous. I do not remember to have spoken of this circumstance where it would be likely to be repeated, and I beg you will be equally discreet.'

'The fact has not come from me, I can assure you, sir. It puts me in too awkward a position to delight me; and I make it a point to say as little as possible of what is disagreeable. I do not relish the idea of being thought selfish by my future constituents. Geniros'ty is my cue before *them*. But they say you work for love, sir.'

'Love!' answered Dunscomb, quickly. – 'Love of what? – or of *whom*?'

'Of your client; – that's the story now. It is said that you admire Miss Monson; that she is young, and handsome, and rich; and she is to marry you, if acquitted. If found guilty and hanged, the bargain is off, of course.

You may look displeased, 'squire; but I give you my word such is the rumour.'

Dunscomb was extremely vexed; but he was too proud to make any answer. He knew that he had done that which, among the mass of this nation, is a very capital mistake, in not placing before its observation an intelligible *motive* — one on the level of the popular mind — to prevent these freaks of the fancy dealing with his affairs. It is true that the natural supposition would be that he worked for his fee, as did Timms, had not the contrary got out; when he became subject to all the crude conjectures of those who ever look for the worst motives for everything. Had he been what is termed a favourite public servant, the very reverse would have been the case, and there was little that he might not have done with impunity; but, having no such claims on the minds of the mass, he came under the common law which somewhat distinguishes their control. Too much disgusted, however, to continue this branch of the subject, the worthy counsellor at once adverted to another.

'Have you looked over the list of the jurors, Timms?' he demanded, continuing to sort his papers.

'That I never fail to do, sir, the first thing. It's my brief, you know, 'Squire Dunscomb. All *safe* York law, now-a-days, is to be found in that learned body; especially in criminal cases. There is but one sort of suit in which the jury counts for nothing, and might as well be dispensed with.'

'Which is——?'

'An ejectment cause. It's not one time in ten that they understand anything about the matter, or care anything about it; and the court usually leads in those actions — but our Duke's county juries are beginning to understand their powers in all others.'

'What do you make of the list?'

'It's what I call reasonable, 'squire. There are two men on it who would not hang Cain, were he indicted for the murder of Abel.'

'Quakers, of course?'

'Not they. The time was when we were reduced to the "thee's" and the "thou's" for this sort of support; but philanthropy is abroad, sir, covering the land. Talk of the school-master? — Why, 'squire, a new philanthropical idea will go two feet to the schoolmaster's one. Pro-nigger, anti-gallows, eternal peace, woman's rights, the people's power, and anything of that sort, sweeps like a tornado through the land. Get a juror who has just come into the anti-gallows notion, and I would defy the State to hang a body-snatcher who lived by murdering his subjects.'

'And you count on two of these partisans for our case?'

'Lord no, sir. The District Attorney himself knows them both; and Davis's counsel have been studying that list for the last week, as if it were Blackstone in the hands of a new beginner. I can tell you, 'Squire

Dunscomb, that the jury-list is a most important part of a case out here
in the country!'

'I am much afraid it is, Timms; though I never examined one in my
life.'

'I can believe you, sir, from what I have seen of your practice. But
principles and facts won't answer in an age of the world when men are
ruled by talk and prejudice. There is not a case of any magnitude tried,
now-a-days, without paying proper attention to the jury. We are pretty
well off, on the whole; and I am tolerably sanguine of a disagreement,
though I fear an acquittal is quite out of the question.'

'You rely on one or two particularly intelligent and disinterested men,
ha! Timms?'

'I rely on five or six particularly ignorant and heated partisans, on the
contrary; – men who have been reading about the abolishing of capital
punishments, and who in gin'ral, because they've got hold of some
notions that have been worn out as far back as the times of the Caesars,
fancy themselves philosophers and the children of progress. The country
is getting to be full of what I call donkeys and racers; the donkey is
obstinate, and backs going up hill; while the racers will not only break
their own necks, but those of their riders too, unless they hold up long
before they reach their goal.'

'I did not know, Timms, that you think so much on such subjects. To
me, you have always appeared to be a purely working-man – no theorist.'

'It is precisely because I am a man of action, and live in the world, and
see things as they were meant to be seen, that I laugh at your theorists.
Why, sir, this country, in my judgment, for the time being, could much
better get along without preaching, than without hanging. I don't say
always; for there is no telling yet what is to be the upshot of preaching. It
may turn out as many think; in which case human natur' will undergo a
change that will pretty much destroy our business. Such a state of things
would be worse for the bar, 'squire, than the code, or the last fee-bill.'

'I'm not so sure of that, Timms; there are few things worse than this
infernal code.'

'Well, to my taste, the fee-bill is the most disagreeable of the two. A
man can stand any sort of law, and any sort of practice: but he can't stand
any sort of pay. I hear the circuit is to be held by one of the new judges –
a people's man, altogether.'

'You mean by that, I suppose, Timms, one of those who did not hold
office under the old system? It is said that the new broom sweeps clean –
it is fortunate ours has not brushed away all the old incumbents.'

'No, that is to come; and come it will, as sure as the sun rises. We must
have rotation on the bench, as well as in all other matters. You see,
'squire, rotation is a sort of *claim* with many men, who have no other.

They fancy the earth to have been created on a sort of Jim Crow principle, because it turns round.'

'That is it; and it explains the clamour that is made about it. But to return to this jury, Timms; on the whole, you like it, I should infer?'

'Not too well, by any means. There are six or eight names on the list that I'm always glad to see; for they belong to men who are friendly to me——'

'Good God, man – it cannot be possible that you count on such assistants in a trial for a human life!'

'Not count on it, 'Squire Dunscomb! I count on it from an action of trespass on the case, to this indictment – count on it, quite as much, and a good deal more rationally, than you count on your law and evidence. Didn't I carry that heavy case *for* the railroad company on that principle altogether? The law was dead against us they say, and the facts were against us; but the verdict was in our favour. That's what I call practising law!'

'Yes; I remember to have heard of that case, and it was always a wonder with the bar how you got along with it. Had it been a verdict *against* a corporation, no one would have thought anything of it – but to carry a bad case *for* a company, now-a-days, is almost an unheard-of thing.'

'You are quite right, sir. I can beat any railroad in the State, with a jury of a neighbourhood, let the question or facts be what they may; but, in this instance, I beat the neighbourhood, and all through the faith the jury had in *me*. It's a blessed institution, this of the jury, 'Squire Dunscomb! – no doubt it makes us the great, glorious, and free people that we are!'

'If the bench continue to lose its influence as it has done, the next twenty years will see it a curse of the worst character. It is now little more than a popular Cabal in all cases in the least calculated to awaken popular feeling or prejudice.'

'There's the rub in this capital case of ours. Mary Monson has neglected popularity altogether; and she is likely to suffer for it.'

'Popularity!' exclaimed Dunscomb, in a tone of horror – 'and this in a matter of life and death! What are we coming to in the law, as well as in politics! No public man is to be found of sufficient moral courage, or intellectual force, to stem this torrent, which is sweeping away everything before it. But in what has our client failed, Timms?'

'In almost everything connected with this one great point; and what vexes me is her wonderful power of pleasing, which is completely thrown away. 'Squire Dunscomb, I would carry this county for Free Sile, or ag'in it, with that lady to back me, as a wife.'

'What, if she should refuse to resort to popular airs and graces?'

'I mean, of course, she aiding and abetting. I would give the world, now, could we get the judge into her company for half an hour. It would make a friend of him; and it is still something to have a friend in the judge in a criminal case.'

'You may well say "*still*," Timms; how much longer it will be so, is another matter. Under the old system it would be hopeless to expect so much complaisance in a judge; but I will not take it on myself to say what a people's judge will not do.'

'If I thought the thing could be managed, by George I would attempt it! The grand jurors visit the gaols, and why not the judges? What do you think, sir, of an anonymous letter hinting to his honour that a visit to Mrs Gott — who is an excellent creature in her way — might serve the ends of justice!'

'As I think of all underhanded movements and trickery. No, no, Timms; you had better let our client remain unpopular, than undertake anything of this nature.'

'Perhaps you are right, sir. Unpopular she is, and will be, as long as she pursues her present course; whereas she might carry all classes of men with her. For my part, 'Squire Dunscomb, I've found this young lady' — here Timms paused, hemmed, and concluded by looking a little foolish — a character of countenance by no means common with one of his shrewdness and sagacity.

'So, so, Master Timms,' said the senior counsel, regarding the junior with a sort of sneer — 'you are as great a fool as my nephew, Jack Wilmeter; and have fallen in love with a pretty face, in spite of the grand jury and the gallows!'

Timms gave a gulp, seemed to catch his breath, and regained enough of his self-command to be able to answer.

'I'm in hopes that Mr Wilmeter will think better of this, sir,' he said, 'and turn his views to a quarter where they will be particularly acceptable. It would hardly do for a young gentleman of his expectations to take a wife out of a gaol.'

'Enough of this foolery, Timms, and come to the point. Your remarks about popularity may have some sense in them, if matters have been pushed too far in a contrary direction. Of what do you complain?'

'In the first place, she will not show herself at the windows; and that offends a great many persons, who think it proud and aristocratic in her not to act as other criminals act. Then, she has made a capital mistake with a leading reporter, who sent in his name, and desired an interview; which she declined granting. She will hear from that man, depend on it, sir.'

'I shall look to him, then — for, though this class of men is fast putting the law under foot, it may be made to turn on them, by one who understands it, and has the courage to use it. I shall not allow the rights of Mary Monson to be invaded by such a fungus of letters.'

'Fungus of letters! Ahem! − if it was anybody but yourself, 'squire, that I was talking to, I might remind you that these funguses flourish on the dunghill of the common mind.'

'No matter; the law *can* be made to touch them, when in good hands; and mine have now some experience. Has this reporter resented the refusal of the prisoner to see him?'

'He is squinting that way, and has got himself sent to Biberry by two or three journals, to report the progress of the trial. I know the man; he is vindictive, impudent, and always uses his craft to indulge his resentments.'

'Ay, many of those gentry are up to that. Is it not surprising, Timms, that in a country for ever boasting of its freedom, men do not see how much abuse there is of a very important interest, in suffering these irresponsible tyrants to ride rough-shod over the community?'

'Lord, 'squire, it is not with the reporters only, that abuses are to be found. I was present, the other day, at a conversation between a judge and a great town lawyer, when the last deplored the state of the juries! "What would you have?" says his honour; "angels sent down from heaven to fill the jury-boxes?" Waal' − Timms never could get over the defects of his early associations, − 'Waal, 'squire,' he continued, with a shrewd leer of the eyes, 'I thought a few saints might be squeezed in between the lowest angel in heaven and the average of our Duke's county panels. This is a great fashion of talking that is growing up among us to meet an objection by crying out, "men are not angels;" as if some men are not better than others.'

'The institutions clearly maintain that some men are better than others, Timms!'

'That's news to me, I will own. I thought the institutions declared all men alike − that is, all white men; I know that the niggers are non-suited.'

'They are unsuited, at least, according to the spirit of the institutions. If all men are supposed to be alike, what use is there in the elections? Why not draw lots for office, as we draw lots for juries? Choice infers inequalities, or the practice is an absurdity. But here comes McBrain, with a face so full of meaning; he must have something to tell us.'

Sure enough, the bridegroom-physician came into the room at that instant; and without circumlocution he entered at once on the topic that was then uppermost in his mind. It was the custom of the neighbourhood to profit by the visits of this able practitioner to his country-place, by calling on him for advice in such difficult cases as existed anywhere in the vicinity of Timbully. Even his recent marriage did not entirely protect him from these appeals, which brought so little pecuniary advantage as to be gratuitous; and he had passed much of the last two days in making professional visits in a circle around his residence that included Biberry. Such were the means by which he had obtained the information that now escaped from him, as it might be, involuntarily.

'I have never known so excited a state of the public mind,' he cried, 'as now exists all around Biberry, on the subject of your client, Tom, and this approaching trial. Go where I may, see whom I will, let the disease be as serious as possible, all, patients, parents, friends and nurses, commence business with asking me what I think of Mary Monson, and of her guilt or innocence.'

'That's because you are married, Ned,' – Dunscomb coolly answered – 'Now, no one thinks of putting such a question to *me*. I see lots of people, as well as yourself; but not a soul has asked me whether I thought Mary Monson guilty or innocent.'

'Poh! You are her counsel, and no one could take the liberty. I dare say that even Mr Timms, here, your associate, has never compared notes with you on that particular point.'

Timms was clearly not quite himself; and he did not look as shrewd as he once would have done at such a remark. He kept in the back-ground, and was content to listen.

'I do suppose association with a brother in the law, and in a case of life and death, is something like matrimony, Dr McBrain. A good deal must be taken for granted, and not a little on credit. As a man is bound to believe his wife the most excellent, virtuous, most amiable and best creature on earth, so is a counsel bound to consider his client innocent. The relation, in each case, is confidential, however; and I shall not pry into your secrets, any more than I shall betray one of my own.'

'I asked for none, and wish none; but one may express surprise at the intense degree of excitement that prevails all through Duke's, and even in the adjacent counties.'

'The murder of a man and his wife in cold blood, accompanied by robbery and arson, are enough to arouse the community. In this particular case the feeling of interest is increased, I make no doubt, by the extraordinary character, as well as by the singular mystery, of the party accused. I have had many clients, Ned, but never one like this before; as you have had many wives, but no one so remarkable as the present Mrs McBrain.'

'Your time will come yet, Master Dunscomb; recollect I have always prognosticated that.'

'You forget that I am approaching sixty. A man's heart is as hard and dry as a bill in chancery at that age; but I beg your pardon, Ned, *you* are an exception.'

'I certainly believe that a man can have affections, even at four-score; and what is more, I believe that when the reason and judgment come in aid of the passions——'

Dunscomb laughed outright; nay, he even gave a little shout, his bachelor habits having rendered him more exuberant in manner than might otherwise have been the case.

'Passions!' he cried, rubbing his hands, and looking round for Timms, that he might have some one to share in what he regarded as a capital joke. 'The passions of a fellow of three-score! Ned, you do not flatter yourself that you have been marrying the Widow Updyke in consequence of any *passion* you feel for her?'

'I do, indeed,' returned the doctor, with spirit; mustering resolution to carry the war into the enemy's country. – 'Let me tell you, Tom Dunscomb, that a warm-hearted fellow can love a woman dearly, long after the age you have mentioned – that is, provided he has not let all feeling die within him for want of watering a plant that is the most precious boon of a most gracious Providence.'

'Ay, if he begin at twenty, and keep even pace with his beloved down the descent of time.'

'That may all be true; but if it has been his misfortune to lose one partner, a second——'

'And a third, Ned, a third – why not foot the bill at once, as they say in the market?'

'Well, a third, too, if circumstances make that demand on him. Anything is better than leaving the affections to stagnate for want of cultivation.'

'Adam in Paradise, by Jove! But I'll not approach you again, since you have got so gentle and kind a creature, and one who is twenty years your junior——'

'Only eighteen, if you please, Mr Dunscomb.'

'Now, I should be glad to know whether you have added those two years to the bride's age, or subtracted them from that of the bridegroom! I suppose the last, however, as a matter of course.'

'I do not well see how you can suppose any such thing, knowing my age as well as you do. Mrs McBrain is forty-two, an age when a woman can be as loveable as at nineteen – more so, if her admirer happens to be a man of sense.'

'And sixty-two. Well, Ned, you are incorrigible; and for the sake of the excellent woman who has consented to have you, I only hope this will be the last exhibition of your weakness. So they talk a good deal of Mary Monson up and down the country, do they?'

'Of little else, I can assure you. I am sorry to say the tide seems to be setting strongly against her.'

'That is bad news, as few jurors, now-a-days, are superior to such an influence. What is said, in particular, Dr McBrain? – In the way of facts, I mean?'

'One report is that the accused is full of money, and that a good deal of that which she is scattering broadcast has been seen by different persons, at different times, in the possession of the deceased Mrs Goodwin.'

'Let them retail that lie far and near, 'squire, and we'll turn it to good account,' said Timms, taking out his note-book and writing down what he had just heard. 'I have reason to think that every dollar Miss Monson has uttered since her confinement——'

'Imprisonment would be a better word, Mr Timms,' interrupted the doctor.

'I see no great difference,' replied the literal attorney; 'but imprisonment, if you prefer it. I have reason to think that every dollar Mary Monson has put in circulation since she entered the gaol at Biberry, has come from either young Mr Wilmeter or myself, in exchange for hundred-dollar notes – and, in one instance, for a note of five hundred dollars. She is well off, I can tell you, gentlemen; and if she is to be executed, her executor will have something to do when all is over.'

'You do not intend to allow her to be hanged, Timms?' demanded McBrain, aghast.

'Not if I can help it, doctor; and this lie about the money, when clearly disproved, will be of capital service to her. Let them circulate it as much as they please, the rebound will be in proportion to the blow. The more they circulate that foolish rumour, the better it will be for our client when we come to trial.'

'I suppose you are right, Timms; though I could prefer plainer dealings. A cause in which you are employed, however, must have more or less of management.'

'Which is better, 'squire, than your law and evidence. But what else has Dr McBrain to tell us?'

'I hear that Peter Goodwin's nephew, who, it seems, had some expectations from the old people, is particularly savage, and leaves no stone upturned to get up a popular feeling against the accused.'

'He had best beware,' said Dunscomb, his usually colourless but handsome face flushing as he spoke. 'I shall not trifle in a matter of this sort – ha! Timms?'

'Lord bless you, 'squire, Duke's county-folks wouldn't understand a denial of the privilege to say what they please in a case of this sort. They fancy this is liberty; and "touch my honour, take your poker," is not more sensitive than the feelin' of liberty in these parts. I'm afraid that not only this Joe Davis, but the reporters, will say just what they please; and Mary Monson's rights will whistle for it. You will remember that our judge is not only a brand-new one, but he drew the two years' term into the bargain. No, I think it will be wisest to let the law, and old principles, and the right, and *true* liberty, quite alone; and to bow the knee to things as they are. A good deal is said about our fathers, and their wisdom, and patriotism, and sacrifices; but nobody dreams of doing as they *did*, or of reasoning as they *reasoned*. Life is made up, in reality, of these little matters in a corner; while the great principles strut about in buckram, for men to admire them, and talk about them. I do take considerable delight, 'Squire Dunscomb, in hearing you enlarge on a principle, whether it be in law, morals, or politics; but I should no more think of prac*t*ysing on 'em, than I should think of refusing a thousand dollar fee.'

'Is that your price?' demanded McBrain, with curiosity. 'Do you work for as large a sum as that, in this case, Timms?'

'I'm paid, doctor; just as you was' – the attorney never stuck at grammar – 'just as you was for that great operation on the Wall Street Millenary'ian——'

'Millionaire, you mean, Timms,' said Dunscomb, coolly; 'it means one worth a million.'

'I never attempt a foreign tongue but I stumble,' said the attorney, simply; for he knew that both his friends were familiar with his origin, education, and advancement in life, and that it was wisest to deny nothing to *them*; 'but since I have been so much with Mary Monson and her woman, I do own a desire to speak the language they use.'

Again Dunscomb regarded his associate intently; something comical gleaming in his eye.

'Timms, you have fallen in love with our handsome client,' he quietly remarked.

'No, sir; not quite as bad as that, *yet*; though I will acknowledge that the lady is very interesting. Should she be acquitted, and could we only get some knowledge of her early history – why, that *might* put a new face on matters.'

'I must drive over to Biberry in the morning, and have another interview with the lady myself. And now, Ned, I will join your wife, and read an epithalamium prepared for this great occasion. You need not trouble yourself to follow, the song being no novelty; for I have read it twice before on your account.'

A hearty laugh at his own wit concluded the discourse on the part of the great York counsellor; though Timms remained some time longer with the Doctor, questioning the latter touching opinion and facts gleaned by the physician in the course of his circuit.

CHAPTER XIV

From his brimstone bed at break of day,
  A-walking the devil is gone,
To visit his little snug farm of the earth,
  And see how his stock went on.

COLERIDGE.

Dunscomb was as good as his word. Next morning he was on his way to Biberry. He was thoughtful; had laid a bundle of papers on the front seat of the carriage, and went his way musing and silent. Singularly enough, his only companion was Anna Updyke, who had asked a seat in the carriage timidly, but with an earnestness that prevailed. Had Jack Wilmeter been at Biberry, this request would not have been made; but she knew he was in town, and that she might make the little excursion without the imputation of indelicacy, so far as he was concerned. Her object will appear in the course of the narrative.

The 'best tavern' in Biberry was kept by Daniel Horton. The wife of this good man had a native propensity to talk that had been essentially cultivated in the course of five-and-twenty years' practice in the inn where she had commenced her career as maid; and was now finishing it as mistress. As is common with persons of her class, she knew hundreds of those who frequented her house; calling each readily by name, and treating every one with a certain degree of professional familiarity that is far from uncommon in country inns.

'Mr Dunscomb, I declare!' cried this woman, as she entered the room, and found the counsellor and his companion in possession of her best parlour. 'This is a pleasure I did not expect until the circuit. It's quite twenty years, 'squire, since I had the pleasure of first waiting on you in this house. And a pleasure it has always been; for I've not forgotten the ejectment suit that you carried for Horton when we was only new-beginners. I am glad to see you, sir; welcome to Biberry, as is this young lady, who is your daughter, I presume, Mr Dunscomb?'

'You forget that I am a bachelor, Mrs Horton — no marrying man, in any sense of the word.'

'I might have known that, had I reflected a moment; for they say Mary Monson employs none but bachelors and widowers in her case; and you are her counsel, I know.'

'This is a peculiarity of which I was not aware. Timms is a bachelor, certainly, as well as myself; but to whom else can you allude? Jack Wilmeter, my nephew, can hardly be said to be employed at all; nor, for that matter, Michael Millington; though neither is married.'

'Yes, sir; we know both of the last well, they having lodged with us. If young Mr Wilmeter is single, I fancy it is not his own fault' – here Mrs Horton looked very wise, but continued talking – 'Young gentlemen of a good appearance and handsome fortunes commonly have not much difficulty in getting wives – not as much as young ladies; for you men make the law, and you give your own sex the best chance, almost as a matter of course——'

'Pardon me, Mrs Horton,' interrupted Dunscomb, a little formally, like one who felt great interest in the subject – 'you were remarking that we have the best chance of getting married; and here have I been a bachelor all my life, trying in vain to enter into the happy state of matrimony – if, indeed, it deserve to be so termed.'

'It could not be very difficult for *you* to find a companion,' said the landlady, shaking her head; 'and for the reason I have just given.'

'Which was——?'

'That you men have made the laws and profit by them. *You* can *ask* whom you please; but a woman is obliged to wait to be asked.'

'You never were in a greater mistake in your life, I do assure you, my good Mrs Horton. There is no such law on the subject. Any woman may put the question, as well as any man. This *was* the law, and I don't think the code has changed it.'

'Yes, I know that well enough and get laughed at, and pointed at, for her pains. I know that a good deal is said about leap-year; but who ever heard of a woman's putting the question? I fancy that even Mary Monson would think twice before she took so bold a step once.'

'Mary Monson!' exclaimed Dunscomb, suddenly turning towards his hostess – 'Has she a reputation for being attentive to gentlemen?'

'Not that I know of; but——'

'Then allow me to say, my good Mrs Horton,' interrupted the celebrated counsellor, with a manner that was almost austere, 'that you have been greatly to blame in hazarding the sort of remark you did. If you *know* nothing of the character you certainly insinuated, you should have said nothing. It is very extraordinary that women, alive as they must be to the consequences to one of their own sex, are ever more ready than men to throw out careless, and frequently malicious hints, that take away a reputation, and do a melancholy amount of harm in the world. Slander is the least respectable, the most unchristian-like, and the most unlady-like vice, of all the secondary sins of your sex. One would think the danger you are all exposed to in common, would teach you greater caution.'

'Yes, sir, that is true; but this Mary Monson is in such a pickle already, that it is not easy to make *her* case much worse,' answered Mrs Horton, a good deal frightened at the austerity of Dunscomb's rebuke; for his reputation was too high to render his good or bad opinion a matter of indifference to her. 'If you only knew the half that is said of her in Duke's, you wouldn't mind a careless word or so about her. Everybody thinks her guilty; and a crime, more or less, can be of no great matter to the likes of *her*.'

'Ah, Mrs Horton, these careless words do a vast deal of harm. They insinuate away a reputation in a breath; and my experience has taught me that they who are the most apt to use them, are persons whose own conduct will least bear the light. Women with a whole log-heap of beams in their own eyes, are remarkable for discovering motes. Give me the female who floats along quietly in her sphere, unoffending and charitable, wishing for the best, and as difficult to be brought to *think* as to *do* evil. But, they talk a good deal against my client, do they?'

'More than I have ever known folks talk against any indicted person, man or woman. The prize-fighters, who were in for murder, had a pretty hard time of it; but nothing to Mary Monson's. In short, until 'Squire Timms came out in her favour, she had no chance at all.'

'This is not very encouraging, certainly – but what is said, Mrs Horton, if you will suffer me to put the question?'

'Why, 'Squire Dunscomb,' answered the woman, pursing up a very pretty American mouth of her own, 'a body is never sure that you won't call what she says slander——'

'Poh – poh – you know me better than that. I never meddle with that vile class of suits. I am employed to defend Mary Monson, you know——'

'Yes, and are well paid for it, too, 'Squire Dunscomb, if all that a body hears is true,' interrupted Mrs Horton, a little spitefully. 'Five thousand dollars, they say, to a cent!'

Dunscomb, who was working literally without other reward than the consciousness of doing his duty, smiled, while he frowned at this fresh instance of the absurdities into which rumour can lead its votaries. Bowing a little apology, he coolly lighted a cigar, and proceeded.

'Where is it supposed that Mary Monson can find such large sums to bestow, Mrs Horton?' he quietly asked, when his cigar was properly lighted. 'It is not usual for young and friendless women to have pockets so well lined.'

'Nor is it usual for young women to rob and murder old ones, 'squire.'

'Was Mrs Goodwin's stocking thought to be large enough to hold sums like that you have mentioned?'

'Nobody knows. Gold takes but little room, as witness Californy. There was General Wilton – every one thought him rich as Caesar——'

'Do you not mean Croesus, Mrs Horton?'

'Well, Caesar or Croesus; both were rich, I do suppose, and General Wilton was thought the equal of either; but, when he died, his estate wouldn't pay his debts. On the other hand, old Davy Davidson was set down by nobody at more than twenty thousand, and he left ten times that much money. So I say nobody knows. Mrs Goodwin was always a saving woman, though Peter would make the dollars fly, if he could get at them. There was certainly a weak spot in Peter, though known to but a few.'

Dunscomb now listened attentively. Every fact of this nature was of importance just then; and nothing could be said of the murdered couple that would not induce all engaged in the cause to prick up their ears.

'I have always understood that Peter Goodwin was a very respectable sort of a man,' observed Dunscomb, with a profound knowledge of human nature, which was far more likely to induce the woman to be communicative, in the way of opposition, than by any other process – 'as respectable a man as any about here.'

'So he might be, but he had his weak points as well as other respectable men; though, as I have said already, his'n wasn't generally known. Everybody is respectable, I suppose, until they're found out. But Peter is dead and gone, and I have no wish to disturb his grave, which I believe to be a sinful act.'

This sounded still more ominously, and it greatly increased Dunscomb's desire to learn more. Still he saw that great caution must be used, Mrs Horton choosing to affect much tenderness for her deceased neighbour's character. The counsellor knew human nature well enough to be aware that indifference was sometimes as good a stimulant as opposition; and he now thought it expedient to try the virtue of that quality. Without making any immediate answer, therefore, he desired the attentive and anxious Anna Updyke to perform some little office for him; thus managing to get her out of the room, while the hostess stayed behind. Then his cigar did not quite suit him, and he tried another, making divers little delays that set the landlady on the tenter-hooks of impatience.

'Yes, Peter is gone – dead and buried – and I hope the sod lies lightly on his remains!' she said, sighing ostentatiously.

'Therein you are mistaken, Mrs Horton,' the counsellor coolly remarked – 'the remains of neither of those found in the ruins of the house are under ground yet; but are kept for the trial.'

'What a time we shall have of it! – so exciting and full of mystery!'

'And you might add "custom," Mrs Horton. The reporters alone, who will certainly come from town like an inroad of Cossacks, will fill your house.'

'Yes, and themselves too. To be honest with you, 'Squire Dunscomb, too many of those gentry wish to be kept for nothing to make them pleasant boarders. I dare say, however, we shall be full enough next week. I sometimes wish there was no such thing as justice, after a hard-working Oyer and Terminer court.'

'You should be under no concern, my good Mrs Horton, on that subject. There is really so little of the thing you have mentioned, that no reasonable woman need make herself unhappy about it. So Peter Goodwin was a faultless man, was he?'

'As far from it as possible, if the truth was said of him; and seeing the man is not absolutely under ground, I do not know why it may not be told. I can respect the grave as well as another; but, as he is not buried, one may tell the truth. Peter Goodwin was by no means the man he seemed to be.'

'In what particular did he fail, my good Mrs Horton?'

To be *good* in Dunscomb's eyes, the landlady well knew, was a great honour; and she was flattered as much by the manner in which the words were uttered, as by their import. Woman-like, Mrs Horton was overcome by this little bit of homage; and she felt disposed to give up a secret which, to do her justice, had been religiously kept now for some ten or twelve years between herself and her husband. As she and the counsel were alone, dropping her voice a little, more for the sake of appearances than for any sufficient reason, the landlady proceeded.

'Why, you must know, 'Squire Dunscomb, that Peter Goodwin was a member of meetin', and a professing Christian, which I suppose was all the better for him, seeing that he was to be murdered.'

'And do you consider his being a "professing Christian," as you call it, a circumstance to be concealed?'

'Not at all, sir – but I consider it a good reason why the facts I am about to tell you ought not to be generally known. Scoffers abound; and I take it that the feelings of a believer ought to be treated more tenderly than those of an unbeliever, for the church's sake.'

'That is a fashion of the times too – one of the ways of the hour, whether it is to last or not. But, proceed if you please, my good Mrs Horton; I am quite curious to know by what particular sin Satan managed to overcome this "professing Christian"?'

'He drank, 'Squire Dunscomb – no, he *guzzled*, for that is the best word. You must know that Dolly was avarice itself – that's the reason she took this Mary Monson in to board, though her house was no ways suited for boarders, standing out of the way, with only one small spare bed-room, and that under the roof. Had she let this stranger woman come to one of the regular houses, as she might have done, and been far better accommodated than it was possible for her to be in a garret, it is not likely she would have been murdered. She lost her life, as I tell Horton, for meddling with other people's business.'

'If such were the regular and inevitable punishment of that particular offence, my good landlady, there would be a great dearth of ladies,' said Tom Dunscomb, a little drily – 'but, you were remarking that Peter

Goodwin, the member of meeting, and Mary Monson's supposed victim, had a weakness in favour of strong liquor?'

'Juleps were his choice — I've heard of a part of the country, somewhere about Virginny, I believe it is, where tee-totallers make an exception in favour of juleps — it may do *there*, 'Squire Dunscomb, but it won't do *here*. No liquor undoes a body, in this part of the country, sooner than mint juleps. I will find you ten constitutions that can hold out ag'in brandy, or plain grog, or even grog, beer and cider, all three together, where you can find me one that will hold out ag'in juleps. I always set down a reg'lar julep fancier as a case — that is, in this part of the country.'

'Very true, my good landlady, and very sensible and just. I consider you a sensible and just woman, whose mind has been enlarged by an extensive acquaintance with human nature.'

'A body does pick up a good deal in and around a bar, 'Squire Dunscomb!'

'Pick up, indeed — I've known 'em picked up by the dozen myself. And Peter *would* take the juleps?'

'Awfully fond of them! He no more dared to take one at home, however, than he dared to go and ask Minister Watch to make him one. No, he know'd better where the right sort of article was to be had, and always came down to our house when he was dry. Horton mixes stiff, or we should have been a good deal better off in the world than we are — not that we're mis'rable, as it is. But Horton takes it strong himself, and he mixes strong for others. Peter soon found this out, and he fancied his juleps more, as he has often told me himself, than the juleps of the great Boweryman, who has a name for 'em, far and near. Horton *can* mix a julep, if he can do nothing else.'

'And Peter Goodwin was in the habit of frequenting your house privately, to indulge this propensity.'

'I'm almost ashamed to own that he did — perhaps it was sinful in us to let him; but a body must carry out the idee of trade — our trade is tavern-keeping, and it's our business to mix liquors, though Minister Watch says, almost every Sabbath, that professors should do nothing out of sight that they wouldn't do before the whole congregation. I don't hold to that, however, for it would soon break up tavern-keeping altogether. Yes, Peter did drink awfully, in a corner.'

'To intoxication, do you mean, Mrs Horton?'

'To delirrum tremus, sir — yes, full up to that. His way was to come down to the village on the pretence of business, and to come right to our house, where I've known him to take three juleps in the first half-hour. Sometimes he'd pretend to go to town to see his sister, when he would stay two or three days up stairs in a room that Horton keeps for what he calls his *cases* – he has given the room the name of his *ward* – hospital-ward he means.'

'Is the worthy Mr Horton a member of the meeting also, my good landlady?'

Mrs Horton had the grace to colour; but she answered without stammering, habit fortifying us in moral discrepancies much more serious than even this.

'He was, and I don't know but I may say he is yet; though he hasn't attended, now, for more than two years. The question got to be between meetin' and the bar; and the bar carried the day, so far as Horton is concerned. I've held out better, I hope, and expect to gain a victory. It's quite enough to have one backslider in a family, I tell my husband, 'squire.'

'A sufficient supply, ma'am – quite a sufficiency. So Peter Goodwin lay in your house drunk, days at a time?'

'I'm sorry to say he did. He was here a week once, with delirrum tremus on him; but Horton carried him through by the use of juleps; for *that's* the time to take 'em, everybody says; and we got him home without old Dolly's knowing that he hadn't been with his sister the whole time. That turn satisfied Peter for three good months.'

'Did Peter pay as he went, or did you keep a score?'

'Ready money, sir. Catch us keeping an account with a man when his wife ruled the roast! No, Peter paid like a king, for every mouthful he swallowed.'

'I am far from certain that the comparison is a good one, kings being in no degree remarkable for paying their debts. But, is it not possible that Peter may have set his own house on fire, and thus have caused all this calamity, for which my client is held responsible?'

'I've thought that over a good deal since the murder, 'squire, but don't well see how it can be made out. Setting the building on fire is simple enough; but who killed the old couple, and who robbed the house, unless this Mary Monson did both?'

'The case has its difficulties, no doubt; but I have known the day to dawn after a darker night than this. I believe that Mrs Goodwin and her husband were very nearly of the same height?'

'Exactly; I've seen them measure, back to back. He was a very short man, and she a very tall woman!'

'Do you know anything of a German female who is said to have lived with the unfortunate couple?'

'There has been some talk of such a person since the fire; but Dolly Goodwin kept no help. She was too stingy for that; then she had no need of it, being very strong and stirring for her time of life.'

'Might not a boarder, like Miss Monson, have induced her to take this foreigner into her family for a few weeks? The nearest neighbours, those who would be most likely to know all about it, say that no wages were given; the woman working for her food and lodging.'

"Squire Dunscomb, you'll never make it out that any German killed Peter and his wife.'

'Perhaps not; though even that is possible. Such, however, is not the object of my present inquiries – but, here comes my associate counsel, and I will take another occasion to continue this conversation, my good Mrs Horton.'

Timms entered with a hurried air. For the first time in his life he appeared to his associate and old master to be agitated. Cold, calculating, and cunning, this man seldom permitted himself to be so much thrown off his guard as to betray emotion; but now he actually did. There was a tremor in his form that extended to his voice; and he seemed afraid to trust the latter even in the customary salutations. Nodding his head, he drew a chair and took his seat.

'You have been to the gaol?' asked Dunscomb.

A nod was the answer.

'You were admitted, and had an interview with our client?'

Nod the third was the only reply.

'Did you put the questions to her, as I desired?'

'I did, sir; but I would sooner cross-examine all Duke's, than undertake to get anything she does not wish to tell, out of that one young lady!'

'I fancy most young ladies have a faculty for keeping such matters to themselves as they do not wish to reveal. Am I to understand that you got no answers?'

'I really do not know, 'squire. She was polite, and obliging, and smiling – but, somehow or other, I do not recollect her replies.'

'You must be falling in love, Timms, to return with such an account,' retorted Dunscomb, a cold but very sarcastic smile passing over his face. 'Have a care, sir; 'tis a passion that makes a fool of a man sooner than any other. I do not think there is much danger of the lady's returning your flame; unless, indeed, you can manage to make her acquittal a condition of the match.'

'I am afraid – dreadfully afraid, her acquittal will be a very desperate affair,' answered Timms, passing his hands down his face, as if to wipe away his weakness. 'The deeper I get into the matter, the worse it appears!'

'Have you given our client any intimation to this effect?'

'I hadn't the heart to do it. She is just as composed, and calm, and tranquil, and judicious – yes, and ingenious, as if *she* were only the counsel in this affair of life and death! I couldn't distrust so much tranquillity. I wish I knew her history!'

'My interrogatories pointed out the absolute necessity of her furnishing us with the means of enlightening the court and jury on that most material point, should the worst come to the worst.'

'I know they did, sir; but they no more got at the truth than my own pressing questions. I should like to see that lady on the stand above all things! I think she would bother saucy Williams, and fairly put him out of countenance. By the way, sir, I hear he is employed against us by the nephew, who is quite furious about the loss of the money, which he pretends was a much larger sum than the neighbourhood has commonly supposed.'

'I have always thought the relations would employ some one to assist the public prosecutor in a case of this magnitude. The theory of our government is that the public virtue will see the laws executed; but, in my experience, Timms, this public virtue is a very acquiescent and indifferent quality, seldom troubling itself even to abate a nuisance, until its own nose is offended, or its own pocket damaged.'

'Roguery is always more active than honesty – I found that out long since, 'squire. But, it is nat'ral for a public prosecutor not to press one on trial for life, and the accused a woman, closer than circumstances seem to demand. It is true, that popular feeling is strong ag'in Mary Monson; but it was well in the nephew to fee such a bull-dog as Williams, if he wishes to make a clean sweep of it.'

'Does our client know this?'

'Certainly; she seems to know all about her case, and has a strange pleasure in entering into the mode and manner of her defence. It would do your heart good, sir, to see the manner in which she listens, and advises, and consults. She's wonderful handsome at such times!'

'You are in love, Timms; and I shall have to engage some other assistant. First Jack, and then you! Umph! This is a strange world, of a verity.'

'I don't think it's quite as bad with me as that,' said Timms, this time rubbing his shaggy eye-brows as if to ascertain whether or not he were dreaming, 'though I must own I do not feel precisely as I did a month since. I wish you would see our client yourself, sir, and make her understand how important it is to her interest that we should know something of her past history.'

'Do you think her name is rightfully set forth in the indictment?'

'By no means – but, as she has called herself Mary Monson, she cannot avail herself of her own acts.'

'Certainly not. I asked merely as a matter of information. She must be made to feel the necessity of fortifying us on that particular point, else it will go far towards convicting her. Jurors do not like aliases.'

'She knows this already; for I have laid the matter before her, again and again. Nothing seems to move her, however; and as to apprehension, she appears to be above all fear.'

'This is most extraordinary! – Have you interrogated the maid?'

'How can I? She speaks no English; and I can't utter a syllable in any foreign tongue.'

'Ha! Does she pretend to that much ignorance? Marie Moulin speaks very intelligible English, as I know from having conversed with her often. She is a clever, prudent Swiss, from one of the French cantons, and is known for her fidelity and trustworthiness. With me she will hardly venture to practise this deception. If she has feigned ignorance of English it was in order to keep her secrets.'

Timms admitted the probability of its being so; then he entered into a longer and more minute detail of the state of the case. In the first place he admitted that, in spite of all his own efforts to the contrary, the popular feeling was setting strong against their client. 'Frank Williams,' as he called the saucy person who bore that name, had entered into the struggle might and main, and was making his customary impressions.

'His fees must be liberal,' continued Timms, 'and I should think are in some way dependent on the result, for I never saw the fellow more engaged in my life.'

'This precious code does allow such a bargain to be made between the counsel and his client, or any other bargain that is not downright conspiracy,' returned Dunscomb; 'but I do not see what is to be shared, even should Mary Monson be hanged.'

'Do not speak in that manner of so agreeable a person,' cried Timms, actually manifesting emotion; 'it is unpleasant to think of. It is true, a conviction will not bring money to the prosecution, unless it should bring to light some of Mrs Goodwin's hoards.'

Dunscomb shrugged his shoulders, and his associate proceeded with his narrative. Two of the reporters were offended, and their allusions to the cause, which were almost daily in their respective journals, were ill-natured, and calculated to do great harm, though so far covered as to wear an air of seeming candour. The natural effect of this 'constant dropping,' in a community accustomed to refer everything to the common mind, had been 'to wear away the stone.' Many of those who, at first, had been disposed to sustain the accused, unwilling to believe that one so young, so educated, so modest in deportment, so engaging in manners, and of the gentler sex, could possibly be guilty of the crimes imputed, were now changing their opinions under the control of this potent and sinister mode of working on the public sentiment. The agents employed by Timms to counteract this malign influence had failed of their object; they working merely for money, while those of the other side were resenting what they regarded as an affront.

The family of the Burtons, the nearest neighbours of the Goodwins, no longer received Timms with the frank cordiality that they had manifested in the earlier period of his intercourse with them. Then, they had been communicative, eager to tell all that they knew, and, as the lawyer fancied, even a little more; while they were now reserved, uneasy, and indisposed to let one-half of the real facts within their knowledge be known. Timms thought they had been worked upon, and that they might expect some hostile and important testimony from that quarter. The consultation ended by an exclamation from Dunscomb on the subject of the abuses that were so fast creeping into the administration of justice, rendering the boasted freemen of America, though in a different mode, little more likely to receive its benefit from an unpolluted stream, than they who live under the worn out and confessedly corrupt systems of the Old World. Such is the tendency of things, and such one of the ways of the hour.

CHAPTER XV

Are those *her* ribs through which the sun
    Did peer, as through a grate?
And is that woman all her crew?
    Is that a Death, and are there two?
    Is Death that woman's mate?

The Phantom Ship.

After a short preparatory interview with Anna Updyke, Dunscomb repaired to the gaol, whither he had already dispatched a note to announce his intended visit. Good Mrs Gott received him with earnest attention; for, as the day of trial approached, this kind-hearted woman manifested a warmer and warmer interest in the fate of her prisoner.

'You are welcome, Mr Dunscomb,' said this well-disposed and gentle turnkey, as she led the way to the door that opened on the gallery of the gaol; 'and welcome, again and again. I do wish this business may fall into good hands; and I'm afraid Timms is not getting on with it as well as he might.'

'My associate has the reputation of being a skilful attorney and a good manager, Mrs Gott.'

'So he has, Mr Dunscomb; but somehow – I scarce know how myself – but somehow, he doesn't get along with *this* cause as well as I have known him to get along with others. The excitement in the county is terrible; and Gott has had seven anonymous letters to let him know that if Mary Monson escape, his hopes from the public are gone for ever. I tell him not to mind such contemptible things; but he is frightened half out of his wits. It takes good courage, 'squire, to treat an anonymous letter with the contempt it merits.'

'It sometimes does, indeed. Then you think we shall have up-hill work with the defence?'

'Dreadful! – I've never known a cause so generally tried out of doors as this. What makes the matter more provoking, Mary Monson might have had it all her own way, if she had been so minded; for, at first, she was popularity itself with all the neighbours. Folks nat'rally like beauty, and elegance, and youth; and Mary has enough of each to make friends anywhere.'

'What! with the ladies?' said Dunscomb, smiling. 'Surely not with your sex, Mrs Gott?'

'Yes, with the women, as well as with the men, if she would only use her means; but she stands in her own light. Crowds have been round the outer windows to hear her play on the harp – they tell me she uses the real Jew's Harp, 'Squire Dunscomb; such as Royal David used to play on; and that she has great skill. There is a German in the village who knows all about music, and he says Mary Monson has been excellently taught – by the very best masters.'

'It is extraordinary; yet it would seem to be so. Will you have the goodness to open the door, Mrs Gott?'

'With all my heart,' answered this, in one sense, very singular turnkey, though in another a very every-day character, jingling her keys, but not taking a forward step to comply: 'Mary Monson expects you. I suppose, sir, you know that saucy Frank Williams is retained by the friends of the Goodwins?'

'Mr Timms has told me as much as that. I cannot say, however, that I have any particular apprehension of encountering Mr Williams.'

'No, sir; not *you*, I'll engage, not in open court; but out of doors he's very formidable.'

'I trust this cause, one involving the life and reputation of a very interesting female, will not be tried out of doors, Mrs Gott. The issue is too serious for such a tribunal.'

'So a body would think; but a great deal of law business is settled, they tell me, under the sheds, and in the streets, and in the taverns; most especially in the jurors' bedrooms, and settled in a way it ought not to be.'

'I am afraid you are nearer right than every just-minded person could wish. But we will talk of this another time – the door if you please, now.'

'Yes, sir, in one minute. It would be *so* easy for Mary Monson to be just as popular with everybody in Biberry as she is with me. Let her come to one of the side-windows of the gallery this evening, and show herself to the folks, and play on that harp of hers, and Royal David himself could not have been better liked by the Jews of old than she would soon be by our people hereabouts.'

'It is probably now too late. The court sits in a few days; and the mischief, if any there be, must be done.'

'No such thing, begging your pardon, 'squire. There's that in Mary Monson that can carry anything she pleases. Folks now think her proud and consequential, because she will not just stand at one of the grates and let them look at her a little.'

'I am afraid, Mrs Gott, your husband has taught you a greater respect for those you call "the people," than they deserve to receive at your hands.'

'Gott is dreadfully afraid of them——'

'And he is set apart by the laws to see them executed on these very people,' interrupted Dunscomb, with a sneer; 'to levy on their possessions, keep the peace, enforce the laws; in short, to make them *feel*, whenever it is necessary, that they are *governed!*'

'Gott says "that the people *will* rule." That's *his* great saying.'

'Will *seem* to rule is true enough, but the most that the mass of any nation *can* do is occasionally to check the proceedings of their governors. The every-day work is most effectually done by a favoured few here, just as it is done by a favoured few everywhere else. The door, now, if you please, my good Mrs Gott.'

'Yes, sir, in one minute. Dear me! how odd that you should think so. Why, I thought that you were a democrat, Mr Dunscomb?'

'So I am, as between forms of government; but I never was fool enough to think that the people can really rule, further than by occasional checks and rebukes.'

'What would Gott say to this! Why, he is so much afraid of the people that he tells me he never does anything without fancying some one is looking over his shoulders.'

'Ay, that is a very good rule for a man who wishes to be chosen *sheriff*. To be a *bishop*, it would be better to remember the omniscient eye.'

'I do declare – oh! Gott never thinks of *that*, more's the pity,' applying the key to the lock. 'When you wish to come out, 'squire, just call at this grate' – then dropping her voice to a whisper – 'try and persuade Mary Monson to show herself at one of the side grates.'

But Dunscomb entered the gallery with no such intention. As he was expected, his reception was natural and easy. The prisoner was carefully, though simply, dressed, and she appeared all the better, most probably, for some of the practised arts of her woman. Marie Moulin herself kept modestly within the cell, where, indeed, she passed most of her time, leaving the now quite handsomely furnished gallery to the uses of her mistress.

After the first few words of salutation, Dunscomb took the chair he was invited to occupy, a good deal at a loss how to address a woman of his companion's mien and general air as a culprit about to be tried for her life. He first attempted words, of course.

'I see you have had a proper regard to your comforts in this miserable place,' he remarked.

'Do not call it by so forbidding a name, Mr Dunscomb,' was the answer given with a sorrowful, but exceedingly winning smile; 'it is *my* place of *refuge.*'

'Do you still persist in refusing to tell me against *what*, Miss Monson?'

'I persist in nothing that ought not to be done, I hope. At another time I may be more communicative. But if what Mrs Gott tells me is correct, I need these walls to prevent my being torn to pieces by those she calls the people outside.'

Dunscomb looked with amazement at the being who quietly made this remark on her own situation. Of beautiful form, with all the signs of a gentle origin and refined education, young, handsome, delicate, nay, dainty of speech and acts, there she sat, indicted for arson and murder, and about to be tried for her life, with the composure of a lady in her drawing-room! The illuminated expression that at times rendered her countenance so very remarkable, had now given place to one of sobered sadness; though apprehension did not appear to be in the least predominant.

'The sheriff has instilled into his wife a very healthful respect for those she calls the people – healthful, for one who looks to their voices for his support. This is very American.'

'I suppose it to be much the same everywhere. I have been a good deal abroad, Mr Dunscomb, and cannot say I perceive any great difference in men.'

'Nor is there any, though circumstances cause different modes of betraying their weaknesses, as well as what there is in them that is good. But the people in this country, Miss Monson, possess a power that, in your case, is not to be despised. As Mrs Gott would intimate, it may be prudent for you to remember *that.*'

'Surely *you* would not have me make an exhibition of myself, Mr Dunscomb, at the window of a gaol!'

'As far from that as possible. I would have you do nothing that is unbecoming one of your habits and opinions – nothing, in short, that would be improper, as a means of defence, by one accused and tried by the State. Nevertheless, it is always wiser to make friends than to make enemies.'

Mary Monson lowered her eyes to the carpet, and Dunscomb perceived that her thoughts wandered. They were not on her critical situation. It was indispensably necessary, however, that he should be explicit, and he did not shrink from his duty. Gently, but distinctly, and with a clearness that a far less gifted mind than that of the accused could comprehend, he now opened the subject of the approaching trial. A few words were first ventured on its grave character, and on the vast importance it was in all respects to his client; to which the latter listened attentively, but without the slightest visible alarm. Next, he alluded to the stories that were in circulation, the impression they were producing, and the danger there was that her rights might be affected by these sinister opinions.

'But I am to be tried by a judge and a jury, they tell me,' said Mary Monson, when Dunscomb ceased speaking; 'they will come from a distance, and will not be prejudiced against me by all this idle gossip.'

'Judges and jurors are only men, and nothing goes farther with less effort than your "idle gossip." Nothing is repeated accurately, or it is very rare to find it so; and those who only half comprehend a subject are certain to relate with exaggerations and false colourings.'

'How, then, can the electors discover the real characters of those for whom they are required to vote?' demanded Mary Monson, smiling; 'or get just ideas of the measures they are to support or to oppose?'

'Half the time they do neither. It exceeds all our present means, at least, to diffuse sufficient information for *that*. The consequence is, that appearances and assertions are made to take the place of facts. The mental food of the bulk of this nation is an opinion simulated by the artful to answer their own purposes. But the power of the masses is getting to be very formidable – more formidable in a way never contemplated by those who formed the institutions, than in any way that was foreseen. Among other things, they begin to hold the administration of justice in the hollow of their hands.'

'I am not to be tried by the masses, I trust. If so, my fate would be very hard, I fear, judging from what I hear in my little excursions in the neighbourhood.'

'Excursions, Miss Monson!' repeated the astonished Dunscomb.

'Excursions, sir; I make one for the benefit of air and exercise, every favourable night, at this fine season of the year. Surely you would not have me cooped up here in a gaol, without the relief of a little fresh air?'

'With the knowledge and concurrence of the sheriff, or that of his wife?'

'Perhaps not strictly with those of either; though I suspect good Mrs Gott has an inkling of my movements. It would be too hard to deny myself air and exercise, both of which are very necessary to my health, because I am charged with these horrid crimes.'

Dunscomb passed a hand over his brow, as if he desired to clear his mental vision by friction of the physical, and, for a moment, sat absolutely lost in wonder. He scarce knew whether he was or was not dreaming.

'And you have actually been outside of these walls, Miss Monson!' he exclaimed, at length.

'Twenty times, at least. Why should I stay within them, when the means of quitting them are always in my power?'

As Mary Monson said this, she showed her counsel a set of keys that corresponded closely with those which good Mrs Gott was in the habit of using whenever she came to open the door of that particular gallery. A quiet smile betrayed how little the prisoner fancied there was anything remarkable in all this.

'Are you aware, Miss Monson, it is felony to assist a prisoner to escape?'

'So they tell me, Mr Dunscomb; but as I have not escaped, or made any attempt to escape, and have returned regularly and in good season to my gaol, no one can be harmed for what I have done. Such, at least, is the opinion of Mr Timms.'

Dunscomb did not like the expression of face that accompanied this speech. It might be too much to say it was absolutely cunning; but there was so much of the manoeuvring of one accustomed to manage in it, that it awakened the unpleasant distrust that existed in the earlier days of his intercourse with this singular young woman, and which had now been dormant for several weeks. There was, however, so much of the cold polish of the upper classes in his client's manner, that the offending expression was thrown off from the surface of her looks, as light is reflected from the ground and silvered mirror. At the very instant which succeeded this seeming gleam of cunning, all was calm, quiet, refined, gentle, and without apparent emotion in the countenance of the accused.

'Timms!' repeated Dunscomb, slowly. 'So *he* has known of this, and I dare say has had an agency in bringing it about?'

'As you say it is felony to aid a prisoner to escape, I can say neither yes nor no to this, Mr Dunscomb, lest I betray an accomplice. I should rather think, however, that Mr Timms is not a person to be easily caught in the meshes of the law.'

Again the counsellor disliked the expression; though Mary Monson looked unusually pretty at that particular moment. He did not pause to analyze his feelings, notwithstanding, but rather sought to relieve his own curiosity, which had been a good deal aroused by the information just received.

'As you have not hesitated to tell me of what you call your "excursions," Miss Monson,' he continued, 'perhaps you will so far extend your confidence as to let me know where you go?'

'I can have no objection to that. Mr Timms tells me the law cannot compel a counsel to betray his client's secrets; and of course I am safe with you. Stop – I have a duty to perform that has been too long delayed. Gentlemen of your profession are entitled to their fees; and, as yet, I have been very remiss in this respect. Will you do me the favour, Mr Dunscomb, to accept that, which you will see has been some time in readiness to be offered.'

Dunscomb was too much of a professional man to feel any embarrassment at this act of justice; but he took the letter, broke the seal, even before his client's eyes, and held up for examination a note for a thousand dollars. Prepared as he was by Timms's account for a liberal reward, this large sum took him a good deal by surprise.

'This is an unusual fee, Miss Monson!' he exclaimed; 'one much more considerable than I should expect from you, were I working for remuneration, as in your case I certainly am not.'

'Gentlemen of the law look for their reward, I believe, as much as others. We do not live in the times of chivalry, when gallant men assisted distressed damsels as a matter of honour; but in what has well been termed a "bank-note world."'

'I have no wish to set myself up above the fair practices of my profession, and am as ready to accept a fee as any man in Nassau Street. Nevertheless, I took your case in hand with a very different motive. It would pain me to be obliged to work for a fee, on the present unhappy occasion.'

Mary Monson looked grateful, and for a minute she seemed to be reflecting on some scheme by which she could devise a substitute for the old-fashioned mode of proceeding in a case of this sort.

'You have a niece, Mr Dunscomb,' she at length exclaimed – 'as Marie Moulin informs me. A charming girl, and who is about to be married?'

The lawyer assented by an inclination of the head, fastening his penetrating black eyes on the full, expressive, greyish-blue ones of his companion.

'You intend to return to town this evening?' said Mary Monson, in continuation.

'Such is my intention. I came here to-day to confer with you and Mr Timms, on the subject of the trial, to see how matters stand on the spot, by personal observation, and to introduce to you one who feels the deepest interest in your welfare, and desires most earnestly to seek your acquaintance.'

The prisoner was now silent, interrogating with her singularly expressive eyes.

'It is Anna Updyke, the step-daughter of my nearest friend, Dr McBrain; and a very sincere, warm-hearted, and excellent girl.'

'I have heard of her, too,' returned Mary Monson, with a smile so strange, that her counsel wished she had not given this demonstration of a feeling that seemed out of place, under all the circumstances. 'They tell me she is a most charming girl, and that she is a very great favourite with your nephew, the young gentleman whom I have styled my legal vidette.'

'Vidette! That is a singular term to be used by *you*.'

'Oh! you will remember that I have been much in countries where such persons abound. I must have caught the word from some of the young soldiers of Europe. But, Mr John Wilmeter is an admirer of the young lady you have named?'

'I hope he is. I know of no one with whom I think he would be more likely to be happy.'

Dunscomb spoke earnestly, and at such times his manner was singularly sincere and impressive. It was this appearance of feeling and nature that gave him the power he possessed over juries; and it may be said to have made no small part of his fortune. Mary Monson seemed to be surprised; and she fastened her remarkable eyes on the uncle, in a way that might have admitted of different interpretations. Her lips moved as if she spoke to herself; and the smile that succeeded was both mild and sad.

'To be sure,' added the prisoner, slowly, 'my information is not on the very best authority, coming, as it does, from a servant – but Marie Moulin is both discreet and observant.'

'She is tolerably well qualified to speak of Anna Updyke, having seen her almost daily for the last two years. But, we are all surprised that *you* should know anything of this young woman.'

'I know her precisely as she is known to your niece and Miss Updyke – in other words, as a maid who is much esteemed by those she serves – but,' apparently wishing to change the discourse – 'we are forgetting the purpose of your visit, all this time, Mr Dunscomb. Do me the favour to write your address in town, and that of Dr McBrain on this card, and we will proceed to business.'

Dunscomb did as desired, when he opened on the details that were the object of his little journey. As had been the case in all his previous interviews with her, Mary Monson surprised him with the coolness with which she spoke of an issue that involved her own fate, for life or for death. While she carefully abstained from making any allusion to circumstances that might betray her previous history, she shrunk from no inquiry that bore on the acts of which she had been accused. Every question put by Dunscomb that related to the murders and the arson, was answered frankly and freely, there being no wish apparent to conceal the minutest circumstance. She made several exceedingly shrewd and useful suggestions on the subject of the approaching trial, pointing out defects in the testimony against her, and reasoning with singular acuteness on particular facts that were known to be much relied on by the prosecution. We shall not reveal these details any further in this stage of our narrative, for they will necessarily appear at length in our subsequent pages; but shall confine ourselves to a few of those remarks that may be better given at present.

'I do not know, Mr Dunscomb,' Mary Monson suddenly said, while the subject of her trial was yet under discussion, 'that I have ever mentioned to you the fact that Mr and Mrs Goodwin were not happy together. One would think, from what was said at the time of the inquest, that they were a very affectionate and contented couple; but my own observation, during the short time I was under their roof, taught me better. The husband drank, and the wife was avaricious and very quarrelsome. I am afraid, sir, there are few really happy couples to be found on earth!'

'If you knew McBrain better, you would not say that, my dear Miss Monson,' answered the counsellor with a sort of glee – 'there's a husband for you! – a fellow who is not only happy with *one* wife, but who is happy with *three*, as he will tell you himself.'

'Not all at the same time, I hope, sir?'

Dunscomb did justice to his friend's character, by relating how the matter really stood; after which he asked permission to introduce Anna Updyke. Mary Monson seemed startled at this request, and asked several questions, which induced her counsel to surmise that she was fearful of being recognised. Nor was Dunscomb pleased with all the expedients adopted by his client, in order to extract information from him. He thought they slightly indicated cunning, a quality that he might be said to abhor. Accustomed as he was to all the efforts of ingenuity in illustrating a principle or maintaining a proposition, he had always avoided everything like sophistry and falsehood. This weakness on the part of Mary Monson, however, was soon forgotten in the graceful manner in which she acquiesced in the wish of the stranger to be admitted. The permission was finally accorded, as if an honour were received, with the tact of female and the easy dignity of a gentlewoman.

Anna Updyke possessed a certain ardour of character that had, more than once, given her prudent and sagacious mother uneasiness, and which sometimes led her into the commission of acts, always innocent in themselves, and perfectly under the restraint of principles, which the world would have been apt to regard as imprudent. Such, however, was far from being her reputation, her modesty and the diffidence with which she regarded herself, being amply sufficient to protect her from the common observation, even while most beset by the weakness named. Her love for John Wilmeter was so disinterested, or to herself so seemed to be, that she fancied she could even assist in bringing about his union with another woman, were that necessary to his happiness. She believed that this mysterious stranger was, to say the least, an object of intense interest with John, which soon made her an object of intense interest with herself; and each hour increased her desire to become acquainted with one so situated, friendless, accused, and seemingly suspended by a thread over an abyss, as she was. When she first made her proposal to Dunscomb to be permitted to visit his client, the wary and experienced counsellor strongly objected to the step. It was imprudent, could lead to no good, and might leave an impression unfavourable to Anna's own character. But this advice was unheeded by a girl of Anna Updyke's generous temperament. Quiet and gentle as she ordinarily appeared to be, there was a deep under-current of feeling and enthusiasm in her moral constitution, that bore her onward in any course which she considered to be right, with a total abnegation of self. This was a quality to lead to good or evil, as it might receive a direction; and happily nothing had yet occurred in her brief existence to carry her away towards the latter goal.

Surprised at the steadiness and warmth with which his young friend persevered in her request, Dunscomb, after obtaining the permission of her mother, and promising to take good care of his charge, was permitted to convey Anna to Biberry in the manner related.

Now that her wish was about to be gratified, Anna Updyke, like thousands of others who have been more impelled by impulses than governed by reason, shrank from the execution of her own purposes. But the generous ardour revived in her in time to save appearances; and she was admitted by well-meaning Mrs Gott to the gallery of the prison, leaning on Dunscomb's arm, much as she might have entered a drawing-room in a regular morning call.

The meeting between these two charming young women was frank and cordial, though slightly qualified by the forms of the world. A watchful and critical observer might have detected less of nature in Mary Monson's manner than in that of her guest, even while the welcome she gave her visitor was not without cordiality and feeling. It is true that her courtesy was more elaborate and European, if one may use the expression, than it is usual to see in an American female, and her air was less ardent than that of Anna; but the last was highly struck with her countenance and general appearance, and, on the whole, not dissatisfied with her own reception.

The power of sympathy and the force of affinities soon made themselves felt, as between these two youthful females. Anna regarded Mary as a stranger most grievously wronged; and forgetting all that there was which was questionable or mysterious in her situation, or remembering it only to feel the influence of its interest, while she submitted to a species of community of feeling with John Wilmeter, as she fancied, and soon got to be as much entranced with the stranger as seemed to be the fate of all who approached the circle of her acquaintance. On the other hand, Mary Monson felt a consolation and gratification in this visit to which she had long been a stranger. Good Mrs Gott was kind-hearted and a woman, but she had no claim to the refinement and peculiar sensibilities of a lady; while Marie Moulin, discreet, respectful, even wise as she was in her own way, was, after all, nothing but an upper servant. The chasm between the cultivated and the uncultivated, the polished and the unpolished, is wide; and the accused fully appreciated the change, when one of her own class in life, habits, associations, and, if the reader will, prejudices, so unexpectedly appeared to sympathize with and to console her. Under such circumstances three or four hours made the two fast and deeply-interested friends, on their own accounts, to say nothing of the effect produced by the generous advances of one and the perilous condition of the other.

Dunscomb returned to town that evening, leaving Anna Updyke behind him, ostensibly under the care of Mrs Gott. Democracy has been carried so far on the high road of ultraism in New York, as in very many interests to become the victim of its own expedients. Perhaps the people are never so far from exercising a healthful, or indeed any authority at all, as when made to seem, by the expedients of demagogues, to possess an absolute control. It is necessary merely to bestow a power which it is impossible for the masses to wield with intelligence, in order to effect this little piece of legerdemain in politics, the quasi people in all such cases becoming the passive instruments in the hands of their leaders, who strengthen their own authority by this seeming support of the majority. In all cases, however, in which the agency of numbers can be felt, its force is made to prevail, the tendency necessarily being to bring down all representation to the level of the majority. The effect of the change has been pretty equally divided between good and evil. In many cases benefits have accrued to the community by the exercise of this direct popular control, while in probably quite as many the result has been exactly the reverse of that which was anticipated. In no one instance, we believe it will be generally admitted, has the departure from the old practice been less advantageous than in rendering the office of sheriff elective. Instead of being a leading and independent man, who has a pride in his position, and regards the character of his county as he does his own, this functionary has got to be, nine times in ten, a mere political manoeuvrer, who seeks the place as a reward for party labours, and fills it very much for his personal benefit, conferring no dignity on it by his own position and character, lessening its authority by his want of the qualities calculated to increase it, and in a good many instances, making it quite as difficult to wrest money from *his* hands, as from those of the original debtor.

It is a consequence of this state of things that the sheriff has quite lost all, or nearly all of the personal consideration that was once connected with his office; and has sunk, in most of the strictly rural counties, into a gaoler, and the head of the active bailiffs. His object is altogether money; and the profit connected with the keeping of the prisoners, now reduced almost entirely to felons, the accused, and persons committed for misdemeanours, is one of the inducements for aspiring to an office once so honourable.

In this state of things, it is not at all surprising that Dunscomb was enabled to make such an arrangement with Mrs Gott as would place Anna Updyke in a private room in the house attached to the gaol, and which formed the sheriff's dwelling. The counsellor preferred leaving her with Mrs Horton; but to this Anna herself objected, both because she had taken a strong dislike to the garrulous but shrewd landlady, and because it would have separated her too much from the person she had come especially to console and sympathize with.

The arrangement made, Dunscomb, as has already been mentioned, took his departure for town, with the understanding that he was to return the succeeding week; the Circuit and Oyer and Terminer sitting on Monday; and the District Attorney, Mr Garth, having given notice to her counsel that the indictment against Mary Monson would be certainly traversed the second day of the sitting, which would be on Tuesday.

CHAPTER XVI

> Let her locks be the reddest that ever were seen,
> And her eyes may be e'en any colour but green;
> Be they light, gray, or black, their lustre and hue,
> I swear I've no choice, only let her have two.
>
> *The Duenna.*

Two days after this, Dunscomb was in his library, late at night, holding a brief discourse with McBrain's coachman, who has been already introduced to the reader. Some orders had been given to the last, in relation to another trip to Biberry, whither the master and our lawyer were to proceed next day. The man was an old and indulged servant, and often took great liberties in these conferences. In this respect the Americans of his class differ very little from the rest of their fellow-creatures, notwithstanding all that has been said and written to the contrary. They obey the impulses of their characters much as the rest of mankind, though not absolutely without some difference in manner.

'I s'poses, 'Squire Dunscomb, that this is like to be the last journey that I and the doctor will have to take soon ag'in, in *that* quarter,' coolly observed Stephen, when his master's friend had told him the hour to be at the door, with the other preparations that would be necessary; 'unless we should happen to be called in at the *post mortal*.'

'*Post mortem*, you must mean, Hoof,' a slight smile flashing on the lawyer's countenance, and as quickly disappearing. 'So you consider it a settled thing that my client is to be found guilty?'

'That's what they say, sir; and things turn out, in this country, pretty much as they say aforehand. For my part, sir, I never quite liked the criminal's looks.'

'Her *looks!* I do not know where you would go to find a more lovely young woman, Stephen!'

This was said with a vivacity and suddenness that startled the coachman a little. Even Dunscomb seemed surprised at his own animation, and had the grace to change colour. The fact was, that he too was feeling the influence of woman, youthful, lovely, spirited, refined, and surrounded with difficulties. This was the third of Mary Monson's conquests since her arrest, if John Wilmeter's wavering admiration could be placed in this category; viz., Timms, the nephew, and the counsellor himself. Neither was absolutely in love; but each and all submitted to an interest of an unusual degree in the person, character, and fortunes of this unknown female. Timms, alone, had got so far as to contemplate a marriage; the idea having crossed his mind that it might be almost as useful as popularity, to become the husband of one possessed of so much money.

'I'll not deny her *good* looks, 'squire,' returned Stephen Hoof – or Stephen Huff, as he called himself – 'but it's her *bad* looks that isn't so much to my fancy. Vhy, sir, once the doctor had a horse that was agreeable enough to the eye, having a good colour and most of the p'ints, but who wasn't no traveller, not a bit on't. One that know'd the animal could see where the fault lay, the fetlock j'int being oncommon longish; and that's what I call *good* looks and *bad* looks.'

'You mean, Stephen,' said Dunscomb, who had regained all his *sang-froid*, 'that Mary Monson has a bad-looking ankle, I suppose, wherein I think you miserably mistaken. No matter; she will not have to travel under your lash very far. But, how is it with the reporters? – Do you see any more of your friend that asks so many questions?'

'They be an axing set, 'squire, if anybody can be so called,' returned Stephen, grinning. 'Would you think it, sir? – one day when I was a comin' in from Timbully empty, one on 'em axed me for a ride! a chap has hadn't his foot in a reg'lar private coach since he was born, a wantin' to drive about in a wehicle as well known as Doctor McBrain's best carriage! Them's the sort of chaps that spreads all the reports that's going up and down the land, they tell me.'

'They do their share of it, Stephen; though there are enough to help them who do not openly belong to their corps. Well; what does your acquaintance want to know now?'

'Oncommon curious, 'squire, about the bones. He axed me more than forty questions; what we thought of them; and about their being male or female bones; and how we know'd; and a great many more sich matters. I answered him accordin' to my abilities; and so he made an article on the subject, and has sent me the papers.'

'An article! Concerning Mary Monson, and on your information?'

'Sartain, sir; and the bones. Vhy they cut articles out of much narrower cloth, I can tell you, 'squire. There's the cooks, and chambermaids, and vaiters about town, none of vich can hold up their heads with a reg'lar, long-established physician's coachman, who goes far ahead of even an omnibus driver in public estimation, as you must know, 'squire – but such sort of folks furnish many an article for the papers now-a-days – yes, and articles that ladies and gentlemen read.'

'That is certainly a singular source of useful knowledge – one must hope they are well-grounded, or they will soon cease to be ladies and gentlemen at all. Have you the paper about you, Stephen?'

Hoof handed the lawyer a journal folded with a paragraph in view that was so much thumbed and dirtied, it was not very easy to read it.

'We understand that the trial of Mary Monson, for the murder of Peter and Dorothy Goodwin,' said the 'article,' 'will come off in the adjoining county of Duke's, at a very early day. Strong attempts have been made to make it appear that the skeletons found in the ruins of Goodwin's dwelling, which our readers will remember was burned at the time of the murders, are not human bones; but, we have been at great pains to investigate this very material point, and have no hesitation in giving it as our profound conviction, that it will be made to appear that these melancholy memorials are all that remain of the excellent couple who were so suddenly taken out of existence. We do not speak lightly on this subject, having gone to the fountain-head for our facts, as well as for our science.'

'Hoof on McBrain!' muttered Dunscomb, arching his brows – 'this is much of a piece with quite one-half of the knowledge that is poured into the popular mind, now-a-days. Thank you, Stephen; I will keep this paper, which may be of use at the trial.'

'I thought our opinions was vorth something more than nothing, sir,' answered the gratified coachman – 'a body doesn't ride at all hours, day and night, year arter year, and come out where he started. I vishes you to keep that 'ere paper, 'squire, a little carefully, for it may be wanted in the college where they reads all sorts of things, one of these days.'

'It shall be cared for, my friend – I hear some one at the street-door bell. – It is late for a call; and I fear Peter has gone to bed. See who is there, and good night.'

Stephen withdrew, the ringing being repeated a little impatiently, and was soon at the street-door. The fellow admitted the visitors, and went ruminating homeward, Dunscomb maintaining a very respectable reputation, in a bachelor point of view, for morals. As for the lawyer himself, he was in the act of reading a second time the precious opinion expressed in the journals, when the door of his library opened, a little hesitatingly it must be confessed, and two females stood on its threshold. Although his entirely unexpected visitors were so much muffled in shawls and veils, it was not possible to distinguish even the outlines of their persons, Dunscomb fancied each was youthful and handsome, the instant he cast his eyes on them. The result showed how well he guessed.

Throwing aside the garments that concealed their forms and faces, Mary Monson and Anna Updyke advanced into the room. The first was perfectly self-possessed and brilliantly handsome; while her companion, flushed with excitement and exercise, was not much behind her in this important particular. Dunscomb started, and fancied there was felony, even in his hospitality.

'You know how difficult it is for me to travel by daylight,' commenced Mary Monson, in the most natural manner in the world; 'that, and the distance we had to drive, must explain the unseasonableness of this visit. You told me once, yourself, that you are both a late and an early man, which encouraged me to venture. Mr Timms has written me a letter which I have thought it might be well to show you. There it is; and when you have cast an eye over it, we will speak of its contents.'

'Why, this is very much like a conditional proposal of marriage!' cried Dunscomb, dropping the hand that held the letter, as soon as he had read the first paragraph. 'Conditional, so far as the result of your trial is concerned!'

'I forgot the opening of the epistle, giving very little thought to its purport; though Mr Timms has not written me a line lately that has not touched on this interesting subject. A marriage between him and me is so entirely out of the way of all the possibilities, that I look upon his advances as mere embellishment. I have answered him directly in the negative once, and that ought to satisfy any prudent person. They tell me no woman should marry a man she has once refused; and I shall plead this as a reason for continued obduracy.'

This was said pleasantly, and without the least appearance of resentment; but in a way to show she regarded her attorney's proposal as very much out of the beaten track. As for Dunscomb, he passed his hand over his brows, and read the rest of a pretty long letter with grave attention. The purely business part of this communication was much to the point; important, clearly put, and every way creditable to the writer. The lawyer read it attentively a second time, ere he once opened his mouth in comments.

'And why is this shown to me?' he asked, a little vexed, as was seen in his manner. 'I have told you it is felony to assist a prisoner in an attempt to escape.'

'I have shown it to you, because I have not the remotest intention, Mr Dunscomb, to attempt anything of the sort. I shall not quit my asylum so easily.'

'Then why are you here, at this hour, with the certainty that most of the night must be passed on the road, if you mean to return to your prison ere the sun reappears?'

'For air, exercise, and to show you this letter. I am often in town, but am compelled, for more reasons than you are acquainted with, to travel by night.'

'May I ask where you obtain a vehicle to make these journeys in?'

'I use my own carriage, and trust to a very long-tried and most faithful domestic. I think Miss Updyke will say he drove us not only carefully, but with great speed. On that score, we have no grounds of complaint. But I am very much fatigued, and must ask permission to sleep for an hour. You have a drawing-room, I take it for granted, Mr Dunscomb?'

'My niece fancies she has two. Shall I put lights in one of them?'

'By no means. Anna knows the house as well as she does her mother's, and will do the honours. On no account let Miss Wilmeter be disturbed. I am a little afraid of meeting *her*, since we have practised a piece of treachery touching Marie Moulin. But, no matter; one hour on a sofa, in a dark room, is all I ask. That will bring us to midnight, when the carriage will again be at the door. You wish to see your mother, my dear, and here is a safe and very suitable attendant to accompany you to her house and back again.'

All this was said pleasantly, but with a singular air of authority, as if this mysterious being were accustomed to plan out and direct the movements of others. She had her way. In a minute or two she was stretched on a sofa, covered with a shawl, the door was closed on her, and Dunscomb was on his way to Mrs McBrain's residence, which was at some distance from his own, with Anna leaning on his arm.

'Of course, my dear,' said the lawyer, as he and his beautiful companion left his own door at that late hour of the night, 'we shall see no more of Mary Monson?'

'Not see her again! I should be very, very sorry to think that, sir!'

'She is no simpleton, and means to take Timms's advice. That fellow has written a strong letter, in no expectation of its being seen, I fancy, in which he points out a new source of danger; and plainly advises his client to abscond. I can see the infatuation of love in this; for the letter, if produced, would bring him into great trouble.'

'And you suppose, sir, that Mary Monson intends to follow this advice!'

'Beyond a question. She is not only a very clever, but she is a very cunning woman. This last quality is one that I admire in her the least. I should be half in love with her myself' – this was exactly the state of the counsellor's feelings towards his client, in spite of his bravado and affected discernment; a woman's charms often overshadowing a philosophy that is deeper even than his – 'but for this very trait, which I find little to my taste. I take it for granted you are sent home to be put under your mother's care, where you properly belong; and I am got out of the way to save me from the pain and penalties of an indictment for felony.'

'I think you do not understand Mary Monson, uncle Tom' – so Anna had long called her friend's relative, as it might be in anticipation of the time when the appellation would be correct. – 'She is not the sort of person to do as you suggest; but would rather make it a point of honour to remain, and face any accusation whatever.'

'She must have nerves of steel to confront justice in a case like hers, and in the present state of public feeling in Duke's. Justice is a very pretty thing to talk about, my dear; but we old practitioners know that it is little more, in human hands, than the manipulations of human passions. Of late years, the outsiders – outside barbarians they might very properly be termed – have almost as much to do with the result of any warmly-contested suit, as the law and evidence. "Who is on the jury?" is the first question asked now-a-days; not what are the facts. I have told all this, very plainly, to Mary Monson——'

'To induce her to fly?' asked Anna, prettily, and a little smartly.

'Not so much that, as to induce her to consent to an application for delay. The judges of this country are so much over-worked, so little paid, and usually are so necessitous, that almost any application for delay is granted. Business at chambers is sadly neglected; for that is done in a corner, and does not address itself to the public eye, or seek public eulogiums; but he is thought the cleverest fellow who will soonest sweep out a crowded calendar. Causes are tried by tallow candles until midnight, with half the jurors asleep; and hard-working men, accustomed to be asleep by eight each night, are expected to keep their thoughts and minds active in the face of all these obstacles.'

'Do you tell me this, uncle Tom, in the expectation that I am to understand it?'

'I beg your pardon, child; but my heart is full of the failing justice of the land. We shout hosannas in praise of the institutions, while we shut our eyes to the gravest consequences that are fast undermining us in the most important of all our interests. But here we are already; I had no notion we had walked so fast. Yes, there is papa McBrain's one-horse vehicle, well emptied of its contents, I hope by a hard day's work.'

'A doctor's life must be so laborious!' exclaimed the pretty Anna. 'I think nothing could tempt me to marry a physician.'

'It is well a certain lady of our acquaintance was not of your way of thinking,' returned Dunscomb, laughing; for his good-humour always returned when he could give his friend a rub on his matrimonial propensities, 'else would McBrain have been troubled to get his last and best. Never mind, my dear; he is a good-natured fellow, and will make a very kind papa.'

Anna made no reply, but rang the bell a little pettishly; for no child likes to have a mother married a second time, there being much greater toleration for fathers, and asked her companion in. As the wife of a physician in full practice, the bride had already changed many of her long-cherished habits. In this respect, however, she did no more than follow the fortunes of woman, who so cheerfully makes any sacrifice in behalf of him she loves. If men were only one-half as disinterested, as self-denying, and as true as the other sex, in all that relates to the affections, what a blessed state would that of matrimony be. Still, there are erring, and selfish, and domineering, and capricious, vain, heartless, and self-willed females, whom nature never intended for married life; and who are guilty of a species of profanation, when they stand up and vow to love, honour, and obey their husbands. Many of these disregard their solemn pledges, made at the altar, and under the immediate invocation of the Deity, as they would disregard a promise made in jest, and think no more of the duties and offices that are so peculiarly the province of their sex, than of the passing and idle promises of vanity. But, if such women exist, and that they do our daily experience proves, they are as exceptions to the great law of female faith, which is tenderness and truth. They are not women in character, whatever they may be in appearance; but creatures in the guise of a sex that they discredit and caricature.

Mrs McBrain was not a person of the disposition just described. She was gentle and good, and bid fair to make the evening of her second husband's days very happy. Sooth to say, she was a good deal in love, notwithstanding her time of life, and the still more mature years of the bridegroom; and had been so much occupied with the duties and cares that belonged to her recent change of condition, as to be a little forgetful of her daughter. At no other period of their joint lives would she have permitted this beloved child to be absent from her, under such circumstances, without greater care for her safety and comforts; but there is a honey-week, as well as a honeymoon; and the intenseness of its feelings might very well disturb the ordinary round of even maternal duties. Glad enough, however, was she now to see her daughter; when Anna, blooming, and smiling, and blushing, flew into her mother's arms.

'There she is, widow – Mrs Updyke – I beg pardon – married woman, and Mrs McBrain,' cried Dunscomb – 'Ned is such an uneasy fellow, he keeps all his friends in a fever with his emotions, and love, and matrimony; and that just suits him, as he has only to administer a pill and set all right again. But, there she is, safe and *unmarried*, thank heaven; which is always a sort of consolation to me. She's back again, and you will do well to keep her, until my nephew, Jack, comes to ask permission to carry her off, for good and all.'

Anna blushed more deeply than ever, while the mother smiled and embraced her child. Then succeeded questions and answers, until Mrs McBrain had heard the whole story of her daughter's intercourse with Mary Monson, so far as it has been made known to the reader. Beyond that, Anna did not think herself authorized to go; or, if she made any revelation, it would be premature for us to repeat it.

'Here we are, all liable to be indicted for felony,' cried Dunscomb, as soon as the young lady had told her tale. 'Timms will be hanged, in place of his client; and we three will have cells at Sing Sing, as accessaries before the act. Yes, my dear bride, you are what the law terms a *particeps criminis*, and may look out for the sheriff before you are a week older.'

'And why all this, Mr Dunscomb?' demanded the half-amused, half-frightened Mrs McBrain.

'For aiding and abetting a prisoner in breaking gaol. Mary Monson is off, beyond a question. She lay down in Sarah's drawing-room, pretending to be wearied, ten minutes since; and has no doubt got through with her nap already, and is on her way to Canada, or Texas, or California, or some other out-of-the-way country; Cuba, for aught I know.'

'Is this so, think you, Anna?'

'I do not, mamma. So far from believing Mary Monson to be flying to any out-of-the-way place, I have no doubt that we shall find her fast asleep on Mr Dunscomb's sofa.'

'*Uncle* Dunscomb's sofa, if you please, young lady.'

'No, sir; I shall call you uncle no longer,' answered Anna, blushing scarlet – 'until – until——'

'You have a legal claim to the use of the word. Well, that will come in due time, I trust; if not, it shall be my care to see you have a title to a still dearer appellation. There, widow – Mrs McBrain, I mean – I think that will do. But, seriously, child, you cannot imagine that Mary Monson means ever to return to her prison, there to be tried for life?'

'If there is faith in woman, she does, sir; else would I not have exposed myself to the risk of accompanying her.'

'In what manner did you come to town, Anna?' asked the anxious mother. 'Are you not now at the mercy of some driver of a hackney-coach, or of some public cabman?'

'I understand that the carriage which was in waiting for us, half a mile from Biberry, is Mrs Monson's——'

'Mrs!' interrupted Dunscomb – 'Is she, then, a married woman?'

Anna looked down, trembled, and was conscious of having betrayed a secret. So very precious to herself had been the communication of Marie Moulin on this point, that it was ever uppermost in her thoughts; and it had now escaped her under an impulse she could not control. It was too late, however, to retreat; and a moment's reflection told her it would every way be better to tell all she knew, on this one point, at least.

This was soon done; for even Marie Moulin's means of information were somewhat limited. This Swiss had formerly known the prisoner by another name; though what name, she would not reveal. This was in Europe, where Marie had actually passed three years in this mysterious person's employment. Marie had even come to America, in consequence of this connection, at the death of her own mother; but, unable to find her former mistress, had taken service with Sarah Wilmeter. Mary Monson was single and unbetrothed when she left Europe. Such was Marie Moulin's statement. But it was understood she was now married; though to whom, she could not say. If Anna Updyke knew more than this, she did not reveal it at that interview.

'Ah! Here is another case of a wife's elopement from her husband,' interrupted Dunscomb, as soon as Anna reached this point in her narration; 'and I dare say something or other will be found in this wretched code to uphold her in her disobedience. You have done well to marry, Mrs McBrain; for, according to the modern opinions in these matters, instead of providing yourself with a lord and master, you have only engaged an upper servant.'

'No true-hearted woman can ever look upon her husband in so degrading a light,' answered the bride, with spirit.

'That will do for three days; but wait to the end of three years. There are runaway wives enough, at this moment, roaming up and down the land, setting the laws of God and man at defiance, and jingling their purses, when they happen to have money, under their lawful husbands' noses: ay, enough to set up a three-tailed bashaw! But this damnable code will uphold them, in some shape or other, my life for it. One can't endure her husband because he smokes; another finds fault with his not going to church but once a day; another quarrels with him for going three times; another says he has too much dinner-company; and another protests she can't get a male friend inside of her house. All these ladies, forgetful as they are of their highest earthly duties, forgetful as they are of woman's very nature, are the models of divine virtues, and lay claim to the sympathies of mankind. They get those of fools; but prudent and reflecting men shake their heads at such wandering *déesses*.'

'You are severe on us women, Mr Dunscomb,' said the bride.

'Not on you, my dear Mrs McBrain – never a syllable on *you*. But, go on, child; I have had the case of one of these vagrant wives in my hands, and know how mistaken has been the disposition to pity her. Men lean to the woman's side; but the frequency of the abuse is beginning to open the eyes of the public. Go on, Anna dear, and let us hear it all – or all you have to tell us.'

Very little remained to be related. Marie Moulin, herself, knew very little of that which had occurred since her separation from her present mistress in France. She did make one statement, however, that Anna had deemed very important; but which she felt bound to keep as a secret in consequence of the injunctions received from the Swiss.

'I should have a good deal to say about this affair,' observed Dunscomb, when his beautiful companion was done, 'did I believe that we shall find Mary Monson on our return to my house. In that case, I should say to you, my dear widow – Mrs McBrain, I mean – the devil take that fellow Ned, he'll have half the women in town bearing his name before he is done. Well, heaven be praised! he can neither marry *me*, nor give me a stepfather, let him do his very best. There's comfort in that consideration, at any rate.'

'You were about to tell us what you would do,' put in the bride, slightly vexed, yet too well assured of the counsellor's attachment to her husband to feel angry – 'you must know how much value we all give to your advice.'

'I was about to say that Anna should not return to this mysterious convict – no, she is not *yet* convicted, but she is indicted, and that is something – but return she should not, were there the least chance of our finding her, on our return home. Let her go, then, and satisfy her curiosity, and pass the night with Sarah, who must be through with her first nap by this time.'

Anna urged her mother to consent to this arrangement, putting forward her engagement with Mary Monson, not to desert her. McBrain driving to the door, from paying his last visit that night, his wife gave her assent to the proposition; the tenderest mother occasionally permitting another and more powerful feeling to usurp the place of maternal care. Mrs McBrain, it must be admitted, thought more of the bridegroom, sixty as he was, than of her charming daughter; nor was she yet quite free from the awkwardness that ever accompanies a new connection of this nature when there are grown-up children; more especially on the part of the female. Then Anna had communicated to her mother a most material circumstance, which it does not suit our present purpose to reveal.

'Now for a dozen pair of gloves that we do not find Mary Monson,' said the lawyer, as he walked smartly towards his own residence, with Anna Updyke under his arm.

'Done!' cried the young lady – 'and you shall *pay* if you lose.'

'As bound in honour. Peter' – the grey-headed black who answered the summons to the door – 'will be glad enough to see us; for the old fellow is not accustomed to let his young rogue of a master in at midnight, with a charming young woman under his arm.'

Anna Updyke was right. Mary Monson was in a deep sleep on the sofa. So profound was her rest, there was a hesitation about disturbing her; though twelve, the hour set for the return of the carriage to Biberry, was near. For a few minutes Dunscomb conversed with his agreeable companion, in his own library.

'If Jack knew of your being in the house, he would never forgive my not having him called.'

'I shall have plenty of occasions for seeing Jack,' returned the young lady, colouring. 'You know how assiduous he is in this cause, and how devoted he is to the prisoner.'

'Do not run away with any such notion, child; Jack is yours, heart and soul.'

'Hist! – there is the carriage; Mary must be called.'

Away went Anna, laughing, blushing, but with tears in her eyes. In a minute Mary Monson made her appearance, somewhat refreshed and calmed by her short nap.

'Make no excuse for waking me, Anna,' said this unaccountable woman. 'We can both sleep on the road. The carriage is as easy as a cradle; and, luckily, the roads are quite good.'

'Still they lead to a prison, Mrs Monson!'

The prisoner smiled, and seemed to be lost in thought. It was the first time any of her new acquaintances had ever addressed her as a married woman; though Marie Moulin, with the exception of her first exclamation at their recent meeting, had invariably used the appellation of Madame. All this, however, was soon forgotten in the leave-taking. Dunscomb thought he had seldom seem a female of higher tone of manners, or greater personal charms than this singular and mysterious young woman appeared to be, as she curtsied her adieu.

CHAPTER XVII

What then avail impeachments, or the law's
Severest condemnation, while the queen
May snatch him from the uplifted hand of justice?

Earl of Essex.

Perhaps the most certain proof that any people can give of a high moral condition is in the administration of justice. Absolute infallibility is unattainable to men; but there are wide chasms in right and wrong, between the legal justice of one state of society and that of another. As the descendants of Englishmen, we in this country are apt to ascribe a higher tone of purity to the courts of the mother country than to those of any other European nation. In this we may be right, without inferring the necessity of believing that even the ermine of England is spotless; for it can never be forgotten that Bacon and Jeffreys once filled her highest judicial seats, to say nothing of many others, whose abuses of their trusts have doubtless been lost in their comparative obscurity. Passing from the parent to its offspring, the condition of American justice, so far as it is dependent on the bench, is a profound moral anomaly. It would seem that every known expedient of man has been resorted to, to render it corrupt, feeble, and ignorant; yet he would be a hardy, not to say an audacious commentator, who should presume to affirm that it is not entitled to stand in the very foremost ranks of human integrity.

Ill paid, without retiring pensions, with nothing to expect in the way of family and hereditary honours and dignities; with little, in short, either in possession or in prospect, to give any particular inducement to be honest, it is certain that, as a whole, the judges of this great republic may lay claim to be classed among the most upright of which history furnishes any account. Unhappily, popular caprice, and popular ignorance, have been brought to bear on the selection of the magistrates, of late; and it is easy to predict the result, which, like that on the militia, is soon to pull down even this all-important machinery of society to the level of the common mind.

Not only have the obvious and well-earned inducements to keep men honest – competence, honours, and security in office – been recklessly thrown away by the open hand of popular delusion, but all the minor expedients by which those who cannot think might be made to feel, have been laid aside, leaving the machinery of justice as naked as the hand. Although the colonial system was never elaborated in these last particulars, there were some of its useful and respectable remains, down as late as the commencement of the present century. The sheriff appeared with his sword, the judge was escorted to and from the court-house to his private dwelling with some show of attention and respect, leaving a salutary impression of authority on the ordinary observer. All this has disappeared. The judge slips into the county town almost unknown; lives at an inn amid a crowd of lawyers, witnesses, suitors, jurors and horse-shedders, as Timms calls them; finds his way to the bench as best he may; and seems to think that the more work he can do in the shortest time is the one great purpose of his appointment. Nevertheless, these men, as *yet*, are surprisingly incorrupt and intelligent. How long it will remain so, no one can predict; if it be for a human life, however, the working of the problem will demonstrate the fallibility of every appreciation of human motives. One bad consequence of the depreciation of the office of a magistrate, however, has long been apparent, in the lessening of the influence of the judge on the juries; the power that alone renders the latter institution even tolerable. This is putting an irresponsible, usually an ignorant, and often a corrupt arbiter in the judgment-seat, in lieu of the man of high qualities for which it was alone intended.

The circuit and Oyer and Terminer for Duke's presented nothing novel in its bench, its bar, its jurors, and we might add its witnesses. The first was a cool-headed, dispassionate man, with a very respectable amount of legal learning and experience, and a perfectly fair character. No one suspected him of acting wrong from evil motives; and when he did err, it was ordinarily from the pressure of business; though, occasionally, he was mistaken, because the books could not foresee every possible phase of a case. The bar was composed of plain, hard-working men, materially above the level of Timms, except in connection with mother-wit; better educated, better mannered, and, as a whole, of materially higher origin; though, as a body, neither profoundly learned nor of very refined deportment. Nevertheless, these persons had a very fair portion of all the better qualities of the northern professional men. They were shrewd, quick in the application of their acquired knowledge, ready in their natural resources, and had that general aptitude for affairs that probably is the fruit of a practice that includes all the different branches of the profession. Here and there was a usurer and extortioner among them; a fellow who disgraced his calling by running up unnecessary bills of cost, by evading the penal statutes passed to prevent abuses of this nature, and by cunning attempts to obtain more for the use of his money than the law sanctioned. But such was not the general character of the Duke's county bar, which was rather to be censured for winking at irregular proceedings out of doors, for brow-beating witnesses, and for regarding the end so intensely as not always to be particular in reference to the means, than for such gross and positively illegal and oppressive measures as those just mentioned. As for the jurors, they were just what that ancient institution might be supposed to be, in a country where so many of the body of the people are liable to be summoned. An unusually large proportion of these men, when all the circumstances are considered, were perhaps as fit to be thus employed as could be obtained from the body of the community of any country on earth; but a very serious number were altogether unsuited to perform the delicate duties of their station. Fortunately, the ignorant are very apt to be influenced by the more intelligent, in cases of this nature; and by this exercise of a very natural power, less injustice is committed than might otherwise occur. Here, however, is the opening for the 'horse-shedding' and 'pillowing,' of which Timms has spoken, and of which so much use is made around every country court-house in the state. This is the crying evil of the times; and, taken in connection with the enormous abuse which is rendering a competition in news a regular, money-getting occupation, one that threatens to set at defiance all laws, principles, and facts.

A word remains to be said of the witnesses. Perhaps the rarest thing connected with the administration of justice all over the world, is an intelligent, perfectly impartial, clear-headed, discriminating witness; one who distinctly knows all he says, fully appreciates the effect of his words on the jury, and who has the disposition to submit what he knows solely to the law and the evidence. Men of experience are of opinion that an oath usually extracts the truth. We think so too; but it is truth as the witness understands it; facts as he has seen them; and opinions that, unconsciously to himself, have been warped by reports, sneers and malice. In a country of popular sway like this, there is not one man in a thousand, probably, who has sufficient independence of mind, or sufficient moral courage, to fancy he has seen even a fact, if it be of importance, differently from what the body of the community has seen it; and nothing is more common than to find witnesses colouring their testimony, lessening its force by feeble statements, or altogether abandoning the truth, under this pressure from without, in cases of a nature and magnitude to awake a strong popular feeling. It is by no means uncommon, indeed, to persuade one class of men, by means of this influence, that they did not see that which actually occurred before their eyes, or that they did see that which never had an existence.

Under no circumstances do men congregate with less meritorious motives than in meeting in and around a court of justice. The object is victory, and the means of obtaining it will not always bear the light. The approaching circuit and Oyer and Terminer of Duke's was no exception to the rule; a crowd of evil passions, of sinister practices, and of plausible pretences, being arrayed against justice and the law, in two-thirds of the causes on the calendar. Then it was that Timms and saucy Williams, or Dick Williams, as he was familiarly termed by his associates, came out in their strength, playing off against each other the out-door practices of the profession. The first indication that the former now got of the very serious character of the struggle that was about to take place between them, was in the extraordinary civility of saucy Williams when they met in the bar-room of the inn they each frequented, and which had long been the arena of their antagonistical wit and practices.

'I never saw you look better, Timms,' said Williams, in the most cordial manner imaginable; 'on the whole, I do not remember to have ever seen you looking so well. You grow younger instead of older, every day of your life. By the way, do you intend to move on Butterfield against Town this circuit?'

'I should be glad to do it, if you are ready. Cross-notices have been given, you know.'

Williams knew this very well; and he also knew that it had been done to entitle the respective parties to costs, in the event of any thing occurring to give either side an advantage; the cause being one of those nuts out of which practitioners are very apt to extract the whole of the kernel before they are done with it.

'Yes, I am aware of that, and I believe we are quite ready. I see that Mr Town is here, and I observe several of his witnesses; but I have so much business, I have no wish to try a long slander cause; words spoken in heat, and never thought of again, but to make a profit of them.'

'You are employed against us in the murder case, I hear?'

'I rather think the friends of the deceased so regard it; but I have scarcely had time to look at the testimony before the coroner' – This was a deliberate mystification, and Timms perfectly understood it as such, well knowing that the other had given the out-door work of the case nearly all of his time for the last fortnight – 'and I don't like to move in one of these big matters without knowing what I am about. Your senior counsel has not yet arrived from town, I believe?'

'He cannot be here until Wednesday, having to argue a great insurance case before the Superior Court to-day and to-morrow.'

This conversation occurred after the grand jury had been charged, the petit jurors sworn, and the judge had heard several motions for correcting the calendar, laying causes over, &c. Two hours later, the District Attorney being absent in his room, engaged with the grand jury, Williams arose and addressed the court, which had just called the first civil cause on the calendar.

'May it please the court,' he said, coolly, but with the grave aspect of a man who felt he was dealing with a very serious matter – 'there is a capital indictment depending, a case of arson and murder, which it is the intention of the State to call on at once.'

The judge looked still more grave than the counsel, and it was easy to see that he deeply regretted it should fall to his lot to try such an issue.

He leaned forward, with an elbow on the very primitive sort of desk with which he was furnished by the public, indented it with the point of his knife, and appeared to be passing in review such of the circumstances of this important case as he had become acquainted with, judicially. We say 'judicially;' for it is not an easy thing for either judge, counsel, or jurors, in the state of society that now exists, to keep distinctly in their minds that which has been obtained under legal evidence, from that which floats about the community on the thousand tongues of rumour – fact from fiction. Nevertheless, the respectable magistrate whose misfortune it was to preside on this very serious occasion, was a man to perform all his duty to the point where public opinion or popular clamour is encountered. The last is a bug-bear that few have moral courage to face; and the evil consequences are visible, hourly, daily, almost incessantly, in most of the interests of life. This popular feeling is the great moving lever of the republic; the wronged being placed beneath the fulcrum, while the outer arm of the engine is loaded with numbers. Thus it is that we see the oldest families among us quietly robbed of their estates, after generations of possession; the honest man proscribed; the knave and demagogue deified; mediocrity advanced to high places; and talents and capacity held in abeyance, if not actually trampled under foot. Let the truth be said: these are evils to which each year gives additional force, until the tyranny of the majority has taken a form and combination which, unchecked, must speedily place every personal right at the mercy of plausible, but wrong-doing, popular combinations.

'Has the prisoner been arraigned?' asked the judge. 'I remember nothing of the sort.'

'No, your honour,' answered Timms, now rising for the first time in the discussion, and looking about him as if to scan the crowd for witnesses. 'The prosecution does not yet know the plea we shall put in.'

'You are retained for the prisoner, Mr Timms?'

'Yes, sir, I appear in her behalf. But Mr Dunscomb is also retained, and will be engaged in the New York Superior Court until Wednesday, in an insurance case of great magnitude.'

'No insurance case can be of the magnitude of a trial for life,' returned Williams. 'The justice of the State must be vindicated, and the person of the citizen protected.'

This sounded well, and it caused many a head in the crowd, which contained both witnesses and jurors, to nod with approbation. It is true, that every thoughtful and observant man must have had many occasions to observe how fallacious such a declaration is, in truth; but it sounded well, and the ears of the multitude are always open to flattery.

'We have no wish to interfere with the justice of the State, or with the protection of the citizen,' answered Timms, looking round to note the effect of his words – 'our object is to defend the innocent; and the great and powerful community of New York will find more pleasure in seeing an accused acquitted than in seeing fifty criminals condemned.'

This sentiment sounded quite as well as that of Williams's, and heads were again nodded in approbation. It told particularly well in a paragraph of a newspaper that Timms had engaged to publish what he considered his best remarks.

'It seems to me, gentlemen,' interposed the judge, who understood the meaning of these *ad captandum* remarks perfectly well, 'that your conversation is premature, at least, if not altogether improper. Nothing of this nature should be said until the prisoner has been arraigned.'

'I submit, your honour, and acknowledge the justice of the reproof,' answered Williams. 'I now move the court on behalf of the District Attorney, that Mary Monson, who stands indicted for murder and arson, *be* arraigned, and her pleas entered——'

'I could wish this step might be delayed until I can hear from the leading counsel for the defence,' objected Timms, 'which must now occur in the course of a very few hours.'

'I perceive that the prisoner is a female,' said the judge, in a tone of regret.

'Yes, your honour; she is, and young and handsome, they tell me,' answered Williams; 'for I have never been able to get a sight of her. She is too much of a great lady to be seen at a grate, by all I can learn of her and her proceedings. Plays on the harp, sir; has a French *valet de chambre*, or something of that sort——'

'This is all wrong, Mr Williams, and must be checked,' again interposed the judge, though very mildly; for, while his experience taught him that the object of such remarks was to create prejudice, and his conscience prompted him to put an end to a proceeding so unrighteous, he stood in so much awe of this particular counsel, who had half-a-dozen presses at his command, that it required a strong inducement to bring him out as he ought to be, in opposition to any of his more decided movements. As for the community, with the best intentions as a whole, it stood passive under this gross wrong. What 'is everybody's business' is literally 'nobody's business,' when the public virtue is the great moving power; the upright preferring their ease to everything else, and the ill-disposed manifesting the ceaseless activity of the wicked. All the ancient barriers to this species of injustice, which have been erected by the gathered wisdom of our fathers and the experience of ages, have been thrown down by the illusions of a seeming liberty, and the whole machinery of justice is left very much at the mercy of an outside public opinion, which, in itself, is wielded by a few of the worst men in the country. These are sober truths, as a close examination will show to any one who may choose to enter into the investigation of the ungrateful subject. It is not what is *said*, we very well know; but it is what is *done*.

Williams received the mild rebuke of the judge like one who felt his position; paying very little respect to its spirit or its letter. He knew his own power, and understood perfectly well that this particular magistrate was soon to run for a new term of office, and might be dealt with more freely on that account.

'I know it is very wrong, your honour — very wrong,' — rejoined the wily counsel to what had been said — 'so wrong, that I regard it as an insult to the State. When a person is capitally indicted, man or woman, it is his or her bounden duty to put all aboveboard, that there may be no secrets. The harp was once a sacred instrument, and it is highly improper to introduce it into our gaols and criminals' cells———'

'There is no criminal as yet — no crime can be established without proof, and the verdict of twelve good men and true,' interrupted Timms — 'I object, therefore, to the learned counsel's remarks, and———'

'Gentlemen, gentlemen,' put in the judge, a little more pointedly than in his former rebuke — 'this is all wrong, I repeat.'

'You perceive, my brother Timms,' rejoined the indomitable Williams, 'the court is altogether against you. This is not a country of lords and ladies, fiddles and harps, but of the *people*; and when the people find a bill for a capital offence, capital care should be taken not to give more offence.'

Williams had provided himself with a set of supporters that are common enough in the courts, whose business it was to grin, and sneer, and smile, and look knowing at particular hits of the counsel, and otherwise to back up his wit, and humour, and logic, by the agency of sympathy. This expedient is getting to be quite common, and is constantly practised in suits that relate, in any manner, to politics or political men. It is not so common, certainly, in trials for life; though it may be, and has been, used with effect, even on such serious occasions. The influence of these wily demonstrations, which are made to have the appearance of public opinion, is very great on the credulous and ignorant; men thus narrowly gifted invariably looking around them to find support in the common mind.

The hits of Williams told, to Timms's great annoyance; nor did he know exactly how to parry them. Had he been the assailant himself, he could have wielded the weapons of his antagonist with equal skill; but his dexterity was very much confined to the offensive in cases of this nature; for he perfectly comprehended all the prejudices on which it was necessary to act, while he possessed but a very narrow knowledge of the means of correcting them. Nevertheless, it would not do to let the prosecution close the business of the day with so much of the air of triumph, and the indomitable attorney made another effort to place his client more favourably before the public eye.

'The harp is a most religious instrument,' he coolly observed, 'and it has no relation to the violin, or any light and frivolous piece of music. David used it as the instrument of praise, and why should not a person who stands charged ——'

'I have told you, gentlemen, that all this is irregular, and cannot be permitted,' cried the judge, with a little more of the appearance of firmness than he had yet exhibited.

The truth was, that he stood less in fear of Timms than of Williams; the connection of the last with the reporters being known to be much the most extensive. But Timms knew his man, and understood very well what the committal of counsel had got to be, under the loose notions of liberty that have grown up in the country within the last twenty years. Time was, and that at no remote period, when the lawyer who had been thus treated for indecorum at the bar would have been a disgraced man, and would have appealed in vain to the community for sympathy; little or none would he have received. Men then understood that the law was their master, established by themselves, and was to be respected accordingly. But that feeling is in a great measure extinct. Liberty is every hour getting to be more and more personal; its concentration consisting in rendering every man his own legislator, his own judge, and his own juror. It is monarchical and aristocratic, and all that is vile and dangerous, to see power exercised by any but the people; those whom the constitution and the laws have set apart expressly to discharge a delegated authority being obliged, by clamours sustained by all the arts of cupidity and fraud, to defer to the passing opinions of the hour. No one knew this better than Timms, who had just as lively a recollection as his opponent that this very judge was to come before the people, in the next autumn, as a candidate for re-election. The great strain of American foresight was consequently applied to this man's conscience, who, over-worked and under-paid, was expected to rise above the weaknesses of humanity, as a sort of sublimated political theory that is getting to be much in fashion, and which, *if true*, would supersede the necessity of any court or any government at all. Timms knew this well, and was not to be restrained by one who was thus stretched, as it might be, on the tenter-hooks of political uncertainty.

'Yes, your honour,' retorted this indomitable individual, 'I am fully aware of its impropriety, and was just as much so when the counsel for the prosecution was carrying it on to the injury of my client; I might say almost unchecked, if not encouraged.'

'The court did its best to stop Mr Williams, sir; and must do the same to keep you within the proper limits of practice. Unless these improprieties are restrained, I shall confine the counsel for the State to the regular officer, and assign new counsel to the accused, as from the court.'

Both Williams and Timms looked amused at this menace, neither having the smallest notion the judge dare put such a threat in execution. What! presume to curb licentiousness when it chose to assume the aspect of human rights? This was an act behind the age, more especially in a country in which liberty is so fast getting to be all means, with so very little regard to the end.

A desultory conversation ensued, when it was finally settled that the trial must be postponed until the arrival of the counsel expected from town. From the beginning of the discussion, Williams knew such must be the termination of that day's work; but he had accomplished two great objects by his motion. In the first place, by conceding delay to the accused, it placed the prosecution on ground where a similar favour might be asked, should it be deemed expedient. This resisting of motions for delay is a common *ruse* of the bar, since it places the party whose rights are seemingly postponed in a situation to demand a similar concession. Williams knew that his case was ready as related to his brief, the testimony, and all that could properly be produced in court; but he thought it might be strengthened out of doors, among the jurors and the witnesses. We say, the witnesses; because even this class of men get their impressions, quite frequently, as much from what they subsequently hear, as from what they have seen and know. A good reliable witness, who relates no more than he actually knows, conceals nothing, colours nothing, and leaves a perfectly fair impression of the truth, is perhaps the rarest of all the parties concerned in the administration of justice. No one understood this better than Williams; and his agents were, at that very moment, actively employed in endeavouring to persuade certain individuals that they knew a great deal more of the facts connected with the murders, than the truth would justify. This was not done openly or directly; not in a way to alarm the consciences or pride of those who were to be duped, but by the agency of hints, and suggestions, and plausible reasonings, and all the other obvious devices, by means of which the artful and unprincipled are enabled to act on the opinions of the credulous and inexperienced.

While all these secret engines were at work in the streets of Biberry, the external machinery of justice was set in motion with the usual forms. Naked, but business-like, the blind goddess was invoked with what is termed 'republican simplicity,' one of the great principles of which, in some men's estimation, is to get the maximum of work at the minimum of cost. We are no advocates for the senseless parade and ruthless expenditure – ruthless, because extracted from the means of the poor –

with which the governments of the old world have invested their dignity; and we believe that the reason of men may be confided in, in managing these matters, to a certain extent; though not to the extent that it would seem to be the fashion of the American theories, to be desirable. Wigs of all kinds, even when there is a deficiency of hair, we hold in utter detestation; and we shall maintain that no more absurd scheme of clothing the human countenance with terror was ever devised, than to clothe it with flax. Nevertheless, as comfort, decency and taste unite in recommending clothing of some sort or other, we do not see why the judicial functionary should not have his appropriate attire as well as the soldier, the sailor, or the priest. It does not necessarily follow that extravagances are to be imitated if we submit to this practice; though we incline to the opinion that a great deal of the nakedness of 'republican simplicity,' which has got to be a sort of political idol in the land, has its origin in a spirit that denounces the past as a species of moral sacrifice to the present time.

Let all this be as it may, it is quite certain that 'republican simplicity' — the slang lever by means of which the artful move the government — has left the administration of justice among us, so far as externals are concerned, as naked as may be. Indeed, so much have the judges become exposed to sinister influences, by means of the intimacies with which they are invested by means of 'republican simplicity,' that it has been found expedient to make a special provision against undue modes of approaching their ears, all of which would have been far more efficiently secured by doubling their salaries, making a respectable provision for old age in the way of pensions, and surrounding them with such forms as would keep the evil-disposed at a reasonable distance. Neither Timms nor 'saucy Williams,' however, reasoned in this fashion. They were, in a high degree, practical men, and saw things as they are; not as they ought to be. Little was either troubled with theories, regrets, or principles. It was enough for each that he was familiar with the workings of the system under which he lived; and which he knew how to pervert in a way the most likely to effect his own purposes.

The reader may be surprised at the active pertinacity with which Williams pursued one on trial for her life; a class of persons with whom the bar usually professes to deal tenderly and in mercy. But the fact was that he had been specially retained by the next of kin, who had large expectations from the abstracted hoards of his aunt; and that the fashion of the day had enabled him to achieve such a *cent per cent* bargain with his client, as caused his own compensation altogether to depend on the measure of his success. Should Mary Monson be sentenced to the gallows, it was highly probable her revelations would put the wronged in the way of being righted, when this limb of the law would, in all probability, come in for a full share of the recovered gold. How different all this was from the motives and conduct of Dunscomb, the reader will readily perceive; for, while the profession in this country abounds with Williams's and Timms's, men of the highest tone of feeling, the fairest practice, and the clearest perceptions of what is right, are by no means strangers to the bar.

CHAPTER XVIII

Thou hast already racked me with thy stay;
Therefore require me not to ask thee twice:
Reply at once to all. What is concluded?

Mourning Bride.

During the interval between the occurrence of the scene in court that has just been related, and the appearance of Dunscomb at Biberry, the community was rapidly taking sides on the subject of the guilt or innocence of Mary Monson. The windows of the gaol were crowded all day; throngs collecting there to catch glimpses of the extraordinary female who was rightly enough reported to be living in a species of luxury in so unusual a place, and who was known to play on an instrument that the popular mind was a good deal disposed to regard as sacred. As a matter of course, a hundred stories were in circulation touching the character, history, sayings and doings of this remarkable person, that had no foundation whatever in truth; for it is an infirmity of human nature to circulate and place its belief in falsehoods of this sort; and more especially of human nature as it is exhibited in a country where care has been taken to stimulate the curiosity of the vulgar, without exactly placing them in a condition to appease its longings, either intelligently or in a very good taste.

This interest would have been manifested, in such a case, had there been no particular moving cause; but the secret practices of Williams and Timms greatly increased its intensity, and was bringing the population of Duke's to a state of excitement that was very little favourable to an impartial administration of justice. Discussions had taken place at every corner, and in all the bar-rooms; and many were the alleged facts connected with the murders, which had their sole existence in rumour, that was adduced in the heat of argument, or to make out a suppositious case. All this time Williams was either in court, attending closely to his different causes, or was seen passing between the court-house and the tavern with bundles of papers under his arms, like a man absorbed in business. Timms played a very similar part, though *he* found leisure to hold divers conferences with several of his confidential agents. Testimony was his aim; and, half a dozen times, when he fancied himself on the point of establishing something new and important, the whole of the ingenious fabric he had reared came tumbling about his ears, in consequence of some radical defect in the foundation.

Such was the state of things on the evening of Wednesday, the day preceding that which had been set down for the trial, when the stage arrived bringing "Squire Dunscomb,' his carpet-bags, his trunk, and his books. McBrain shortly after drove up in his own carriage, and Anna was soon in her mother's arms. The excitement so general in the place had naturally enough extended to these females, and Mrs McBrain and her daughter were soon closeted, talking over the affair of Mary Monson.

About eight that evening Dunscomb and Timms were busy looking over minutes of testimony, briefs, and other written documents that were connected with the approaching trial. Mrs Horton had reserved the best room in her house for this distinguished counsel; an apartment in a wing that was a good deal removed from the noise and bustle of a leading inn during a circuit. Here Dunscomb had been duly installed, and here he early set up 'his traps,' as he termed his flesh-brushes, sponges, briefs, and calfskin-covered volumes. Two tallow candles threw a dim, lawyer-like light on the scene; while unrolled paper-curtains shut out as much of night as such an imperfect screen could exclude. The odour of cigars – excellent Havannas, by the way – was fragrant in the place; and one of the little fountains of smoke was stuck knowingly in a corner of the eminent counsel's mouth, while Timms had garnished his skinny lips with the short stump of a pipe. Neither said anything; one of the parties presenting documents that the other read in silence. Such was the state of matters when a slight tap at the door was succeeded by the unexpected appearance of 'saucy Williams.' Timms started, gathered together all his papers with the utmost care, and awaited the explanation of this unlooked-for visit with the most lively curiosity. Dunscomb, on the other hand, received his guest with urbanity, and like one who felt that the wrangling of the bar, in which, by the way, he had too much self-respect and good-temper to indulge, had no necessary connection with the courtesies of private life.

Williams had scarcely a claim superior to those of Timms, to be considered a gentleman; though he had the advantage of having been what is termed liberally educated – a phrase of very doubtful import, when put to the test of old-fashioned notions on such subjects. In manners, he had the defects, and we may add the merits, of the school in which he had been educated. All that has been said of Timms on this subject, in the way of censure, was equally applicable to Williams; but the last possessed a self-command, an admirable reliance on his own qualities, which would have fitted him, as regards this one quality, to be an emperor. Foreigners wonder at the self-possession of Americans in the presence of the great; and it is really one of the merits of the institutions that it causes every person to feel that he is a man, and entitled to receive the treatment due to a being so high in the scale of earthly creations. It is true, that this feeling often degenerates into a vulgar and over-sensitive jealousy, frequently rendering its possessor exacting and ridiculous; but, on the whole, the effect is manly, not to say ennobling.

Now, Williams was self-possessed by nature, as well as by association and education. Though keenly alive to the differences and chances of fortune, he never succumbed to mere rank and wealth. Intriguing by disposition, not to say by education, he could affect a deference he did not feel; but, apart from the positive consequences of power, he was not to be daunted by the presence of the most magnificent sovereign who ever reigned. No wonder, then, that he felt quite at home in the company of his present host; though fully aware that he was one of the leading members of the New York bar. As a proof of this independence may be cited the fact that he had no sooner paid his salutations and been invited to be seated, than he deliberately selected a cigar from the open box of Dunscomb, lighted it, took a chair, raised one leg coolly on the corner of a table, and began to smoke.

'The calendar is a little crowded,' observed this free-and-easy visitor, 'and is likely to carry us over into the middle of next week. Are you retained in Daniels against Fireman's Insurance?'

'I am not – a brief was offered by the plaintiff, but I declined taking it.'

'A little conscientious, I suppose. Well, I leave all the sin of my suits on the shoulders of my clients. It is bad enough to *listen* to their griefs, without being called on to *smart* for them. I have heard you are in Cogswell against Davidson?'

'In that cause I have been retained. I may as well say, at once, we intend to move it on.'

'It's of no great moment – if you beat us at the circuit, our turn will come on execution.'

'I believe, Mr Williams, your clients have a knack at gaining the day in that mode. It is of no great interest to me, however, as I rarely take the management of a cause after it quits the courts.'

'How do you like the code, brother Dunscomb?'

'Damnable, sir. I am too old, in the first place, to like change. Then change from bad to worse is adding folly to imbecility. The Common Law practice had its faults, I allow; but this new system has no merits.'

'I do not go as far as that, and I rather begin to like the new plan of remuneration. We are nothing out of pocket, and sometimes are a handsome sum in. You defend Mary Monson?'

Timms felt assured that his old antagonist had now reached the case that had really brought him to the room. He fidgeted, looked eagerly round to see that no stray paper could fall beneath the hawk-like eye of the other party, and then sat in comparative composure, waiting the result.

'I do,' Dunscomb quietly replied; 'and I shall do it *con amore* – I suppose you know what that means, Mr Williams?'

A sarcastic smile passed over the steeled countenance of the other, his appearance being literally sardonic for an instant.

'I presume I do. We know enough Latin in Duke's to get along with such a quotation; though our friend Timms here despises the classics. "Con amore" means, in this instance, a "lover's zeal," I suppose; for they tell me that all who approach the criminal submit to her power to charm.'

'The *accused*, if you please,' put in the opposing attorney; 'but no *criminal*, until the word "*guilty*" has been pronounced.'

'I am convicted. They say you are to be the happy man, Timms, in the event of an acquittal. It is reported all over the county that you are to become Mr Monson as a reward for your services; and if half that I hear be true, you will deserve her, with a good estate in the bargain.'

Here Williams laughed heartily at his own wit; but Dunscomb looked grave, while his associate counsel looked angry. In point of fact the nail had been hit on the head; and consciousness lighted the spirit within, with its calm, mild glow. The senior counsel was too proud and too dignified to make any reply; but Timms was troubled with no such feeling.

'If there are any such rumours in old Duke's,' retorted the last, 'it will not need mesmerism to discover their author. In my opinion, the people ought to carry on their suits in a spirit of liberality and justice; and not in vindictive, malicious temper.'

'We are all of the same way of thinking,' answered Williams with a sneer. 'I consider it liberal to give you a handsome young woman with a full purse; though no one can say how, or by whom, it has been filled. By the way, Mr Dunscomb, I am instructed to make a proposal to you; and as Timms is in the court, this may be as good a moment as another to present it for consideration. My offer is from the nephew, next of kin, and sole heir of the late Peter Goodwin; by whom, as you probably know, I am retained. This gentleman is well assured that his deceased relatives had a large sum in gold by them, at the time of the murder——'

'No verdict has yet shown that there has been any murders at all,' interrupted Timms.

'We have the verdict of the inquest, begging your pardon, brother Timms – that is something, surely: though not enough, quite likely, to convince your mind. But, to proceed with my proposition: – My client is well assured that such a secret fund existed. He also knows that *your* client, gentlemen, is flush of money, and money in gold coins that correspond with many pieces that have been seen by different individuals in the possession of our aunt――'

'Ay, eagles and half-eagles,' interrupted Timms – 'a resemblance that comes from the stamp of the mint.'

'Go on with your proposition Mr Williams,' – said Dunscomb.

'We offer to withdraw all our extra counsel, myself included, and to leave the case altogether with the State, which is very much the same thing as an acquittal; provided you will *return* to us five thousand dollars in this gold coin. Not *pay*, for that might be compounding a felony; but *return.*'

'There could be no compounding a felony, if the indictment be not quashed, but traversed,' said the senior counsel for the defence.

'Very true; but we prefer the word "return." That leaves everything clear, and will enable us to face the county. Our object is to get our *rights* – let the State take care of its justice for itself.'

'You can hardly expect that such a proposition should be accepted, Williams?'

'I am not so sure of that, Timms; life is sweeter than money even. I should like to hear the answer of your associate, however. You, I can see, have no intention of lessening the marriage portion, if it can be helped.'

Such side-hits were so common in court, as between these worthies, that neither thought much of them out of court. But Williams gave a signal proof of the acuteness of his observation, when he expressed a wish to know in what light his proposal was viewed by Dunscomb. That learned gentleman evidently paid more respect to the offer than had been manifested by his associate; and now sat silently ruminating on its nature. Thus directly appealed to, he felt the necessity of giving some sort of an answer.

'You have come expressly to make this proposition to us, Mr Williams?' Dunscomb demanded.

'To be frank with you, sir, such is the main object of my visit.'

'Of course it is sanctioned by your client, and you speak by authority?'

'It is fully sanctioned by my client, who would greatly prefer the plan; and I act directly by his written instructions. Nothing short of these would induce me to make the proposition.'

'Very well, sir. Will an answer by ten o'clock this evening meet your views?'

'Perfectly so. An answer at any time between this and the sitting of the court to-morrow morning, will fully meet our views. The terms, however, cannot be diminished. Owing to the shortness of the time, it may be well to understand *that.*'

'Then, Mr Williams, I ask a little time for reflection and consultation. We may meet again to-night.'

The other assented, rose, coolly helped himself to another cigar, and had got as far as the door, when an expressive gesture from Timms induced him to pause.

'Let us understand each other,' said the last, with emphasis. 'Is this a truce, with a complete cessation of hostilities; or is it only a negotiation to be carried on in the midst of war?'

'I hardly comprehend your meaning, Mr Timms. The question is simply one of taking certain forces – allied forces they may be called – from the field, and leaving you to contend only with the main enemy. There need be nothing said of a truce, since nothing further can be done until the court opens.'

'That may do very well, Williams, for those that haven't practised in Duke's as long as myself; but it will not do for me. There is an army of reporters here, at this moment; and I am afraid that the allies of whom you speak have whole corps of skirmishers.'

Williams maintained a countenance so unmoved that even the judicious Timms was a little shaken; while Dunscomb, who had all the reluctance of a gentleman to believe in an act of meanness, felt outraged by his associate's suspicions.

'Come, come, Mr Timms,' the last exclaimed, 'I beg we may have no more of this. Mr Williams has come with a proposition worthy of our consideration; let us meet it in the spirit in which it is offered.'

'Yes,' repeated Williams, with a look that might well have explained his *sobriquet* of 'saucy;' 'yes, in the spirit in which it is offered. What do you say to that, Timms?'

'That I shall manage the defence precisely as if no such proposition had been made, or any negotiation accepted. You can do the same for the prosecution.'

'Agreed!' Williams rejoined, making a sweeping gesture with his hand, and immediately quitting the room.

Dunscomb was silent for a minute. A thread of smoke arose from the end of his cigar; but the volume no longer poured from between his lips. He was ruminating too intensely even to smoke. Rising suddenly, he took his hat, and motioned towards the door.

'Timms, we must go to the gaol,' he said; 'Mary Monson must be spoken to at once.'

'If Williams had made his proposition ten days ago, there might be some use in listening to it,' returned the junior, following the senior counsel from the room, carrying all the papers in the cause under an arm; 'but, now that all the mischief is done, it would be throwing away five thousand dollars to listen to his proposition.'

'We will see – we will see,' answered the other, hurrying down stairs – 'what means the rumpus in that room, Timms? Mrs Horton has not treated me well, to place a troublesome neighbour so near me. I shall stop and tell her as much, as we go through the hall.'

'You had better not, 'squire. We want all our friends just now; and a sharp word might cause us to lose this woman, who has a devil of a tongue. She tells me that a crazy man was brought here privately; and, being well paid for it, she has consented to give him what she calls her "drunkard's parlour," until the court has settled his affair. His room, like your own, is so much out of the way, that the poor fellow gives very little trouble to the great body of the boarders.'

'Ay, very little trouble to *you*, and the rest of you, in the main building; but a great deal to me. I shall speak to Mrs Horton on the subject, as we pass out.'

'Better not, 'squire. The woman is our friend now, I know; but a warm word may turn her to the right-about.'

It is probable Dunscomb was influenced by his companion; for he left the house without putting his threat in execution. In a few minutes he and Timms were at the gaol. As counsel could not well be refused admission to their client on the eve of trial, the two lawyers were admitted to the gallery within the outer door that has been so often mentioned. Of course, Mary Monson was notified of the visit; and she received them with Anna Updyke, the good, gentle, considerate Anna, who was ever disposed to help the weak and to console the unhappy at her side. Dunscomb had no notion that the intimacy had grown to this head; but when he came to reflect that one of the parties was to be tried for her life next day, he was disposed to overlook the manifest indiscretion of his old favourite in being in such a place. Mrs McBrain's presence released him from all responsibility; and he returned the warm pressure of Anna's hand in kindness, if not with positive approbation. As for the girl herself, the very sight of 'Uncle Tom,' as she had so long been accustomed to call the counsellor, cheered her heart, and raised new hopes in behalf of her friend.

In a few clear, pointed words, Dunscomb let the motive of his visit be known. There was little time to throw away, and he went directly at his object, stating everything succinctly, but in the most intelligible manner. Nothing could have been more calm than the manner in which Mary Monson listened to his statement; her deportment being as steady as that of one sitting in judgment herself, rather than that of a person whose own fate was involved in the issue.

'It is a large sum to raise in so short a time,' continued the kind-hearted Dunscomb; 'but I deem the proposition so important to your interest, that, rather than lose this advantage, I would not hesitate about advancing the money myself, should you be unprepared for so heavy a demand.'

'As respects the money, Mr Dunscomb,' returned the fair prisoner, in the most easy and natural manner, '*that* need give us no concern. By sending a confidential messenger to town – Mr John Wilmeter, for instance' – here Anna pressed less closely to her friend's side – 'it would be very easy to have five hundred eagles or a thousand half-eagles here, by breakfast-time to-morrow. It is not on account of any such difficulty that I hesitate a moment. What I dislike is the injustice of the thing, I have never touched a cent of poor Mrs Goodwin's hoard; and it would be false to admit that I am *returning* that which I never received.'

'We must not be particular, ma'am, on immaterial points, when there is so much at stake.'

'It may be immaterial whether I pay money under one form or another, Mr Dunscomb; but it cannot be immaterial to my future standing, whether I am acquitted in the teeth of this Mr William's opposition, or under favour of his purchase.'

'Acquitted! Our case is not absolutely clear, Miss Monson – it is my duty to tell you as much!'

'I understand such to be the opinion of both Mr Timms and yourself, sir; I like the candour of your conduct, but am not converted to your way of thinking. I shall be acquitted, gentlemen – yes, honourably, triumphantly acquitted; and I cannot consent to lessen the impression of such a termination to my affair, by putting myself in the way of being even suspected of a collusion with a man like this saucy Williams. It is far better to meet him openly, and to defy him to do his worst. Perhaps some such trial, followed by complete success, will be necessary to my future happiness.'

Anna now pressed nearer to the side of her friend; passing an arm, unconsciously to herself, around her waist. As for Dunscomb, he gazed at the handsome prisoner in a sort of stupefied wonder. The place, the hour, the business of the succeeding day, and all the accessories of the scene, had an effect to increase the confusion of his mind, and, for the moment, to call in question the fidelity of his senses. As he gazed at the prison-like aspect of the gallery, his eye fell on the countenance of Marie Moulin, and rested there in surprise for half a minute. The Swiss maid was looking earnestly at her mistress, with an expression of concern and of care so intense, that it caused the counsellor to search for their cause. For the first time it flashed on his mind that Mary Monson might be a lunatic, and that the defence so often set up in capital cases as to weary the common mind, might be rendered justly available in this particular instance. The whole conduct of this serving-woman had been so singular; the deportment of Mary Monson herself was so much out of the ordinary rules; and the adhesion of Anna Updyke, à girl of singular prudence of conduct, notwithstanding her disposition to enthusiasm, so marked, that the inference was far from unnatural. Nevertheless, Mary Monson had never looked more calm, more intellectual; never manifested more of a mien of high intelligence, than at that very instant. The singular illumination of the countenance to which we have had occasion already to allude, was conspicuous, but it was benignant and quiet; and the flush of the cheeks added lustre to her eyes. Then the sentiments expressed were just and noble, free from the cunning and mendacity of a maniac; and such as any man might be proud to have the wife of his bosom entertain. All these considerations quickly chased the rising distrust from Dunscomb's mind, and his thoughts reverted to the business that had brought him there.

'You are the best judge, ma'am, of what will most contribute to your happiness,' rejoined the counsellor, after a brief pause. 'In the ignorance in which we are kept of the past, I might well add, the *only* judge; though it is possible that your female companions know more, in this respect, than your legal advisers. It is proper I should say, once more, and probably for the last time, that your case will be greatly prejudiced unless you enable us to dwell on your past life freely and truly.'

'I am accused of murdering an unoffending female and her husband; of setting fire to the dwelling, and of robbing them of their gold. These are accusations that can properly be answered only by a complete acquittal, after a solemn investigation. No half-way measures will do. I must be found not guilty, or a blot rests on my character for life. My position is singular – I had almost said cruel – in some respects owing to my own wilfulness——'

Here Anna Updyke pressed closer to her friend's side, as if she would defend her against these self-accusations; while Marie Moulin dropped her needle, and listened with the liveliest curiosity.

'In *many* respects, perhaps,' continued Mary, after a short pause, 'and I must take the consequences. Wilfulness has ever been my greatest enemy. It has been fed by perfect independence and too much money. I doubt if it be good for woman to be thus tried. We were created for dependence, Mr Dunscomb; dependence on our fathers, on our brothers, and perhaps on our husbands' – here there was another pause; and the cheeks of the fair speaker flushed, while her eyes became brilliant to light.

'*Perhaps!*' repeated the counsellor, with solemn emphasis.

'I know that men think differently from us on this subject——'

'From *us* – do you desire me to believe that most women wish to be independent of their husbands? Ask the young woman at your side, if *that* be her feeling of the duties of her sex.'

Anna dropped her head on her bosom, and blushed scarlet. In all her day-dreams of happiness with John Wilmeter, the very reverse of the feeling now alluded to, had been uppermost in her mind; and to her nothing had ever seemed half as sweet as the picture of leaning on him for support, guidance, authority, and advice. The thought of independence would have been painful to her; for a principle of nature, the instinct of her sex, taught her that the part of woman was 'to love, honour, and obey.' As for Mary Monson, she quailed a little before the severe eye of Dunscomb; but education, the accidents of life, and possibly a secret principle of her peculiar temperament, united to stimulate her to maintain her original ground.

'I know not what may be the particular notions of Miss Updyke,' returned this singular being, 'but I can feel my own longings. They are all for independence. Men have not dealt fairly by women. Possessing the power, they have made all the laws, fashioned all the opinions of the world, in their own favour. Let a woman err, and she can never rise from her fall; while men live with impunity in the midst of their guilt. If a woman think differently from those around her, she is expected to conceal her opinions, in order to receive those of her masters. Even in the worship of God, the highest and most precious of all our duties, she is expected to play a secondary part, and act as if the Christian Faith favoured the sentiment of another, which teaches that women have no souls.'

'All this is as old as the repinings of a very treacherous nature, young lady,' answered Dunscomb, coolly; 'and I have often heard it before. It is not surprising, however, that a young, handsome, highly-educated, and I presume rich, person of your sex, should be seduced by notions seemingly so attractive, and long for what she will be apt to term the emancipation of her sex. This is an age of emancipation; prudent grey-headed men become deluded, and exhibit their folly by succumbing to a wild and exceedingly silly philanthropical hurrah! Even religion is emancipated! There are churches, it is true; but they exist as appendages of society, instead of being divine institutions, established for the secret purposes of unerring wisdom; and we hear men openly commending this or that ecclesiastical organization, because it has more or less of the savour of republicanism. But one new dogma remains to be advanced – that the government of the universe is democratical – in which the "music of the spheres" is a popular song; and the disappearance of a world a matter to be referred to the people in their primary capacity. Among other absurdities of the hour is a new law, giving to married women the control of their property, and drawing a line of covetousness across the bolster of every marriage-bed in the State!'

'Surely, Mr Dunscomb, a man of your integrity, character, manliness, and principles, would defend the weaker sex in the maintenance of its rights against prodigality, tyranny, and neglect!'

'These are so many words, my dear ma'am, and are totally without meaning, when thoroughly sifted. God created woman to be a help-meet to man — to comfort, solace, and aid him in his pursuit after worldly happiness; but always in a dependent relation. The marriage condition, viewed in its every-day aspect, has sufficient causes of disagreement, without drawing in this of property. One of the dearest and nearest of its ties, indeed, that of a perfect identification of interests, is at once cut off by this foolish, not to say wicked attempt to light the torch of contention in every household. It were better to teach our women not to throw themselves away on men who cannot be trusted; to inculcate the necessity of not marrying in haste to repent at leisure, than to tinker the old, venerable, and long-tried usages of our fathers, by crotchets that come far more from the feverish audacity of ignorance, than from philosophy or wisdom. Why, unless the courts interpose their prudence to rectify the blunders of the legislature, as they have already done a hundred times, the labourer's wife may have her action against her husband for the earthen bowl he has broken; and the man may be sued by the wife for rent! The happiness of every home is hourly put in jeopardy, in order that, now and then, a wife may be saved from the courses of a speculator or a spendthrift.'

'Might not this have been done before, uncle Tom, by means of settlements!' asked Anna, with interest.

'Certainly; and that it is which renders all this silly quackery so much the worse. In those cases in which the magnitude of the stake might seem to demand extraordinary care, the means already existed for providing all useful safeguards; and any new legislation was quite unnecessary. This very law will produce twenty-fold more unhappiness in families, than it will prevent of misery, by setting up distinct, and often conflicting interests, among those who ought to live as "bone of their bone, and flesh of their flesh."'

'You do not give to woman her proper place in society, Mr Dunscomb,' returned Mary Monson, haughtily; 'your comments are those of a bachelor. I have heard of a certain Miss Millington, who once had an interest with you, and who, if living, would have taught you juster sentiments on this subject.'

Dunscomb turned as white as a sheet; his hand and lip quivered; and all desire to continue the discourse suddenly left him. The gentle Anna, ever attentive to his wishes and ailings, stole to his side, silently offering a glass of water. She had seen this agitation before, and knew there was a leaf in 'Uncle Tom's' history that he did not wish every vulgar eye to read.

As for Mary Monson, she went into her cell, like one who declined any further communication with her counsel. Timms was struck with her lofty and decided manner; but stood too much in awe of her, to interpose a remonstrance. After a few minutes taken by Dunscomb to regain his self-command, and a brief consultation together, the two lawyers quitted the prison. All this time, the accused remained in her cell, in resentful silence, closely and anxiously watched by the searching eye of her senior attendant.

CHAPTER XIX

Methinks, if, as I guess, the fault's but small,
It might be pardoned.

The Orphan.

Perhaps no surer test of high principles, as it is certain no more accurate test of high breeding can be found, than a distaste for injurious gossip. In woman, subject as she is unquestionably by her education, habits, and active curiosity, to the influence of this vice, its existence is deplorable, leading to a thousand wrongs, among the chief of which is a false appreciation of ourselves; but, when men submit to so vile a propensity, they become contemptible, as well as wicked. As a result of long observation, we should say that those who are most obnoxious to the just condemnation of the world, are the most addicted to finding faults in others; and it is only the comparatively good, who are so because they are humble, that abstain from meddling and dealing in scandal.

When one reflects on the great amount of injustice that is thus inflicted, without even the most remote hope of reparation, how far a loose, ill-considered, and ignorant remark will float on the tongues of the idle, how much unmerited misery is often times entailed by such unweighed assertions and opinions, and how small is the return of benefit in any form whatever, it would almost appear a necessary moral consequence that the world, by general consent, would determine to eradicate so pernicious an evil, in the common interest of mankind. That it does not, is probably owing to the power that is still left in the hands of the Father of Sin, by the Infinite Wisdom that has seen fit to place us in this condition of trial. The parent of all lies, gossip, is one of the most familiar of the means he employs to put his falsehoods in circulation.

This vice is heartless and dangerous when confined to its natural limits, the circles of society; but, when it invades the outer walks of life, and, most of all, when it gets mixed up with the administration of justice, it becomes a tyrant as ruthless and injurious in its way, as he who fiddled while Rome was in flames. We have no desire to exaggerate the evils of the state of society in which we live; but an honest regard to truth will, we think, induce every observant man to lament the manner in which this power, under the guise of popular opinion, penetrates into all the avenues of the courts, corrupting, perverting, and often destroying, the healthful action of their systems.

Biberry furnished a clear example of the truth of these remarks on the morning of the day on which Mary Monson was to be tried. The gaol-window had its crowd, of course; and though the disposition of curtains, and other similar means of concealment, completely baffled vulgar curiosity, they could not cloak the resentful feelings to which this reserve gave birth. Most of those who were drawn thither belonged to a class who fancied it was not affliction enough to be accused of two of the highest crimes known to the laws; but that to this grievous misfortune should be added a submission to the stare of the multitude. It was the people's laws the accused was supposed to have disregarded; and it was their privilege to anticipate punishment, by insult.

'Why don't she show herself, and let the public look on her?' demanded one curious old man, whose head had whitened under a steadily increasing misconception of what the rights of this public were. 'I've seen murderers afore now, and ain't a bit afeared on 'em, if they be well ironed and look'd a'ter.'

This sally produced a heartless laugh; for, sooth to say, where *one* feels, under such circumstances, as reason and justice, and revelation would tell them to feel, ten feel as the demons prompt.

'You cannot expect that a lady of fashion, who plays on the harp and talks French, will show her pretty face to be gazed at by common folk,' rejoined a shabby-genteel sort of personage, out of whose waistcoat-pocket obtruded the leaves of a small note-book, and the end of a gold pen. This man was a reporter, rendered malignant by meeting with opposition to his views of imagining that the universe was created to furnish paragraphs for newspapers. He was a half-educated European, who pronounced all his words in a sort of boarding-school dialect, as if abbreviation offended a taste 'sicken'd over by learning.'

Another laugh succeeded this supercilious sneer; and three or four lads, half-grown and clamorous, called aloud the name of 'Mary Monson,' demanding that she should show herself. At that moment the accused was on her knees, with Anna Updyke at her side, praying for that support which, as the crisis arrived, she found to be more and more necessary!

Changing from the scene to the open street, we find a pettifogger, one secretly prompted by Williams, spreading a report that had its origin no one knew where, but which was gradually finding its way to the ears of half the population of Duke's, exciting prejudice and inflicting wrong.

'It's the curi'stest story I ever heard,' said Sam Tongue, as the pettifogger was usually styled, though his real name was Hubbs; 'and one so hard to believe, that, though I tell it, I call on no man to believe it. You see, gentlemen' – the little group around him was composed of suitors, witnesses, jurors, grand-jurors, and others of a stamp that usually mark these several classes of men – 'that the account now is, that this Mary Monson was sent abroad for her schoolin' when only ten years old; and that she staid in the old countries long enough to l'arn to play the harp, and other deviltries of the same natur'. It's a misfortin', as I say, for any young woman to be sent out of Ameriky for an edication. Edication, as everybody knows, is the great glory of *our* country; and a body would think that what can't be l'arn't *here*, isn't worth knowin'.'

This sentiment was well received, as would be any opinion that asserted American superiority, with that particular class of listeners. Eye turned to eye, nod answered nod, and a murmur expressive of approbation passed through the little crowd.

'But there was no great harm in that,' put in a person named Hicks, who was accustomed to connect consequences with their causes, and to trace causes down to their consequences. 'Anybody might have been edicated in France as well as Mary Monson. *That* will hardly tell ag'in her on the trial.'

'I didn't say it would,' answered Sam Tongue; 'though it's gin'rally conceded that France is no country for religion or true freedom. Give me religion and freedom, say I; a body can get along with bad crops, or disapp'intments in gin'ral, so long as he has plenty of religion and plenty of freedom.'

Another murmur, another movement in the group, and other nods denoted the spirit in which this was received too.

'All this don't make ag'in Mary Monson; 'specially as you say she was sent abroad so young. It wasn't her fault if her parents——'

'She had no parents – there's the great mystery of her case. Never had, so far as can be discovered. A gal without parents, without fri'nds of any sort, is edicated in a foreign land, l'arns to speak foreign tongues, plays on foreign music, and comes home a'ter she's grown up, with her pockets as full as if she'd been to Californy and met a vein; and no one can tell where it all come from!'

'Well, *that* won't tell ag'in her, ne'ther,' rejoined Hicks, who had now defended the accused so much, that he began to take an interest in her acquittal. 'Evidence must be direct, and have a p'int, to tell ag'in man or woman. As for Californy, it's made lawful by treaty, if Congress will only let it alone.'

'I know that as well as the best lawyer in Duke's; but *character* can tell ag'in an accused, as is very likely to be shown in the Oyer and Tarminer of this day. Character counts, let me tell you, when the facts get a little confused; and this is just what I was about to say. Mary Monson has money; where does it come from?'

'Those that think her guilty say that it comes from poor Mrs Goodwin's stockin',' returned Hicks, with a laugh; 'but, for my part, I've *seen* that stockin', and am satisfied it didn't hold five hundred dollars, if it did four.'

Here the reporter out with his notes, scribbling away for some time. That evening a paragraph, a little altered to give it point and interest, appeared in an evening paper, in which the conflicting statements of Tongue and Hicks were so presented, that neither of these worthies could have recognised his own child. That paper was in Biberry next morning, and had no inconsiderable influence, ultimately, on the fortunes of the accused.

In the bar-room of Mrs Horton, the discussion was also lively and wily on this same subject. As this was a place much frequented by the jurors, the agents of Timms and Williams were very numerous in and around that house. The reader is not to suppose that these men admitted directly to themselves even, the true character of the rascally business in which they were engaged; for their employers were much too shrewd not to cover, to a certain degree, the deformity of their own acts. One set had been told that they were favouring justice, bringing down aristocratic pride to the level of the rights of the mass, demonstrating that this was a free country, by one of the very vilest procedures that ever polluted the fountains of justice at their very source. On the other hand, the agents of Timms had been persuaded that they were working in behalf of a persecuted and injured woman, who was pressed upon by the well-known avarice of the nephew of the Goodwins, and who was in danger of becoming the victim of a chain of extraordinary occurrences that had thrown her into the meshes of the law. It is true, this reasoning was backed by liberal gifts; which, however, were made to assume the aspect of compensation fairly earned; for the biggest villain going derives a certain degree of satisfaction in persuading himself that he is acting under the influence of motives to which he is, in truth, a stranger. The homage which vice pays to virtue is on a much more extended scale than is commonly supposed.

Williams's men had much the best of it with the mass. They addressed themselves to prejudices as wide as the dominion of man; and a certain personal zeal was mingled with their cupidity. Then they had, by far, the easiest task. He who merely aids the evil principles of our nature, provided he conceal the cloven foot, is much more sure of finding willing listeners than he who looks for support in the good. A very unusual sort of story was circulated in this bar-room at the expense of the accused, and which carried with it more credit than common, in consequence of its being so much out of the beaten track of events as to seem to set invention at defiance.

Mary Monson was said to be an heiress, well connected, and well educated – or, as these three very material circumstances were stated by the Williams's men – 'well to do herself, of friends well to do, and of excellent schooling.' She had been married to a person of equal position in society, wealth, and character, but many years her senior – too many, the story went, considering her own time of life; for a great difference, when one of the parties is youthful, is apt to tax the tastes too severely – and that connection had not proved happy. It had been formed abroad, and more on foreign than on American principles; the bridegroom being a Frenchman. It was what is called a *mariage de raison*, made through the agency of friends and executors, rather than through the sympathies and feelings that should alone bring man and woman together in this, the closest union known to human beings. After a year of married life abroad, the unmatched couple had come to America, where the wife possessed a very ample fortune. This estate the recently enacted laws gave solely and absolutely to herself; and it soon became a source of dissension between man and wife. The husband, quite naturally, considered himself entitled to advise and direct, and, in some measure, to control, while the affluent, youthful, and pretty wife, was indisposed to yield any of the independence she so much prized; but which, in sooth, was asserted in the very teeth of one of the most salutary laws of nature. In consequence of this very different manner of viewing the marriage relation, a coolness ensued, which was shortly followed by the disappearance of the wife. This wife was Mary Monson, who had secreted herself in the retired dwelling of the Goodwins, while the hired agents of her husband were running up and down the land in search of the fugitive in places of resort. To this account, so strange, and yet in many respects so natural, it was added that a vein of occult madness existed in the lady's family; and it was suggested that, as so much of her conduct as was out of the ordinary course might be traced to this malady, so was it also possible that the terrible incidents of the fire and the deaths were to be imputed to the same deep affliction.

We are far from saying that any rumour expressed in the terms we have used, was circulating in Mrs Horton's bar-room; but one that contained all their essentials was. It is one of the curious effects of the upward tendency of truth that almost every effort to conceal it altogether fails; and this at the very time when idle and heartless gossip is filling the world with lies. The tongue does a thousand times more evil than the sword; destroys more happiness, inflicts more incurable wounds, leaves deeper and more indelible scars. Truth is rarely met with unalloyed by falsehood.

'This or that unmix'd, no mortal e'er shall find'–

was the judgment of Pope a century since; nor has all the boasted progress of these later times induced a change. It is remarkable that a country which seems honestly devoted to improvement of every sort, that has a feverish desire to take the lead in the warfare against all sorts and species of falsehood, gives not the slightest heed to the necessity of keeping the channels of intelligence *pure*, as well as *open!* Such is the fact; and it is a melancholy, but a just, admission to acknowledge that with all the means of publicity preserved by America, there is no country in which it is more difficult to get unadulterated truth impressed on the common mind. The same wire that transmits a true account of the price of cotton from Halifax to New Orleans, carries a spark that imparts one that is false. The two arrive together; and it is not until each has done its work that the real fact is ascertained.

Notwithstanding these undoubted obstacles to the circulation of unalloyed truth, that upward tendency to which we have alluded occasionally brings out clear and strong rays of the divine quality, that illumine the moral darkness on which they shine, as the sun touches the verge of the thunder-cloud. It is in this way that an occasional report is heard, coming from no one knows where; originating with, no one knows whom; circulating in a sort of under-current beneath the torrents of falsehood, that is singularly, if it be not absolutely correct.

Of this character was the strange rumour that found its way into Biberry on the morning of Mary Monson's trial, touching the history of that mysterious young woman's past life. Wilmeter heard it, first, with a pang of disappointment, though Anna had nearly regained her power in his heart; and this pang was immediately succeeded by unbounded surprise. He told the tale to Millington; and together they endeavoured to trace the report to something like its source. All efforts of this nature were in vain. One had heard the story from another; but no one could say whence it came originally. The young men gave the pursuit up as useless, and proceeded together towards the room of Timms, where they knew Dunscomb was to be found, just at that time.

'It is remarkable that a story of this nature should be in such general circulation,' said John, 'and no one be able to tell who brought it to Biberry. Parts of it seem extravagant. Do they not strike you so, sir?'

'There is nothing too extravagant for some women to do,' answered Millington, thoughtfully. 'Now, on such a person as Sarah, or even on Anna Updyke, some calculations might be made – certain calculations, I might say; but there are women, Jack, on whom one can no more depend, than on the constancy of the winds.'

'I admire your – "even on Anna Updyke!"'

'Do you not agree with me?' returned the unobservant Millington. 'I have always considered Sarah's friend as a particularly reliable and safe sort of person.'

'Even on Anna Updyke! – and a particularly reliable and safe sort of person! – You have thought this, Mike, because she is Sarah's bosom friend!'

'That *may* have prejudiced me in her favour, I will allow; for I like most things that Sarah likes.'

John looked at his friend and future brother-in-law with an amused surprise; the idea of liking Anna Updyke on any account but her own, striking him as particularly absurd. But they were soon at Timms's door, and the conversation dropped as a matter of course.

No one who has ever travelled much in the interior of America, can easily mistake the character of one of the small edifices, with the gable to the street, ornamented with what are erroneously termed Venetian blinds, painted white, and with an air of tobacco-smoke and the shabby-genteel about it, notwithstanding its architectural pretensions. This is a lawyer's office, thus brought edgeways to the street, as if its owner felt the necessity of approaching the thoroughfare of the world a little less directly than the rest of mankind. It often happens that these buildings, small as they usually are, contain two, or even three rooms; and that the occupants, if single men, sleep in them as well as transact their business. Such was the case with Timms, his 'office,' as the structure was termed, containing his bed-room, in addition to an inner and an outer apartment devoted to the purposes of the law. Dunscomb was in the sanctum, while a single clerk and three or four clients, countrymen of decent exterior and very expecting countenances, occupied the outer room. John and Millington went into the presence with little or no hesitation.

Wilmeter was not accustomed to much circumlocution; and he at once communicated the substance of the strange rumour that was in circulation, touching their interesting client. The uncle listened with intense attention, turning pale as the nephew proceeded. Instead of answering or making any comment, he sank upon a chair, leaned his hands on a table and his head on his hands for fully a minute. All were struck with these signs of agitation, but no one dared to interfere. At length this awkward pause came to a close, and Dunscomb raised his head, the face still pale and agitated. His eye immediately sought that of Millington.

'You had heard this story, Michael?' demanded the counsellor.

'I had, sir. John and I went together, to try to trace it to some authority.'

'With what success?'

'None whatever. It is in every one's mouth, but no one can say whence it came. Most rumours have a clue, but this seems to have none.'

'Do you trace the connection which has struck – which has *oppressed* me?'

'I do, sir, and was so struck the moment I heard the rumour; for the facts are in singular conformity with what you communicated to me some months since.'

'They are, indeed, and create a strong probability that there is more truth in this rumour than is commonly to be found in such reports. What has become of Timms?'

'On the ground, 'squire,' answered that worthy from the outer room – 'just despatching my clerk' – this word he pronounced 'clurk' instead of 'clark,' by way of showing he knew how to spell – 'with a message to one of my men. He will find him, and be with us in a minute.'

In the mean time Timms had a word to say to each client in succession, getting rid of them all by merely telling each man in his turn there was not the shadow of doubt that he would get the better of his opponent in the trial that was so near at hand. It may be said here, as a proof how much a legal prophet may be mistaken, Timms was subsequently beaten in each of these three suits, to the great disappointment of as many anxious husbandmen, each of whom fondly counted on success, from the oily promises he had received.

In a very few minutes the agent expected by Timms appeared in the office. He was plain-looking, rather rough and honest in appearance, with a most wily, villainous leer of the eye. His employer introduced him as Mr Johnson.

'Well, Johnson, what news?' commenced Timms. 'These are friends to Mary Monson, and you can speak out, always avoiding partic'lar partic'lars.'

Johnson leered, helped himself to a chew of tobacco with great deliberation, a trick he had when he needed a moment of thought before he made his revelations, bowed respectfully to the great York lawyer, took a good look at each of the young men, as if to measure their means of doing good or harm, and then condescended to reply.

'Not very good,' was the answer. 'That foreign instrument, which they say is just such a one as David used when he played before Saul, has done a good deal of harm. It won't do, 'Squire Timms, to fiddle off an indictment for murder! Mankind gets engaged in such causes; and if they desire music on the trial, it's the music of law and evidence that they want.'

'Have you heard any reports concerning Mary Monson's past life – if so, can you tell where they come from?'

Johnson knew perfectly well whence a portion of the rumours came; those which told in favour of the accused; but these he easily comprehended were not the reports to which Timms alluded.

'Biberry is full of all sorts of rumours,' returned Johnson, cautiously, 'as it commonly is in court-time. Parties like to make the most of their causes.'

'You know my meaning; we have no time to lose; answer at once.'

'I suppose I do know what you mean, 'Squire Timms; and I have heard the report. In my judgment the person who set it afloat is no friend of Mary Monson's.'

'You think, then, it will do her damage?'

'To the extent of her neck. Eve, before she touched the apple, could not have been acquitted in the face of such a rumour. I look upon your client as a lost woman, 'Squire Timms.'

'Does that seem to be the common sentiment – that is, so far as you can judge?'

'Among the jurors it does.'

'The jurors!' exclaimed Dunscomb; – 'what can you possibly know of the opinions of the jurors, Mr Johnson?'

A cold smile passed over the man's face, and he looked steadily at Timms, as if to catch a clue that might conduct him safely through the difficulties of his case. A frown that was plain enough to the agent, though admirably concealed from all others in the room, told him to be cautious.

'I only know what I see and hear. Jurors are men, and other men can sometimes get an insight into their feelings, without running counter to law. I heard the rumour related myself, in the presence of seven of the panel. It's true nothing was said of the murder or the arson; but such a history of the previous life of the accused was given as Lady Washington couldn't have stood up ag'in, had she been livin', and on trial for her life.'

'Was anything said of insanity?' asked Dunscomb.

'Ah, that plea will do no good now-a-days; it's worn out. They'd hang a murderer from Bedlam. Insanity has been overdone, and can't be depended on any longer.'

'Was anything said on the subject?' repeated the counsellor.

'Why, to own the truth, there was; but as that told *for* Mary Monson, and not *ag'in* her, it was not pressed.'

'You think, then, that the story has been circulated by persons in favour of the prosecution?'

'I know it. One of the other side said to me, not ten minutes ago, – "Johnson," said he, "we are old friends;" – he always speaks to me in that familiar way, – "Johnson," said he, "you'd a done better to have gi'n up. What's five thousand dollars to the likes of her? and them, you know, is the figures."'

'This is a pretty exhibition of the manner of administering justice!' exclaimed the indignant Dunscomb. 'Long as I have been at the bar, I had no conception that such practices prevailed. At all events this illegality will give a fair occasion to demand a new trial.'

'Ay, the sharpest lawyer that ever crossed Harlem bridge can l'arn something in old Duke's,' said Johnson, nodding. ''Squire Timms will stand to *that*. As for new trials, I only wonder the lawyers don't get one each time they are beaten, for the law would bear them out.'

'I should like to know how, Master Johnson,' put in Timms. 'That would be a secret worth knowing.'

'A five-dollar note will buy it.'

'There's one of ten – now, tell me your secret.'

'Well, 'squire, you *be* a gentleman, whatever folks may say and think of you. I'd rather do business with you, by one-half, than do business with Williams; notwithstanding he has such a name, up and down the country. Stick to it, and you'll get the nomination to the Sinat'; and the nomination secured, you're sure of the seat. Nomination is the government of Ameriky; and that's secured by a wonderful few!'

'I believe you are more than half right, Johnson.' Here Dunscomb, his nephew, and Millington, left the office, quite unnoticed by the two worthies, who had entered on a subject as engrossing as that of Timms's elevation to the Senate. And, by the way, as this book is very likely to be introduced to the world, it may be well enough to explain that we have two sorts of 'Senates' in this country; wheels within wheels. There is the Senate of each State, without an exception now, we believe; and there is the Senate of the United States; the last being, in every sense, much the most dignified and important body. It being unfortunately true, that 'nominations' are the real people of America, unless in cases which arouse the nation, the State Senates very often contain members altogether unsuited to their trusts; men who have obtained their seats by party legerdemain; and who had much better, on their own account, as well as on that of the public, be at home attending to their own private affairs. This much may be freely said by any citizen, of a State Senate, a collection of political partisans that commands no particular respect; but, it is very different with that of the United States; and we shall confine ourselves to saying, in reference to that body, which it is the fashion of the times to reverence as the most illustrious political body on earth, that it is not quite as obnoxious to this judgment as the best of its sisterhood of the several States; though very far from being immaculate, or what, with a little more honesty in political leaders, it might be.

'I believe you are half right, Johnson,' answered Timms. 'Nomination *is* the government in this country; liberty, people, and all! Let a man get a nomination on the *right* side, and he's as good as elected. But, now for this mode of getting new trials, Johnson?'

'Why, 'squire, I'm amazed a man of your experience should ask the question! The law is sharp enough in keeping jurors, and constables, and door-keepers, in their places; but the jurors, and constables, and door-keepers, don't like to be kept in their places; and there isn't one cause in ten, if they be of any length, in which the jurors don't stray, or the constables don't get into the jury-rooms. You can't pound free-born Americans like cattle!'

'I understand you, Johnson, and will take the hint. I knew there was a screw loose in this part of our jurisprudence, but did not think it as important as I now see it is. The fact is, Johnson, we have been telling the people so long that they are perfect, and every man that he, in his own person, is one of these people, that our citizens don't like to submit to restraints that are disagreeable. Still, we are a law-abiding people, as every one says.'

'That may be so, 'squire; but we are not jury-room-abiding, nor be the constables outside-of-the-door-abiding, take my word for it. As you say, sir, every man is beginning to think he is a part of the people, and a great part, too; and he soon gets the notion that he can do as he has a mind to do.'

'Where is Mr Dunscomb?'

'He stepp'd out with the young gentlemen, a few moments since. I dare say, 'Squire Timms, he's gone to engage men to talk down this rumour about Mary Monson. That job should have been mine, by rights!'

'Not he, Johnson – not he. Your grand lawyers don't meddle with such matters; or, when they do, they pretend not to. No, he has gone to the gaol, and I must follow him.'

At the gaol was Dunscomb, sure enough. Mary Monson, Anna and Sarah, with Marie Moulin, all dressed for the court; the former with beautiful simplicity, but still more beautiful care; the last three plainly, but in attire well suited to their respective stations in life. There was a common air of concern and anxiety; though Mary Monson still maintained her self-command. Indeed, the quiet of her manner was truly wonderful for the circumstances.

'Providence has placed me in a most trying situation,' she said; 'but I see my course. Were I to shrink from this trial, evade it in any manner, a blot would rest on my name as long as I am remembered. It is indispensable that I should be *acquitted*. This, by God's blessing on the innocent, must come to pass, and I may go forth and face my friends with a quiet mind.'

'These friends ought to be known,' answered Dunscomb, 'and should be here to countenance you with their presence.'

'They! – He! – Never – while I live, never!'

'You see this young man, Mary Monson – I believe he is known to you by name?'

Mary Monson turned her face towards Millington, smiled coldly, and seemed undisturbed.

'What is he to me? – Here is the woman of his heart; – let him turn to *her*, with all his care.'

'You understand me, Mary Monson – it is important that I should be assured of *that*.'

'Perhaps I do, Mr Dunscomb, and perhaps I do *not*. You are enigmatical this morning; I cannot be certain.'

'In one short half-hour the bell of yonder court-house will ring, when you are to be tried for your life.'

The cheek of the accused blanched a little; but its colour soon returned, while her eye assumed a look even prouder than common.

'Let it come,' – was her quiet answer – 'the innocent need not tremble. These two pure beings have promised to accompany me to the place of trial, and to give me *their* countenance. Why, then, should I hesitate?'

'I shall go too,' – said Millington, steadily, like one whose mind was made up.

'You! – Well, for the sake of this dear one, you may go, too.'

'For no other reason, Mary?'

'For no other reason, sir. I am aware of the interest you and Mr Wilmeter have taken in my case; and I thank you both from the bottom of my heart. Ah! kindness was never lost on me——'

A flood of tears, for the first time since her imprisonment, so far as any one knew, burst from this extraordinary being; and, for a few minutes, she became woman in the fullest meaning of the term.

During this interval Dunscomb retired, perceiving that it was useless to urge anything on his client while weeping almost convulsively; and aware that he had several things to do before the court met. Besides, he left the place quite satisfied on an all-important point; and he and Millington walked by themselves towards the court-house, their heads close together, and their voices reduced nearly to whispers.

CHAPTER XX

> 'I blush, and am confounded to appear
> Before thy presence, Cato.'
> 'What's thy crime?'
> 'I am a Numidian.'
>
> *Cato.*

Within the half hour mentioned by Dunscomb the court-house bell rang, and there was a rush towards that building, in order to secure seats for the approaching trial. All that has been related in the preceding chapter occurred between the hours of six and nine that morning, it being one of the 'ways of the hour' in the march of improvement, to drive the administration of justice with as near an approach to railroad speed as is practicable. Many of the modern judges go to work as early as eight in the morning – perhaps most do in the country circuits – and continue to call causes until nine and ten at night, illustrating the justice of the land by means of agents who are half asleep, and stupid from fatigue.

We have said that everything like dignity, except as it is to be found in the light character of its duties, and the manner in which they are performed, has been banished from the courts of New York. Even on this solemn occasion, when a human being was to be put on trial for her life, and she a woman, there was no departure from the naked simplicity that has been set up on the pedestal of reason, in open opposition to the ancient accessories by which the Law asserted its power. It remains to be seen whether human nature has not been as much over-estimated under the new arrangement as it was underrated by the old. There is a medium, in truth, that it is ever safe to respect; and there is reason to apprehend that in throwing away the useless vestments of idle parade, those necessary to decency were cast aside with them.

Quite a fourth of the audience assembled in Duke's county court-house, on this occasion, were females. The curiosity, which is said to be so natural to the sex, was, on this occasion, quickened by the peculiar circumstances of the case, a woman having been murdered, and a woman accused of having committed the offence. It was said, however, that many were summoned as witnesses, it being generally understood that the State had subpoenaed the country far and near.

At length, a general and expecting silence succeeded the bustle of the crowds entering and obtaining seats, and the eyes of the spectators were very generally turned towards the door, in the wish to get a glimpse of the principal personage in the approaching scene. We know not why it is that the spectacle of others' woes has so great a charm for most persons. Nature has given us sympathy, and compassion, and a desire to alleviate misery; yet most of us like to look upon it, as a mere spectacle, when we have neither the wish nor the power to be more than useless spectators. Thousands will assemble to see a man hanged, when all know that the law has a grasp too tight to be unloosed, and that the circle of the gallows is no place for feelings of commiseration. But, so it is; and many a female, that day, who would have gladly alleviated any distress that it was in her power to lessen, sat there, a curious and interested observer of all that passed; to note the workings of the countenance, the writhings of the inner soul, if any such there should be, or the gleams of hope, that might, at intervals, lighten the gloom of despair.

The court was occupied for half an hour with hearing motions, and in granting orders, nothing seeming to impede its utilitarian progress. Then the movement within the bar ceased, and an expectation that was even solemn, fell on the whole mass of human beings that were collected in that narrow space.

'This is the day for which the trial of Mary Monson was, by arrangement, set down,' observed the judge. 'Mr District Attorney are you ready?'

'We are, sir – entirely so, I believe. If the court please, Mr Williams and Mr Wright will be associated with me in this case. It is one of importance, and I do not like the responsibility of trying it alone.'

'The court has so understood it. Who is for the accused?'

'I am retained to defend Mary Monson,' answered Dunscomb, rising with dignity, and speaking with the self-possession of one long accustomed to the courts. 'Mr Timms will assist me.'

'Are you ready, gentlemen?'

'I believe we are, your honour; though the prisoner has not yet been arraigned.'

'Mr District Attorney, we will proceed.'

As the sheriff now left the room, in person, rather an unusual thing in bringing a prisoner into court, expectation was at its height. In the midst of a breathing silence the door swung round – court-room doors are now made to swing like turnpikes in order to prevent noise – and Mr Gott entered, followed by Mary Monson, Anna, Sarah, Marie Moulin, and the two young men. The kind-hearted wife of the sheriff was already in the room, and, by means of a constable, had managed to keep seats reserved for those who might attend the prisoner. To these seats the party now retired, with the exception of Marie Moulin, who attended her mistress within the bar.

Every observer was struck with the unexpected air, manner, and attire of the prisoner. Dunscomb saw, at a glance, that her appearance had made a most favourable impression. This was something, and he hoped it might counteract much of the manoeuvring of Davis and Williams. The judge, in particular, a kind-hearted and very well meaning man, was taken altogether by surprise. There is nothing in which there is more freemasonry than in the secret symptoms of social castes. Each individual is more or less of a judge of these matters up to the level of his own associations, while all beyond is mystery. It happened that the judge, now about to try Mary Monson, belonged to an old, historical, New York family, a thing of rather rare occurrence in the great movements of the times, and he possessed an hereditary tact in discerning persons of his own habits of life. Almost at a glance he perceived that the prisoner had the air, manners, countenance and finesse of one accustomed, from infancy, to good company. The reader may smile at this, but he must pardon us if we say the smile will betray ignorance, rather than denote the philosophy that he may fancy controls his opinions. Dunscomb was much gratified when the judge rather earnestly interposed against the act of the sheriff, who was about to place the prisoner at the bar in the little barricaded space allotted to the use of ordinary criminals, directing him to –

'Give the prisoner a chair *within* the bar, Mr Sheriff. Gentlemen, be so good as to make room, that the accused may sit near her counsel. Mr Attorney, let the prisoner be arraigned as soon as she has rested from the fatigue and agitation of appearing here.'

This ceremony, now little more than a blank form, was soon ended, and the plea of 'Not Guilty' was entered. The next step was to empannel the jury, a task of infinite difficulty, and one that has got to be so much an outwork, in the proceedings in criminal cases, as almost to baffle the powers of the law. It is no unusual thing for the time of the court to be occupied a week or two in this preliminary proceeding, until the evil has got to be so crying as to induce the executive to recommend that the legislature may devise some mode of relief. One of the most besetting vices of all American legislation, in those cases in which abuses are not the offspring of party, is a false philanthropy, in which the wicked and evil doer has been protected at the expense of the upright and obedient. The abuse just mentioned is one of those in which the bottom has been reached somewhat sooner than common; but, it is hazarding little to predict, that more than half which has been done within the last few years, under the guise of liberty and philanthropy, will have to be undone, ere the citizen will be left to the quiet enjoyment of his rights, or can receive the just protection of the laws.

One of the common-sense and real improvements of the day, is to swear the jurors, in all the causes that are to be tried, by one process. This is a saving of time; and though the ceremony might be, and ought to be made, much more solemn and impressive than it is, as by causing all other business to cease, and to make every one present rise, and stand in reverential silence, while the name of the God of heaven and earth is invoked, still it is a great improvement on the ancient mode, and has reason to sustain it. It gives us pleasure to note such circumstances in the 'ways of the hour,' whenever a sense of right can induce one who loaths the flattery of the people quite as much as he loaths that of princes, and flattery of all sorts, to say aught in favour of what has been done, or is yet doing around him.

The clerk called the name of Jonas Wattles, the first juror drawn. This man was a respectable mechanic, of no great force in the way of mind, but meaning well, and reputed honest. Timms gave the senior counsel a look, which the other understood to mean, 'he may do.' No objection being made on account of the State, Jonas Wattles took his seat in the jury-box, which was thought great good luck for a capital case.

'Ira Trueman,' cried the clerk.

A meaning pause succeeded the announcement of this name. Trueman was a person of considerable local influence, and would probably carry great weight in a body composed principally of men even less instructed than he was himself. What was more, both Timms and Williams knew that their respective agents had been hard at work to gain his ear, though neither knew exactly with what degree of success. It was consequently equally hazardous to accept or to oppose, and the two legal gladiators stood at bay, each waiting for the other to betray his opinion of the man. The judge soon became wearied, and inquired if the juror was accepted. It was a somewhat amusing sight, now, to observe the manner in which Timms proceeded with Williams, and Williams met Timms.

'I should like to hear the gentleman's objections to this juror,' observed Timms, 'as I do not see that his challenge is peremptory.'

'I have not challenged the juror at all,' answered Williams, 'but have understood the challenge comes from the defence.'

'This is extr'or'nary! The gentleman looks defiance at the jurors, and now declares he does not challenge!'

'Looks! If looks made a challenge, the State might at once suffer these foul murders to go unpunished, for I am sure the gentleman's countenance is a perfect thunder-cloud——'

'I trust that counsel will recollect the gravity of this cause, and suffer it to be conducted with the decorum that ought never to be wanting in a court of justice,' interposed the judge. 'Unless there is a direct challenge, from one side or the other, the juror must take his seat, of course.'

'I should like to ask the juror a question or two,' Timms replied, speaking very cautiously, and like one who was afraid of hurting the feelings of the party under examination; and in truth wary, lest on investigation he might discover that Trueman was likely to be the sort of person he wanted. 'You have been at Biberry, juror, since the opening of the court?'

Trueman nodded his head.

'Of course, you have been round among your friends and neighbours, that you have met with here?'

Another nod from Trueman, with a sort of affirmative grunt.

'You have probably heard more or less said concerning Mary Monson – I mean in a legal and proper way?'

A third nod of assent.

'Can you speak anything, in particular, that has been said in your presence?'

Trueman seemed to tax his memory; then he raised his head, and answered deliberately and with great clearness.

'I was going from the tavern to the court-house, when I met David Johnson.'

'Never mind those particulars, Mr Trueman,' interrupted Timms, who saw that the juror had been talking with one of his own most confidential agents – 'what the court wishes to know is, if any one has been reporting circumstances *unfavourable* to Mary Monson in your presence?'

'Or in her *favour*,' put in Williams, with a sneer.

'Juror,' interposed the judge – 'tell us if any one has spoken to you on the merits of this case – for or against!'

'*Merits*' – repeated Trueman, seeming to reflect again – 'No, your honour; I can't say that there has.'

Now, this was as bold a falsehood as was ever uttered; but Trueman reconciled the answer to his conscience by choosing to consider that the conversation he had heard had been on the *demerits* of the accused.

'I do not see, gentlemen, that you can challenge for cause,' observed his Honour – 'unless you have further facts.'

'Perhaps we have, sir,' answered Williams. 'You were saying, Mr Trueman, that you met David Johnson as you were going from the inn to the court-house – Did I understand you correctly?'

'Just so, 'squire. I had been having a long talk with Peter Titus' – one of Williams's most active and confidential agents – 'when Johnson came up. Johnson says, says he, "a pleasant day, gentlemen – I'm glad to see you both out; for the faces of old friends is getting scarce——"'

'I see no objection to the juror's being received,' Williams carelessly remarked; satisfied that Titus had not neglected his duty in that long talk.

'Yes, he is as good a juror as Duke's can furnish,' observed Timms, perfectly sure Johnson had turned to account the advantage of having the last word. Trueman was accordingly admitted to the box, as the second man of the twelve. The two managers of this cause were both right. Titus *had* crammed his old acquaintance Trueman with all that was circulating to the prejudice of the prisoner; expressing surprise when he had said all he had to say, at hearing that his friend was on the panel.

'Well,' said Titus, as Johnson approached, 'if questioned, you'll remember I said I didn't dream of your being a juryman – but, just as like as not, you'll not be drawn for the case at all.' On the other hand, Johnson was quite eloquent and pathetic in giving his old acquaintance the history of Mary Monson's case, whom he pronounced 'a most injured and parsecuted woman.' Trueman, a shrewd, managing fellow in general, fancied himself just as impartial and fit to try the cause, after he had heard the stories of the two men, as he had ever been; but in this he was mistaken. It requires an unusually clear head, exceedingly high principles, and a great knowledge of men, to maintain perfect impartiality in these cases; and certainly Trueman was not the man to boast of all these rare qualities. In general, the last word tells; but it sometimes happens that first impressions become difficult to eradicate.

Such was the fact in the present instance; Trueman taking his seat in the jury-box with an exceedingly strong bias against the accused.

We are aware that these are not the colours in which it is the fashion to delineate the venerable and much vaunted institution of the jury; certainly a most efficient agent in curtailing the power of a prince; but just as certainly a most irresponsible, vague, and quite often an unprincipled means of administering the law, when men are not urged to the desire of doing right by political pressure from without, and are left to the perverse and free workings of a very evil nature. We represent things as we believe them to exist, knowing that scarce a case of magnitude occurs in which the ministers of corruption are not at work among the jurors, or a verdict rendered in which the fingers of the Father of Lies might not be traced, were the veil removed, and the facts exposed to the light of day. It is true, that in trials for life, the persecution of the prisoner rarely takes so direct a form as has been represented in the case of Mary Monson; but the press and the tongue do an incalculable amount of evil, even in such cases; all the ancient safeguards of the law having been either directly removed by ill-considered legislation, or rendered dead-letters by the 'ways of the hour.'

It was regarded as exceedingly good progress to get two jurors into the box, in a capital case, in the first half-hour. His honour had evidently resigned himself to a twenty-four hours' job; and great was his satisfaction when he saw Wattles and Trueman safely seated on their hard and uncomfortable seats; for it would almost seem that discomfort has been brought into the court-houses as a sort of auxiliary to the old practice of starving a jury into a verdict.

Whether it was owing to a suspicion, on the part of Timms, of the truth in regard to his being over-reached in the case of Trueman, or to some other cause, he raised no objections to either of the six jurors next called. His moderation was imitated by Williams. Then followed two peremptory challenges; one in behalf of the prisoner, and one in behalf of the people, as it is termed. This was getting on so much better than everybody expected, that all were in good humour; and it is not exceeding the truth if we add, in a slight degree more disposed to view the prisoner and her case with favour. On such trifles do human decisions very often depend.

All this time, fully an hour, did Mary Monson sit in resigned submission to her fate, composed, attentive, and singularly lady-like. The spectators were greatly divided in their private speculations on her guilt or innocence. Some saw in her quiet manner, curious interest in the proceedings, and unchanging colour, proofs not only of a hardened conscience, but of an experience in scenes similar to that in which she was now engaged; overlooking all the probabilities, to indulge in conjectures so severe against one so young.

'Well, gentlemen,' cried the judge, 'time is precious. Let us proceed.'

The ninth juror was drawn, and it proved to be a country trader of the name of Hatfield. This person was known to be a man of considerable influence among persons of his own class, and to have a reputation for judgment, if not for principles. 'They might as well send the other eleven home, and let Hatfield pronounce the verdict,' whispered one lawyer to another; 'there is no material in that box to withstand his logic.'

'Then he will hold this young woman's life in his hand,' was the reply.

'It will be pretty much so. The glorious institution of the jury is admirably devised to bring about such results.'

'You forget the judge. He has the last word, you will remember.'

'Thank God it is so; else would our condition be terrible! Lynch law is preferable to laws administered by jurors who fancy themselves so many legislators.'

'It cannot be concealed that the spirit of the times has invaded the jury-box; and the court has not one-half its ancient influence. I should not like to have this Hatfield against me.'

It would seem that Williams was of the same way of thinking; for he muttered to himself, desired the juror not to enter the box, and seemed to be pondering on the course he ought to pursue. The truth was that he himself had recently sued Hatfield for debt, and the proceedings had been a little vindictive. One of the dangers that your really skilful lawyer has to guard against, is the personal animosity that is engendered by his own professional practice. Many men have minds so constituted that their opinions are affected by prejudices thus created; and they do not scruple to transfer their hostility from the counsel to the cause he is employed to defend. It is consequently incumbent on the prudent lawyer to make his estimate of character with judgment, and be as sure as the nature of the case will allow, that his client is not to suffer for his own acts. As hostility to the counsel is not a legal objection to a juror, Williams was under the necessity of presenting such as would command the attention of the court.

'I wish the juror may be sworn true answers to make' – said Williams.

Timms now pricked up his ears; for, if it were of importance for Williams to *oppose* the reception of this particular individual, it was probably of importance to Mary Monson to have him received. On this principle, therefore, he was ready to resist the attack on the juror, who was at once sworn.

'You reside in the adjoining town of Blackstone, I believe, Mr Hatfield?' asked Williams.

A simple assent was the reply.

'In practice there, in one of the learned professions?'

Hatfield was certain his interrogator knew better, for Williams had been in his store fifty times; but he answered with the same innocent manner as that with which the question was put.

'I'm in trade.'

'In trade! – Keep a store, I dare say, Mr Hatfield?'

'I do – and one in which I have sold you hundreds myself.'

A general smile succeeded this sally; and Timms looked round at the audience, with his nose pointing upwards, as if he scented his game.

'I dare say – I pay as I go,' returned Williams; 'and my memory is not loaded with such transactions——'

'Mr Williams,' interrupted the judge, a little impatiently, 'the time of the court is very precious.'

'So is the dignity of the outraged laws to the State, your Honour. We shall soon be through, sir. – Many people in the habit of frequenting your store, Mr Hatfield?'

'As much so as is usual in the country.'

'Ten or fifteen at a time, on some occasions?'

'I dare say there may be.'

'Has the murder of Peter Goodwin ever been discussed by your customers in your presence?'

'I don't know but it has – such a thing is very likely; but one hears so much, I can't say.'

'Did you never join in such a discussion yourself?'

'I may, or I may not.'

'I ask you, now, distinctly, if you had no such discussion on the 26th of May last, between the hours of eleven and twelve in the forenoon?'

The sharpness of the manner in which this question was put, the minuteness of the details, and the particularity of the interrogatories, quite confounded the juror, who answered accordingly.

'Such a thing *might* have taken place, and it might *not*. I do not remember.'

'Is Jonas White (a regular country loafer) in the habit of being in your store?'

'He is – it is a considerable lounge for labouring men.'

'And Stephen Hook?'

'Yes; he is there a good deal of his time.'

'Now, I beg you to remember – did not such a conversation take place, in which you bore a part, between the hours of eleven and twelve in the forenoon; White and Hook being present?'

Hatfield seemed perplexed. He very conscientiously desired to tell the truth, having nothing to gain by an opposite course; but he really had no recollection of any such discussion, as well might be the case; no such conversation ever having taken place. Williams knew the habits of the loafers in question, had selected the time a little at random, and adopted the particularity merely as a means of confounding the juror, of whom he was seriously afraid.

'Such a thing *may* have happened,' answered Hatfield, after a pause – 'I don't remember.'

'It *may* have happened – Now, sir, allow me to ask you if, in that conversation, you did not express an opinion that you did not, and *could* not believe that a lady, educated and delicate, like the prisoner at the bar, did, or would, under any circumstances, commit the offence with which Mary Monson is charged?'

Hatfield grew more and more confounded; for Williams's manner was more and more confident and cool. In this state of feeling he suffered the reply to escape him –

'I *may* have said as much – it seems quite natural.'

'I presume, after this,' observed Williams, carelessly, 'your Honour will order the juror not to enter the box?'

'Not so fast – not so fast, brother Williams,' put in Timms, who felt it was now his turn to say a word, and who was thumbing a small pocket-almanac very diligently the while.

'This discussion, I understand the learned gentleman, took place in the juror's store?'

'It did, sir,' was the answer – 'a place where such discussions are very apt to occur. Hook and White loaf half their time away in that store.'

'All quite likely – very likely to happen – Mr Hatfield, do you open your store on the Sabbath?'

'Certainly not – I am very particular to do nothing of the sort.'

'A church-member, I suppose, sir?'

'An undeserving one, sir.'

'Never, on any account, in the practice of opening your store of a Sabbath, I understand you to say?'

'Never, except in cases of sickness. We must all respect the wants of the sick.'

'Are Hook and White in the habit of loafing about on your premises of a Sunday?'

'Never – I wouldn't tolerate it. The store is a public place of a week-day, and they can come in if they please; but I wouldn't tolerate such visits on the Sabbath.'

'Yet, if the court please, the 26th of last May happened to fall on the Sabbath day! My brother Williams forgot to look into the almanac before he made up his brief.'

Here Timms sat down, cocking his nose still higher, quite certain of having made a capital hit towards his views on the Senate, though he actually gained nothing for the cause. There was a general simper in the audience; and Williams felt that he had lost quite as much as his opponent had gained.

'Well, gentlemen, time is precious – let us get on,' interposed the judge. – 'Is the juror to enter the box or not?'

'I trust a trifling mistake as to the day of the month is not about to defeat the ends of justice,' answered Williams, raising himself higher on his stilts, as he found himself sinking lower in his facts. 'I put it on the 26th by a miscalculation, I can now see. It was probably on the 25th – Saturday is the loafer's holiday; – yes, it must have been on Saturday the 25th that the conversation took place.'

'Do you remember this fact, juror?'

'I remember, now so much has been said on the subject,' answered Hatfield, firmly, 'that I was not at home at all between the 20th and the 27th of May last. I could have held no such conversation on the 25th or 26th of May; nor do I know that I think Mary Monson either innocent or guilty.'

As all this was true, and was uttered with the confidence of truth, it made an impression on the audience. Williams doubted; for so fine was his skill in managing men, that he often succeeded in gaining jurors by letting them understand he suspected them of being prejudiced against his case. With the weak and vain, this mode of proceeding has frequently more success than a contrary course; the party suspected being doubly anxious to illustrate his impartiality in his verdict. This was what Williams, and indeed the bar, very generally calls 'standing so erect as to lean backward.'

'Mr Williams,' said the judge, 'you must challenge peremptorily, or the juror will be received.'

'No, your Honour, the State will accept the juror; I now see that my information has been wrong.'

'We challenge for the defence,' said Timms, deciding on the instant, on the ground that if Williams was so ready to change his course of proceeding, there must be a good reason for it. 'Stand aside, juror.'

'Peter Bailey,' called the clerk.

No objection being made, Peter Bailey took his seat. The two next jurors were also received unquestioned; and it only remained to draw the twelfth man. This was so much better luck than commonly happens in capital cases, that everybody seemed more and more pleased, as if all were anxious to come to the testimony. The judge evidently felicitated himself, rubbing his hands with very great satisfaction. The bar, generally, entered into his feelings; for it helped along its business.

'On the whole,' observed one of the lawyers who was in extensive practice, speaking to another at his side, 'I would as soon try one of these murder-cases as to go through with a good water-cause.'

'Oh! *they* are excruciating! Get into a good water-cause, with about thirty witnesses on a side, and you are in for a week. I was three days at one, only last circuit.'

'Are there many witnesses in this case?'

'About forty, I hear,' glancing towards the benches where most of the females sat. 'They tell me there will be a very formidable array as to character. Ladies from York by the dozen!'

'They will be wanted, if all they say is true.'

'If all you hear is true, we have reached a new epoch in the history of mankind. I have never seen the day when half of that I hear is more than half true. I set the rest down as "leather and prunella."'

'Robert Robinson,' cried the clerk.

A respectable-looking man of fifty presented himself, and was about to enter the box without stopping to ascertain whether or not he would be welcome there. This person had much more the air of the world than either of the other jurors; and with those who are not very particular, or very discriminating in such matters, might readily enough pass for a gentleman. He was neatly dressed, wore gloves, and had certain chains, an eye-glass, and other appliances of the sort, that it is not usual to see at a country circuit. Neither Williams nor Timms seemed to know the juror; but each looked surprised, and undecided how he ought to act. The peremptory challenges were not exhausted; and there was a common impulse in the two lawyers, first to accept one so respectable in mien, and attire, and general air; and then, by a sudden revolution of feeling, to reject one of whom they knew nothing.

'I suppose the summons is all right,' William carelessly remarked. 'The juror resides in Duke's?'

'I do,' was the answer.

'Is a freeholder, and entitled to serve?'

A somewhat supercilious smile came over the countenance of the juror; and he looked round at the person who could presume to make such a remark, with something very like an air of contempt.

'I am *Doctor* Robinson!' he then observed, laying emphasis on his learned appellation.

Williams seemed at a loss; for, to say the truth, he had never heard of any such physician in the county. Timms was quite as much mystified; when a member of the bar leaned across a table, and whispered to Dunscomb that the juror was a celebrated quack, who made pills that would cure all diseases; and who, having made a fortune, had bought a place in the county, and was to all legal purposes entitled to serve.

'The juror can stand aside,' said Dunscomb, rising in his slow dignified manner. 'If it please the court, *we* challenge peremptorily.'

Timms looked still more surprised; and when told the reason for the course taken by his associate, he was even sorry.

'The man is a *quack*,' said Dunscomb, 'and there is quackery enough in this system of a jury, without calling in assistance from the more open practitioners.'

'I'm afraid, 'squire, he is just the sort of man we want. I can work on such spirits, when I fail altogether with more every-day-kind of men. A little quackery does no harm to some causes.'

'Ira Kingsland,' called out the clerk.

Ira Kingsland appeared, a staid, solid, respectable husbandman – one of those it is a mistaken usage of the country to term yeomen; and of a class that contains more useful information, practical good sense and judgment, than might be imagined under all the circumstances.

As no objection was raised, this juror was received, and the panel was complete. After cautioning the jurors about listening and talking, in the usual way, the judge adjourned the court for dinner.

CHAPTER XXI

> I know it is dreadful! I feel the
> Anguish of thy generous soul – but I was born
> To murder all who love me.
>
> *George Barnwell.*

Dunscomb was followed to his room by Millington, between whom and himself, John Wilmeter had occasion to remark, a sudden intimacy had sprung up. The counsellor had always liked his student, or he would never have consented to give him his niece; but it was not usual for him to hold as long, or seemingly as confidential conversations with the young man as now proved to be the case. When the interview was over, Millington mounted a horse and galloped off, in the direction of town, in that almost exploded manner of moving. Time was, and that within the memory of man, when the gentlemen of New York were in their saddles hours each day; but all this is changing with the times. We live in an age of buggies, the gig, phaeton, and curricle having disappeared, and the utilitarian vehicle just named having taken their places. Were it not for the women, who still have occasion for closer carriages, the whole nation would soon be riding about in buggies! Beresford is made, by one of his annotators, to complain that everything like individuality is becoming lost in England, and that the progress of great improvements must be checked, or independent thinkers will shortly be out of the question. If this be true of England, what might not be said on the same subject of America? Here, where there is so much community as to have completely engulfed everything like individual thought and action, we take it the most imitative people on earth are to be found. This truth is manifested in a thousand things. Every town is getting its Broadway, thus defeating the very object of names; to-day the country is dotted with Grecian temples, to-morrow with Gothic villages, all the purposes of domestic architecture being sadly forgotten in each; and as one of the Spensers is said to have introduced the article of dress which bears his name, by betting he could set the fashion of cutting off the skirts of the coat, so might one who is looked up to, in this country, almost set the fashion of cutting off the nose.

Dunscomb, however, was a perfectly original thinker. This he manifested in his private life, as well as in his public profession. His opinions were formed in his own way, and his acts were as much those of the individual as circumstances would at all allow. His motives in despatching Millington so suddenly to town were known to himself, and will probably be shown to the reader, as the narrative proceeds.

'Well, sir, how are we getting on?' asked John Wilmeter, throwing himself into a chair, in his uncle's room, with a heated and excited air. 'I hope things are going to your mind?'

'We have got a jury, Jack, and that is all that can be said in the matter,' returned the uncle, looking over some papers as the conversation proceeded. 'It is good progress, in a capital case, to get a jury empanelled in the first forenoon.'

'You'll have the verdict in, by this time to-morrow, sir, I'm afraid!'

'Why afraid, boy? The sooner the poor woman is acquitted, the better will it be for *her*.'

'Ay, if she be acquitted; but I fear everything is looking dark in the case.'

'And this from *you*, who fancied the accused an angel of light only a week since!'

'She is certainly a most fascinating creature, *when she chooses to be*,' said John, with emphasis; 'but she does not always choose to appear in that character.'

'She is most certainly a fascinating creature *when she chooses to be!*' returned the uncle, with very much the same sort of emphasis.

But Dunscomb's manner was very different from that of his nephew. John was excited, petulant, irritable, and in a state to feel and say disagreeable things; dissatisfied with himself, and consequently not very well pleased with others. A great change had come over his feelings, truly, within the last week, and the image of the gentle Anna Updyke was fast taking the place of that of Mary Monson. As the latter seldom saw the young man, and then only at the grate, the former had got to be the means of communication between the youthful advocate and his client, throwing them constantly in each other's way. On such occasions Anna was always so truthful, so gentle, so earnest, so natural, and so sweetly feminine, that John must have been made of stone, to remain insensible of her excellent qualities. If women did but know how much their power, not to say charms, are increased by gentleness, by tenderness in lieu of coldness of manner, by keeping within the natural circle of their sex's feelings, instead of aping an independence and spirit more suited to men than to their own condition, we should see less of discord in domestic life, happier wives, better mothers, and more reasonable mistresses. No one knew this better than Dunscomb, who had not been an indifferent spectator of his nephew's course, and who fancied this a favourable moment to say a word to him, on a subject that he felt to be important.

'This *choosing* to be is a very material item in the female character,' continued the counsellor, after a moment of silent and profound thought. 'Whatever else you may do, my boy, in the way of matrimony, marry a gentle and feminine woman. Take my word for it, there is no true happiness with any other.'

'Women have their tastes and caprices, and like to indulge them, sir, as well as ourselves.'

'All that may be true, but avoid what is termed a woman of independent spirit. They are usually so many devils incarnate. If they happen to unite moneyed independence with moral independence, I am not quite certain that their tyranny is not worse than that of Nero. A tyrannical woman is worse than a tyrannical man, because she is apt to be capricious. At one moment she will blow hot, at the next cold; at one time she will give, at the next clutch back her gifts; to-day she is the devoted and obedient wife, to-morrow the domineering partner. No, no, Jack, marry a *woman*; which means a kind, gentle, affectionate, thoughtful creature, whose heart is so full of *you*, there is no room in it for herself. Marry just such a girl as Anna Updyke, if you can get her.'

'I thank you, sir,' answered John, colouring. 'I dare say the advice is good, and I shall bear it in mind. What would you think of a woman like Mary Monson, for a wife?'

Dunscomb turned a vacant look at his nephew, as if his thoughts were far away, and his chin dropped on his bosom. This abstraction lasted but a minute, however, when the young man got his answer.

'Mary Monson *is* a wife, and I fear a bad one,' returned the counsellor. 'If she be the woman I suppose her to be, her history, brief as it is, is a very lamentable one. John, you are my sister's son, and my heir. You are nearer to me than any other human being, in one sense, though I certainly love Sarah quite as well as I do you, if not a little better. These ties of feeling are strange links in our nature! At one time I loved your mother with a tenderness such as a father might feel for a child; in short, with a brother's love – a brother's love for a young, and pretty, and good girl, and I thought I could never love another as I loved Elizabeth. She returned my affection, and there was a period of many years when it was supposed that we were to pass down the vale of life in company, as brother and sister – old bachelor and old maid. Your father deranged all this, and at thirty-four my sister left me. It was like pulling my heartstrings out of me, and so much the worse, boy, because they were already sore.'

John started. His uncle spoke hoarsely, and a shudder, that was so violent as to be perceptible to his companion, passed through his frame. The cheeks of the counsellor were usually colourless; now they appeared absolutely pallid.

'This, then,' thought John Wilmeter, 'is the insensible old bachelor, who was thought to live altogether for himself. How little does the world really know of what is passing within it! Well may it be said, "there is a skeleton in every house."'

Dunscomb soon recovered his self-command. Reaching forth an arm, he took his nephew's hand, and said affectionately –

'I am not often thus, Jack, as you must know. A vivid recollection of days that have long been past came freshly over me, and I believe I have been a little unmanned. To you, my early history is a blank; but a very few words will serve to tell all you need ever know. I was about your time of life, Jack, when I loved, courted, and became engaged to Mary Millington – Michael's great-aunt. Is this new to you?'

'Not entirely, sir; Sarah has told me something of the same sort – you know the girls get hold of family anecdotes sooner than we men.'

'She then probably told you that I was cruelly, heartlessly jilted, for a richer man. Mary married, and left one daughter; who also married early, her own cousin, Frank Millington, the cousin of Michael's father. You may now see why I have ever felt so much interest in your future brother-in-law.'

'*He* is a good fellow, and quite free from all jilting blood, I'll answer for it. But, what has become of this Mrs Frank Millington? I remember no such person.'

'Like her mother, she died young, leaving an only daughter to inherit her name and very ample fortune. The reason you never knew Mr Frank Millington is probably because he went to Paris early, where he educated his daughter, in a great degree – there, and in England – and when he died, Mildred Millington, the heiress of both parents, is said to have had quite twenty thousand a year. Certain officious friends made a match for her, I have heard, with a Frenchman of some family, but small means; and the recent Revolution has driven them to this country, where, as I have been told, she took the reins of domestic government into her own hands, until some sort of a separation has been the consequence.'

'Why, this account is surprisingly like the report we have had concerning Mary Monson, this morning!' cried Jack, springing to his feet with excitement.

'I believe her to be the same person. Many things unite to create this opinion. In the first place, there is certainly a marked family resemblance to her grandmother and mother; then the education, manners, languages, money, Marie Moulin, and the initials of the assumed name, each and all have their solution in this belief. The "Mademoiselle" and the "Madame" of the Swiss maid are explained; in short, if we can believe this Mary Monson to be Madame de Larocheforte, we can find an explanation of everything that is puzzling in her antecedents.'

'But, why should a woman of twenty thousand a year be living in the cottage of Peter Goodwin?'

'Because she *is* a woman of twenty thousand a year. Mons. de Larocheforte found her money was altogether at her own command, by this new law, and, naturally enough, he desired to play something more than a puppet's part in his own abode and family. The lady clings to her dollars, which she loves more than her husband; a quarrel ensues, and she chooses to retire from his protection, and conceal herself, for a time, under Peter Goodwin's roof, to evade pursuit. Capricious and wrong-headed women do a thousand strange things, and thoughtless gabblers often sustain them in what they do.'

'This is rendering the marriage tie very slight!'

'It is treating it with contempt; setting at naught the laws of God and man – one's duties and the highest obligations of woman. Still, many of the sex fancy if they abstain from one great and distinct offence, the whole catalogue of the remaining misdeeds is at their mercy.'

'Not to the extent of murder and arson, surely! Why should such a woman commit these crimes?'

'One never knows. We are fearfully constituted, John, morally and physically. The fairest form often conceals the blackest heart, and *vice versâ*. But I am now satisfied that there is a vein of insanity in this branch of the Millingtons; and it is possible Madame de Larocheforte is more to be pitied than to be censured.'

'You surely do not think her guilty, uncle Tom?'

The counsellor looked intently at his nephew, shaded his brow a moment, gazed upward, and answered:–

'I do. There is such a chain of proof against her as will scarce admit of explanation. I am afraid, Jack – I am afraid that she has done these deeds, terrible as they are! Such has been my opinion, now, for some time; though my mind has vacillated, as I make no doubt will prove to be the case with those of most of the jurors. It is a sad alternative, but I see no safety for her except in the plea of insanity. I am in hopes that something may be made out in that respect.'

'We are quite without witnesses to the point; are we not, sir?'

'Certainly; but Michael Millington has gone to town to send by telegraph for the nearest connections of Madame de Larocheforte, who are in the neighbourhood of Philadelphia. The husband himself is somewhere on the Hudson. He must be hunted up too. Michael will see to all this. I shall get the judge to adjourn early this evening; and we must spin out the trial for the next day or two in order to collect our forces. The judge is young and indulgent. He has certain ridiculous notions about saving the time of the public, but does not feel secure enough in his seat to be very positive.'

At this instant Timms burst into the room in a high state of excitement, exclaiming, the moment he was sure that his words would not reach any hostile ears:—

'Our case is desperate! All the Burtons are coming out dead against us; and neither "the new philanthropy," nor "Friends," nor "anti-gallows," can save us. I never knew excitement get up so fast. It's the infernal aristocracy that kills us! Williams makes great use of it; and our people will not stand aristocracy. See what a magnanimous report to the legislature the learned Attorney-General has just made on the subject of aristocracy. How admirably he touches up the kings and countesses!'

'Pshaw!' exclaimed Dunscomb, with a contemptuous curl of the lip — 'not one in a thousand knows the meaning of the word, and he among the rest. The report you mention is that of a refined gentleman, to be sure, and is addressed to his equals. What exclusive political privilege does Mary Monson possess? or what does the patroon, unless it be the privilege of having more stolen from him, by political frauds, than any other man in the State? This cant about social aristocracy, even in a state of society in which the servant deserts his master with impunity, in the midst of a dinner, is very miserable stuff. Aristocracy, forsooth! If there be aristocracy in America the blackguard is the aristocrat. Away, then, with all this trash, and speak common sense in future.'

'You amaze me, sir! Why, I regard *you* as a sort of aristocrat, Mr Dunscomb.'

'Me! — and what do you see aristocratic about me, pray?'

'Why, sir, you don't *look* like the rest of us. Your very *walk* is different — your language, manners, dress, habits and opinions, all differ from those of the Duke's county bar. Now, to my notion, that is being exclusive and peculiar; and whatever is peculiar is aristocratic, is it not?'

Here Dunscomb and his nephew burst out in a laugh; and, for a few minutes, Mary Monson was forgotten. Timms was quite in earnest; for he had fallen into the every-day notions, in this respect, and it was not easy to get him out of them.

'Perhaps the Duke's county bar contains the aristocrats, and I am the serf!' said the counsellor.

'That cannot be – you *must* be the aristocrat, if any there be among us. I don't know *why* it is so, but so it is; yes, *you* are the aristocrat, if there be one at our bar.'

Jack smiled, and looked funny; but he had the discretion to hold his tongue. *He* had heard that a Duke of Norfolk, the top of the English aristocracy, was so remarkable for his personal habits as actually to be offensive; a man who, according to Timms's notions, would have been a long way down the social ladder; but who, nevertheless, was a top-peer, if not a top-sawyer. It was easy to see that Timms confounded a gentleman with an aristocrat; a confusion in ideas that is very common, and which is far from being unnatural, when it is remembered how few formerly acquired any of the graces of deportment who had not previously attained positive, exclusive, political rights. As for the Attorney-General and his report, Jack had sufficient sagacity to see it was a document that said one thing and meant another; professing deference for a people that it did not stop to compliment with the possession of either common honesty or good manners.

'I hope *my* aristocracy is not likely to affect the interests of my client.'

'No; there is little danger of that. It is the democracy of the Burtons which will do that. I learn from Johnson that they are coming out stronger and stronger; and I feel certain Williams is sure of their testimony. By the way, sir, I had a hint from him, as we left the court-house, that the five thousand dollars might *yet* take him from the field.'

'This Mr Williams, as well as yourself, Timms, must be more cautious, or the law will yet assert its power. It is very much humbled, I am aware, under the majesty of the people and a feeble administration of its authority; but its arm is long, and its gripe potent, when it chooses to exert its force. Take my advice, and have no more to do with such arrangements.'

The dinner-bell put an end to the discussion. Timms vanished like a ghost; but Dunscomb, whose habits were gentlemanlike, and who knew that Mrs Horton had assigned a particular seat to him, moved more deliberately; following his nephew about the time Timms was half through the meal.

An American tavern-dinner, during the sitting of the circuit, is every way worthy of a minute and graphic description; but our limits will hardly admit of our assuming the task. If 'misery makes a man acquainted with strange bed-fellows,' so does the law. Judges, advocates, witnesses, sheriffs, clerks, constables, and not unfrequently the accused, dine in common, with rail-road speed. The rattling of knives, forks, and spoons, the clatter of plates, the rushing of waiters, landlords, landlady, chambermaids, ostler and bar-keeper included, produce a confusion that would do honour to the most profound 'republican simplicity.' Everything approaches a state of nature but the eatables; and they are invariably overdone. On an evil day, some Yankee invented an article termed a 'cooking stove;' and since its appearance everything like good cookery has vanished from the common American table. There is plenty spoiled; abundance abused. Of made dishes, with the exception of two or three of very simple characters, there never were any; and these have been burned to cinders by the baking processes of the 'cook-stoves.'

It matters little, however, to the *convives* of a circuit-court dinner, what the dishes are called, or of what they are composed. 'Haste' forbids 'taste;' and it actually occurred that day, as it occurs almost invariably on such occasions, that a very clever country practitioner was asked the *matériel* of the dish he had been eating, and he could not tell it! Talk of the mysteries of French cookery! The 'cook-stove' produces more mystery than all the art of all the culinary artists of Paris; and this, too, on a principle that tallies admirably with that of the purest 'republican simplicity;' since it causes all things to taste alike.

To a dinner of this stamp Dunscomb now sat down, just ten minutes after the first clatter of a plate was heard, and just as the only remove was seen, in the form of slices of pie, pudding, and cake. With his habits, railroad speed of lightning-line eating could find no favour; and he and Jack got their dinner, as best they might, amid the confusion and remnants of the close of such a repast. Nine-tenths of those who had so lately been at work as trencher-men were now picking their teeth, smoking cigars, or preparing fresh quids for the afternoon. A few clients were already holding their lawyers by the button; and here and there one of the latter led the way to his room to 'settle' some slander cause in which the plaintiff had got frightened.

It is a bad sign when eating is carried on without conversation. To converse, however, at such a table, is morally if not physically impossible. Morally, because each man's mind is so intent on getting as much as he wants, that it is almost impossible to bring his thoughts to bear on any other subject; physically, on account of the clatter, a movement in which an eclipse of a plate by the body of a waiter is no unusual thing, and universal activity of the teeth. Conversation under such circumstances would be truly a sort of ventriloquism; the portion of the human frame included in the term being all in all just at that moment.

Notwithstanding these embarrassments and unpleasant accompaniments, Dunscomb and his nephew got their dinners, and were about to quit the table as McBrain entered. The doctor would not expose his bride to the confusion of the common table, where there was so much that is revolting to all trained in the usages of good company, singularly blended with a decency of deportment, and a consideration for the rights of each, that serve to form bright spots in American character; but he had obtained a more private room for the females of his party.

'We should do pretty well,' observed McBrain, in explaining his accommodations, 'were it not for a troublesome neighbour in an adjoining room, who is either insane or intoxicated. Mrs Horton has put us in your wing, and I should think you must occasionally hear from him too?'

'The man is constantly drunk, they tell me, and is a little troublesome at times. On the whole, however, he does not annoy me much. I shall take the liberty of dining with you to-morrow, Ned; this eating against time does not agree with my constitution.'

'To-morrow! – I was thinking that my examination would be ended this afternoon, and that we might return to town in the morning. You will remember I have patients to attend to.'

'You will have more reason for *patience*. If you get through in a week, you will be lucky.'

'It is a curious case! I find all the local faculty ready to swear through thick and thin against her. My own opinion is fixed — but what is the opinion of one man against those of several in the same profession?'

'We will put that question to Mrs Horton, who is coming to ask how we have dined – Thank'ee, my good Mrs Horton, we have done *remarkably* well, considering all the circumstances.'

The landlady was pleased, and smirked, and expressed her gratification. The *sous entendu* of Dunscomb was lost upon her; and human vanity is very apt to accept the flattering, and to overlook the disagreeable. She was pleased that the great York lawyer was satisfied.

Mrs Horton was an American landlady in the strictest sense of the word. This implies many features distinct from her European counterpart; some of which tell greatly in her favour, and others not so much so. Decency of exterior, and a feminine deportment, are so characteristic of the sex in this country that they need scarcely be adverted to. There were no sly jokes, no *doubles entendres* with Mrs Horton; who maintained too grave a countenance to admit of such liberties. Then, she was entirely free from the little expedients of a desire to gain that are naturally enough adopted in older communities, where the pressure of numbers drives the poor to their wits'-end in order to live. American abundance had generated American liberality in Mrs

Horton; and if one of her guests asked for bread she would give him the loaf. She was, moreover, what the country round termed 'accommodating;' meaning that she was obliging and good-natured. Her faults were a fierce love of gossip, concealed under a veil of great indifference and modesty, a prying curiosity, and a determination to know everything, touching everybody, who ever came under her roof. This last propensity had got her into difficulties, several injurious reports having been traced to her tongue, which was indebted to her imagination for fully one-half of what she had circulated. It is scarcely necessary to add, that, among the right set, Mrs Horton was a great talker. As Dunscomb was a favourite, he was not likely to escape on the present occasion, the room being clear of all the guests but those of his own party.

'I am glad to get a little quiet talk with you, 'Squire Dunscomb,' the landlady commenced; 'for a body can depend on what is heard from such authority. Do they mean to hang Mary Monson?'

'It is rather premature to ask that question, Mrs Horton. The jury is empanelled, and there we stand at present.'

'Is it a good jury? Some of our Duke's county juries are none too good, they tell me.'

'The whole institution is a miserable contrivance for the administration of justice. Could a higher class of citizens compose the juries the system might still do, with a few improvements.'

'Why not elect them?' demanded the landlady, who was, *ex officio*, a politician, much as women are usually politicians in this country. In other words, she *felt* her opinions, without knowing their reasons.

'God forbid, my good Mrs Horton – we have elective judges; that will do for the present. Too much of a good thing is as injurious as the positively bad. I prefer the present mode of drawing lots.'

'Have you got a Quaker in the box? – If you have, you are safe enough.'

'I doubt if the District Attorney would suffer that; although he appears to be kind and considerate. The man who goes into that box must be prepared to hang if necessary.'

'For my part, I wish all hanging was done away with. I can see no good that hanging can do a man.'

'You mistake the object, my dear Mrs Horton, though your argument is quite as good as many that are openly advanced on the same side of the question.'

'Just hear me, 'squire,' rejoined the woman, for she loved dearly to get into a discussion on any question that she was accustomed to hear debated among her guests. 'The country hangs a body to reform a body; and what good can that do when a body is dead?'

'Very ingeniously put,' returned the counsellor, politely offering his box to the landlady, who took a few grains; and then deliberately helping himself to a pinch of snuff – 'quite as ingeniously as much of the argument that appears in public. The objection lies to the premises, and not to the deduction, which is absolutely logical and just. A hanged body is certainly an unreformed body; and, as you say, it is quite useless to hang in order to reform.'

'There!' exclaimed the woman in triumph – 'I told 'Squire Timms that a gentleman who knows as much as you do must be on our side. Depend on one thing, lawyer Dunscomb, and you too, gentlemen – depend on it, that Mary Monson will never be hanged.'

This was said with a meaning so peculiar, that it struck Dunscomb, who watched the woman's earnest countenance while she was speaking, with undeviating interest and intensity.

'It is my duty and my wish, Mrs Horton, to believe as much, and to make others believe it also, if I can,' he answered, now anxious to prolong a discourse that a moment before he had found tiresome.

'You can, if you will only try. I believe in dreams – and I dreamt a week ago that Mary Monson would be acquitted. It would be ag'in all our new notions to hang so nice a lady.'

'Our *tastes* might take offence at it; and taste is of *some* influence yet, I am bound to agree with you.'

'But you do agree with me in the uselessness of hanging, when the object is to reform?'

'Unfortunately for the force of that argument, my dear landlady, society does not punish for the purposes of reformation – that is a very common blunder of superficial philanthropists.'

'Not for the purposes of reformation, 'squire! – You astonish me! Why, for what else should it punish?'

'For its own protection. To prevent others from committing murder. Have you no other reason than your dream, my good Mrs Horton, for thinking Mary Monson will be acquitted?'

The woman put on a knowing look, and nodded her head significantly. At the same time, she glanced towards the counsellor's companions, as much as to say that their presence prevented her being more explicit.

'Ned, do me the favour to go to your wife, and tell her I shall step in, and say a kind word as I pass her door; – and, Jack, go and bid Sarah be in Mrs McBrain's parlour, ready to give me my morning's kiss.'

The Doctor and John complied, leaving Dunscomb alone with the woman.

'May I repeat the question, my good landlady? – Why do you think Mary Monson is to be acquitted?' asked Dunscomb, in one of his softest tones.

Mrs Horton mused, seemed anxious to speak, but struggling with some power that withheld her. One of her hands was in a pocket where the jingling of keys and pence made its presence known. Drawing forth this hand mechanically, Dunscomb saw that it contained several eagles. The woman cast her eyes on the gold, returned it hastily to her pocket, rubbed her forehead, and seemed the wary, prudent landlady once more.

'I hope you like your room, 'squire,' she cried, in a thoroughly innkeeping spirit. 'It's the very best in this house; though I'm obliged to tell Mrs McBrain the same story as to her apartment. But you have the best. You have a troublesome neighbour between you, I'm afraid; but he'll not be there many days, and I do all I can to keep him quiet.'

'Is that man crazy?' asked the counsellor, rising, perceiving that he had no more to expect from the woman just then; 'or is he only drunk? I hear him groan and then I hear him swear; though I cannot understand what he says.'

'He's sent here by his friends; and your wing is the only place we have to keep him in. When a body is well paid, 'squire, I suppose you know that the fee must not be forgotten? Now, inn-keepers have fees, as well as you gentlemen of the bar. How wonderfully Timms is getting along, Mr Dunscomb!'

'I believe his practice increases; and they tell me he stands next to Mr Williams in Duke's.'

'He does, indeed; and a "bright particular star," as the poet says, has he got to be!'

'If he be a star at all,' answered the counsellor, curling his lip, 'it must be a very particular one, indeed. I am sorry to leave you, Mrs Horton; but the intermission is nearly up.'

Dunscomb gave a little friendly nod, which the landlady returned; the former went his way with singular coolness of manner, when it is remembered that on him rested the responsibility of defending a fellow-creature from the gallows. What rendered this deliberation more remarkable, was the fact that he had no faith in the virtue of Mrs Horton's dream.

CHAPTER XXII

Wilt thou behold me sinking in my woes,
And wilt thou not reach out a friendly arm,
To raise one from amidst this plunge of sorrow?

ADDISON.

'Call the names of the jurors, Mr Clerk,' said the judge. 'Mr Sheriff, I do not see the prisoner in her place.'

This produced a stir. The jurors were called, and answered to their names; and shortly after Mary Monson appeared. The last was accompanied by the ladies, who might now be said to belong to her party, though no one but herself and Marie Moulin came within the bar.

There was profound stillness in the hall, for it was felt that now the issue of life or death was actually approaching. Mary Monson gazed, not with disquietude but interest, at the twelve men who were to decide on her innocence or guilt – men of habits and opinions so different from her own – men so obnoxious to prejudices against those whom the accidents of life had made objects of envy or hatred – men too much occupied with the cares of existence to penetrate the arcana of thought, and who consequently held their opinions at the mercy of others – men unskilled, because without practice, in the very solemn and important office now imposed on them by the law – men who might, indeed, be trusted, so long as they would defer to the court and reason, but who were terrible and dangerous, when they listened, as is too apt to be the case, to the suggestions of their own impulses, ignorance, and prejudice. Yet these men were Mary Monson's peers, in the eyes of the law; would have been so viewed and accepted in a case involving the feelings and practices of social castes, about which they knew absolutely nothing, or what is worse than nothing, a very little through the medium of misrepresentation and mistaken conclusions.

It is the fashion to extol the institution of the jury. Our own experience, by no means trifling, as foreman, as suitor, and as a disinterested spectator, does not lead us to coincide in this opinion. A narrative of the corrupt, misguided, partial, prejudiced, or ignorant conduct that we have ourselves witnessed in these bodies, would make a legend of its own. The power that most misleads such men is one unseen by themselves, half the time, and is consequently so much the more dangerous. The feelings of neighbourhood, political hostility, or party animosities, are among the commonest evils that justice has to encounter, when brought in contact with tribunals thus composed. Then come the feelings engendered by social castes, an inexhaustible source of evil passions. Mary Monson had been told of the risks she ran from that source; though she had also been told, and with great truth, that so much of the Spirit of God still remains in the hearts and minds of men, as to render a majority of those who were to be the arbiters of her fate conscientious and careful in a capital case. Perhaps, as a rule, the singularity of his situation, with a man who finds himself, for the first time, sitting as a juror in a trial for a human life, is one of the most available correctives of his native tendencies to do evil.

'Mr District Attorney, are you ready to proceed?' inquired the judge.

This functionary rose, bowed to the court and jury, and commenced his opening. His manner was unpretending, natural, and solemn. Although high talent and original thought are very rare in this country, as

they are everywhere else, there is a vast fund of intellect of a secondary
order ever at the command of the public. The District Attorney of
Duke's was a living witness of this truth. He saw all within his reach
clearly, and, possessing great experience, he did his duty on this occasion
in a very creditable manner. No attempt was made to awaken prejudice
of any sort against the accused. She was presented by the grand inquest,
and it was his and their painful duty, including his honour on the bench,
to investigate this matter, and make a solemn decision, on their oaths.
Mary Monson was entitled to a fair hearing, to all the advantages that the
lenity of the criminal law of a very humane state of society could afford,
and 'for God's sake let her be acquitted should the State fail to establish
her guilt!'

Mr District Attorney then proceeded to give a narrative of the events
as he supposed them to have occurred. He spoke of the Goodwins as
'*poor,* but *honest*' people, a sort of illustration that is in much favour, and
deservedly so, when true. 'It seems, gentlemen,' the District Attorney
continued, 'that the wife had a propensity, or a fancy, to collect gold
pieces, no doubt as a store against the wants of age. This money was kept
in a stocking, according to the practice of country ladies, and was often
exhibited to the neighbours. We may have occasion, gentlemen, to show
you that some fifteen or twenty persons, at different times, have seen and
handled this gold. You need not be told what natural curiosity is, but
must all know how closely persons little accustomed to see money of this
sort would be apt to examine the more rare pieces in particular. There
happened to be several of these pieces among the gold of Mrs Goodwin,
and one of them was an Italian or a Dutch coin, of the value of four
dollars, which commonly goes by the name of the king whose likeness is
on the piece. This Dutch or Italian coin, no matter which, or William,
was seen, and handled, and examined, by several persons, as we shall
show you.

'Now, gentlemen, the stocking that contained the gold coins was kept
in a bureau, which bureau was saved from the fire, with all its contents:
but the stocking and the gold were missing! These facts will be shown to
you by proof that puts them beyond a peradventure. We shall next show
to you, gentlemen, that on a public examination of the prisoner at the
bar, the contents of her purse were laid open, and the Dutch or Italian
coin I have mentioned was found, along with more than a hundred
dollars of other pieces, which being in American coin, cannot so readily
be identified.

'The prosecution relies, in a great degree, on the proof that will be
offered in connection with this piece of money, to establish the guilt of
the prisoner. We are aware that, when this piece of money was found on
her person, she affirmed it was hers; that she had been possessed of *two*

such pieces, and that the one seen in Mrs Goodwin's stocking had been a present from herself to that unfortunate woman.

'Gentlemen, if persons accused of crimes could vindicate themselves by their own naked statements, there would be very few convictions. Reason tells us that proof must be met by proof. Assertions will not be received, as against the accused, nor will they be taken in her favour. Your own good sense will tell you, gentlemen, that if it be shown that Dorothy Goodwin possessed this particular piece of gold, valued it highly, and was in the practice of hoarding all the gold she could lay her hands on lawfully; that the said Dorothy Goodwin's residence was burned, she herself murdered by a savage and cruel blow or blows on the occiput, or head; that Mary Monson, the prisoner at the bar, knew of the existence of this little stock of gold coins, had seen it, handled it, and doubtless *coveted* it; residing in the same house, with easy access to the bedside of the unhappy couple, with easy access to the bureau, to the keys which opened that bureau, for its drawers were found locked, just as Mrs Goodwin was in the habit of leaving them; – but, gentlemen, if all this be shown to you, and we then trace the aforesaid piece or coin to the pocket of Mary Monson, we make out a *primâ facie* case of guilt, as I conceive; a case that will throw on her the *onus* of showing that she came in possession of the said piece or coin lawfully, and by no improper means. Failing of this, your duty will be plain.

'It is incumbent on the prosecution to make out its case, either by direct proof, on the oaths of credible witnesses, or by such circumstances as shall leave no doubt in your minds of the guilt of the accused. It is also incumbent that we show that the crimes, of which the prisoner is accused, have been committed, and committed by her.

'Gentlemen, we shall offer you this proof. We shall show you that the skeletons of which I have spoken, and which lie under that pall, sad remains of a most ruthless scene, are beyond all question the skeletons of Peter and Dorothy Goodwin. This will be shown to you by proof; though all who knew the parties, can almost see the likeness in these sad relics of mortality. Peter Goodwin, as will be shown to you, was a very short, but sturdy man, while Dorothy, his wife, was a woman of large size. The skeletons meet this description exactly. They were found on the charred wood of the bedstead the unhappy couple habitually used, and on the very spot where they had passed so many previous nights in security and peace. Everything goes to corroborate the identity of the persons whose remains have been found, and I regret it should be my duty to add, that everything goes to fasten the guilt of these murders on the prisoner at the bar.

'Gentlemen, although we rely mainly on the possession of the Dutch or Italian coin, no matter which, to establish the case for the State, we shall offer you a great deal of sustaining and secondary proof. In the first place, the fact that a female, young, handsome, well, nay, expensively educated, coming from nobody knows whence, to go nobody knows whither, should suddenly appear in a place as retired as the house of Peter Goodwin, why no one can say, are in themselves very suspicious. Gentlemen, "all is not gold that glitters." Many a man, and many a woman, in places as large as New York, are not what they seem to be. They dress, and laugh, and sing, and appear to be among the gayest of the gay, when they do not know where to lay their heads at night. Large towns are moral blotches, they say, on the face of the community, and they conceal many things that will not bear the light. From one of these large towns, it is to be presumed from her dress, manners, education, amusements, and all belonging to her, came Mary Monson, to ask an asylum in the dwelling of the Goodwins. Gentlemen, why did she come? Had she heard of the hoard of Mrs Goodwin, and did she crave the possession of the gold? These questions it will be your duty to answer in your verdict. Should the reply be in the affirmative, you obtain, at once, a direct clue to the motives for the murder.

'Among the collateral proof that will be offered are the following circumstances, to which I now ask your particular attention, in order that you may give to the testimony its proper value. It will be shown that Mary Monson had a large sum in gold in her possession, *after* the arson and murders, and consequently *after* the robbery, but no one knew of her having any *before*. It will be shown that she has money in abundance, scattering it right and left, as we suppose to procure her acquittal, and this money we believe she took from the bureau of Mrs Goodwin – how much, is not known. It is thought that the sum was very large; the gold alone amounted to near a thousand dollars, and two witnesses will testify to a still larger amount in bank notes. The Goodwins talked of purchasing a farm, valued at five thousand dollars; and as they were known never to run in debt, the fair inference is, that they must have had at least that sum by them. A legacy was left Dorothy Goodwin within the last six months, which we hear was very considerable, and we hope to be able to put a witness on the stand who will tell you all about it.

'But, gentlemen, a circumstance worthy of all attention in an investigation like this, is connected with an answer to this question – Who is Mary Monson? What are her parentage, birth-place, occupation, and place of residence? Why did she come to Biberry at all? In a word, what is her past history? Let this be satisfactorily explained, and a great step is taken towards her vindication from these most grave charges. Shall we have witnesses to character? No one will be happier to listen to them than myself. My duty is far from pleasant. I sincerely hope the prisoner will find lawful means to convince you of her innocence. There is not one within the walls of this building who will hear such a verdict, if sustained by law and evidence, with greater pleasure than it will be heard by me.'

After pursuing this vein some time longer, the worthy functionary of the State showed a little of that cloven foot which seems to grow on all, even to the cleanest heels, who look to the popular voice for preferment. No matter who the man is, rich or poor, young or old, foolish or wise, he bows down before the idol of Numbers, and there worships. Votes being the one thing wanted, must be bought by sacrifices on the altar of conscience. Now it is by wild, and, half the time, impracticable schemes of philanthropy, that while they seem to work good to the majority, are quite likely to disregard the rights of the minority; now they are flourishes against negro slavery, or a revolution in favour of the oppressed inhabitants of Crim-Tartary, of the real state of which country we are all as ignorant as its inhabitants are ignorant of us; now, it's an exemption law, to enable a man to escape from the payment of his just debts, directly in the teeth of the sound policy, not to say morality, that if a man owe he should be made to pay as long as he has anything to do it with; now, it is a hymn in praise of a liberty that the poet neither comprehends nor cares to look into farther than may suit his own selfish patriotism; and now, it is some other of the thousand modes adopted by the designing to delude the masses and advance themselves.

On this occasion the District Attorney was very cautious, but he showed the cloven foot. He paid a passing tribute to the god of Numbers, worshipped before the hierarchy of votes. 'Gentlemen,' he continued, 'like myself, you are plain, unpretending citizens. Neither you, nor your wives and daughters, speak in foreign tongues, or play on foreign instruments of music. We have been brought up in republican simplicity [God bless it! say we, could we ever meet with it], and lay no claims to superiority of any sort. Our place is in the body of the nation, and there we are content to remain. We shall pay no respect to dress, accomplishments, foreign languages, or foreign music; but, the evidence sustaining us, will show the world that the law frowns as well on the great as on the little; on the pretending, as well as on the unpretending.'

As these grandiose sentiments were uttered, several of the jurors half rose from their seats, in the eagerness to hear, and looks of approbation passed from eye to eye. This was accepted as good republican doctrine; no one there seeing, or feeling, as taste and truth would have shown, that the real pretension was on the side of an exaggerated self-esteem, that prompted to resistance ere resistance was necessary, under the influence of, perhaps, the lowest passion of human nature – we allude to envy. With a little more in the same vein, the District Attorney concluded his opening.

The great coolness, not to say indifference, with which Mary Monson listened to this speech, was the subject of general comment among the members of the bar. At times she had been attentive, occasionally betraying surprise; then indignation would just gleam in her remarkable eye; but, on the whole, an uncommon calmness reigned in her demeanour. She had prepared tablets for notes; and twice she wrote in them as the District Attorney proceeded. This was when he adverted to her past life, and when he commented on the Dutch coin. While he was speaking of castes, flattering one set under the veil of pretending humility, and undermining their opposites, a look of quiet contempt was apparent in every feature of her very expressive face.

'If it please the court,' said Dunscomb, rising in his deliberate way, 'before the prosecution proceeds with its witnesses, I could wish to appeal to the courtesy of the gentlemen on the other side for a list of their names.'

'I believe we are not bound to furnish any such list,' answered Williams, quickly.

'Perhaps not bound exactly in law; but, it strikes me, bound in justice. This is a trial for a life; the proceedings are instituted by the State. The object is justice, not vengeance – the protection of society, through the agency of an impartial, though stern justice. The State cannot wish to effect anything by surprise. We are accused of murder and arson, with no other notice of what is to be shown, or *how* anything is to be shown, than what is contained in the bill or complaint. Any one can see how important it may be to us, to be apprised of the names of the witnesses a little in advance, that we may inquire into character and note probabilities. I do not insist on any *right*; but I ask a favour that humanity sanctions.'

'If it please the court,' said Williams, 'we have an important trust. I will here say that I impute nothing improper to either of the prisoner's counsel; but it is my duty to suggest the necessity of our being cautious. A great deal of money has been expended already in this case; and there is always danger of witnesses being bought off. On behalf of my client, I protest against the demand's being complied with.'

'The court has no objection to the course asked by the prisoner's counsel,' observed the judge, 'but cannot direct it. The State can never wish its officers to be harsh or exacting; but it is their duty to be prudent. Mr District Attorney, are you ready with your evidence? Time is precious, sir.'

The testimony for the prosecution was now offered. We shall merely advert to most of it, reserving our details for those witnesses on whom the cause might be said to turn. Two very decent-looking and well-behaved men, farmers who resided in the vicinity of Biberry, were put on the stand to establish the leading heads of the case. They had known Peter and Dorothy Goodwin; had often stopped at the house; and were familiarly acquainted with the old couple, as neighbours. Remembered the fire – were present at it, towards its close. Saw the prisoner there; saw her descend, by a ladder; and assisted in saving her effects. Several trunks, carpet-bags, bandboxes, writing-desks, musical instruments, &c. All were saved. '*It seemed to them that they had been placed near the windows in a way to be handy.*' After the fire, had never seen or heard anything of the old man and his wife, unless two skeletons that had been found were their skeletons. Supposed them to be the skeletons of Peter Goodwin and his wife. – Here the remains were for the first time on that trial exposed to view. 'Those are the same skeletons, should say – had no doubt of it; they are about the size of the old couple. The husband was short; the wife tall. Little or no difference in their height. Had never seen the stocking or the gold; but had heard a good deal of talk of them, having lived near neighbours to the Goodwins five-and-twenty years.'

Dunscomb conducted the cross-examination. He was close, discriminating, and judicious. Separating the hearsay and gossip from the facts known, he at once threw the former to the winds, as matter not to be received by the jury. We shall give a few of his questions and their answers that have a bearing on the more material points of the trial.

'I understand you to say, witness, that you knew both Peter Goodwin and his wife?'

'I did – I knew them well – saw them almost every day of my life.'

'For how long a time?'

'This many a day. For five-and-twenty years, or a little more.'

'Will you say that you have been in the habit of seeing Peter Goodwin and his wife daily, or almost daily, for five-and-twenty years?'

'If not right down daily, quite often; as often as once or twice a week, certainly.'

'Is this material, Mr Dunscomb!' inquired the judge. 'The time of the court is very precious.'

'It *is* material, your honour, as showing the looseness with which witnesses testify; and as serving to caution the jury how they receive their evidence. The opening of the prosecution shows us that if the charge is to be made out at all against the prisoner, it is to be made out on purely circumstantial evidence. It is not pretended that any one *saw* Mary Monson kill the Goodwins; but the crime is to be *inferred* from a series of collateral facts, that will be laid before the court and jury. I think your honour will see how important it is, under the circumstances, to analyze the testimony, even on points that may not seem to bear directly on the imputed crimes. If a witness testify loosely, the jury ought to be made to see it. I have a life to defend, your honour will remember.'

'Proceed, sir; the court will grant you the widest latitude.'

'You now say as often as once or twice a week, witness; on reflection, will you swear to even *that?*'

'Well, if not twice, I am sure I can say once.'

Dunscomb was satisfied with this answer, which went to show that the witness could reply a little at random, and was not always certain of his facts, when pressed.

'Are you certain that Dorothy Goodwin is dead?'

'I suppose I am as certain as any of the neighbours.'

'That is not an answer to my question. Will you, and do you swear on your oath, that Peter Goodwin, the person named in the indictment, is actually dead?'

'I'll swear that I *think* so.'

'That is not what I want. You see those skeletons – will you say, on your oath, that you *know* them to be the skeletons of Peter and Dorothy Goodwin?'

'I'll swear that I believe it.'

'That does not meet the question. Do you *know* it?'

'How can I know it? I'm not a doctor, or a surgeon. No, I do not absolutely *know* it. Still, I believe that one is the skeleton of Peter Goodwin, and the other the skeleton of his wife.'

'Which do you suppose to be the skeleton of Peter Goodwin?'

This question puzzled the witness not a little. To the ordinary eye, there was scarcely any difference in the appearance of these sad remains; though one skeleton had been ascertained by actual measurement to be about an inch and a half longer than the other. This fact was known to all in Biberry; but it was not easy to say which was which, at a glance. The witness took the safe course, therefore, of putting his opinion altogether on a different ground.

'I do not pretend to tell one from the other,' was the answer. 'What I know of my own knowledge is this, and this only. I knew Peter and Dorothy Goodwin; knew the house they lived in; know that the house has been burnt down, and that the old folks are not about their old ha'nts. The skeletons I never saw until they were moved from the place where they tell me they were found; for I was busy helping to get the articles saved under cover.'

'Then you do not pretend to know which skeleton is that of a man, or which that of a woman?'

This question was ingeniously put, and had the effect to make all the succeeding witnesses shy on this point; for it created a belief that there was a difference that might be recognized by those who are skilled in such matters. The witness assented to the view of Dunscomb; and having been so far sifted as to show he knew no more than all the rest of the neighbours, he was suffered to quit the stand. The result was, that very little was actually established by means of this testimony. It was evident that the jury was now on the alert, and not disposed to receive all that was said as gospel.

The next point was to make out all the known facts of the fire, and of the finding of the skeletons. The two witnesses just examined had seen the close of the fire, had *heard* of the skeletons, but had said very little more to the purpose. Dunscomb thought it might be well to throw in a hint to this effect in the present state of the case, as he now did by remarking –

'I trust that the District Attorney will see precisely where he stands. All that has yet been shown by legal proof are the facts that there were such persons as Peter and Dorothy Goodwin; facts we are not at all disposed to deny——'

'And that they have not appeared in the flesh since the night of the fire?' put in Williams.

'Not to the witnesses; but, to how many others does not appear.'

'Does the learned counsel mean to set up the defence that Goodwin and his wife are not dead?'

'It is for the prosecution to show the contrary affirmatively. If it be so, it is fair to presume they can do it. All I now contend for, is the fact that we have no proof as yet that either is dead. We have proof that the house was burnt; but we are now traversing an indictment for murder, and not that for arson. As yet, it strikes me, therefore, nothing material has been shown.'

'It is certainly material, Mr Dunscomb, that there should have been such persons as the Goodwins, and that they have disappeared since the night of the fire; and this much is proved, unless you impeach the witnesses,' observed the judge.

'Well, sir, that much we are not disposed to deny. There *were* such persons as the Goodwins, and they have disappeared from the neighbourhood. We believe that much ourselves.'

'Crier, call Peter Bacon.'

Bacon came forward, dressed in an entire new suit of clothes, and appearing much more respectable than was his wont. This man's testimony was almost word for word as it has already been given in the coroner's inquest. He established the facts of the fire, about which there could be no prudent contention indeed, and of the finding of the skeletons; for he had been one of those who aided in first searching the ruins for the remains. This man told his story in an extremely vulgar dialect, as we have had already occasion to show; but in a very clear, distinct manner. He meant to tell the truth, and succeeded reasonably well; for it does not occur to all who have the same upright intentions to effect their purposes as well as he did himself. Dunscomb's cross-examination was very brief; for he perceived it was useless to attempt to deny what had been thus proved.

'Jane Pope' — called out the District Attorney — 'Is Mrs Jane Pope in court?'

The widow Pope was on the spot, and ready and willing to answer. She removed her bonnet, took the oath, and was shown to the seat with which it is usual to accommodate persons of her sex.

'Your name,' said Dunscomb, holding his pen over the paper.

'Pope — Jane Pope since my marriage; but Jane Anderson from my parents.'

Dunscomb listened politely, but recorded no more than the appellation of the widow. Mrs Pope now proceeded to tell her story, which she did reasonably well, though not without a good deal of unnecessary amplitude, and some slight contradictions. It was *her* intention, also, to tell nothing but the truth; but persons whose tongues move as nimbly as that of this woman's, do not always know exactly what they do say. Dunscomb detected the contradictions; but he had the tact to see their cause, saw that they were not material, and wisely abstained from confounding whatever of justice there was in the defence with points that the jury had probably sufficient sagacity to see were of no great moment. He made no note, therefore, of these little oversights, and allowed the woman to tell her whole story uninterrupted. When it came to his turn to cross-examine, however, the duty of so doing was not neglected.

'You say, Mrs Pope, that you had often seen the stocking in which Mrs Goodwin kept her gold. Of what material was that stocking?'

'Wool — yes, of blue woollen yarn. A stocking knit by hand, and very darny.'

'Should you know the stocking, Mrs Pope, were you to see it again?'

'I think I might. Dolly Goodwin and I looked over the gold together more than once; and the stocking got to be a sort of acquaintance.'

'Was this it?' continued Dunscomb, taking a stocking of the sort described from Timms, who sat ready to produce the article at the proper moment.

'If it please the court,' cried Williams, rising in haste, and preparing eagerly to interrupt the examination.

'Your pardon, sir,' put in Dunscomb, with great self-command, but very firmly, 'words must not be put into the witness's mouth, nor ideas into her head. She has sworn, may it please your honour, to a certain stocking, which stocking she described in her examination in chief; and we now ask her if this is that stocking. All this is regular, I believe, and I trust we are not to be interrupted.'

'Go on, sir,' said the judge; 'the prosecution will not interrupt the defence. But time is very precious.'

'Is this the stocking?' repeated Dunscomb.

The woman examined the stocking, looking inside and out, turning it over and over, and casting many a curious glance at the places that had been mended.

'It's dreadful darny, isn't it?' she said, looking inquiringly at the counsellor.

'It is as you see, ma'am. I have made no alteration in it.'

'I declare I believe this *is* the very stocking.'

'At the proper time, your honour, we shall show that this is *not* the stocking, if indeed there ever was such a stocking at all,' said Timms, rolling up the article in question, and handing it to the clerk to keep.

'You saw a certain piece of gold, you say,' resumed Dunscomb, 'which piece of gold, I understand you to say was afterwards found in the pocket of Mary Monson. Will you have the goodness to say whether the piece of gold which you saw in Mrs Goodwin's possession is among these?' showing a dozen coins; 'or whether one resembling it is here?'

The woman was greatly puzzled. She meant to be honest; had told no more than was true, with the exception of the little embellishments that her propensity to imagine and talk rendered almost unavoidable; but, for the life of her, she could not distinguish the piece of money, or its counterpart. After examining the coins for several minutes she frankly admitted her ignorance.

'It is scarcely necessary to continue this cross-examination,' said Dunscomb, looking at his watch. 'I shall ask the court to adjourn, and to adjourn over until morning. We have reached the hour for lighting candles; but we have agents out in quest of most important witnesses; and we ask the loss of this evening as a favour. It can make no great difference as to the length of the trial; and the jurors will be all the fresher for a good night's rest.'

The court acquiesced, and allowed of the adjournment, giving the jury the usual charge about conversing or making up their opinions until they had heard the whole testimony; a charge that both Williams and Timms took very good care to render of no use in several instances, or as regarded particular individuals.

A decided impression was made in favour of the prisoner by Mrs Pope's failure to distinguish the piece of money. In her examination in chief she saw no difficulty in recognising the single piece then shown to her, and which was the Dutch coin actually found in Mary Monson's purse; but when it was put among a dozen others resembling it, more or less, she lost all confidence in herself, and, to a certain point, completely broke down as a witness. But Dunscomb saw that the battle had not yet in truth begun. What had passed was merely the skirmishing of light troops, feeling the way for the advance of the heavy columns and the artillery that were to decide the fortunes of the day.

CHAPTER XXIII

'Tis the wisest way, upon all tender-topics, to be silent; for he who takes upon himself to defend a lady's reputation, only publishes her favours to the world.

CUMBERLAND.

The wing of 'Horton's Inn' that contained the room of Dunscomb, was of considerable extent, having quite a dozen rooms in it, though mostly of the diminutive size of an American tavern bed-room. The best apartment in it, one with two windows, and of some dimensions, was that appropriated to the counsellor. The doctor and his party had a parlour, with two bed-rooms; while, between these and the room occupied by Dunscomb, was that of the troublesome guest – the individual who was said to be insane. Most of the remainder of the wing, which was much the most quiet and retired portion of the house, was used for a better class of bed-rooms. There were two rooms, however, that the providence of Horton and his wife had set apart for a very different purpose. These were small parlours, in which the initiated smoked, drank, and played.

Nothing sooner indicates the school in which a man has been educated, than his modes of seeking amusement. One who has been accustomed to see innocent relaxation innocently indulged, from childhood up, is rarely tempted to abuse those habits which have never been associated, in his mind, with notions of guilt, and which, in themselves, necessarily imply no moral delinquency. Among the liberal, cards, dancing, music, all games of skill and chance that can interest the cultivated, and drinking, in moderation and of suitable liquors, convey no ideas of wrong doing. As they have been accustomed to them from early life, and have seen them practised with decorum and a due regard to the habits of refined society, there is no reason for concealment or consciousness. On the other hand, an exaggerated morality, which has the temerity to enlarge the circle of sin beyond the bounds for which it can find any other warranty than its own metaphysical inferences, is very apt to create a factitious conscience, that almost invariably takes refuge in that vilest of all delinquency – direct hypocrisy. This, we take it, is the reason that the reaction of ultra godliness so generally leaves its subjects in the mire and sloughs of deception and degradation. The very same acts assume different characters, in the hands of these two classes of persons; and that which is perfectly innocent with the first, affording a pleasant, and in that respect a useful relaxation, becomes low, vicious, and dangerous with the other, because tainted with the corrupting and most dangerous practices of deception. The private wing of Horton's inn, to which there has been allusion, furnished an example in point of what we mean, within two hours of the adjournment of the court.

In the parlour of Mrs McBrain, late Dunscomb's Widow Updyke, as he used to call her, a little table was set in the middle of the room, at which Dunscomb himself, the doctor, his new wife and Sarah were seated, at a game of whist. The door was not locked, no countenance manifested either a secret consciousness of wrong, or an overweening desire to transfer another's money to its owner's pocket, although a sober sadness might be said to reign in the party, the consequence of the interest all took in the progress of the trial.

Within twenty feet of the spot just mentioned, and in the two little parlours already named, was a very different set collected. It consisted of the rowdies of the bar, perhaps two-thirds of the reporters in attendance on Mary Monson's trial, several suitors, four or five country doctors, who had been summoned as witnesses, and such other equivocal gentry as might aspire to belong to a set as polished and exclusive as that we are describing. We will first give a moment's attention to the party around the whist-table, in the parlour first described.

'I do not think the prosecution has made out as well, to-day, all things considered, as it was generally supposed it would,' observed McBrain. 'There is the ace of trumps, Miss Sarah, and if you can follow it with the king, we shall get the odd trick.'

'I do not think I shall follow it with anything,' answered Sarah, throwing down her cards. 'It really seems heartless to be playing whist, with a fellow-creature of our acquaintance on trial for her life.'

'I have not half liked the game,' said the quiet Mrs McBrain, 'but Mr Dunscomb seemed so much bent on a rubber, I scarce knew how to refuse him.'

'Why, true enough, Tom,' put in the doctor, 'this is all your doings, and if there be anything wrong about it, you will have to bear the blame.'

'Play anything but a trump, Miss Sarah, and *we* get the game. You are quite right, Ned' – throwing down the pack – 'the prosecution has not done as well as I feared they might. That Mrs Pope was a witness I dreaded, but her testimony amounts to very little, in itself; and what she has said, has been pretty well shaken by her ignorance of the coin.'

'I really begin to hope the unfortunate lady may be innocent,' said the doctor.

'Innocent!' exclaimed Sarah – 'surely, uncle Ned, you can never have doubted it!'

McBrain and Dunscomb exchanged significant glances, and the last was about to answer, when raising his eyes, he saw a strange form glide stealthily into the room, and place itself in a dark corner. It was a short, sturdy figure of a man, with all those signs of squalid misery in his countenance and dress that usually denote mental imbecility. He seemed anxious to conceal himself, and did succeed in getting more than half of his person beneath a shawl of Sarah's, ere he was seen by any of the party but the counsellor. It at once occurred to the latter that this was the being who had more than once disturbed him by his noise, and who Mrs Horton had pretty plainly intimated was out of his mind; though she had maintained a singularly discreet silence for her, touching his history and future prospects. She believed 'he had been brought to court by his friends, to get some order, or judgment – may be, his visit had something to do with the new code, about which 'Squire Dunscomb said so many hard things.'

A little scream from Sarah soon apprised all in the room of the presence of this disgusting-looking object. She snatched away her shawl, leaving the idiot, or madman, or whatever he might be, fully exposed to view, and retreated, herself, behind her uncle's chair.

'I fancy you have mistaken your room, my friend,' said Dunscomb, mildly. 'This, as you see, is engaged by a card-party – I take it, you do not play.'

A look of cunning left very little doubt of the nature of the malady with which this unfortunate being was afflicted. He made a clutch at the cards, laughed, then drew back, and began to mutter.

'She won't let me play,' mumbled the idiot – 'she never *would*.'

'Whom do you mean by she?' asked Dunscomb. 'Is it any one in this house – Mrs Horton, for instance?'

Another cunning look, with a shake of the head, for an answer in the negative.

'Be you 'Squire Dunscomb, the great York lawyer?' asked the stranger, with interest.

'Dunscomb is certainly my name – though I have not the pleasure of knowing yours.'

'I haven't got any name. They may ask me from morning to night, and I won't tell. She won't let me.'

'By *she*, you again mean Mrs Horton, I suppose?'

'No, I don't. Mrs Horton's a *good* woman; she gives me victuals and drink.'

'Tell us whom you do mean, then.'

'Won't you tell?'

'Not unless it be improper to keep the secret. Who is this *she*?'

'Why, *she*.'

'Ay, but who?'

'Mary Monson. If you're the great lawyer from York, and they say you be, you must know all about Mary Monson.'

'This is very extraordinary!' said Dunscomb, regarding his companion, in surprise. 'I *do* know something about Mary Monson, but not *all* about her. Can you tell me anything?'

Here the stranger advanced a little from his corner, listened, as if fearful of being surprised, then laid a finger on his lip, and made the familiar sound for 'hush.'

'Don't let her hear you; if you do, you may be sorry for it. She's a witch!'

'Poor fellow! – she seems in truth to have bewitched you, as I dare say she may have done many another man.'

'That has she! I wish you'd tell me what I want to know, if you really be the great lawyer from York.'

'Put your questions, my friend; I'll endeavour to answer them.'

'Who set fire to the house? Can you tell me *that*?'

'That is a secret yet to be discovered – do you happen to know anything about it?'

'Do I? – I think I do. Ask Mary Monson; *she* can tell you.'

All this was so strange, that the whole party now gazed at each other in mute astonishment; McBrain bending his looks more intently on the stranger, in order to ascertain the true nature of the mental malady with which he was obviously afflicted. In some respects the disease wore the appearance of idiocy; then again there were gleams of the countenance that savoured of absolute madness.

'You are of opinion, then, that Mary Monson knows who set fire to the house.'

'Sartain, she does. I know, too, but I won't tell. They might want to hang me, as well as Mary Monson, if I told. I know too much to do anything so foolish. Mary has said they would hang *me*, if I tell. I don't want to be hanged, a bit.'

A shudder from Sarah betrayed the effect of these words on the listeners; and Mrs McBrain actually rose with the intention of sending for her daughter, who was then in the gaol, consoling the much-injured prisoner, as Anna Updyke firmly believed her to be, by her gentle but firm friendship. A word from the doctor, however, induced her to resume her seat, and to await the result with a greater degree of patience.

'Mary Monson would seem to be a very prudent counsellor,' rejoined Dunscomb.

'Yes; but she isn't the great counsellor from York – you be that gentleman, they tell me.'

'May I ask who told you anything about me?'

'Nancy Horton – and so did Mary Monson. Nancy said if I made so much noise, I should disturb the great counsellor from York, and he might get me hanged for it. I was only singing hymns, and they say it is good for folks in trouble to sing hymns. If you be the great counsellor from York, I wish you would tell me one thing. Who got the gold that was in the stocking?'

'Do you happen to know anything of that stocking, or of the gold?'

'Do I – ' looking first over one shoulder, then over the other, but hesitating to proceed. 'Will they hang me, if I tell?'

'I should think not; though I can only give you an opinion. Do not answer, unless it be agreeable to you.'

'I want to tell – I want to tell *all*, but I'm afeared. I don't want to be hanged.'

'Well, then, speak out boldly, and I will promise that you shall not be hanged. Who got the gold that was in the stocking?'

'Mary Monson. That's the way she has got so much money.'

'I cannot consent to leave Anna another instant in such company!' exclaimed the anxious mother. 'Go, McBrain, and bring her hither at once.'

'You are a little premature,' coolly remarked Dunscomb. 'This is but a person of weak mind; and too much importance should not be attached to his words. Let us hear what further he may have to say.'

It was too late. The footstep of Mrs Horton was heard in the passage; and the extraordinary being vanished as suddenly and as stealthily as he had entered.

'What can be made of this?' McBrain demanded, when a moment had been taken to reflect.

'Nothing, Ned; I care not if Williams knew it all. The testimony of such a man cannot be listened to for an instant. It is wrong in us to give it a second thought; though I perceive that you do. Half the mischief in the world is caused by misconceptions, arising from a very numerous family of causes; one of which is a disposition to fancy a great deal from a little. Do you pronounce the man an idiot – or is he a madman?'

'He does not strike me as absolutely either. There is something peculiar in his case; and I shall ask permission to look into it. I suppose we are done with the cards – shall I go for Anna?'

The anxious mother gave a ready assent; and McBrain went one way, while Dunscomb retired to his own room, not without stopping before his neighbour's door, whom he heard muttering and menacing within.

All this time the two little parlours mentioned were receiving their company. The law is doubtless a very elevated profession, when its practice is on a scale commensurate with its true objects. It becomes a very different pursuit, however, when its higher walks are abandoned, to choose a path amid its thickets and quagmires. Perhaps no human pursuit causes a wider range of character among its votaries, than the practice of this profession. In the first place, the difference, in an intellectual point of view, between the man who sees only precedents, and the man who sees the principles on which they are founded, is as marked as the difference between black and white. To this great distinction in mind, is to be added another that opens a still wider chasm, the results of practice, and which depends on morals. While one set of lawyers turn to the higher objects of their calling, declining fees in cases of obviously questionable right, and struggle to maintain their honesty in direct collision with the world and its temptations, another, and much the largest, falls readily into the practices of their craft – the word seems admirably suited to the subject – and live on, encumbered and endangered not only by their own natural vices, but greatly damaged by those that in a manner they adopt, as it might be *ex officio*. This latter course is unfortunately that taken by a vast number of the members of the bar all over the world, rendering them loose in their social morality, ready to lend themselves and their talents to the highest bidder, and causing them to be at first indifferent, and in the end blind, to the great features of right and wrong. These are the moralists who advance the doctrine that 'the advocate has a right to act as his client would act;' while the class first named allow that 'the advocate has a right to do what his client *has a right* to do,' and no more.

Perhaps there was not a single member of the profession present that night in the two little parlours of Mrs Horton, who recognized the latter of these rules; or who did not, at need, practise on the former. As has been already said, these were the rowdies of the Duke's county bar. They chewed, smoked, drank, and played, each and all coarsely. To things that were innocent in themselves they gave the aspect of guilt by their own manners. The doors were kept locked; even amid their coarsest jokes, their ribaldry, their oaths that were often revolting and painfully frequent, there was an uneasy watchfulness, as if they feared detection. There was nothing frank and manly in the deportment of these men. Chicanery, management, double-dealing, mixed up with the outbreakings of a coarse standard of manners, were visible in all they said or did, except, perhaps, at those moments when hypocrisy was paying its homage to virtue. This hypocrisy, however, had little, or at most a very indirect connection with anything religious. The offensive offshoots of the exaggerations that were so abounding among us half a century since, are giving place to hypocrisy of another school. The homage that was then paid to principles, however erroneous and forbidding, is now paid to the ballot-boxes. There was scarcely an individual around those card-tables, at which the play was so obviously for the stakes as to render the whole scene revolting, who would not have shrunk from having his amusements known. It would seem as if conscience consulted taste. Everything was coarse and offensive; the attitudes, oaths, conversation, liquors, and even the manner of drinking them. Apart from the dialogue, little was absolutely done that might not have been made to lose most of its repulsiveness, by adopting a higher school of manners; but of this these scions of a noble stock knew no more than they did of the parent stem.

It is scarcely necessary to say that both Williams and Timms were of this party. The relaxation was, in fact, in conformity with their tastes and practices; and each of these excrescences of a rich and beneficent soil counted on the meetings in Mrs Horton's private rooms, as the more refined seek pleasure in the exercise of their tastes and habits.

'I say, Timms,' bawled out an attorney of the name of Crooks, 'you play'd a trump, sir – all right – go a-head – first rate – good play, that – ours dead. I say, Timms, you're going to save Mary Monson's neck. When I came here, I thought she was a case; but the prosecution is making out miserably.'

'What do you say to that, Williams?' put in Crooks's partner, who was smoking, playing, and drinking, with occasional 'asides' of swearing, all, as might be, at the same time. 'I trump that, sir, by your leave – what do you say to that, Williams?'

'I say that this is not the court; and trying such a cause once ought to satisfy a reasonable man.'

'He's afraid of showing his hand, which I am not,' put in another, exposing his cards as he spoke. 'Williams always has some spare trumps, however, to get him out of all his difficulties.'

'Yes, Williams has a spare trump, and there it is, giving me the trick,' answered the saucy lawyer, as coolly as if he had been engaged in an inferior slander-suit. 'I shall be at Timms pretty much by the same process to-morrow.'

'Then you will do more than you have done to-day, Master Williams. This Mrs Jane Pope *may be* a trump, but she is not the ace. I never knew a witness break down more completely.'

'We'll find the means to set her up again – I think that knave is yours, Green – yes, I now see my game, which is to take it with the queen – very much, Timms, as we shall beat you to-morrow. I keep my trump card always for the last play, you know.'

'Come, come, Williams,' put in the oldest member of the bar, a man whose passions were cooled by time, and who had more gravity than most of his companions – 'Come, come, Williams, this is a trial for a life, and joking is a little out of place.'

'I believe there is no juror present, Mr Marvin, which is all the reserve the law exacts.'

'Although the law may tolerate this levity, feeling will not. The prisoner is a fine young woman; and for my part, though I wish to say nothing that may influence any one's opinion, I have heard nothing yet to justify an indictment, much less a conviction.'

Williams laid down his cards, rose, stretched his arms, gaped, and taking Timms by the arm, he led the latter from the room. Not content with this, the wary limb of the law continued to move forward, until he and his companion were in the open air.

'It is always better to talk secrets outside than inside of a house,' observed Williams, as soon as they were at a safe distance from the inn-door. 'It is not too late yet, Timms – you must see how weak we are, and how bunglingly the District Attorney has led off. Half those jurors will sleep to-night with a feeling that Mary Monson has been hardly dealt by.'

'They may do the same to-morrow night, and every night in the month,' answered Timms.

'Not unless the arrangement is made. We have testimony enough to hang the governor.'

'Show us your list of witnesses, then, that we may judge of this for ourselves.'

'That would never do. They might be bought off for half the money that is necessary to take us out of the field. Five thousand dollars can be no great matter for such a woman and her friends.'

'Whom do you suppose to be her friends, Williams? – If you know them, you are better informed than her own counsel.'

'Yes, and a pretty point *that* will make, when pressed against you. No, no, Timms; your client has been ill-advised, or she is unaccountably obstinate. She has friends, although you may not know who they are; and friends who can, and who *would* very promptly help her, if she would consent to ask their assistance. Indeed, I suspect she has cash enough on hand to buy us off.'

'Five thousand dollars is a large sum, Williams, and is not often to be found in Biberry gaol. But if Mary Monson has these friends, name them, that we may apply for their assistance.'

'Harkee, Timms; you are not a man so ignorant of what is going on in the world as to require to be told the letters of the alphabet. You know that there are extensive associations of rogues in this young country, as well as in most that are older.'

'What has that to do with Mary Monson and our case?'

'Everything. This Mary Monson has been sent here to get at the gold of the poor old dolt, who has not been able to conceal her treasure after it was hoarded. She made a sub-treasury of her stocking, and exhibited the coin, like any other sub-treasurer. Many persons like to look at it, just to feast their eyes.'

'More to finger it; and you are of the number, Williams!'

'I admit it. The weakness is general in the profession, I believe. But this is idle talk, and we are losing very precious time. Will you, or will you not, apply again to your client for the money?'

'Answer me candidly, a question or two, and I will do as you desire. You know, Williams, that we are old friends, and never had any serious difficulty since we have been called to the bar.'

'Oh, assuredly,' answered Williams, with an ironical smile that it might have been fortunate for the negotiation the obscurity concealed from his companion; 'excellent friends from the beginning, Timms, and likely to continue so, I trust, to the last. Men who *know* each other as well as you and I, ought to be on the best of terms. For my part I never harboured a wrangle at the bar in my mind five minutes after I left the court. Now for your question.'

'You surely do not set down Mary Monson as the stool-pigeon of a set of York thieves!'

'Who or what else can she be, Mr Timms? Better educated, and belonging to an "upper ten" in villany, but of a company of rogues. Now, these knaves stand by each other much more faithfully than the body of the citizens stand by the law; and the five thousand will be forthcoming for the asking.'

'Are you serious in wishing me to believe you think my client guilty!'

Here Williams made no bones of laughing outright. It is true that he suppressed the noise immediately, lest it should attract attention; but laugh he did, and with right good will.

'Come, Timms, you have asked your question, and I leave you to answer it yourself. One thing I will say, however, in the way of admonition, which is this – we shall make out such a case against her to-morrow as would hang a governor, as I have already told you.'

'I believe you've done your worst already; why not let me know the names of your witnesses?'

'You know the reason. We wish the whole sum ourselves, and have no fancy to its being scattered all over Duke's. I give you my honour, Timms – and you know what *that* is – I give you my honour that we hold this testimony in reserve.'

'In which case the District Attorney will bring the witnesses on the stand; and we shall gain nothing, after all, by your withdrawal.'

'The District Attorney has left the case very much to me. I have prepared his brief, and have taken care to keep to myself enough to turn the scales. If I quit, Mary Monson will be acquitted; if I stay, she will be hanged. A pardon for *her* will be out of the question – she is too high among the "upper ten" to expect *that* – besides, she is not an anti-renter.'

'I wonder the thieves do not combine, as well as other folks, and control votes.'

'They do; these anti-renters belong to the gangs, and have already got their representatives in high places. They are "land-pirates," while *your* client goes for the old stockings. The difference in principle is by no means important, as any clear-headed man may see. It is getting late, Timms.'

'I cannot believe that Mary Monson is the sort of person you take her for! Williams, I've always looked upon you, and treated you as a friend. You may remember how I stood by you in the Middlebury case?'

'Certainly; you did your duty by me in that matter, and I have not forgot it.'

The cause alluded to was an action for a 'breach of promise,' which, at one time, threatened all of Williams's 'future usefulness,' as it is termed; but which was put to sleep in the end by means of Timms's dexterity in managing the 'out-door' points of a difficult case.

'Well, then, be *my* friend in this matter. I will be honest with you, and acknowledge that, as regards my client, I have had – that is provided she is acquitted, and her character comes out fair – that I have had – and *still* have, for that matter – what——'

'Are called "ulterior views." I understand you, Timms, and have suspected as much these ten days. A great deal depends on what you consider a fair character. Taking the best view of her situation, Mary Monson will have been tried for murder and arson.'

'Not if acquitted of the first. I have the District Attorney's promise to consent to a *nolle prosequi* on the last indictment, if we traverse the first successfully.'

'In which case Mary Monson will have been tried for murder only,' returned Williams, smiling. 'Do you really think, Timms, that your heart is soft enough to receive and retain an impression as deep as that made by the seal of the court?'

'If I thought, as you do, that my client is or has been connected with thieves, and burglars, and counterfeiters, I would not think of her for a moment as a wife. But there is a vast difference between a person overtaken by sudden temptation and one who sins on calculation, and by regular habit. Now, in my own case, I sometimes act wrong – yes, I admit as much as that——'

'It is quite unnecessary,' said Williams, drily.

'It is not according to Christian doctrine to visit old offences on a sinner's head, when repentance has washed away the crime.'

'Which means, Timms, that you will marry Mary Monson, although she may be guilty; provided always, that two very important contingencies are favourably disposed of.'

'What contingencies do you allude to, Williams? I know of none.'

'One is, provided she will have you; the other is, provided she is not hanged.'

'As to the first, I have no great apprehension; women that have been once before a court, on a trial for a capital offence, are not very particular. On my side, it will be easy enough to persuade the public that, as counsel in a most interesting case, I became intimately acquainted with her virtues, touched by her misfortunes, captivated by her beauty and accomplishments, and finally overcome by her charms. I don't think, Williams, that such an explanation would fail of its effect, before a caucus even. Men are always favourably disposed to those they think worse off than they are themselves. A good deal of capital is made on that principle.'

'I do not know that it would. Now-a-days the elections generally turn more on public principles than on private conduct. The Americans are a most forgiving people, unless you tell them the *truth*. *That* they will not pardon.'

'Nor any other nation, I fancy. Human natur' revolts at it. But *that*' — snapping his fingers — 'for your elections; it is the caucuses that I lay myself out to meet. Give me the *nomination*, and I am as certain of my seat as, in the old countries, a first-born is to his father's throne.'

'It is pretty safe as a rule, I allow; but nominations sometimes fail.'

'Not when regular, and made on proper principles. A nomination is about as good as popularity.'

'Often better; for men are just asses enough to work in the collar of party, even when overloaded. But all this time the night is wearing away. If I go into court in the morning, it will be too late. This thing must be settled at once, and that in a very explicit manner.'

'I wish I knew what you have picked up concerning Mary Monson's early life!' said Timms, like a man struggling with doubt.

'You have heard the rumour as well as myself. Some say she is a wife already; while others think her a rich widow. My opinion you know; I believe her to be the stool-pigeon of a York gang, and no better than she should be.'

This was plain language to be addressed to a lover; and Williams meant it to be so. He had that sort of regard for Timms which proceeds from a community in practices, and was disposed to regret that a man with whom he had been so long connected, either as an associate or an antagonist, should marry a woman of the pursuits that he firmly believed marked the career of Mary Monson.

The gentlemen of the bar are no more to be judged by appearances than the rest of mankind. They will wrangle, and seem to be at sword's points with each other, at one moment, when the next may find them pulling together in harmony in the next case on the calendar. It was under this sort of feeling that Williams had a species of friendship for his companion.

'I will try, Williams,' said the last, turning towards the gaol. 'Yes, I will make one more trial.'

'Do, my good fellow — and, Timms, remember one thing; you can never marry a woman that has been hanged.'

CHAPTER XXIV

The time is precious; I'll about it straight.

Earl of Essex.

The gaol presented a very different scene. A solemn stillness reigned in its gallery; and even good Mrs Gott had become weary with the excitement of the day, and had retired to rest. A single lamp was burning in the cell; and dark forms were dimly visible in the passage, without the direct influence of its rays. Two were seated, while a third paced the stone but carpeted pavement, with a slow and quiet step. The first were the shadowy forms of Anna Updyke and Marie Moulin; the last that of Mary Monson. For half an hour the prisoner had been on her knees, praying for strength to endure a burden that surpassed her expectations; and, as is usual with those who look above for aid, more especially women, she was reaping the benefit of her petition. Not a syllable had she uttered, however, since quitting the cell. Her voice, soft, melodious, and lady-like, was now heard for the first time.

'My situation is most extraordinary, Anna,' she said; 'it proves almost too much for my strength! This has been a terrible day, calm as I may have appeared; and I fear that the morrow will be still harder to be borne. There is an expression about the eyes of that man Williams, that both alarms and disgusts me. I am to expect in him a most fiery foe.'

'Why, then, do you not escape from scenes for which you are so unsuited, and leave this saucy Williams to himself, and his schemes of plunder?'

'That would not do. Several sufficient reasons exist for remaining. Were I to avail myself of the use of the keys I possess, and quit the gaol not to return, good Mrs Gott and her husband would, probably, both be ruined. Although they are ignorant of what money and ingenuity have done for me, it would be difficult to induce the world to believe them innocent. But a still higher reason for remaining, is the vindication of my own character.'

'No one will think of confounding *you* with Mary Monson; and by going abroad as you say it is your intention to do, you would effectually escape from even suspicion.'

'You little know the world, my dear. I see that all the useful lessons I gave you as your school-mamma, are already forgotten. The six years between us in age have given me an experience that tells me to do nothing of the sort. Nothing is so certain to follow us as a bad name; though the good one is easily enough forgotten. As Mary Monson, I am indicted for these grievous crimes; as Mary Monson will I be acquitted of them. I feel an affection for the character, and shall not degrade it by any act as base as that of flight.'

'Why not, then, resort to the other means you possess, and gain a speedy triumph in open court?'

As Anna put this question, Mary Monson came beneath the light and stopped. Her handsome face was in full view, and her friend saw an expression on it that gave her pain. It lasted only a moment; but that moment was long enough to induce Anna to wish she had not seen it. On several previous occasions this same expression had rendered her uneasy; but the evil look was soon forgotten in the quiet elegance of manners that borrowed charms from a countenance usually as soft as the evening sky in September. Ere she resumed her walk, Mary Monson shook her head in dissent from the proposition of her friend, and passed on, a shadowy but graceful form, as she went down the gallery.

'It would be premature,' she said, 'and I should fail of my object. I will not rob that excellent Mr Dunscomb of his honest triumph. How calm and gentlemanlike he was to-day; yet how firm and prompt, when it became necessary to show these qualities.'

'Uncle Tom is all that is good; and we love him as we would love a parent.'

A pause succeeded, during which Mary Monson walked along the gallery once, in profound thought.

'Yours promises to be a happy future, my dear,' she said. 'Of suitable ages, tempers, stations, country — yes, country; for an American woman should never marry a foreigner!'

Anna Updyke did not reply; and a silence succeeded that was interrupted by the rattling of a key in the outer door.

'It is your new father, Anna, come to see you home. Thank you, kind-hearted and most generous-minded girl. I feel the sacrifices that you and your friend are making in my behalf, and shall carry the recollection of them to the grave. On her, I had no claims at all; and on you, but those that are very slight. You have been to me, indeed, most excellent friends, and a great support when both were most needed. Of my own sex, and of the same social level, I do not now see how I should have got on without you. Mrs Gott is kindness and good-nature themselves; but she is so different from us in a thousand things, that I have often been pained by it. In our intercourse with you, how different! Knowing so much, you pry into nothing. Not a question, not a look to embarrass me; and with a perfect and saint-like reliance on my innocence, were I a sister, your support could not be more warm-hearted or firm.'

After a short pause, in which this singular young woman smiled, and appeared to be talking to herself, she continued, after kissing her companion most affectionately for good-night, and walking with her as far as the door of the gallery, where it had been announced that the doctor was waiting for his step-daughter —

'I wish I knew whether the same faith goes through the connection – Mr John Wilmeter?'

'Oh! He is persuaded of your entire innocence. It was he who excited so much interest in me, on your behalf, before I had the least idea of our having ever met before.'

'He is a noble-hearted young man, and has many excellent qualities – a little romantic, but none the worse for that, my dear, as you will find in the end. Alas! alas! Those marriages that are made over a rent-roll, or an inventory, need a great deal of something very different from what they possess, to render them happy! Mr Wilmeter has told me that *no evidence* could make him believe in my guilt. There is a confidence that might touch a woman's heart, Anna, did circumstances admit of such a thing. I like that Michael Millington, too; the *name* is dear to me, as is the race of which he comes. No matter; the world *va son train*, let us regret and repine as we may. And Uncle Tom, Anna – what do you think of his real opinion? Is it in my favour or not?'

Anna Updyke had detected in Dunscomb a disposition to doubt, and was naturally averse to communicating a fact so unpleasant to her friend. Kissing the latter affectionately, she hurried away to meet McBrain, already waiting for her without. In quitting the dwelling of the building annexed to the gaol, the doctor and Anna met Timms hurrying forward to seek an interview with his client before she retired to rest. An application at once obtained permission for the limb of the law to enter.

'I have come, Miss Mary,' as Timms now called his client, 'on what I fear will prove a useless errand; but which I have thought it my duty to see performed, as your best friend, and one of your legal advisers. You have already heard what I had to say on the subject of a certain proposal of the next of kin to withdraw from the prosecution, which will carry with him this Williams, with whom I should think you would, by this time, be heartily disgusted. I come now to say that this offer is repeated with a good deal of emphasis, and that you have still an opportunity of lessening the force that is pressing on your interests, by at least one-half. Williams may well count for more than half of the vigour and shrewdness of what is doing for the State in your case.'

'The proposal must be more distinctly made, and you must let me have a clear view of what is expected from me, Mr Timms, before I can give any reply,' said Mary Monson. 'But you may wish to be alone with me before you are more explicit. I will order my woman to go into the cell.'

'It might be more prudent were we to go into the cell ourselves, and leave your domestic outside. These galleries carry sounds like ear-trumpets; and we never know who may be our next neighbour in a gaol.'

Mary Monson quietly assented to the proposal, calling to her woman in French to remain outside, in the dark, while she profited by the light of the lamp in the cell. Timms followed, and closed the door.

In size, form, and materials, the cell of Mary Monson was necessarily like that of every other inmate of the gaol. Its sides, top, and bottom, were of massive stones; the last two being flags of great dimensions. But taste and money had converted even this place into an apartment that was comfortable in all respects but that of size. Two cells opening on the section of gallery that the consideration of Mrs Gott had caused to be screened off, and appropriated to the exclusive use of the fair prisoner, one had been furnished as a sleeping apartment, while that in which Timms was now received, had more the air of a sort of *boudoir*. It was well carpeted, like all the rest of what might be termed the suite; and had a variety of those little elegancies that women of cultivated tastes and ample means are almost certain to gather about them. The harp which had occasioned so much scandal, as well as a guitar, stood near by; and chairs of different forms and various degrees of comfort, crowded the room, perhaps to superfluity. As this was the first time Timms had been admitted to the cell, he was all eyes, gazing about him at the numerous signs of wealth it contained, with inward satisfaction. It was a minute after he was desired to be seated before he could comply, so lively was the curiosity to be appeased. It was during this minute that Mary Moulin lighted four candles, that were already arranged in bronzed candlesticks, making a blaze of light for that small room. These candles were of spermaceti, the ordinary American substitute for wax. Nothing that he then saw, or had ever seen in his intercourse with his client, so profoundly impressed Timms as this luxury of light. Accustomed himself to read and write by a couple of small inferior articles in tallow, when he did not use a lamp, there seemed to be something regal to his unsophisticated imagination, in this display of brilliancy.

Whether Mary Monson had a purpose to answer in giving Timms so unusual a reception, we shall leave the reader to discover by means of his own sagacity; but circumstances might well lead one to the conclusion that she had. There was a satisfied look, as she glanced around the cell and surveyed its arrangements, that possibly led fairly enough to such an inference. Nevertheless, her demeanour was perfectly quiet, betraying none of the fidgeting uneasiness of an underbred person, lest all might not be right. Every arrangement was left to the servant; and when Mary Moulin finally quitted the cell and closed the door behind her, every thought of the apartment and what it contained seemed to vanish from the mind of her extraordinary mistress.

'Before you proceed to communicate the purpose of your visit, Mr Timms,' Mary Monson said, 'I shall ask permission to put a few questions of my own, touching the state of our cause. Have we gained or lost by this day's proceedings?'

'Most clearly gained, as every man at the bar will confirm by his opinion.'

'That has been my own way of thinking, and I am glad to hear it corroborated by such competent judges. I confess the prosecution does not seem to me to show the strength it really possesses. This Jane Pope made a miserable blunder about the piece of coin.'

'She has done the other side no great good, certainly.'

'How stands the jury, Mr Timms?'

Although this question was put so directly, Timms heard it with uneasiness. Nor did he like the expression of Mary Monson's eyes, which seemed to regard him with a keenness that might possibly imply distrust. But it was necessary to answer; though he did so with caution, and with a due regard to his own safety.

'It is pretty well,' he said, 'though not quite as much opposed to capital punishment as I had hoped for. We challenged off one of the sharpest chaps in the county, and have got in his place a man who is pretty much under my thumb.'

'And the stories – the reports – have they been well circulated?'

'A little too well, I'm afraid. That concerning your having married a Frenchman, and having run away from him, has gone through all the lower towns of Duke's like wild-fire. It has even reached the ears of 'Squire Dunscomb, and will be in the York papers to-morrow?'

A little start betrayed the surprise of the prisoner; and a look accompanied it, which would seem to denote dissatisfaction that a tale put in circulation by herself, as it would now appear, had gone quite so far.

'Mr Dunscomb!' she repeated, musingly. 'Anna Updyke's Uncle Tom; and one whom such a story may very well set thinking. I wish it had not reached *him*, of all men, Mr Timms.'

'If I may judge of his opinions by some little acts and expressions that have escaped him, I am inclined to think he believes the story to be, in the main, true.'

Mary Monson smiled; and, as was much her wont when thinking intensely, her lips moved; even a low muttering became audible to a person as near as her companion then was.

'It is now time, Mr Timms, to set the other story in motion,' she said quickly. 'Let one account follow the other; that will distract people's belief. We must be active in this matter.'

'There is less necessity for our moving in the affair, as Williams has got a clue to it, by some means or other, and his men will spread it far and near, long before the cause goes to the jury.'

'That is fortunate!' exclaimed the prisoner, actually clapping her pretty gloved hands together in delight. 'A story as terrible as *that* must react powerfully, when its falsehood comes to be shown. I regard that tale as the cleverest of all our schemes, Mr Timms.'

'Why – yes – that is – I think, Miss Mary, it may be set down as the *boldest.*'

'And this saucy Williams, as you call him, has got hold of it already, and believes it true!'

'It is not surprising; there are so many small and probable facts accompanying it.'

'I suppose you know what Shakespeare calls such an invention, Mr Timms?' said Mary Monson, smiling.

'I am not particularly acquainted with that author, ma'am. I know there was such a writer, and that he was thought a good deal of, in his day; but I can't say I have ever read him.'

The beautiful prisoner turned her large expressive blue eyes on her companion with a gaze of wonder; but her breeding prevented her from uttering what she certainly thought and felt.

'Shakespeare is a writer very generally esteemed,' she answered, after one moment of muttering, and one moment to control herself; 'I believe he is commonly placed at the head of our English literature, if not at the head of that of all times and nations – Homer, perhaps, excepted.'

'What! higher, do you think, Miss Mary, than Blackstone and Kent?'

'Those are authors of whom I know nothing, Mr Timms; but now, sir, I will listen to your errand here to-night.'

'It is the old matter. Williams has been talking to me again, touching the five thousand dollars.'

'Mr Williams has my answer. If five thousand *cents* would buy him off, he should not receive them from me.'

This was said with a frown; and then it was that the observer had the opportunity of tracing, in a face otherwise so lovely, the lines that indicate self-will, and a spirit not easily controlled. Alas! that women should ever so mistake their natural means to influence and guide, as to have recourse to the exercise of agents that they rarely wield with effect; and ever with a sacrifice of womanly character and womanly grace. The person who would draw the sex from the quiet scenes that they so much embellish, to mingle in the strifes of the world; who would place them in stations that nature has obviously intended men should occupy, is not their real friend, any more than the weak adviser, who resorts to reputed specifics when the knife alone can effect a cure. The Creator intended woman for a 'help-meet,' and not for the head of the family circle; and most fatally ill-judging are the laws that would fain disturb the order of a domestic government which is directly derived from divine wisdom as from divine benevolence.

'I told him as much, Miss Mary,' answered Timms; 'but he does not seem disposed to take "no" for an answer. Williams has the true scent for a dollar.'

'I am quite certain of an acquittal, Mr Timms; and having endured so much, and hazarded so much, I do not like to throw away the triumph of my approaching victory. There is a powerful excitement in my situation; and I like excitement to weakness, perhaps. No, no; my success must not be tarnished by any such covert bargain. I will not listen to the proposal for an instant.'

'I understand that the raising of the sum required would form no particular obstacle to the arrangement?' asked Timms, in a careless sort of way that was intended to conceal the real interest he took in the reply.

'None at all. The money might be in his hands before the court sits in the morning; but it never shall be as coming from me. Let Mr Williams know this definitively; and tell him to do his worst.'

Timms was a little surprised, and a good deal uneasy at this manifestation of a spirit of defiance, which could produce no good, and which might be productive of evil. While he was delighted to hear, for the fourth or fifth time, how easy it would be for his fair client to command a sum as large as that demanded, he secretly determined not to let the man who had sent him on his present errand know the temper in which it had been received. Williams was sufficiently dangerous as it was; and he saw all the hazard of giving him fresh incentives to increase his exertions.

'And now, as this matter is finally disposed of, Mr Timms – for I desire that it may not be again mentioned to me' – resumed the accused, 'let us say a word more on the subject of our new report. Your agent has set on foot a story that I belong to a gang of wretches who are combined to prey on society; and that, in this character, I came into Duke's to carry out one of its nefarious schemes?'

'That is the substance of the rumour we have started at your own desire; though I could wish it were not quite so strong, and that there were more time for the reaction.'

'The strength of the rumour is its great merit; and, as for time, we have abundance for our purposes. Reaction is the great power of popularity, as I have heard, again and again. It is always the most effective, too, at the turn of the tide. Let the public once get possessed with the notion that a rumour so injurious has been in circulation at the expense of one in my cruel condition, and the current of feeling will set the other way in a torrent that nothing can arrest!'

'I take the idea, Miss Mary, which is well enough for certain cases, but a little too hazardous for this. Suppose it should be ascertained that this report came from us?'

'It never can be, if the caution I directed was observed. You have not neglected my advice, Mr Timms?'

The attorney had not; and great had been his surprise at the ingenuity and *finesse* manifested by this singular woman, in setting afloat a report that would certainly act to her injury, unless arrested and disproved at a moment most critical in her future fate. Nevertheless, in obedience to Mary Monson's positive commands, this very bold measure had been undertaken; and Timms was waiting with impatience for the information by means of which he was to counteract these self-inflicted injuries, and make them the instruments of good on the reaction.

If that portion of society which takes delight in gossip could be made to understand the real characters of those to whom they commit the control of their opinions, not to say principles, there would be far more of reserve and self-respect observed in the submission to this social evil than there is at present. Malice, the inward impulses of the propagators of a lie, and cupidity, are at the bottom of half the tales that reach our ears; and in those cases in which the world in its ignorance fancies it has some authority for what it says, it as often happens that some hidden motive is at the bottom of the exhibition as the one which seems so apparent. There are a set of vulgar vices that may be termed the 'stereotyped,' they lie so near the surface of human infirmities. They who are most subject to their influence always drag these vices first into the arena of talk; and fully one-half of that of this nature which we hear, has its origin as much in the reflective nature of the gossip's own character, as in any facts truly connected with the acts of the subjects of his or her stories.

But Mary Monson was taking a far higher flight than the circulation of an injurious rumour. She believed herself to be putting on foot a master-stroke of policy. In her intercourse with Timms, so much was said of the power of opinion, that she had passed hours, nay days, in the study of the means to control and counteract it. Whence she obtained her notion of the virtue of reaction it might not be easy to say; but her theory was not without its truth; and it is certain that her means of producing it were of remarkable simplicity and ingenuity.

Having settled the two preliminaries of the rumour and of Williams's proposition, Timms thought the moment favourable to making a demonstration in his own affairs. Love he did not yet dare to propose openly; though he had now been, for some time, making covert demonstrations towards the tender passion. In addition to the motive of cupidity, one of great influence with such a man, Timms's heart, such as it was, had really yielded to the influence of a beauty, manners, accomplishments, and information, all of a class so much higher than he had been accustomed to meet with, as to be subjects of wonder with him, not to say of adoration. This man had his affections as well as another; and, while John Wilmeter had submitted to a merely passing inclination, as much produced by the interest he took in an unknown female's situation as by any other cause, poor Timms had been hourly falling more and more in love. It is a tribute to nature, that this passion can be, and is, felt by all. Although a purifying sentiment, the corrupt and impure can feel its power, and, in a greater or less degree, submit to its influence, though their homage may be tainted by the grosser elements that are so largely mixed up with the compound of their characters. We may have occasion to show hereafter how far the uncouth attorney of Mary Monson succeeded in his suit with his fair client.

CHAPTER XXV

I challenge envy,
Malice, and all the practices of hell,
To censure all the actions of my past
Unhappy life, and taint me if they can.

The Orphan.

It is to be presumed that Timms found the means to communicate to Williams the rejection of the latter's offer, before the court met next morning. It is certain that the counsel associated with the Attorney-General, manifested unusual zeal in the performance of duties that most men would have found unpleasant, if not painful, and that he was captious, short, and ill-natured. Just as Mary Monson came within the bar, a letter was put into the hands of Dunscomb, who quietly broke the seal, and read it twice, as the observant Timms fancied; then put it in his pocket, with a mien so undisturbed that no mere looker-on would have suspected its importance. The letter was from Millington, and it announced a general want of success in his mission. The whereabouts of M. de Larocheforte could not be ascertained; and those who knew anything about his movements, were of opinion that he was travelling in the West, accompanied by his fair, accomplished, and affluent young consort. None of those who would naturally have heard of such an event, had it occurred, could say there had ever been a separation between the French husband and the American wife. Millington, himself, had never seen his kinswoman, there being a coolness of long standing between the two branches of the family, and could give little or no information on the subject. In a word, he could discover nothing to enable him to carry out the clue obtained in the rumour; while, on the other hand, he found a certain set, who occupied themselves a good deal with intelligence of that sort, were greatly disposed to believe the report, set on foot by herself, that Mary Monson was a stool-pigeon of a gang of marauders, and doubtless guilty of everything of which she had been accused. Millington would remain in town, however, another day, and endeavour to push his inquiries to some useful result. Cool, clear-headed, and totally without romance, Dunscomb knew that a better agent than his young friend could not be employed, and was fain to wait patiently for the discoveries he might eventually succeed in making. In the meantime the trial proceeded.

'Mr Clerk,' said his honour, 'let the jury be called.'

This was done, and Mary Monson's lips moved, while a lurking smile lighted her countenance, as her eyes met the sympathy that was expressed in the countenances of several of the grave men who had been drawn as arbiters, in her case, between life and death. To her it was apparent that her sex, her youth, perhaps her air and beauty, stood her friends, and that she might largely count on the compassion of that small but important body of men. One of her calculations had succeeded to the letter. The tale of her being a stool-pigeon had been very actively circulated, with certain additions and embellishments that it was very easy to disprove; and another set of agents had been hard at work, all the morning, in brushing away such of the collateral circumstances as had, at first, been produced to confirm the main story, and which, in now being pulled to pieces as of no account, did not fail to cast a shade of the darkest doubt over the whole rumour. All this Mary Monson probably understood, and understanding, enjoyed; a vein of wild wilfulness certainly running through her character, leading in more directions than one.

'I hope there will be no delay on account of witnesses,' observed the judge. 'Time is very precious.'

'We are armed at all points, your honour, and intend to bring the matter to an early conclusion,' answered Williams, casting one of those glances at the prisoner which had obtained for him the merited *sobriquet* of 'saucy.' 'Crier, call Samuel Burton.'

Timms fairly started. This was breaking ground in a new spot, and was producing testimony from a source that he much dreaded. The Burtons had been the nearest neighbours of the Goodwins, and were so nearly on a social level with them, as to live in close and constant communication. These Burtons consisted of the man, his wife, and three maiden sisters. At one time, the last had conversed much on the subject of the murders; but, to Timms's great discontent, they had been quite dumb of late. This had prevented his putting in practice a method of anticipating testimony, that is much in vogue, and which he had deliberately attempted with these sometime voluble females. As the reader may not be fully initiated in the mysteries of that sacred and all-important master of the social relations, the law, we shall set forth the manner in which justice is often bolstered, when its interests are cared for by practitioners of the Timms's and Williams's school.

No sooner is it ascertained that a particular individual has a knowledge of an awkward fact, than these worthies of the bar set to work to extract the dangerous information from him. This is commonly attempted, and often effected, by inducing the witness to relate what he knows, and by leading him on to make statements that, on being sworn to in court, will either altogether invalidate his testimony, or throw so much doubt on it as to leave it of very little value. As the agents employed to attain this end are not very scrupulous, there is great danger that their imaginations may supply the defects in the statements, and substitute words and thoughts that the party never uttered. It is so easy to mistake another's meaning, with even the best intentions, that we are not to be surprised if this should seriously happen when the disposition is to mislead. With the parties to suits, this artifice is often quite successful, admissions being obtained, or supposed to be obtained, that they never, for an instant, intended to make. In the States where speculation has cornered men, and left them loaded with debt, these devices of the eaves-droppers and suckers are so common, as to render their testimony no immaterial feature in nearly every cause of magnitude that is tried. In such a state of society it is, indeed, unsafe for a suitor to open his lips on his affairs, lest some one near him be employed to catch up his words, and carry them into court with shades of meaning gathered from his own imagination.

At first, Timms was under the impression that the Burtons were going to sustain the defence, and he was placing himself on the most amiable footing with the females, three of whom might very reasonably be placed within the category of matrimony with this rising lawyer; but, it was not long ere he ascertained that Williams was getting to be intimate, and had proved to be a successful rival. Davis, the nephew and heir of the Goodwins, was a single man, too, and it is probable that his frequent visits to the dwelling of the Burtons had a beneficial influence on his own interests. Let the cause be what it might, the effect was clearly to seal the lips of the whole family, not a member of which could be induced, by any art practised by the agents of Timms, to utter a syllable on a subject that now really seemed to be forbidden. When, therefore, Burton appeared on the stand, and was sworn, the two counsel for the defence waited for him to open his lips, with a profound and common interest.

Burton knew the deceased, had lived all his life near them, was at home the night of the fire, went to assist the old people, saw the two skeletons, had no doubt were the remains of Peter Goodwin and his wife, observed the effects of a heavy blow across the foreheads of each, the same that was still to be seen, inferred that this blow had destroyed them, or so far stunned them as to leave them incapable of escaping from the fire.

This witness was then questioned on the subject of the stocking, and Mrs Goodwin's hoard of money. He had seen the stocking but once, had often heard it mentioned by his sisters, did not think his wife had ever alluded to it, did not know the amount of the gold, but supposed it might be very considerable, saw the bureau examined, and knew that the stocking could not be found. In a word, his testimony in chief went generally to sustain the impression that prevailed relative to the murders, though it is unnecessary to repeat it in this form, as the cross-examination will better explain his statements and opinions.

'Mr Burton,' said Dunscomb, 'you knew the Goodwins well?'

'Very well, sir. As well as near neighbours generally know each other.'

'Can you swear that those are the skeletons of Peter and Dorothy Goodwin?'

'I can swear that I *believe* them to be such – have no doubt of the fact.'

'Point out that which you suppose to be the skeleton of Peter Goodwin.'

This request embarrassed the witness. In common with all around him, he had no other clue to his facts than the circumstances under which these vestiges of mortality had been found, and he did not know what ought to be his reply.

'I suppose the shortest of the skeletons to be Peter Goodwin's, and the longest that of his wife,' he at length answered. 'Peter was not as tall as Dorothy.'

'Which is the shortest of these remains?'

'That I could not say, without measuring. I know that Goodwin was not as tall as his wife by half an inch, for I have seen them measure.'

'Then you would say that, in your opinion, the longest of these two skeletons is that of Dorothy Goodwin, and the shortest that of her husband?'

'Yes, sir; that is my opinion – formed to the best of my knowledge. I have seen them measure.'

'Was this measurement accurate?'

'Very much so. They used to dispute about their height, and they measured several times, when I was by; generally in their stocking feet, and once barefoot.'

'The difference being half an inch in favour of the wife?'

'Yes, sir, as near as could be; for I was umpire more than once.'

'Did Peter Goodwin and his wife live happily together?'

'Tolerable – much as other married folks get along.'

'Explain what you mean by that.'

'Why, there's ups and downs, I suppose, in all families. Dorothy was high-tempered and Peter was sometimes cross-grained.'

'Do you mean that they quarrelled?'

'They got r'iled with each other, now and then.'

'Was Peter Goodwin a sober man?'

The witness now appeared to be bothered. He looked around him, and meeting everywhere with countenances which evidently reflected 'yes,' he had not the moral courage to run counter to public opinion, and say 'no.' It is amazing what a tyrant this concentration of minds gets to be over those who are not very clear-headed themselves, and who are not constituted, morally, to resist its influence. It almost possesses a power to persuade these persons not to put faith in their own senses, and disposes them to believe what they hear, rather than what they have seen. Indeed, one effect is to cause them to see with the eyes of others. As the 'neighbours,' those inquisitors who know so much of persons of their association and intimacy, and so little of all others, very generally fancied Peter a sober man, Burton scarce knew what to answer. Circumstances had made him acquainted with the delinquency of the old man, but his allegations would not be sustained were he to speak the whole truth, since Peter had succeeded in keeping his infirmity from being generally known. To a man like the witness, it was easier to sacrifice the truth than to face a neighbourhood.

'I suppose he was much as others,' answered Burton, after a delay that caused some surprise. 'He was human, and had a human natur'. Independence days, and other rejoicings, I've known him give in more than the temperance people think is quite right; but I shouldn't say he was downright intemperate.'

'He drank to excess, then, on occasions?'

'Peter had a very weak head, which was his greatest difficulty.'

'Did you ever count the money in Mrs Goodwin's stocking?'

'I never did. There was gold and paper; but how much I do not know.'

'Did you see any strangers in or about the house of the Goodwins, the morning of the fire?'

'Yes; two strange men were there, and were active in helping the prisoner out of the window, and afterwards in getting out the furniture. They were very particular in saving Mary Monson's property.'

'Were those strangers near the bureau?'

'Not that I know. I helped carry the bureau out myself; and I was present afterwards in court when it was examined for the money. We found none.'

'What became of those strangers?'

'I cannot tell you. They were lost to me in the confusion.'

'Had you ever seen them before?'

'Never.'

'Nor since?'

'No, sir.'

'Will you have the goodness to take that rod, and tell me what is the difference in length between the two skeletons?'

'I trust, your honour, that this is testimony which will not be received,' put in Williams. 'The fact is before the jury, and they can take cognizance of it for themselves.'

Dunscomb smiled as he answered –

'The zeal of the learned gentleman runs ahead of his knowledge of the rules of evidence. Does he expect the jury to measure the remains; or are we to show the fact by means of witnesses?'

'This is a cross-examination; and the question is one in chief. The witness belongs to the defence, if the question is to be put at all.'

'I think not, your honour. The witness has testified, in chief, that he believes these remains to be those of Peter and Dorothy Goodwin; he has further said, on his cross-examination, that Dorothy was half an inch taller than Peter; we now wish to put to the test the accuracy of the first opinion, by comparing the two facts – his knowledge of the difference by the former measurement as compared with the present. It has been said that these two skeletons are very nearly of a length. We wish the truth to be seen.'

'The witness will answer the question,' said the judge.

'I doubt the power of the court to compel a witness to obtain facts in this irregular mode,' observed the pertinacious Williams.

'You can note your exceptions, brother Williams,' returned the judge, smiling; 'although it is not easy to see with what useful consequences. If the prisoner be acquitted, you can hardly expect to try her again; and, if convicted, the prosecution will scarcely wish to press any objection.'

Williams, who was as much influenced by a bull-dog tenacity, as by any other motive, now submitted; and Burton took the rod and measured the skeletons, an office he might have declined, most probably, had he seen fit. The spectators observed surprise in his countenance; and he was seen to repeat the measurement, seemingly with more care.

'Well, sir, what is the difference in the length of those skeletons?' inquired Dunscomb.

'I make it about an inch and a half, if these marks are to be relied on,' was the slow, cautious, well-considered reply.

'Do you now say that you believe these skeletons to be the remains of Peter and Dorothy Goodwin?'

'Whose else can they be? They were found on the spot where the old couple used to sleep.'

'I ask you to answer *my* question; I am not here to answer *yours*. Do you still say that you believe these to be the skeletons of Peter and Dorothy Goodwin?'

'I am a good deal non-plussed by this measurement – though the flesh, and skin, and muscles, may have made a considerable difference in life.'

'Certainly,' said Williams, with one of his withering sneers – sneers that had carried many a cause purely by their impudence and sarcasm – 'Every one knows how much more muscle a man has than a woman. It causes the great difference in their strength. A bunch of muscles, more or less in the heel, would explain all this, and a great deal more.'

'How many persons dwelt in the house of Goodwin at the time of the fire?' demanded Dunscomb.

'They tell me Mary Monson was there, and I saw her there during the fire; but I never saw her there before.'

'Do you know of any other inmate besides the old couple and the prisoner?'

'I did see a strange woman about the house for a week or two before the fire, but I never spoke to her. They tell me she was High Dutch.'

'Never mind what they *tell* you, Mr Burton' – observed the judge – 'testify only to what you *know*.'

'Did you see this strange woman at the fire, or after the fire?' continued Dunscomb.

'I can't say that I did. I remember to have looked round for her, too; but I did not find her.'

'Was her absence spoken of in the crowd at the time?'

'Something was said about it; but we were too much taken up with the old couple to think a great deal of this stranger.'

This is an outline of Burton's testimony; though the cross-examination was continued for more than an hour, and Williams had him again examined in chief. That intrepid practitioner contended that the defence had made Burton its own witness in all that related to the measurement of the skeletons; and that he had a right to a cross-examination. After all this contest, the only fact of any moment elicited from the witness related to the difference in stature between Goodwin and his wife, as has been stated already.

In the meantime, Timms ascertained that the last report set on foot by his own agents, at the suggestion of Mary Monson herself, was circulating freely; and, though it was directly opposed to the preceding rumour, which had found great favour with the gossips, this extravagant tale was most greedily swallowed. We conceive that those persons who are so constituted, morally, as to find pleasure in listening to the idle rumours that float about society, are objects of pity; their morbid desire to talk of the affairs of others being a disease that presses them down beneath the level they might otherwise occupy. With such persons, the probabilities go for nothing; and they are more inclined to give credit to a report that excites their interest, by running counter to all the known

laws of human action, than to give faith to its contradiction, when
sustained by every reason that experience sustains. Thus was it on the
present occasion. There was something so audacious in the rumour that
Mary Monson belonged to a gang of rogues in town, and had been sent
especially to rob the Goodwins, that vulgar curiosity found great delight
in it; the individual who heard the report usually sending it on with
additions of his own, that had their authority purely in the workings of a
dull imagination. It is in that way that this great faculty of the mind is
made to perform a double duty; which in the one case is as pure and
ennobling, as in the other it is debasing and ignoble. The man of a rich
imagination, he who is capable of throwing the charms of poetical feeling
around the world in which we dwell, is commonly a man of truth. The
high faculty which he possesses seems, in such cases, to be employed in
ferreting out facts which, on proper occasions, he produces distinctly,
manfully, and logically. On the other hand, there is a species of
subordinate imagination that is utterly incapable of embellishing life with
charms of any sort, and which delights in the false. This last is the
imagination of the gossip. It obtains some modicum of fact, mixes it with
large quantities of stupid fiction, delights in the idol it has thus fashioned
out of its own head, and sends it abroad to find worshippers as dull, as
vulgar-minded, and as uncharitable, as itself.

Timms grew frightened at the success of his client's scheme, and felt
the necessity of commencing the reaction at once, if the last were to have
time in which to produce its effect. He had been warmly opposed to the
project in the commencement, and had strenuously resisted its adoption;
but Mary Monson would not listen to his objections. She even
threatened to employ another, should he fail her. The conceit seemed to
have taken a strong hold on her fancy; and all the wilfulness of her
character had come in aid of this strange scheme. The thing was done;
and it now remained to prevent its effecting the mischief it was so well
adapted to produce.

All this time, the fair prisoner sat in perfectly composed silence,
listening attentively to everything that was said, and occasionally taking a
note. Timms ventured to suggest that it might be better were she to
abstain from doing the last, as it gave her the air of knowing too much,
and helped to deprive her of the interesting character of an unprotected
female; but she turned a perfectly deaf ear to his admonitions, hints, and
counsel. He was a safe adviser, nevertheless, in matters of this sort; but
Mary Monson was not accustomed so much to follow the leadings of
others, as to submit to her own impulses.

The sisters of Burton were next examined. They proved all the
admitted facts; testified as to the stocking and its contents; and two of
them recognised the piece of gold which was said to have been found in

Mary Monson's purse, as that which had once been the property of Dorothy Goodwin. On this head, the testimony of each was full, direct, and explicit. Each had often seen the piece of gold, and they had noted a very small notch or scratch near the edge, which notch or scratch was visible on the piece now presented in court. The cross-examination failed to shake this testimony, and well it might, for every word these young women stated was strictly true. The experiment of placing the piece of coin among other similar coin, failed with them. They easily recognised the true piece by the notch. Timms was confounded; Dunscomb looked very grave; Williams raised his nose higher than ever; and Mary Monson was perfectly surprised. When the notch was first mentioned, she arose, advanced far enough to examine the coin, and laid her hand on her forehead, as if she pondered painfully on the circumstance. The testimony that this was the identical piece found in her purse was very ample, the coin having been sealed up and kept by the coroner, who had brought it into court; while it must now be admitted that a very strong case was made out to show that this foreign coin had once been among the hoards of Dorothy Goodwin. A very deep impression was made by this testimony on all who heard it, including the court, the bar, the jury, and the audience. Every person present, but those who were in the immediate confidence of the accused, was firmly convinced of Mary Monson's guilt. Perhaps the only other exceptions to this mode of thinking were a few experienced practitioners, who, from long habit, knew the vast importance of hearing both sides, before they made up their minds in a matter of so much moment.

We shall not follow Dunscomb through his long and arduous cross-examination of the sisters of Burton; but confine ourselves to a few of the more pertinent of the interrogatories that he put to the eldest, and which were duly repeated when the other two were placed on the stand.

'Will you name the persons dwelling in the house of the Goodwins at the time of the fire?' asked Dunscomb.

'There were the two old folks, this Mary Monson, and a German woman named Yatty (Jette), that Aunt Dorothy took in to wait on her boarders.'

'Was Mrs Goodwin your aunt, then?'

'No; we wasn't related no how; but being such near neighbours, and she so old, we just called her aunt by way of a compliment.'

'I understand that,' said Dunscomb, arching his brows; 'I am called uncle, and by very charming young persons, on the same principle. Did you know much of this German?'

'I saw her almost every day for the time she was there, and talked with her as well as I could; but she spoke very little English. Mary Monson was the only person who could talk with her freely; she spoke her language.'

'Had you much acquaintance with the prisoner at the bar?'

'I was some acquainted, as a body always is when they live such near neighbours.'

'Were your conversations with the prisoner frequent or at all confidential?'

'To own the truth, I never spoke to her in my life. Mary Monson was much too grand for me.'

Dunscomb smiled; he understood how common it was for persons in this country to say they are 'well acquainted' with this or that individual, when their whole knowledge is derived from the common tongue. An infinity of mischief is done by this practice; but the ordinary American who will admit that he lives near any one, without having an acquaintance with him, if acquaintance is supposed to confer credit, is an extraordinary exception to a very general rule. The idea of being 'too grand' was of a nature to injure the prisoner and to impair her rights; and Dunscomb deemed it best to push the witness a little on this point.

'Why did you think Mary Monson was "too grand" for you?' he demanded.

'Because she *looked* so.'

'*How* did she look? – In what way does or did her looks indicate that she was, or thought herself "too grand" for your association?'

'Is this necessary, Mr Dunscomb?' demanded the judge.

'I beg your honour will suffer the gentleman to proceed,' put in Williams, cocking his nose higher than ever, and looking round the court-room with an air of intelligence that the great York counsellor did not like. 'It is an interesting subject; and we poor, ignorant Duke's county folks may get useful ideas, to teach us how to look "too grand!"'

Dunscomb felt that he had made a false step, and he had the self-command to stop.

'Had you any conversation with the German woman?' he continued, bowing slightly to the judge to denote submission to *his* pleasure.

'She couldn't talk English. Mary Monson talked with her. I didn't, to any account.'

'Were you at the fire?'

'I was.'

'Did you see anything of this German during the fire, or afterwards?'

'I didn't. She disappeared, unaccountable!'

'Did you visit the Goodwins as often after Mary Monson came to live with them, as you had done previously?'

'I didn't – grand looks and grand language isn't agreeable to me.'

'Did Mary Monson ever speak to you?'

'I think, your honour,' objected Williams, who did not like the question, 'that this is travelling out of the record.'

'Let the gentleman proceed – time is precious, and a discussion would lose us more of it than to let him proceed – go on, Mr Dunscomb.'

'Did Mary Monson ever speak to you?'

'She never did, to my knowledge.'

'What, then, do you mean by "grand language?"'

'Why, when she spoke to Aunt Dorothy, she didn't speak as I was used to hear folks speak.'

'In what respect was the difference?'

'She was grander in her speech, and more pretending like.'

'Do you mean louder?'

'No – perhaps she wasn't as loud as common – but 'twas more like a book, and uncommon.'

Dunscomb understood all this perfectly, as well as the feeling which lay at its bottom, but he saw that the jury did not; and he was forced to abandon the inquiry, as often happens on such occasions, on account of the ignorance of those to whom the testimony was addressed. He soon after abandoned the cross-examination of the sister of Burton; when his wife was brought upon the stand by the prosecution.

This woman, coming from a different stock, had none of the family characteristics of the sisters. As they were garrulous, forward, and willing enough to testify, she was silent, reserved in manner, thoughtful, and seemingly so diffident that she trembled all over, as she laid her hand on the sacred volume. Mrs Burton passed for a very good woman among all who dwelt in or near Biberry; and there was much more confidence felt in her revelations than in those of her sisters-in-law. Great modesty, not to say timidity of manner, an air of singular candour, a low, gentle voice, and an anxious expression of countenance, as if she weighed the import of every syllable she uttered, soon won for this witness the sympathy of all present, as well as perfect credence. Every word she uttered had a direct influence on the case; and this so much the more since she testified reluctantly, and would gladly have been permitted to say nothing.

The account given by Mrs Burton, in her examination in chief, did not materially differ from that previously stated by her sisters-in-law. She knew more, in some respects, than those who had preceded her, while, in others, she knew less. She had been more in the confidence of Dorothy Goodwin than any other member of her family, had seen her oftener, and knew more of her private affairs. With the stocking and its contents she admitted that she was familiarly acquainted. The gold exceeded twelve hundred dollars in amount; she had counted it, in her own hands. There was paper, also, but she did not know how much, exactly, as Dorothy kept *that* very much to herself. She knew, however, that her neighbours talked of purchasing a farm, the price of which was quite five thousand dollars, a sum that Dorothy often talked of paying down. She thought the deceased must have had money to that amount, in some form or other.

On the subject of the piece of gold found in Mary Monson's purse, Mrs Burton gave her testimony with the most amiable discretion. Every one compared the reserve and reluctance of her manner most favourably with the pert readiness of Mrs Pope and the sisters. This witness appeared to appreciate the effect of all she said, and uttered the facts she knew with a gentleness of manner that gave great weight to her testimony. Dunscomb soon saw that this was the witness the defence had most reason to dread, and he used the greatest care in having every word she said written out with precision.

Mrs Burton swore point blank to the piece of notched gold, although she fairly trembled as she gave her testimony. She knew it was the very piece that she had often seen in Dorothy Goodwin's possession; she had examined it, at least a dozen times, and could have selected it among a thousand similar coins, by means of its private marks. Besides the notch, there was a slight defect in the impression of the date. This had been pointed out to her by Dorothy Goodwin herself, who had said it was a good mark by which to know the piece, should it be stolen. On this head, the witness's testimony was firm, clear, and full. As it was corroborated by so much other evidence, the result was a deep and very general impression of the prisoner's guilt.

It was late when the examination in chief of Mrs Burton terminated. She stated that she was much fatigued, and was suffering under a severe headache; and Williams asked, in her behalf, that the court would adjourn over, until next day, ere the cross-examination was gone into. This suited Dunscomb's views altogether, for he knew he might lose an essential advantage by allowing the witness a night to arrange her thoughts, pending so searching a process. There being no resistance on the part of the prisoner, to the request of the prosecution, the judge so far waived his regard for the precious time of the court, as to consent to adjourn at eight o'clock in the evening, instead of pushing the case to ten or eleven. As a consequence the jurors took their rest in bed, instead of sleeping in the jury-box.

Dunscomb left the court-house, that night, dejected, and with no great expectation of the acquittal of his client. Timms had a better feeling, and thought nothing had yet appeared that might not be successfully resisted.

CHAPTER XXVI

'I've not wrong'd her.'
'Far be it from my fears.'
'Then why this argument?'
'My lord, my nature's jealous, and you'll bear it.'

OTWAY.

So great was the confidence of Sarah Wilmeter and Anna Updyke in the innocence of their friend, that almost every step that the trial advanced, appeared to them as so much progress towards an eventual acquittal. It was perhaps a little singular, that the party most interested, she who knew her own guilt or innocence, became dejected, and for the first half hour after they had left the court-room, she was silent and thoughtful. Good Mrs Gott was quite in despair, and detained Anna Updyke, with whom she had established a sort of intimacy, as she opened the door of the gallery for the admission of the party, in order to say a word on the subject that lay nearest to her heart.

'Oh! Miss Anna,' said the sheriff's wife, 'it goes from bad to worse! It was bad enough last evening, and it is worse to-night.'

'Who tells you this, Mrs Gott? So far from thinking as you do, I regard it as appearing particularly favourable.'

'You must have heard what Burton said and what his wife said, too. They are the witnesses I dread.'

'Yes, but who will mind what such persons say! I am sure if fifty Mr and Mrs Burtons were to testify that Mary Monson had taken money that did not belong to her, I should not believe them.'

'You are not a Duke's county jury! Why, Miss Anna, these men will believe almost anything you tell them. Only swear to it, and there's no accounting for their credulity. No; I no more believe in Mary Monson's guilt than I do in my own; but law is law, they say, and rich and poor must abide by it.'

'You view the matter under a false light, my kind-hearted Mrs Gott, and after a night's rest will see the case differently. Sarah and I have been delighted with the course of things. You must have remarked no one said that Mary Monson had been seen to set fire to the house, or to harm the Goodwins, or to touch their property, or to do anything that was wrong; and of course she must be acquitted.'

'I wish that piece of gold had not been found in her pocket! It's that which makes all the trouble.'

'I think nothing of that, my good friend. There is nothing remarkable in two pieces of money having the same marks on them; I have seen that often, myself. Besides, Mary Monson explains all that, and her declaration is as good as that of this Mrs Burton's, any day.'

'Not in law, Miss Anna; no, not in law. Out of doors it might be much better, and probably is; but not in court, by what they tell me. Gott says it is beginning to look very dark, and that we, in the gaol, here, must prepare for the very worst. I tell him, if I was he, I'd resign before I'd execute such a beautiful creature!'

'You make me shudder with such horrid thoughts, Mrs Gott, and I will thank you to open the door. Take courage; we shall never have to lament such a catastrophe, or your husband to perform so revolting a duty.'

'I hope not – I'm sure I hope not with all my heart. I would prefer that Gott should give up all hopes of ever rising any higher, than have him do this office. One never knows, Miss Anna, what is to happen in life, though I was as happy as a child when he was made sheriff. If my words have any weight with him, and he often says they have, I shall never let him execute Mary Monson. You are young, Miss Anna; but you've heard the tongue of flattery, I make no doubt, and know how sweet it is to woman's ear.'

Mrs Gott had been wiping her eyes with one hand, and putting the key into the lock with the other, while talking, and she now stood regarding her young companion with a sort of motherly interest, as she made this appeal to her experience. Anna blushed 'rosy red,' and raised her gloved hand to turn the key, as if desirous of getting away from the earnest look of the matron.

'That's just the way with all of us, Miss Anna!' continued Mrs Gott. 'We listen, and listen, and listen; and believe, and believe, and believe, until we are no longer the gay, light-hearted creatures that we were, but become mopy, and sighful, and anxious, to a degree that makes us forget father and mother, and fly from the paternal roof.'

'Will you have the kindness, now, to let me into the gaol?' said Anna, in the gentlest voice imaginable.

'In a minute, my dear – I call you my dear, because I like you; for I never use what Gott calls "high flown." There is Mr John Wilmeter, now, as handsome and agreeable a youth as ever came to Biberry. He comes here two or three times a day, and sits and talks with me in the most agreeable way, until I've got to like him better than any young man of my acquaintance. He talks of you quite half the time; and when he is not *talking* of you, he is *thinking* of you, as I know by the way he gazes at this very door.'

'Perhaps his thoughts are on Mary Monson,' answered Anna, blushing scarlet. 'You know she is a sort of client of his, and he has been here in her service, for a good while.'

'She hardly ever saw him; scarcely ever except at this grate. His foot never crossed this threshold, until his uncle came; and since, I believe he has gone in but once. Mary Monson is not the being he worships.'

'I trust he worships the Being we all worship, Mrs Gott,' struggling gently to turn the key, and succeeding. 'It is not for us poor frail beings to talk of being worshipped.'

'Or of worshipping, as I tell Gott,' said the sheriff's wife, permitting her companion to depart.

Anna found Mary Monson and Sarah walking together in the gallery, conversing earnestly.

'It is singular that nothing reaches us from Michael Millington!' exclaimed the last, as Anna interlocked arms with her, and joined the party. 'It is now near eight-and-forty hours since my uncle sent him to town.'

'On my business?' demanded Mary Monson, quickly.

'Certainly; on no other; though what it was that took him away so suddenly I have not been told. I trust you will be able to overturn all that these Burtons have said, and to repair the mischief they have done?'

'Fear nothing for me, Miss Wilmeter,' answered the prisoner, with singular steadiness of manner. 'I tell you, as I have often told your friend, *I must be acquitted*. Let justice take its course, say I, and the guilty be punished. I have a clue to the whole story, as I believe, and must make provision for to-morrow. Do you two, dear, warm-hearted friends as you are, now leave me; and when you reach the inn, send Mr Dunscomb hither as soon as possible. Not that Timms; but noble, honest, upright Mr Dunscomb. Kiss me, each of you, and so good night. Think of me in your prayers. I am a great sinner, and have need of your prayers.'

The wishes of Mary Monson were obeyed, and the young ladies left the gaol for the night. Ten minutes later Dunscomb reached the place, and was admitted. His conference with his client was long, intensely interesting, and it quite unsettled the notions he had now for some time entertained of her guilt. She did not communicate anything concerning her past life, nor did she make any promises on that subject; but she did communicate facts of great importance, as connected with the result of her trial. Dunscomb left her at a late hour, with views entirely changed, hopes revived, and his resolution stimulated. He made ample entries in his brief; nor did he lay his head on his pillow until it was very late.

The little court-house bell rang as usual next morning, and judge, jurors, witnesses, lawyers, and the curious in general, collected as before, without any ceremony, though in decent quiet. The case was now getting to be so serious that all approached it as truly a matter of life and death; even the reporters submitting to an impulse of humanity, and viewing the whole affair less in a business point of view than as one which might carry a singularly gifted woman into the other world. The first act of the day opened by putting Mrs Burton on the stand, for her cross-examination. As every intelligent person present understood that on

her testimony depended the main result, the fall of a pin might almost have
been heard, so profound was the general wish to catch what was going on.

The witness, however, appeared to be calm, while the advocate was
pale and anxious. He had the air of one who had slept little the past
night. He arranged his papers with studied care, made each movement
deliberately, compressed his lips, and seemed to be bringing his thoughts
into such a state of order and distinctness that each might be resorted to
as it was needful. In point of fact, Dunscomb foresaw that a human life
depended very much on the result of this cross-examination, and like a
conscientious man, he was disposed to do his whole duty. No wonder,
then, that he paused to reflect, was deliberate in his acts, and
concentrated in feeling.

'We will first give our attention to this piece of gold, Mrs Burton,' the
counsel for the prisoner mildly commenced, motioning to the coroner,
who was in court, to show the witness the piece of money so often
examined. 'Are you quite certain that it is the very coin that you saw in
the possession of Mrs Goodwin?'

'Absolutely certain, sir. As certain as I am of anything in the world.'

'Mrs Burton, I wish you to remember that the life of the prisoner at
the bar will, most probably, be affected by your testimony. Be kind
enough, then, to be very guarded and close in your answers. Do you still
say this is the precise coin that you once saw in Mrs Goodwin's stocking?'

The witness seemed suddenly struck with the manner of the advocate.
She trembled from head to foot. Still, Dunscomb spoke mildly, kindly
even; and the idea conveyed in the present, was but a repetition of that
conveyed in the former question. Nevertheless, those secret agencies, by
means of which thought meets thought, unknown to all but their
possessors; that set in motion, as it might be, all the covert currents of the
mind, causing them to flow towards similar streams in the mind of another,
were now at work, and Dunscomb and the witness had a clue to each
other's meaning that entirely escaped the observation of all around them.
There is nothing novel in this state of secret intelligence. It doubtless
depends on a mutual consciousness, and a common knowledge of certain
material facts, the latter being applied by the former, with promptitude and
tact. Notwithstanding her sudden alarm, and the change it brought over
her entire manner, Mrs Burton answered the question as before; what was
more, she answered it truly. The piece of gold found in Mary Monson's
purse, and now in possession of the coroner, who had kept it carefully, in
order to identify it, had been in Dorothy Goodwin's stocking.

'Quite certain, sir. I know that to be the same piece of money that I
saw at different times, in Mrs Goodwin's stocking.'

'Did you ever have that gold coin in your own hand, Mrs Burton,
previously to this trial?'

This was a very natural and simple interrogatory; one that might be, and probably was, anticipated; yet it gave the witness uneasiness, more from the manner of Dunscomb, perhaps, than from anything in the nature of the inquiry itself. The answer, however, was given promptly, and, as before, with perfect truth.

'On several occasions, sir. I saw that notch, and talked with Mrs Goodwin about it, more than once.'

'What was the substance of Mrs Goodwin's remarks, in relation to that notch?'

'She asked me, one time, if I thought it lessened the weight of the coin; and if so, how much I thought it might take away from its value?'

'What was your answer?'

'I believe I said I did not think it could make any great difference.'

'Did Mrs Goodwin ever tell you how, or where she got that piece of money?'

'Yes, sir, she did. She told me it came from Mary Monson.'

'In pay for board; or, for what purpose did it pass from one to the other?'

This, too, was a very simple question, but the witness no longer answered promptly. The reader will remember that Mary Monson had said, before the coroner, that she had two of these coins, and that she had given one of them to the poor unfortunate deceased, and had left the other in her own purse. This answer had injured the cause of the accused, inasmuch as it was very easy to tell such a tale, while few in Biberry were disposed to believe that gold passed thus freely, and without any consideration, from hand to hand. Mrs Burton remembered all this, and, for a reason best known to herself, she shrunk a little from making the required reply. Still she did answer this question also, and answered it truly.

'I understood Aunt Dolly to say that Mary Monson made her a present of that piece of money.'

Here Timms elevated his nose, and looked around him in a meaning manner, that appealed to the audience to know if his client were not a person of veracity. Sooth to say, this answer made a strong impression in favour of the accused, and Dunscomb saw with satisfaction that, in-so-much, he had materially gained ground. He was not a man to gain it, however, by dramatic airs; he merely paused for a few moments, in order to give full effect to this advantage.

'Mrs Goodwin, then, owned to you that she had the coin from Mary Monson, and that it was a present?' was the next question.

'She did, sir.'

'Did she say anything about Mary Monson's having another piece of money, like the one before you, and which was given by her to Dorothy Goodwin?'

A long pause succeeded. The witness raised a hand to her brow, and appeared to meditate. Her reputation for taciturnity and gravity of deportment was such, that most of those in court believed she was endeavouring to recollect the past, in order to say neither more nor less than the truth. In point of fact, she was weighing well the effect of her words, for she was a person of extreme caution, and of great reputed probity of character. The reply came at length –

'She did speak on the subject,' she said, 'and did state something of the kind.'

'Can you recollect her words? – if so, give them to the jury – if not her very words, their substance.'

'Aunt Dolly had a way of her own in talking, which makes it very difficult to repeat her precise words; but she said, in substance, that Mary Monson had two of these pieces of money, one of which was given to *her*.'

'Mary Monson, then, kept the other?'

'So I understood it, sir.'

'Have you any knowledge yourself, on this subject? – If so, state it to the jury.'

Another pause, one even longer than before, and again the hand was raised to the brow. The witness now spoke with extreme caution, seeming to feel her way among the facts, as a cat steals on its prey.

'I believe I have – a little – some – I have seen Mary Monson's purse, and I *believe* I saw a piece of money in it which resembled this.'

'Are you not certain of the fact?'

'Perhaps I am.'

Here Dunscomb's face was lighted with a smile; he evidently was encouraged.

'Were you present, Mrs Burton, when Mary Monson's purse was examined, in presence of the inquest?'

'I was.'

'Did you then see its contents?'

'I did' – after the longest pause of all.

'Had you that purse in your hand, ma'am?'

The brow was once more shaded, and the recollection seemingly taxed.

'I think I had. It was passed round among us, and I believe that I touched it, as well as others.'

'Are you not certain that you did so?'

'Yes, sir. Now, I reflect, I know that I did. The piece of money found in Mary Monson's purse, was passed from one to another, and to me among the rest.'

'This was very wrong,' observed his honour.

'It was wrong, sir; but not half as wrong as the murders and arson,' coolly remarked Williams.

'Go on, gentlemen – time is precious.'

'Now, Mrs Burton, I wish to ask you a very particular question, and I beg that your answer may be distinct and guarded – did you ever have access to the piece of gold found, or said to be found, in Mary Monson's purse, except on the occasion of the inquest?'

The longest pause of all, and the deepest shading of the brow. So long was the self-deliberation this time, as to excite a little remark among the spectators. Still, it was no more than prudent to be cautious, in a cause of so much importance.

'I certainly have, sir,' was the reply that came at last. 'I saw it in Dorothy Goodwin's stocking, several times; had it in my hand, and examined it. This is the way I came to discover the notch. Aunt Dolly and I talked about that notch, as I have already told the court.'

'Quite true, ma'am, we remember that; all your answers are carefully written out——'

'I'm sure nothing that I have said can be written out, which is not true, sir.'

'We are to suppose that. And now, ma'am, permit me to ask if you ever saw that piece of money at any other time than at those you have mentioned. Be particular in the answer.'

'I may,' after a long pause.

'Do you not *know*?'

'I do not, sir.'

'Will you say, on your oath, that you cannot recollect any one occasion, other than those you have mentioned, on which you have seen and handled that piece of money?'

'When Aunt Dolly showed it to me, before the coroner, and here in court. I recollect no other time.'

'Let me put this question to you again, Mrs Burton – recalling the solemnity of the oath you have taken – have you, or have you not, seen that piece of money on any other occasion than those you have just mentioned?'

'I do not remember ever to have seen it at any other time,' answered the woman, firmly.

Mary Monson gave a little start, and Dunscomb appeared disappointed. Timms bit his lip, and looked anxiously at the jury, while Williams once more cocked *his* nose, and looked around him in triumph. If the witness spoke the truth, she was now likely to adhere to it; if, on the other hand, there were really any ground for Dunscomb's question, the witness had passed the Rubicon, and would adhere to her falsehood even more tenaciously than she would adhere to the truth. The remainder of this cross-examination was of very little importance. Nothing further was obtained from the witness that went to shake her testimony.

Our limits will not permit a detailed account of all the evidence that was given in behalf of the prosecution. All that appeared before the inquest was now introduced, methodized and arranged by Williams; processes that rendered it much more respectable than it had originally appeared to be. At length it came to the turn of the defence to open. This was a task that Dunscomb took on himself, Timms, in his judgment, being unequal to it. His opening was very effective, in the way of argument, though necessarily not conclusive, the case not making in favour of his client.

The public expected important revelations as to the past history of the prisoner, and of this Timms had apprised Dunscomb. The latter, however, was not prepared to make them. Mary Monson maintained all her reserve, and Millington did not return. The cause was now so far advanced as to render it improbable that any facts, of this nature, could be obtained in sufficient season to be used, and the counsel saw the necessity of giving a new turn to this particular point in the case. He consequently complained that the prosecution had neglected to show anything in the past life of the accused to render it probable she had been guilty of the offences with which she was charged. 'Mary Monson appears here,' he went on to say, 'with a character as fair as that of any other female in the community. This is the presumption of law, and you will truly regard her, gentlemen, as one that is innocent until she is proved to be guilty.' The inference drawn from the silence of the prosecution was not strictly logical, perhaps; but Dunscomb managed at least to mystify the matter in such a way as to prepare the jury to hear a defence that would be silent on this head, and to leave a doubt whether this silence were not solely the fault of the counsel for the prosecution. While he was commenting on this branch of the subject, Williams took notes furiously, and Timms foresaw that he meant to turn the tables on them, at the proper moment.

Pretty much as a matter of course, Dunscomb was compelled to tell the court and jury that the defence relied principally on the insufficiency of the evidence of the other side. This was altogether circumstantial; and the circumstances, as he hoped to be able to convince the jury, were of a nature that admitted of more than one construction. Whenever this was the case, it was the duty of the jury to give the accused the full benefit of these doubts. The rest of the opening had the usual character of appeals to the sympathy and justice of the jury, very prudently and properly put.

Dr McBrain was now placed upon the stand, when the customary questions were asked, to show that he was a witness entitled to the respect of the court. He was then further interrogated, as follows:–

'Have you seen the two skeletons that are now in court, and which are said to have been taken from the ruins of the house of the Goodwins?'

'I have. I saw them before the inquest; and I have again examined them here, in court.'

'What do you say, as to their sex?'

'I believe them both to be the skeletons of females.'

'Do you feel certain of this fact?'

'Reasonably so, but not absolutely. No one can pronounce with perfect certainty in such a case; more especially when the remains are in the state in which these have been found. We are guided principally by the comparative size of the bones; and, as these are affected by the age of the subject, it is hazardous to be positive. I can only say that I think both of these skeletons belonged to female subjects; particularly the shortest.'

'Have you measured the skeletons?'

'I have, and find one rather more than an inch and a half shorter than the other. The longest measures quite five feet seven and a half, in the state in which it is; while the shortest measures a trifle less than five feet six. If women, both were of unusual stature; particularly the first. I think that the bones of both indicate that they belonged to females; and I should have thought the same had I known nothing of the reports which have reached my ears touching the persons whose remains these are said to be.'

'When you first formed your opinion of the sex of those to whom these remains belonged, had you heard that there was a German woman staying in the house of the Goodwins at the time of the fire?'

'I think not; though I have taken so little heed of these rumours as to be uncertain when I first heard this circumstance. I do remember, however, that I was under the impression the remains were, beyond a doubt, those of Peter Goodwin and his wife, when I *commenced* the examination of them; and I very distinctly recollect the surprise I felt when the conviction crossed my mind that both were the skeletons of women. From the nature of this feeling, I rather think I could not have heard anything of the German female at that time.'

The cross-examination of Dr McBrain was very long and searching; but it did not materially affect the substance of his testimony. On the contrary, it rather strengthened it; since he had it in his power to explain himself more fully under the interrogatories of Williams, than he could do in an examination in chief. Still he could go no farther than give his strong belief; declining to pronounce positively on the sex of either individual, in the state in which the remains were found.

Although nothing positive was obtained from this testimony, the minds of the jurors were pointedly directed to the circumstance of the sudden and unexplained disappearance of the German woman; thus making an opening for the admission of a serious doubt connected with the fate of that person.

It was a sad thing to reflect that, beyond this testimony of McBrain, there was little other direct evidence to offer in behalf of the accused. It is true, the insufficiency of that which had been produced by the prosecution might avail her much; and on this Dunscomb saw that his hopes of an acquittal must depend; but he could not refrain from regretting, and that bitterly, that the unmoved resolution of his client not to let her past life be known, must so much weaken his case, were she innocent, and so much fortify that of the prosecution, under the contrary supposition. Another physician or two were examined to sustain McBrain; but, after all, the condition of the remains was such as to render any testimony questionable. One witness went so far as to say, it is true, that he thought he could distinguish certain unerring signs of the sex in the length of the lower limbs, and in other similar proof; but even McBrain was forced to admit that such distinctions were very vague and unsatisfactory. His own opinion was formed more from the size of the bones, generally, than from any other proof. In general there was little difficulty in speaking of the sex of the subject, when the skeleton was entire and well-preserved, and particularly when the teeth furnished some clue to the age; but in this particular case, as has already been stated, there could be no such thing as absolute certainty.

It was with a heavy heart, and with many an anxious glance cast towards the door, in the hope of seeing Michael Millington enter, that Dunscomb admitted the prisoner had no further testimony to offer. He had spun out the little he did possess, in order to give it an appearance of importance which it did not actually bring with it, and to divert the minds of the jurors from the impression they had probably obtained, of the remains necessarily being those of Goodwin and his wife.

The summing up on both sides was a grave and solemn scene. Here Williams was thrown out, the District Attorney choosing to perform his own duty on an occasion so serious. Dunscomb made a noble appeal to the justice of the court and jury; admonishing both of the danger of yielding too easily to circumstantial evidence. It was the best possible proof, he admitted, when the circumstances were sufficiently clear and sufficiently shown to be themselves beyond controversy. That Mary Monson dwelt with the Goodwins, was in the house at the time of the arson and murder, if such crimes were ever committed at all; that she escaped and all her property was saved, would of themselves amount to nothing. The testimony, indeed, on several of these heads, rather told in her favour than the reverse. The witnesses for the prosecution proved that she was in her room, beneath the roof, when the flames broke out, and was saved with difficulty. This was a most material fact, and Dunscomb turned it to good account. Would an incendiary be apt to place herself in a situation in which her own life was in danger; and this, too, under circumstances that rendered no such measure necessary? Then, all the facts connected with Mary Monson's residence and habits told in her favour. Why should she remain so long at the cottage, if robbery was her only purpose? The idea of her belonging to a gang that had sent her to make discoveries and to execute its plans, was preposterous; for what hindered any of the men of that gang from committing the crimes in the most direct manner, and with the least loss of time? No; if Mary Monson were guilty, she was undoubtedly guilty on her own account; and had been acting with the uncertain aim and hand of a woman. The jury must discard all notions of accomplices, and consider the testimony solely in connection with the acts of the accused. Accomplices, and those of the nature supposed, would have greatly simplified the whole of the wretched transaction. They would have rendered both the murders and arson unnecessary. The bold and strong do not commit these crimes, except in those cases in which resistance renders them necessary. Here was clearly no resistance, as was shown by the quiet positions in which the skeletons had been found. If a murder was directly committed, it must have been by the blow on the heads; and the jury was asked to consider whether a delicate female like Mary Monson had even the physical force necessary to strike such a blow. With what instrument was it done? Nothing of the sort was found near the bodies; and no proof of any such blow was before the jury. One witness had said that the iron-work of a plough lay quite near the remains; and it had been shown that Peter Goodwin kept such articles in a loft over his bed-room. He would suggest the possibility of the fire having commenced in that loft, through which the pipe of a cooking-stove led; of its having consumed the beams of the floor; letting down this plough and share upon the heads of the sleeping couple below, stunning, if not killing them; thus leaving them unresisting subjects to the action of the element. McBrain had been examined on this point, which we omitted to state in its place, to prevent repetition. He and the two other doctors brought forward for the defence, had tried to place the ploughshare on the skulls; and were of opinion that the injuries might have been inflicted by that piece of iron. But Mary Monson could not use such an instrument. This was beyond all dispute. If the ploughshare inflicted the blow – and the testimony on this point was at least entitled to respect – then was Mary Monson innocent of any murder committed by *direct* means. It is true, she was responsible for all her acts; and if she set fire to the building, she was probably guilty of murder as well as of arson. But would she have done this, and made no provision for her own escape? The evidence was clear that she was rescued by means of a ladder, and through a window; and that there was no other means of escape.'

Dunscomb reasoned on these several points with great force and ingenuity. So clear were his statements, so logical his inferences, and so candid his mode of arguing, that he had produced a great effect ere he closed this branch of his subject. It is true that one far more difficult remained to be met; to answer which he now set about with fear and trembling.

We allude to the piece of money alleged to have been found in Mary Monson's purse. Dunscomb had very little difficulty in disposing of the flippant widow Pope; but the Burton family gave him more trouble. Nevertheless, it was his duty to endeavour to get rid of them, or at least so far to weaken their testimony as to give his client the benefit of the doubt. There was, in truth, but one mode of doing this. It was to impress on the jury the probability that the coin had been changed in passing from hand to hand. It is true, it was not easy to suggest any plausible reason why such an act of treachery should have been committed; but it was a good legal point to show that this piece of money had not, at all times, been absolutely under the eye or within the control of the coroner. If there were a possibility of a change, the fact should and ought to tell in favour of his client. Mrs Burton had made admissions on this point which entitled the prisoner to press the facts on the minds of the jurors; and her counsel did not fail so to do with clearness and energy. After all, this was much the most difficult point of the case; and it would not admit of a perfectly satisfactory solution.

The conclusion of Dunscomb's summing up was manly, touching, even eloquent. He spoke of a lone and defenceless female, surrounded by strangers, being dragged to the bar on charges of such gravity; pointed to his client where she sat enthralled by his language, with all the signs of polished refinement on her dress, person, and manners; delicate, feminine, and beautiful; and asked if any one who had the soul and feelings of a man, could believe that such a being had committed the crimes imputed to Mary Monson.

The appeal was powerful, and was dwelt on just long enough to give it full and fair effect. It left the bench, the bar, the jury-box, the whole audience, in fact, in tears. The prisoner alone kept an unmoistened eye; but it was in a face flushed with feeling. Her self-command was almost supernatural.

CHAPTER XXVII

I'll brave her to her face:
I'll give my anger its free course against her.
Thou shalt see, Phoenix, how I'll break her pride.
The Distressed Mother.

The District-Attorney was fully impressed with the importance of the duty which had now devolved on him. Although we have daily proofs on all sides of us, of the truth of that remark of Bacon's, 'that no man rises to eminence in the State without a mixture of great and mean qualities,' this favourite of the people had his good points as well as another. He was a humane man; and, contrary to the expectations, and greatly to the disappointment of Williams, he now took on himself the office of summing up.

The public functionary commenced in a mild, quiet manner, manifesting by the key on which he pitched his voice a natural reluctance to his painful duty: but he was steady and collected. He opened with a brief summary of the facts. A strange female, of high personal pretensions, had taken lodgings in an humble dwelling. That dwelling contained a considerable sum of money. Some counted it by thousands – all by hundreds. In either case it was a temptation to the covetous and ill-disposed. The lodgings were unsuited to the habits of the guest; but she endured them for several weeks. A fire occurred, and the house was consumed. The remains of the husband and wife were found, as the jury saw them, with marks of violence on their skulls. A deadly blow had been struck by some one. The bureau containing the money was found locked, but the money itself was missing. One piece of that money was known, and it was traced to the purse of the female lodger. This stranger was arrested; and, in her mode of living in the gaol, in her expenditures of every sort, she exhibited the habits and profusion of one possessed of considerable sums. Doubtless many of the reports in circulation were false; exaggerations ever accompanied each statement of any unusual occurrence; but enough was proved to show that Mary Monson had a considerable amount of money at command. Whence came these funds? That which was lightly obtained went lightly. The jury were exhorted to reject every influence but that which was sustained by the evidence. All that had been here stated rested on uncontradicted unresisted testimony.

There was no desire to weaken the force of the defence. This defence had been ingeniously and powerfully presented; and to what did it amount? The direct, unequivocal evidence of Mrs Burton, as to her knowledge of the piece of money, and all that related to it, and this evidence sustained by so much that was known to others, the coroner included, was met by a *conjecture*! This conjecture was accompanied by an insinuation that some might suppose reflected on the principal witness; but it was only an insinuation. There were two legal modes of attacking the credibility of a witness. One was by showing habitual mendacity; the other by demonstrating from the evidence itself, that the testimony could not be true. Had either been done in the present instance? The District Attorney thought not. One, and this the most common course, had not even been attempted. Insinuations, rather than just deductions, he was compelled to say, notwithstanding his high respect for the learned counsel opposed to him, had been the course adopted. That counsel had contended that the circumstances were not sufficient to justify a verdict

of guilty. Of this, the jury were the sole judges. If they believed Mrs
Burton, sustained as she was by so much other testimony, they must
admit that Dorothy Goodwin's money was found in Mary Monson's
purse. This was the turning point of the case. All depended on the
construction of this one fact. He left it to the jury, to their good sense, to
their consciences.

On the part of the defence, great stress had been laid on the
circumstance that Mary Monson was herself rescued from the flames with
some difficulty. But for assistance, she would most probably have perished.
The District Attorney desired to deny nothing that could justly go to prove
the prisoner's innocence. The fact was unquestionably as stated. But for
assistance, Mary Monson *might* have perished. But assistance was *not*
wanting; for strangers were most *opportunely* at hand, and they did this piece
of good service. They remained until all was over and vanished. No one
knew them; whence they came, or whither they went. Important agents in
saving a life, they had gone without their reward, and were not even
named in the newspaper accounts of the occurrence. Reporters generally
tell more than happens; in this instance, they were mute.

As for the danger of the prisoner, it might have happened in a variety of
ways that affected neither her guilt nor her innocence. After committing
the murders, she may have gone into her room and been unexpectedly
enclosed by the flames; or the whole may have been previously planned,
in order to give her the plea of this very dangerous situation, as a proof of
innocence. Such immaterial circumstances were not to overshadow the
very material facts on which the prosecution rested.

Another important question was to be asked by the jury. If Mary
Monson did not commit these crimes, who did? It had been suggested
that the house might have taken fire by accident, and that the
ploughshare was the real cause of the death of its owners. If this were so,
did the ploughshare remove the money? – did the ploughshare put the
notched piece in Mary Monson's purse?

Such is an outline of the manner in which the District Attorney
reasoned on the facts. His summing up made a deep impression; the
moderation of the manner in which he pressed the guilt of the accused,
telling strongly against her. Nothing was said of aristocracy, or harps, or
manners, or of anything else that did not fairly belong to the subject. A
great deal more was said, of course; but we do not conceive it necessary
to advert to it.

The charge was exceedingly impartial. The judge made a full
exposition of all the testimony, pointed out its legitimate bearing, and
dissected its weak points. As for the opinion of McBrain and his
associates, the court conceived it entitled to a great deal of consideration.
Here were several highly respectable professional men testifying that, in

their judgment, both the skeletons were those of females. The German woman was missing. What had become of her? In any case, the disappearance of that woman was very important. She may have committed the crimes and absconded; or one of the skeletons may have been hers. It was in evidence that Peter Goodwin and his wife did not live always in the most happy mood; and he may have laid hands on the money, which was probably his in the eyes of the law, and left the place. He had not been seen since the fire. The jury must take all the facts into their consideration, and decide according to their consciences.

This charge was deemed rather favourable to the accused than otherwise. The humanity of the judge was conspicuous throughout; and he leaned quite obviously to Dunscomb's manner of treating the danger of Mary Monson from the flames, and dwelt on the fact that the piece of money was not sufficiently watched to make out an absolute case of identity. When he had done, the impression was very general that the prisoner would be acquitted.

As it was reasonably supposed that a case of this importance would detain the jury a considerable time, the court permitted the prisoner to withdraw. She left the place, attended by her two friends; the latter in tears, while Mary herself was still seemingly unmoved. The thoughtful Mrs Gott had prepared refreshments for her; and, for the first time since her trial commenced, the fair prisoner ate heartily.

'I shall owe my triumph, not to money, my dear girls,' she said, while at table, 'not to friends, nor to a great array of counsel; but to truth. I did not commit these crimes; and on the testimony of the State alone, with scarcely any of my own, the jury will have to say as much. No stain will rest on my character, and I can meet my friends with the unclouded brow of innocence. This is a very precious moment to me; I would not part with it for all the honours that riches and rank can bestow.'

'How strange that you, of all women, my dear mamma,' said Anna, kissing her cheek, 'should be accused of crimes so horrible to obtain a little money; for this poor Mrs Goodwin could have had no great sum after all, and you are so rich!'

'More is the pity that I have not made a better use of my money. You are to be envied, girls, in having the fortunes of gentlewomen, and in having no more. I do believe it is better for our sex barely to be independent in their respective stations, and not to be rendered rich. Man or woman, money is a dangerous thing, when we come to consider it as a part of our natural existence; for it tempts us to fancy that money's worth gives rights that nature and reason both deny. I believe I should have been much happier, were I much poorer than I am.'

'But those who are rich are not very likely to rob!'

'Certainly not, in the sense that you mean, my dear. Send Marie

Moulin on some errand, Anna; I wish to tell you and Sarah what I think of this fire, and of the deaths for which I am now on trial.'

Anna complied; and the handsome prisoner, first looking cautiously around to make certain she was not overheard, proceeded with her opinion.

'In the first place, I make no doubt Dr. McBrain is right, and that both the skeletons are those of women. The German woman got to be very intimate with Mrs Goodwin; and as the latter and her husband quarrelled daily, and fiercely, I think it probable that she took this woman into her bed, where they perished together. I should think the fire purely accidental, were it not for the missing stocking.'

'That is just what the District Attorney said,' cried Anna, innocently. 'Who, then, *can* have set the house on fire?'

Mary Monson muttered to herself; and she smiled as if some queer fancies crowded her brain, but no one was the wiser for her ruminations. These she kept to herself and continued.

'Yes, that missing stocking renders the arson probable. The question is, who did the deed; I, or Mrs Burton?'

'Mrs Burton!' exclaimed both the girls in a breath. 'Why, her character is excellent – no one has ever suspected her! You cannot suppose that she is the guilty person!'

'It is she, or it is I; which, I will leave you to judge. I was aware that the notch was in the coin, for I was about to give the other piece to Mrs Goodwin, but preferred to keep the perfect specimen myself. The notched piece must have been in the stocking until *after* the fire; and it was changed by some one while my purse was under examination.'

'And you suppose that Mrs Burton did it?'

'I confess to a suspicion to that effect. Who else could or *would* have done it? I have mentioned this distrust to Mr Dunscomb, and he cross-examined in reference to this fact; though nothing very satisfactory was extracted. After my acquittal, steps will be taken to push the inquiry further.'

Mary Monson continued discussing this subject for quite an hour; her wondering companions putting questions. At the end of that time, Mr Gott appeared to say that the jury had come into court; and that it was his duty to take the prisoner there to meet them.

Perhaps Mary Monson never looked more lovely than at that moment. She had dressed herself with great simplicity, but with exceeding care; excitement gave her the richest colour; hope, even delight, was glowing in her eyes; and her whole form was expanding with the sentiment of triumph. There is no feeling more general than sympathy with success. After the judge's charge, few doubted of the result; and on every side, as she walked with a light firm step to her chair, the prisoner read kindness, sympathy, and exultation. After all that had been said, and all the prejudices that had been awakened, Mary Monson was about to be acquitted! Even the reporters became a little humanized; had juster perceptions than common of the rights of their fellow-creatures; and a more smiling, benignant assembly was never collected in that hall. In a few minutes silence was obtained, and the jurors were called. Every man answered to his name, when the profound stillness of expectation pervaded the place.

'Stand up, Mary Monson, and listen to the verdict,' said the clerk, not without a little tremor in his voice. 'Gentlemen, what do you say – is the prisoner guilty or not guilty?'

The foreman arose, stroked down a few scattering grey hairs, then in a voice barely audible, he pronounced the portentous word 'Guilty.' Had a bomb suddenly exploded in the room it could not have produced greater astonishment, and scarcely more consternation. Anna Updyke darted forward, and, as with a single bound, Mary Monson was folded in her arms.

'No, no!' cried this warm-hearted girl, totally unconscious of the impropriety of her acts; 'she is *not* guilty. You do not know her. I *do*. She was my school mamma. She is a lady, incapable of being guilty of such crimes. No, no, gentlemen, you will think better of this, and alter your verdict – perhaps it was a mistake, and you meant to say, "Not Guilty!"'

'Who is this young lady?' asked the judge, in a tremulous voice – 'a relative of the prisoner's?'

'No, sir,' answered the excited girl, 'no relative, but a very close friend. She was my "school mamma" once, and I know she is not a person to rob, and murder, and set fire to houses. Her birth, education, character, all place her above it. You will think better of this, gentlemen, and change your verdict. Now, go at once and do it, or you may distress her!'

'Does any one know who this young lady is?' demanded his honour, his voice growing more and more tremulous.

'I am Anna Updyke – Dr McBrain's daughter, now, and Uncle Tom's niece,' answered Anna, scarce knowing what she said. 'But never mind *me* – it is Mary Monson, here, who has been tried, and who has so wrongfully been found guilty. She never committed these crimes, I tell you, sir – is incapable of committing them – had no motive for committing them; and I beg you will put a stop to these proceedings before they get so far as to make it difficult to recede. Just tell the jury to alter their verdict. No, no, Mary Monson is no murderess! She would no more hurt the Goodwins, or touch a particle of their gold, than either of us all. You do not know her, sir. If you did, you would smile at this mistake of the jury, for it is all a cruel mistake. Now do, my dear sir, send them away again, and tell them to be more reasonable.'

'The young lady had better be removed,' interposed the judge, wiping his eyes. 'Such scenes may be natural, and the court looks on them leniently; but time is precious, and my duty renders it necessary to interpose my authority to maintain the order of our proceedings. Let some of the ladies remove the young lady; she is too delicate for the touch of a constable – but time is precious.'

The judge was not precisely conscious, himself, of what he was saying, though he knew the general drift of his remarks. The process of blowing his nose interrupted his speech, more than once, and Anna was removed by the assistance of Marie Moulin, Sarah Wilmeter, and good Mrs Gott; the latter sobbing like a child, while the other two scarce realized the consequences of the momentous word that had just been pronounced. Dunscomb took care that the whole group should quit the building, and be removed to the tavern.

If the bar, and the spectators in general, had been surprised at the calmness of exterior maintained by the prisoner, previously to the verdict, their wonder was sensibly increased by the manner which succeeded it. Mary Monson's beauty shone with increasing radiance as the justice of her country seemed to threaten her existence more and more; and at the particular moment when she was left alone, by the withdrawal of her female companions, many present fancied that she had increased in stature. Certainly, it was a rare sight to observe the illuminated countenance, the erect mien, and the offended air, with which one of the weaker sex, and one so youthful and charming, met a doom so terrible. Of the jury, she took no notice. Her eye was on the judge, who was endeavouring to muster sufficient fortitude to pronounce the final decision of the law.

'Before the court pronounces sentence, Mr Dunscomb,' observed that functionary, 'it will cheerfully hear anything you may have to offer in behalf of the prisoner, or it will hear the prisoner herself. It is better, on every account, that all my painful duties be discharged at once, in order that the prisoner may turn her attention to the only two sources of mercy that now remain open to her – the earthly and the heavenly. My duty, as you well know, cannot now be avoided; and the sooner it is performed, perhaps, the better for all concerned. It shall be my care to see that the condemned has time to make all her appeals, let them be to the authorities here, or to the more dreaded power above.'

'I am taken so much by surprise, your honour, at a verdict that, to say the least, is given on very doubtful testimony, that I hardly know what to urge. As the court, however, is disposed to indulgence, and there will be time to look at the law of the case, as well as to address our petitions and affidavits to the authority at Albany, I shall interpose no objection; and, as your honour well remarks, since the painful duty *must* be discharged, it were better, perhaps, that it were discharged now.'

'Prisoner at the bar,' resumed the judge, 'you have heard the finding of the jury in your case. A verdict of "guilty" has been rendered, and it has become my painful duty to pronounce the awful sentence of the law. If you have anything to say previously to this, the last and most painful of all my duties, the court will give your words a kind and lenient hearing.'

In the midst of a stillness that seemed supernatural, the sweet, melodious voice of Mary Monson was heard, 'first gentle, almost inaudible,' but gathering strength as she proceeded, until it became clear, distinct, and silvery. There are few things that impart a higher charm than the voice; and the extraordinary prisoner possessed an organ which, while it was feminine and sweet, had a depth and richness that at once denoted her power in song. On the present occasion it was not even tremulous.

'I believe I understand you, sir,' Mary Monson commenced. 'I have been tried and found guilty of having murdered Peter and Dorothy Goodwin, after having robbed them, and then of setting fire to the house.'

'You have been tried for the murder of Peter Goodwin, only, the indictments for the second murder, and for the arson, not having yet been tried. The court has been obliged to separate the cases, lest the law be defeated on mere technicalities. This verdict renders further proceedings unnecessary, and the two remaining indictments will probably never be traversed.'

'I believe I still understand you, sir; and I thank you sincerely for the kind manner in which you have communicated these facts, as well as for the consideration and gentleness you have manifested throughout these proceedings. It has been very kind in you, sir; and whatever may come of this, God will remember and reward you for it.'

'The court will hear you, Mary Monson, if you have anything to say, before sentence be passed.'

'Perhaps I might say and do much to affect your decision, sir,' returned the prisoner, leaning her fair brow, for a moment, on her hand, 'but there would be little satisfaction in it. It was my wish to be acquitted on the testimony of the State. I did hope that this jury would not have seen the proofs of guilt, in the evidence that has been brought against me; and I confess there would be very little satisfaction to me in any other acquittal. As I understand the case, should I be acquitted as respects Peter Goodwin, I must still be tried as respects his wife; and lastly, for setting fire to the house.'

'You are not acquitted of the murder of Peter Goodwin,' mildly interposed the judge; 'the finding of the court has been just to the contrary.'

'I am aware of this, sir. America has many enemies. I have lived in foreign lands, and know this from near and long observation. There are those, and those, too, who are in power, that would gladly see the great example in prosperity, peace and order, that this country has hitherto given to the world, beaten down by our own vices, and the mistaken uses to which the people put the blessings of Divine Providence. I do not reverence the justice of my country, as I did: it is impossible that I should do so. I now see plainly that its agents are not all of the character they should be; and that, so far from Justice's being blind through her impartiality alone, she is also blind through her ignorance. Why am I found guilty of this act? On what evidence – or even on what probability? The whole of the proof is connected with that piece of money. Mrs Burton has testified that Mrs Goodwin, herself, admitted that I had given her that coin – just what I told the coroner, and which I then saw was not believed, for it has been my misfortune to be tried by strangers. Will these gentlemen ask themselves why I have committed the crime of which they have found me guilty? It could not be for money; as of that I have, of my own, more than I want, more, perhaps, than it is good for me to be mistress of.'

'Why have not these facts been shown to the jury, at the proper time and in the proper manner, if true?' demanded the judge, kindly. 'They are material, and might have influenced the verdict.'

The jury was discharged, but not one of them all had left the box. One or two of them now arose, and looks of doubt and indecision began to flicker over their countenances. They had been influenced by one man, a friend and political confidant of Williams, who had led the undecided to his own opinions. We do not mean to say that this man was perjured, or that he was himself conscious of the extent of the wrong he was doing; but his mind had been perverted by the serpent-like report, and he had tried the cause under the influence of rumours, which had no foundation in truth. The case was one of honest doubt, as no one will deny; but instead of giving the accused the benefit of this doubt, as by law and in reason he was bound to do, he had taken a bias altogether from outside influences, and that bias he communicated to others, until by the sheer force of numbers, the few who wavered were driven into a corner, and soon capitulated. Then, there was a morbid satisfaction in the minds of several of the jurors in running counter to the charge of the judge. This was a species of independence that is grateful to some men, and they are guided by their vanity, when they fancy they are only led by conscience. These malign influences were unknown to themselves; for not one of the twelve was absolutely corrupt, but neither of them all was qualified by nature, or education, to be a judge, freed from the influence of the bench, in a case affecting a human life.

Any one in the least observant of what is going on around him, must have had many opportunities of perceiving how strangely juries render their verdicts, and how much the last appear to be opposed to the inferences of the looker-on, as well as to the expressed opinions of the courts. The falling off in the power of the judges over the minds of the jurors, we suppose to be derived from a combination of causes. The tendency of the times is to make men confident in their own judgments, and to defer less than formerly to knowledge and experience. Seeing this very general trait, the judges themselves defer to the tendency, manifest less confidence in their station and knowledge, and perhaps really feel it; while the unceasing cry of the infallibility of the common mind, induces the vulgar, or average intellect, to shrink from any collision with that which wears the semblance, even though simulated, of the popular will. In this way is the institution of the jury gradually getting to be perverted, rendering that which is safe as a human tribunal can well be, when under the guidance of the court, as dangerous as ignorance, party, self-will, and obstinacy can well make it.

'I do not know,' resumed Mary Monson, 'that one is yet obliged, in America, to lay open her account-books, and show her rent-roll, or her bonds and mortgages, in order to avoid the gallows. I have been told that crime must be brought home by unanswerable proof, in order to convict. Who can say that such proof has been adduced in my case? It has not even been made certain that a man was killed at all. Most respectable witnesses have testified that they believe those revolting remains of poor humanity belonged once to women. Nor has it been shown that any one has been murdered. The fire may have been accidental, the deaths a simple consequence of the fire, and no one guilty.'

'You forget, Mary Monson,' interposed the judge, mildly, 'that the robbery, and the piece of money found in your purse, give a colour to the supposition of crime. The jury have doubtless been influenced by these facts, and important facts they are. No one can deny this; and I think you overlook that feature of your case. If, however, your counsel has any good reason to offer why sentence should not now be pronounced, the court will hear it. There is no impatience on the part of justice, which would much rather draw in than stretch forth its arm. Perhaps, Mary Monson, you might do well to leave to your counsel the objections you wish to urge, and let them be presented to us in a form that we can recognise.'

'I see no great use in deferring the sentence,' Dunscomb remarked, quietly enough for the circumstances. 'It must be pronounced; and any question of law, should one occur to my mind, though I confess none does at present, can as well be raised after this ceremony as before.'

'I am disposed to wait, if a good reason can be urged for the delay. I will acknowledge that the case is one involved in a great deal of doubt and uncertainty, and am much inclined to do all the law will sanction. Still, I leave you to decide on your own course.'

'In my judgment, may it please your honour, we shall have to go to the executive, and it were, perhaps, better to get all the most revolting parts of the case over, while the accused——'

'Convicted, Mr Dunscomb – it is a distinction painful to make, but one that cannot now be avoided.'

'I beg pardon of the court – convicted.'

'Yes,' said Mary Monson, solemnly, 'I am convicted, and of the revolting crime of murder. All my hopes of a triumphant acquittal are blasted; and, whatever may be the termination of this extraordinary affair, a dark spot will always rest on my name. Sir, I am as innocent of this crime as the youngest child in your county. I may have been wilful, perverse, ill-judging, unwise, and have a hundred other failings; but neither Peter nor Dorothy Goodwin did I ever harm. I had not been long in the house before I discovered that the old couple were not happy together. They quarrelled often, and bitterly. The wife was managing, dictatorial, and sordidly covetous, while he used every shilling he could obtain, for the purchase of liquors. His mind was affected by his debauches, and he drivelled. In this state he came to me for sympathy and advice.

'There were passages in my own past life, short as it has been, which disposed me to feel for one who was not happy in the married state. It is no matter what my own experience has been; I had sympathy for that poor man. So far from wishing to do him harm, I desired to do him good. I advised him to quit the house, and live apart from his wife, for a time, at least; and this he consented to do, if I would furnish him with the means. Those means I promised; and, that he might not suffer, being of only feeble intellect, and in order to keep him from liquor, I had directed two of my agents to come to the house early in the morning of the very day that the fire happened, that they might convey Peter Goodwin to another residence, where he would be secret and safe, until his wife might repent of her treatment of him. It was fortunate for me that I had done this. Those two men, servants of my own, in the dress of countrymen, were the instruments of saving my life; without their aid, I should have perished in the flames. What they did, and how they did it, it would be premature now to say. Alas! alas! I have not been acquitted as I desired to be, and a dark shadow will for ever rest on my name!'

For the first time a doubt of the sanity of the prisoner crossed the mind of the judge. It was not so much the incoherence of her language, as her eye, the flushed cheek, and a certain air of stealthy cunning that awakened this distrust. Nevertheless, Mary Monson's manner was sincere, her language chosen and perfectly proper, and her explanations not without their force. There was something so strange, however, in a portion of her statements; so irreconcilable with a sound discretion, that, taken with the little which had come to light concerning this singular woman's past life, the doubt arose.

'Perhaps it were better, Mr District Attorney,' the judge observed, 'if we delay the sentence.'

'As your honour may think fit. The State is not over-anxious for life.'

'What say you, Mr Dunscomb – shall there be delay, or shall I sentence?'

'As the sentence *must* come, the sooner it is over the better. We have no ground on which to carry up the case, the jury being judges of the facts. Our principal hope must be in the discretion of the governor.'

'Mary Monson,' continued the judge, evidently treating the affair as purely a matter of form, 'you have been tried for feloniously depriving Peter Goodwin of his life——'

'I never did it,' interrupted the prisoner, in a voice so low as to be melodious, yet so clear as to be audible as the sound of a clarion. 'These men have been influenced by the rumours they have heard, and were not fit to act as my judges. Men should have minds superior to mere reports, to sit in that box.'

'My duty is to pronounce the sentence of the law. After a fair trial, and so far as it appears to us, by an impartial jury, you have been found guilty. For reasons that are of sufficient weight to my mind, I shall not dwell on the character of the awful change you will have to undergo, should this decree be put in force, but confine myself simply to the duty of pronouncing the sentence of the law, which is this: – that you be carried back to the gaol, and there be guarded, until Friday, the sixth day of September next, when between the hours of twelve and two p.m., you be carried to the place of execution, and hanged by the neck until you are dead – and God have mercy on your soul!'

A shudder passed through the audience, at hearing language like this applied to a person of Mary Monson's appearance, education, and sex. This feeling might have manifested itself more strongly, had not Mrs Horton attracted attention to herself, by forcing her way through the crowd, until she stood within the bar. Here the good woman, accustomed to bandy words with her guests, did not scruple to make her presence known to the court, by calling out –

'They tell me, your honour, that Mary Monson has just been found guilty of the murder of Peter Goodwin?'

'It is so, my good woman – but that case is ended. Mr Sheriff, remove the prisoner – time is precious——'

'Yes, you honour, and so is eternity. Mary Monson is no more guilty of taking the life of Peter Goodwin than I am guilty. I've always said some great disgrace would befall our juries, one of these days, and now my prophecy will come true. Duke's is disgraced. Constable, let that poor man come within the bar.'

The drivelling creature who entered the room of McBrain tottered forward, when twenty voices cried aloud the name of '*Peter Goodwin!*' Every word that Mary Monson had stated, was true!

CHAPTER XXVIII

Now, Marcia, now call up to thy assistance,
Thy wonted strength and constancy of mind;
Thou can'st not put it to a greater trial.

ADDISON.

Bench, bar, jury, witnesses and audience, were all astounded. The trial had been carried on in the most perfect good faith; and not a human being but the few who had felt the force of McBrain's testimony, doubted of the death of the individual who now appeared alive, if not well, in open court. The reader can better imagine than we can describe, the effects of a resurrection so entirely unexpected.

When the confusion naturally produced by such a scene had a little subsided; when all had actually seen, and many had actually felt, the supposed murdered man, as if to assure themselves of his being really in the flesh, order was restored: and the court and bar began to reflect on the course next to be pursued.

'I suppose, Mr District Attorney,' observed his honour, 'there is no mistake in the person of this individual; but it were better if we had an affidavit or two. Will you walk this way, sir?'

A long, private conference now took place between the public prosecutor and the judge. Each expressed his astonishment at the result, as well as some indignation at the deception which had been practised on the court. This indignation was a little mollified by the impression, now common to both, that Mary Monson was a person not exactly in her right mind. There was so much deception practised among persons accused of crimes, however, and in connection with this natural infirmity, that public functionaries like themselves were necessary very cautious in admitting the plea. The most offensive part of the whole affair was the discredit brought on the justice of Duke's! It was not in nature for these individuals to be insensible to the sort of disgrace the reappearance of Peter Goodwin entailed on the county and circuit; and there was a very natural desire to wipe off the stain. The conference lasted until the affidavits to establish the facts connected with Goodwin's case were ready.

'Had these affidavits been presented earlier,' said his honour, as soon as the papers were read, 'sentence would not have been pronounced. The case is novel, and I shall want a little time to reflect on the course I am to take. The sentence must be gotten rid of by some means or other; and it shall be my care to see it done. I hope, brother Dunscomb, the counsel for the accused have not been parties to this deception?'

'I am as much taken by surprise as your honour can possibly be,' returned the party addressed, with earnestness, 'not having had the most remote suspicion of the existence of the man said to have been murdered; else would all the late proceedings have been spared. As to the course to be taken next, I would respectfully suggest that the code be examined. It is an *omnium gatherum*; and must contain something to tell us how to undo all we have done.'

'It were better for all parties had they so been. There are still two indictments pending over Mary Monson; one for the arson, and the other for the murder of Dorothy Goodwin. Mr District Attorney feels the necessity of trying these cases, or one of them at least, in vindication of the justice of the State and county; and I am inclined to think that, under all the circumstances, this course should be taken. I trust we shall have no more surprises, and that Dorothy Goodwin will be brought forward at once, if still living – time is precious!'

'Dorothy Goodwin is dead,' said Mary Monson, solemnly. 'Poor woman! she was called away suddenly, and in her sins. Little fear of her ever coming here to flout your justice.'

'It may be well to caution your client Mr Dunscomb, against hasty and indiscreet admissions. Let the accused be arraigned, and a jury be empanelled. Which case do you choose to move on, Mr District Attorney?'

Dunscomb saw that his honour was offended and much in earnest. He was offended himself, and half disposed to throw up his brief; but he felt for the situation of a lovely and defenceless woman. Then his doubts touching his client's sanity began to take the character of certainty; and he saw how odious it would be to abandon one so afflicted in her emergency. He hinted his suspicion to the court; but was told that the fact, under all the circumstances of the case, was one properly for the jury. After reflection, the advocate determined not to desert his trust.

We pass over the preliminary proceedings. A jury was empanelled with very little difficulty; not a challenge having been made. It was composed, in part, of those who had been in the box on the late occasion; and, in part, of new men. There was an air of earnestness and business about them all, that Timms did not like; but it was too late to raise objections. To own the truth, the senior counsel cared much less than before for the result; feeling satisfied that his contemplated application at Albany would meet with consideration. It is true, Mary Monson was no anti-renter. She could not come forward with her demand for mercy with hands dyed in the blood of an officer of that public which lives under the deception of fancying it rules the land; murderers who added to their crimes the hateful and pestilent fraud of attempting to cloak robbery in the garb of righteous liberty; nor could she come sustained by numbers around the ballot-box, and bully the executive into acts which the reason and conscience of every honest man condemn; but Dunscomb believed that she might come with the plea of a being visited by the power of her

Creator, in constituting her as she was, a woman not morally accountable for her acts.

All the leading facts, as shown on the former trial, were shown on this. When the country practitioners were called on to give their opinions concerning the effect of the blow, they necessarily became subject to the cross-examination of the counsel for the prisoner, who did not spare them.

'Were you examined, sir, in the late trial of Mary Monson for the murder of Peter Goodwin?' demanded Dunscomb of the first of these modern Galens who was put on the stand.

'I was, sir.'

'What did you say on that occasion' – looking at his notes of the other trial, – 'touching the sex of the persons to whom those skeletons were thought to have belonged?'

'I said I *believed*, not *knew*, but *believed*, they were the remains of Peter and Dorothy Goodwin.'

'Did you not use stronger language than that?'

'Not that I remember, I may have done so; but I do not remember it.'

'Did you not say you had "*no doubt*" that those were the remains of Peter and Dorothy Goodwin?'

'I may have said as much as that. Now you mention the words, I believe I did.'

'Do you think so now?'

'Certainly not. I cannot think so, after what I have seen.'

'Do you know Peter Goodwin, personally!'

'Very well. I have practised many years in this neighbourhood.'

'Whom, then, do you say that this unfortunate man here, whom we see alive, though a driveller, really is?'

'Peter Goodwin – he who was thought to have been murdered. We are all liable to mistakes.'

'You have testified in chief that, in your judgment, the two persons, of whom we have the remains here in court, were stunned, at least, if not absolutely killed, by the blow that you think fractured each of their skulls. Now, I would ask if you think the prisoner at the bar possesses the physical force necessary to enable her to strike such a blow?'

'That would depend on the instrument she used. A human skull may be fractured easily enough, by a moderate blow struck by a heavy instrument.'

'What sort of instrument, for instance?'

'A sword – a bar of iron – or anything that has weight and force.'

'Do you believe those fractures were given by the same blow?'

'I do. By one and the same blow.'

'Do you think Mary Monson possesses the strength necessary to cause those two fractures at a single blow?'

Witness had no opinion on the subject.

'Are the fractures material?'

'Certainly – and must have required a heavy blow to produce them.'

This was all that could be got from either of the witnesses on that material point. As respected McBrain, he was subsequently examined in reference to the same facts. Dunscomb made good use of this witness, who now commanded the respect of all present. In the first place, he was adroitly offered to the jury, as the professional man who had, from the first, given it as his opinion that both the skeletons were those of females; and this in the face of all the collected wisdom of Duke's county; an opinion that was now rendered so probable as almost to amount to certainty. He (Dunscomb) believed most firmly that the remains were those of Dorothy Goodwin and the German woman who was missing.

'Have you examined those skeletons, Dr McBrain?' Dunscomb asked.

'I have, sir; and carefully, since the late trial.'

'How do you think the persons to whom they belonged came to their deaths?'

'I find fractures in the skulls of both. If they lie now as they did when the remains were found (a fact that had been proved by several witnesses), I am of opinion that a single blow inflicted the injuries on both; it may be, that blow was not sufficient to produce death; but it must have produced a stupor, or insensibility, which would prevent the parties from seeking refuge against the effect of the flames——'

'Is the learned witness brought here to sum up the cause?' demanded Williams, with one of those demoniacal sneers of his, by means of which he sometimes carried off a verdict. 'I wish to know, that I may take notes of the course of his argument.'

McBrain drew back, shocked and offended. He was naturally diffident, as his friend used to admit, in everything but wives; and as regarded them 'he had the impudence of the devil. Ned would never give up the trade until he had married a dozen, if the law would see him out in it. He ought to have been a follower of the great Mahomet, who made it a point to take a new wife at almost every new moon!' The judge did not like this sneer of Williams; and this so much the less, because, in common with all around him, he had imbibed a profound respect for the knowledge of the witness. It is true, he was very much afraid of the man, and dreaded his influence at the polls; but he really had too much conscience to submit to everything. A judge may yet have a conscience – if the Code will let him.

'This is very irregular, Mr Williams, not to say improper,' his honour mildly remarked. 'The witness has said no more than he has a right to say; and the court must see him protected. Proceed with your testimony, sir.'

'I have little more to say, if it please the court,' resumed McBrain, too much dashed to regain his self-possession in a moment. As this was all Williams wanted, he permitted him to proceed in his own way; and all the doctor had to say was soon told to the jury. The counsel for the prosecution manifested great tact in not cross-examining the witness at all. In a subsequent stage of the trial, Williams had the impudence to insinuate to the jury that they did not attach sufficient importance to his testimony, to subject him to this very customary ordeal.

But the turning point of this trial, as it had been that of the case which preceded it, was the evidence connected with the piece of money. As the existence of the notch was now generally known, it was easy enough to recognise the coin that had been found in Mary Monson's purse; thus depriving the accused of one of her simplest and best means of demonstrating the ignorance of the witnesses. The notch, however, was Mrs Burton's great mark, under favour of which her very material testimony was now given as it had been before.

Dunscomb was on the point of commencing the cross-examination, when the clear melodious voice of Mary Monson herself was heard for the first time since the commencement of the trial.

'Is it permitted to *me* to question this witness?' demanded the prisoner.

'Certainly,' answered the judge. 'It is the right of every one who is arraigned by the country. Ask *any* question that you please.'

This was a somewhat liberal decision as to the right of cross-examining; and the accused put on it a construction almost as broad as the privilege. As for the witness, it was very apparent she had little taste for the scrutiny that she probably foresaw she was about to undergo; and her countenance, attitude, and answers, each and all betrayed how much distaste she had for the whole procedure. As permission was obtained, however, the prisoner did not hesitate to proceed.

'Mrs Burton,' said Mary Monson, adopting, as well as she knew how, the manner of the gentlemen of the bar, 'I wish you to tell the court and jury *when* you first saw the notched piece of money?'

'When I first saw it? I saw it first, when Aunt Dolly first showed it to me,' answered the witness.

Most persons would have been dissatisfied with this answer, and would probably have caused the question to be repeated in some other form; but Mary Monson seemed content, and went on putting her questions, just as if she had obtained answers to meet her views.

'Did you examine it well?'

'As well as I desired to. There was nothing to prevent it.'

'Did you know it immediately, on seeing it in my purse?'

'Certainly – as soon as I saw the notch.'

'Did Mrs Goodwin point out the notch to you, or did you point out the notch to her?'

'She pointed it out to me; she feared that the notch might lessen the value of the coin.'

'All this I have heard before; but I now ask you, Mrs Burton, in the name of that Being whose eye is everywhere, did you not yourself put that piece of money in my purse, when it was passing from hand to hand, and take out of it the piece without a notch? Answer me, as you have a regard for your soul!'

Such a question was altogether out of the rules regulating the queries that may be put to witnesses, an answer in the affirmative going directly to criminate the respondent; but the earnest manner, solemn tones, and, we may add, illuminated countenance of Mary Monson, so far imposed on the woman, that she quite lost sight of her rights, if she ever knew them. What is much more remarkable, neither of the counsel for the prosecution interposed an objection. The District Attorney was willing that justice should have its way, and Williams began to think it might be prudent to manifest less anxiety for a conviction than he had done in the case in which the party murdered had been resuscitated. The judge was entranced by the prisoner's manner.

'I believe I have as much regard for my soul as any of the neighbours have for theirs,' answered Mrs Burton, sullenly.

'Let us learn that in your reply – Did you, or did you not, change those pieces of gold?'

'Perhaps I might – it's hard to say, when so much was said and done.'

'How came you with the other piece, with which to make the exchange? Answer, Sarah Burton, as you fear God?'

The witness trembled like an aspen-leaf. So remarkable was the scene, that no one thought of interfering; but the judge, the bar, and the jury, seemed equally willing to leave the two females to themselves, as the most efficient means of extorting the truth. Mary Monson's colour heightened; her mien and countenance grew, as it were, with the occasion, while Sarah Burton's became paler and paler, as each question was put, and the reply pressed.

'I can have money, I hope, as well as other folks,' answered the witness.

'That is no reply. How came you with the piece of gold that is notched, that you could exchange it for the piece which was not notched, and which was the one really found in my purse? Answer me that, Sarah Burton; here, where we both stand in the presence of our great Creator?'

'There's no need of your pressing a body so awfully – I don't believe it's law.'

'I repeat the question – or I will answer it for you. When you fired the house——'

The woman screamed, and raised her hands in natural horror.

'I never set the house on fire,' she cried: 'it took from the stove-pipe in the garret, where it had taken twice before.'

'How can you know *that*, unless you saw it? How see it, unless present?'

'I was *not* there, and did not see it; but I know the garret had caught twice before from that cook-stove-pipe. Aunt Dolly was very wrong to neglect it as she did.'

'And the blows on the head – who struck those blows, Sarah Burton?'

'How can I tell? I wasn't there – no one but a fool could believe *you* have strength to do it.'

'How, then, *was* it done? Speak – I see it in your mind?'

'I saw the ploughshare lying on the heads of the skeletons; and I saw Moses Steen throw it off, in the confusion of first raking the embers. Moses will be likely to remember it, if sent for, and questioned.'

Here was a most important fact elicited under the impulse of self-justification; and a corresponding expression of surprise passed in a murmur through the audience. The eye of Mary Monson kindled with triumph; and she continued with renewed powers of command over the will and conscience of the witness.

'This is well, Sarah Burton – it is right, and what you ought to say. You think that the fire was accidental, and that the fractured skulls came from the fall of the plough?'

'I do. I know that the plough stood in the garret, directly over the bed, and the stove-pipe passed quite near it. There was an elbow in that pipe, and the danger was at that elbow.'

'This is well; and the eye above looks on you with less displeasure, Sarah Burton.' As this was said the witness turned her looks timidly upwards, as if to assure herself of the fact. 'Speak holy truth, and it will soon become benignant and forgiving. Now tell me how you came by the stocking and its contents?'

'The stocking!' said the witness, starting, and turning white as a sheet. 'Who says I took the stocking?'

'I do. I know it by that secret intelligence which has been given me to discover truth. Speak, then, Sarah, and tell the court and jury the truth, the whole truth, and nothing but the truth.'

'Nobody saw me take it; and nobody can say I took it.'

'Therein you are mistaken. You *were* seen to take it. I saw it, for one; but there was another who saw it, with its motive, whose eye is ever on us. Speak, then, Sarah, and keep nothing back.'

'I meant no harm, if I did take it. There was so many folks about, I was afraid that some stranger might lay hands on it. That's all.'

'You were seen to unlock the drawers, as you stood alone near the bureau, in the confusion and excitement of the finding of the skeletons. You did it stealthily, Sarah Burton.'

'I was afraid some one might snatch the stocking from me. I always meant to give it up, as soon as the law said to whom it belongs. Davis wants it, but I'm not sure it is his.'

'What key did you use? Keep nothing back.'

'One of my own. My keys unlocked many of Aunt Dolly's drawers. She knew it, and never found any fault with it. Why should she? Her keys unlocked *mine!*'

'Another word – where is that stocking, and where are its contents?'

'Both are safe in the third drawer of my own bureau, and here is the key,' taking one from her bosom. 'I put them there for security, as no one opens that drawer but myself.'

Timms took the key from the unresisting hand of the woman, and followed by Williams, Davis, and one or two more, he left the court-house. At that instant Sarah Burton fainted. In the confusion of removing her into another room Mary Monson resumed her seat.

'Mr District Attorney, it can hardly be your intention to press this indictment any further?' observed the judge, wiping his eyes, and much delighted with the unexpected termination of the affair.

The functionary addressed was glad enough to be rid of his unwelcome office, and at once signified his willingness to enter a *nolle prosequi*, by an application to the bench, in the case of the arson, and to submit to an acquittal in that now being traversed. After a brief charge from the judge, the jury gave a verdict of acquittal, without leaving the box; and just as this was done, Timms and his companions returned, bringing with them the much-talked-of stocking.

It required months completely to elucidate the whole affair; but so much is already known, and this part of our subject being virtually disposed of, we may as well make a short summary of the facts, as they were already in proof, or as they have since come to light.

The fire was accidental, as has been recently ascertained by circumstances it is unnecessary to relate. Goodwin had left his wife, the night before the accident, and she had taken the German woman to sleep with her. As the garret-floor above this pair was consumed, the plough fell, its share inflicting the blow which stunned them, if it did not inflict even a greater injury. That part of the house was first consumed, and the skeletons were found, as has been related, side by side. In the confusion of the scene, Sarah Burton had little difficulty in opening the drawer, and removing the stocking. She fancied herself unseen; but Mary Monson observed the movement, though she had then no idea what was abstracted. The unfortunate delinquent maintains that her intention, at the time was good; or, that her sole object was to secure the gold; but, is obliged to confess that the possession of the treasure gradually excited her cupidity, until she began to hope that this hoard might eventually become her own. The guilty soonest suspect guilt. As to 'the pure, all things are pure,' so it is with the innocent, who are the least inclined to suspect others of wicked actions. Thus was it with Mrs Burton. In the commission of a great wrong herself, she had little difficulty in supposing that Mary Monson was the sort of person that rumour made her out to be. She saw no great harm, then, in giving a shove to the descending culprit. When looking into the stocking, she had seen, and put in her own pocket, the notched piece, as a curiosity, there being nothing more unusual in the guilty thus incurring unnecessary risks, than there is in the moth's temerity in fluttering around the candle. When the purse of Mary Monson was examined, as usually happens on such occasions, we had almost said as *always* happens, in the management of cases that are subsequently to form a part of the justice of the land, much less attention was paid to the care of that purse than ought to have been bestowed on it. Profiting by the neglect, Sarah Burton exchanged the notched coin for the perfect piece, unobserved, as she again fancied; but once more the watchful eye of Mary Monson was on her. The first time the woman was observed by the last, it was accidentally; but suspicion once aroused, it was natural enough to keep a look-out on the suspected party. The act was seen, and at the moment that the accused thought happy, the circumstance was brought to bear on the trial. Sarah Burton maintains that, at first, her sole intention was to exchange the imperfect for the perfect coin; and that she was induced to swear to the piece subsequently produced, as that found on Mary Monson's person, as a literal fact, ignorant of what might be its consequences. Though the devil, doubtless, leads us on, step by step, deeper and deeper, into crime and sin, it is probable that, in this particular, the guilty woman applied a flattering unction to her conscience, that the truth would have destroyed.

Great was the wonder, and numberless were the paragraphs that this unexpected issue of the 'great Biberry murders' produced. As respects the last, anything that will fill a column is a god-send, and the falsehood has even a value that is not to be found in the truth, as its contradiction will help along quite as much as the original statements. If the public could only be brought to see what a different thing publicity becomes in the hands of those who turn it to *profit*, from what it is thought to be, by those who fancy it is merely a mode of circulating facts, a great step towards a much-needed reformation would be taken, by confining the last within their natural limits.

Mary Monson's name passed from one end of the Union to the other, and thousands heard and read of this extraordinary woman, who never had the smallest clue to her real character or subsequent history. How few reflected on the defects of the system that condemned her to the gallows on insufficient testimony: or, under another phase of prejudice, might have acquitted her when guilty! The random decisions of the juries, usually well-meaning, but so rarely discriminating, or as intelligent as they ought to be, attract very little attention beyond the bar; and even the members of that often strike a balance in error, with which they learn to be content; gaining in one cause as much as they lose in another.

There was a strong disposition in the people assembled at Biberry, on the occasion of the trial, to make a public spectacle of Mary Monson. The right to do this, with all things in heaven and earth, seems to belong to 'republican simplicity,' which is beginning to rule the land with a rod of iron. Unfortunately for this feeling, the subject of momentary sympathy was not a person likely to allow such a license. She did not believe, because she had endured one set of atrocious wrongs, that she was bound to submit to as many more as gaping vulgarity might see fit to inflict. She sought the protection of good Mrs Gott and her gaol, some forms being necessary before the sentence of death could be legally gotten rid of. In vain were the windows again crowded, with the virtuous wish of seeing how Mary Monson *looked*, now she was acquitted, just as they had been previously thronged in order to ascertain how she looked when there was a chance of her being condemned to the gallows. The most extraordinary part of the affair, was the circumstance that the harp became popular; the very sentiment, act, or thing that, in one condition of the common mind, is about to be 'cut down and cast into the fire,' becoming in another, all that is noble, commendable, or desirable. The crowd about the windows of the gaol, for the first few hours after the acquittal, was dying to hear the prisoner sing and play, and would gladly have tolerated the harp and a 'foreign tongue' to be thus gratified.

But Mary Monson was safe from all intrusion, under the locks of the delighted Mrs Gott. This kind-hearted person kissed her prisoner, over and over again, when she admitted her within the gallery, and then she went outside, and assured several of the more respectable persons in the crowd how thoroughly she had been persuaded, from the first, of the innocence of her friend. The circumstances of this important trial rendered Mrs Gott a very distinguished person herself, in that crowd, and never was a woman happier than she while delivering her sentiments on the recent events.

'It's altogether the most foolish trial we have ever had in Duke's, though they tell me foolish trials are getting to be only too common,' said the kind-hearted wife of the sheriff, addressing half a dozen of the more respectable of the crowd. 'It gave me a big fright, I will own. When Gott was elected sheriff, I did hope he would escape all executions but debt executions. The more he has of them, the better. It's bad enough to escort thieves to Sing-sing; but the gallows is a poor trade for a decent man to meddle with. Then, to have the very first sentence, one against Mary Monson, who is as much above such a punishment as virtue is above vice. When I heard those dreadful words, I felt as if a cord was round my own neck. But I had faith to the last; Mary has always told me that she should be acquitted, and here it has all come true, at last.'

'Do you know, Mrs Gott,' said one of her friends, 'it is reported that this woman – or lady, I suppose one must *now* call her – has been in the habit of quitting the gaol whenever she saw fit.'

'Hu-s-h, neighbour Brookes; there is no need of alarming the county! I believe you are right; though it was all done without my knowledge, or it never would have been permitted. It only shows the power of money. The locks are as good as any in the State; yet Mary certainly did find means, unbeknown to me, to open them. It can't be called breaking gaol, since she always came back! I had a good fright the first time I heard of it, but use reconciles us to all things. I never let Gott into the secret, though he's responsible, as he calls it, for all his prisoners.'

'Well, when a matter turns out happily, it does no good to be harping on it always.'

Mrs Gott assented, and in this case, as in a hundred others, the end was made to justify the means. But Mary Monson was felt to be an exception to all rules, and there was no longer any disposition to cavil at any of her proceedings. Her innocence had been established so very triumphantly, that every person regarded her vagaries and strange conduct with indulgence.

At that very moment, when Mrs Gott was haranguing her neighbours at the door of the gaol, Dunscomb was closeted with Michael Millington at the inn; the young man having returned at hot-speed only as the court adjourned. He had been successful, notwithstanding his original disappointment, and had ascertained all about the hitherto mysterious prisoner of the Biberry gaol. Mary Monson was, as Dunscomb suspected, Mildred Millington by birth – Mad. de Larocheforte by marriage – and she was the grand-daughter of the very woman to whom he had been betrothed in youth. Her insanity was not distinctly recognised, perhaps could not have been legally established, though it was strongly suspected by many who knew her intimately, and was a source of great uneasiness with all who felt an interest in her welfare. Her marriage was unhappy, and it was supposed she had taken up her abode in the cottage of the Goodwins to avoid her husband. The command of money gave her a power to do very much as she pleased, and, though the breath of calumny had never yet blown its withering blast on her name, she erred in many things that are duties as grave as that of being chaste. The laws came in aid of her whims and caprices. There is no mode by which an errant wife can be made to perform her duties in boldly experimenting New York, though she can claim a support and protection from her husband. The 'cup and saucer' law comes in aid of this power, and the men who cannot keep their wives in the chains of Hymen in virtue of the affections, may just as well submit, with a grace, to be the victims of an ill-judging and most treacherous regard for the rights of what are called the weaker sex.

CHAPTER XXIX

Why wilt thou add to all the griefs I suffer,
Imaginary ills, and fancied tortures?

Cato.

The scene must now be shifted to Rattletrap. Biberry was deserted. Even the rumours with which its streets had been so lately filled, were already forgotten. None have memories as frail as the gossip. Not only does this class of persons – and a numerous class it is, including nearly all whose minds are not fitted to receive more elevated materials – not only, we say, does this class of persons overlook the contradictions and absurdities of the stories they repeat, but they forget the stories themselves almost as soon as heard. Such was now the case at Biberry. Scarce an individual could be found in the place who would acknowledge that he or she had ever heard that Mary Monson was connected with robbers, or who could recollect that he once fancied the accused guilty.

We may as well say here, that nothing has ever been done with Sarah Burton. She is clearly guilty; but the law, in these times of progress, disdains to pursue the guilty. Their crimes are known; and of what use can it be to expose those who every one can see are offenders! No; it is the innocent who have most reason to dread the law. *They* can be put to trouble, cost, vexation and loss, if they cannot be exactly condemned. We see how thousands regard the law in a recent movement in the legislature, by which suits have been ordered to try the titles of most of the large landed proprietors, with the very honest and modest proposal annexed, that their cases shall be prejudged, and the landlords deprived of the means of defending themselves, by sequestering their rents! Everybody says this is the freest country on earth; the only country that is truly free; but we must be permitted to say, that such a law, like twenty more that have been passed in the same interest within the last ten years, savours a good deal of the character of a Ukase.

Our characters, with the exception of McBrain and his bride, were now assembled at Rattletrap. Dunscomb had ascertained all it was necessary to know concerning Mildred, and had taken the steps necessary to protect her. Of her qualified insanity he did not entertain a doubt; though it was a madness so concealed by the blandishments of education and the graces of a refined woman, that few saw it, and fewer still wished to believe it true. On most subjects this unhappy lady was clear-minded and intelligent enough, more especially on that of money; for, while her expenditures were generous, and her largesses most liberal, she manifested wonderful sagacity in taking care of her property. It was this circumstance that rendered it so difficult to take any steps to deprive her of its control;

though Dunscomb had seen enough, in the course of the recent trial, to satisfy him that such a measure ought to be resorted to in the interest of her own character.

It was in cunning, and in all the low propensities connected with that miserable quality, that Mildred Millington, as she now insisted on calling herself, most betrayed her infirmity. Many instances of it have been incidentally related in the course of our narrative, however unpleasant such an exhibition has been. There is nothing more repugnant to the principles or tastes of the right thinking and right feeling than the practices which cunning engenders. Timms, however, was a most willing agent in all the schemes of his client; though some of her projects had puzzled him by their elaborate duplicity, as much as they had astounded him by their boldness. These were the schemes that had their origin in obliquity of mind. Still they were not without merit in the eyes of Timms, who was cunning without being mad.

Before quitting Biberry, Timms was liberally paid and dismissed. Dunscomb explained to him the situation of his handsome client, without adverting to the state of her mind; when the attorney at once caught at the chances of a divorce. Among the other 'ways of the hour,' that of dissolving the marriage tie has got to be a sort of fashionable mania. Neither time, nor duties, nor children, seem to interpose any material obstacle; and, if our own laws do not afford the required facilities, those of some of our more liberal neighbours do. Timms keeps this principle in his mind, and is at this moment ruminating on the means by which he can liberate his late client from her present chains, and bind her anew in some of his own forging. It is scarcely necessary to add, that Mildred troubles herself very little in the premises, so far as this covert lover is concerned.

The ridicule of Williams was, at first, the sorest portion of Timms's disappointment. Bachelors alike, and rivals for popular favour, these two worthies had long been looking out for advantageous marriages. Each had the sagacity to see that his chances of making a more and more eligible connexion were increasing slowly, and that it was a great thing for a rising man to ascend without dragging after him a wife chosen from among those that prop the base of the great social ladder. It was nuts to one of these competitors for the smiles of the ladies to discover that his rival was in love with a married woman; and this so much the more, because the prospects of Timms's success, arising from his seeming intimacy with the fair occupant of the gaol, had given Williams a very serious fright. Place two men in competition, no matter in what, and all their energies become concentrated in rivalry. Again and again, had these two individuals betrayed their mutual jealousy; and now that one of them had placed himself in a position so false, not to say ridiculous, the other did not fail to enjoy his disappointment to the top of his bent. It was in this manner that Saucy Williams took his revenge for the defeat in the trial.

Mrs Gott was also at Rattletrap. Dunscomb retained much of his original tenderness for Mildred, the grandmother of his guest of that name, and he granted her descendant every indulgence she could ask. Among other things, one of the requests of the liberated prisoner was to be permitted to manifest this sense of her gratitude for the many acts of kindness received from the wife of the sheriff. Gott, accordingly, was left to take care of himself, while his nice little companion was transported to a scene that she found altogether novel, or a temporary residence in a gentleman's dwelling. Sarah's housekeeping, Sarah's good nature, attentions, neatness, attire and attractions, would have been themes to monopolise all of the good little woman's admiration, had not Anna Updyke, then on a visit at Rattletrap, quite fairly come in for her full share. She might almost be said to be in love with both.

It was just after breakfast that Mildred locked an arm in that of Anna, and led her young friend by one of the wooded paths that runs along the shores of the Hudson, terminating in a summer-house, with a most glorious view. In this, there was nothing remarkable; the eye rarely resting on any of the 'bits' that adorn the banks of that noble stream, without taking in beauties to enchant it. But to all these our two lovely young women were momentarily as insensible as they were to the fact that their own charming forms, floating among shrubbery as fragrant as themselves, added in no slight degree to the beauty of the scene. In manner, Mildred was earnest, if not ardent, and a little excited; on the other hand, Anna was placid, though sensitive; changing colour without ceasing, as her thoughts were drawn nearer and nearer to that theme which now included the great object of her existence.

'Your uncle brought me letters from town last evening, Anna, dear,' commenced the liberated lady: 'one of them is from Mons. de Larocheforte. Is that not strange?'

'What is there so strange in a husband's writing to his wife? To me, it seems the most natural thing in the world.'

'It does? I am surprised to hear you say so – you, Anna, whom I regarded as so truly my friend. I have discarded Mons. de Larocheforte, and he ought to respect my pleasure.'

'It would have been better, my dear mamma, had you discarded him before marriage, instead of after.'

'Ah! your dear mamma, indeed! I was your school mamma, Anna, and well had it been for me had I been left to finish my education in my own country. Then, I should have escaped this most unfortunate marriage. Do not marry, Anna; take my advice, and never marry. Matrimony is unsuited to ladies.'

'How long have you been of this opinion, dear mamma?' asked the young girl, smiling.

'Just as long as I have been made to feel how it crushes a woman's independence, and how completely it gives her a master, and how very, very humiliating and depressing is the bondage it inflicts. Do you not feel the force of my reasons?'

'I confess I do not,' answered Anna, in a subdued, yet clear and distinct voice. 'I see nothing humiliating or depressing in a woman's submission to her husband. It is the law of nature, and why should we wish to alter it? My mother has ever inculcated such opinions, and you will excuse me if I say I think the Bible does, also.'

'The Bible! Yes, that is a good book, though I am afraid it is very little read in France. I ought, perhaps, to say, "read very little by strangers resident in France." The French women, themselves, are not one half as negligent of their duties, in this respect, as are the strangers who go to reside among them. When the roots that have grown to any size in their native soil, are violently transplanted to another, it is not often that the tree obtains its proper dimensions and grace. I wish I had never seen France, Anna, in which case I should never have been Mad. de Larocheforte – *vicomtesse*, by the old law, and I am afraid it was that idle appellation that entrapped me. How much more truly respectable I should have been as Mrs John Smith, or Mrs John Brown, or Mrs David Smith, the wife of a countryman, if I must be a wife, at all!'

'Choose at least some name of higher pretension,' said Anna, laughing. 'Why not a Mrs Van Rensselaer, or a Mrs Van Cortlandt, or a Mrs Livingston, or a Mrs Somebody else, of one of our good old families?'

'Families! – Do you know, child, it is treason to talk of families in this age of anti-rentism. They tell me that the man who makes an estate, may enjoy it, should he happen to know how, and this, though he may have cheated all he ever dealt with, in order to become rich; but, that he who inherits an estate, has no claim. It is his tenants who have the high moral claim to his father's property.'

'I know nothing of all this, and would rather talk of things I understand.'

'By which you mean wedlock, and its cares! No, my dear, you little understand what matrimony is, or how much humiliation is required of us women to become wives, or you would never think of marrying.'

'I have never told you that I *do* think of marrying – that is, not much.'

'There spoke your honest nature, which will not permit even an unintended deception. This it was that so much attached me to you as a child; for, though I am not very ingenuous myself, I can admire the quality in another.'

'This admission does not exactly prove the truth of your words, mamma!' said Anna, smiling.

'No matter – let us talk of matrimony. Has John Wilmeter proposed to you, Anna?'

This was a home question; no wonder the young lady started. After a short, musing pause, however, the native candour of Anna Updyke prevailed, and she admitted that he had.

'Thank you for this confidence; but you must go further. Remember, I am your mamma. Is the gentleman accepted?'

A rosy blush, succeeded by a nod of the head, was the answer.

'I am sorry I was not consulted before all this happened; though I have managed my own matters so ill as to have very few claims to your confidence. You scarce know what you undertake, my child.'

'I undertake to become Jack Wilmeter's wife,' answered the betrothed, in a very low but a very firm voice; 'and I hope I shall make him a good one. Most of all, do I pray to be obedient and submissive.'

'To no man that breathes, Anna! – no, to no man breathing! It is *their* business to submit to *us*; not we to them!'

'This is not my reading of the great rule of woman's conduct. In my view of our duties, it is the part of woman to be affectionate, mild, patient and sympathising, – if necessary, forgiving. I firmly believe that, in the end, such a woman cannot fail to be as happy as is permitted to us to be, here on earth.'

'Forgiving!' repeated Mildred, her eyes flashing; 'yes, that is a word often used, yet how few truly practise its teachings! Why should I forgive any one that has wronged me? Our nature tells us to resent, to punish, if necessary, as you say – to revenge.'

A slight shudder passed through the frame of Anna, and she unconsciously moved farther from her companion, though their arms still continued locked.

'There must be a great difference between France and America, if revenge is ever taught to a woman as a part of her duty,' returned the younger female, now speaking with an earnestness she had not before betrayed; 'here, we are told that Christianity forbids the very thought of it, and that to forgive is among the very first of our duties. My great instructor in such things has told me that one of the surest evidences of a hopeful state of the feelings, is the banishment of everything like resentment, and a desire to be at peace with all around us – to have a perception that we love the race as beings of our own wants and hopes.'

'Is this the sort of love, then, with which you give your hand to young Wilmeter?'

Scarlet is not brighter than was the colour that now glowed in the cheeks of Anna, stole into her temples, and even diffused itself over her neck and chest. To herself it seemed as if her very hands blushed. Then the power of innocence came to sustain her, and she became calm and steady.

'It is *not* the feeling with which I shall marry John,' she said. 'Nature has given us another sentiment, and I shall not endeavour to be superior to all of my sex and class. I love John Wilmeter, I own, and I hope to make him happy.'

'To be a dutiful, obedient wife, for ever studying his tastes and caprices!'

'I trust I shall not be *for ever* studying the indulgence of my own. I see nothing degrading to a woman in her filling the place nature and Christianity have assigned to her, and in her doing her duty as a wife.'

'These are not *my* feelings, receiving your terms as you wish them to be understood. But several have told me I ought never to have married; I myself know that I should have been an American, and not a French wife.'

'I have ever heard that greater latitude is given to our sex in France than in this country.'

'That is true in part only. Nothing can exceed the *retenue* of a French girl, or anything that is decent exceed the want of it that is manifested by many Americans. On the other hand, a married woman here has no privileges at all, not even in society; while in France, under an air of great seeming propriety, she does very much as she sees fit. It is a mistake, however, to suppose that faithful wives and devoted mothers, most especially the last, are not to be found all over Europe – in France, in particular.'

'I am glad to hear it,' cried Anna, with a really gratified air; 'it gives me pleasure when I hear of any of our sex behaving as they should behave.'

'Should behave! I fear, Anna, a little covert reproach is intended, in that remark. Our estimate of the conduct of our friends must depend on our notions of our own duties. Now, hearken to my manner of reasoning on this subject. In a physical sense, man is strong, woman is weak; while, in a moral sense, woman is strong and man is weak. You admit my premises?'

'The first part of them, certainly,' said Anna, laughing, 'while I pretend to no knowledge of the last.'

'You surely do not believe that John Wilmeter is as pure, ingenuous, good, as you are yourself?'

'I see no reason why he should not be. I am far from certain Jack is not even better.'

'It is useless to discuss such a subject with you. The principle of pride is wanting, without which you can never enter into my feeling.'

'I am glad it is so. I fancy John will be all the happier for it. Ah! my dear mamma, I never knew any good come of what you call this "principle of pride." We are told to be humble, and not to be proud. It may be all the better for us females that rulers are given to us here, in the persons of our husbands.'

'Anna Updyke, do you marry John Wilmeter with the feeling that he is to rule? You overlook the signs of the times, the ways of the hour, child, if you do aught so weak! Look around you, and see how everybody, almost everything is becoming independent, our sex included. Formerly as I have heard elderly persons say, if a woman suffered in her domestic relations, she was compelled to suffer all. The quarrel lasted for a life. Now, no one thinks of being so unreasonably wretched. No, the wronged wife, or even the offended wife – Monsieur de Larocheforte snuffs abominably – abominably – yes, abominably; but no wife is obliged, in these times of independence and reason, to endure a snuffy husband——'

'No,' broke in Dunscomb, appearing from an adjoining path, 'she has only to pack up her spoons and be off. The code can never catch her. If it could on one page, my life for it there is a hole for her to get out of its grasp on the next. Your servant, ladies; I have been obliged to overhear more of your conversation than was intended for my ears, perhaps; these paths running so close to each other, and you being so animated; and now, I mean to take an old man's privilege, and speak my mind. In the first place, I shall deal with the agreeable. Anna, my love, Jack is a lucky fellow – far luckier than he deserves to be. You carry the right sentiment into wedlock. It is the right of the husband to be the head of his family; and the wife who resists his authority is neither prudent nor a Christian. He may abuse it, it is true; but, even then, so long as criminality is escaped, it were better to submit. I approve of every word you have uttered, dear, and thank you for it all in my nephew's name. And now, Mildred, as one who has a right to advise you, by his avowed love for your grandmother, and recent close connection with yourself, let me tell you what I think of those principles that you avow, and also of the state of things that is so fast growing up in this country. In the first place, he is no true friend of your sex who teaches it this doctrine of independence. I should think – it is true, I am only a bachelor, and have no experience to back me – but, I should think that a woman who truly loves her husband, would find a delight in her dependence——'

'Oh! certainly!' exclaimed Anna; biting her tongue at the next instant, and blushing scarlet at her own temerity.

'I understand you, child, and approve again – but there comes Jack, and I shall have to turn you over to him, that you may receive a good scolding from head-quarters, for this abject servitude feeling that you have betrayed. Go – go – his arm is held out already; and, harkee, young folk, remember that a new maxim in morals has come in with the code – "Principles depend on Circumstances." That is the rule of conduct now-a-days – that, and anti-rentism, and "republican simplicity," and the "cup-and-saucer law," and – and – yes – and the everblessed code!'

Dunscomb was obliged to stop for breath, which gave the young couple an opportunity to walk away. As for Mildred, she stood collected, extremely lady-like in mien, but with a slight degree of *hauteur* expressed in her countenance.

'And now, sir, that we are alone,' she said, 'permit me to inquire what *my* part of the lecture is to be. I trust you will remember, however, that while I am Mildred Millington by birth, the law which you so much reverence and admire, makes me Madame de Larocheforte.'

'You mean to say that I have the honour of conversing with a married woman?'

'Exactly so, Mr Dunscomb.'

'I comprehend you, ma'am, and shall respect your position. You are not about to become my niece, and I can claim no right to exceed the bounds of friendship——'

'Nay, my dear sir, I do not wish to say this. You have every right to advise. To me, you have been a steady and well-judging friend, and this, in the most trying circumstances. I am ready to hear you, sir, in deference, if not in your beloved humility.'

'That which I have to say refers solely to your own happiness, Mildred. Your return to America has, I fear, been most inopportune. Among other innovations that are making on every side of us, even to the verge of the dissolution of civilized society, comes the liberty of woman. Need I tell you, what will be the next step in this downward career?'

'You needs must, Mr Dunscomb – I do not comprehend you. – What will that step be?'

'Her licentiousness. No woman can throw off the most sacred of all her earthly duties, in this reckless manner, and hope to escape from the doom of her sex. After making a proper allowance for the increase of population, the increase in separated married people is getting to be out of all proportion. Scarce a month passes that one does not hear of some wife who has left her husband, secreted herself with a child perhaps, as you did, in some farm-house, passing by a different name, and struggling for her rights, as she imagines. Trust me, Mildred, all this is as much opposed to nature as it is to prescribed duties. That young woman spoke merely what an inward impulse, that is incorporated with her very being, prompted her to utter. A most excellent mother – oh! what a blessing is that to one of your sex – how necessary, how heavenly, how holy! – an excellent mother has left her in ignorance of no one duty, and her character has been formed in what I shall term harmony with her sex. I must be plain, Mildred – you have not enjoyed this advantage. Deprived of your parent young, known to be rich, and transplanted to another soil, your education has necessarily been entrusted to hirelings, flatterers, or persons indifferent to your real well-being; those who have consulted most the reputation of their instruction, and have paid the most attention to those arts which soonest strike the eye, and most readily attract admiration. In this, their success has been complete.'

'While you think it has not been so much so, sir, in more material things?' said the lady, haughtily.

'Let me be sincere. It is due to my relation to you – to your grandmother – to the past – to the present time. I know the blood that runs in your veins, Mildred. You are self-willed by descent, rich by inheritance, independent by the folly of our legislators. Accident has brought you home, at the very moment when our ill-considered laws are unhinging society in many of its most sacred interests; and, consulting only an innate propensity, you have ventured to separate from your husband, to conceal yourself in a cottage, a measure, I dare say, that comported well with your love of the romantic——'

'Not so – I was oppressed, annoyed, unhappy at home, and sought refuge in that cottage. Mons. de Larocheforte has such a passion for snuff! – He uses it night and day.'

'Then followed the serious consequences which involved you in so many fearful dangers——'

'True,' interrupted the lady, laying her small, gloved hand hastily on his arm – 'very true, dear Mr Dunscomb; but how cleverly I contrived to escape them all! – how well I managed your Mr Timms, good Mrs Gott, the puffy, pompous sheriff, that wily Williams, too, whose palm felt the influence of my gold – óh! the excitement of the last two months has been a gift of paradise to me, and, for the first time since my marriage, have I known what true happiness was!'

Dunscomb turned, astonished, to his companion, and stared her in the face. Never was the countenance more lovely to the cursory glance, the eye brighter, the cheek with a richer glow on it, or the whole air, mien and attitude more replete with womanly loveliness and womanly graces; but the observant eye of the lawyer penetrated beyond all these, and detected the unhappy spirit which had gained possession of a tenement so lovely. The expression of the countenance denoted the very triumph of cunning. We pretend not to a knowledge of the arcana of nature, to be able to detect the manner in which the moving principles prompt to good or evil, but we must reject all sacred history, and no small portion of profane, not to believe that agencies exist that are not visible to our ordinary senses; and that our boasted reason, when abandoned to its own support, becomes the victim of those that are malign. We care not by what names these agents are called, imps, demons, evil spirits, or evil passions; but this we do know, let him beware who submits to their control. Better, far better, were it that such an one had never been born!

Three days later Mildred Millington was in a state that left no doubt of her infirmity. The lucid intervals were long, however, and at such times her mind seemed clear enough on all subjects but one. Divorce was her 'ruling passion,' and, in order to effect her purpose, all the extraordinary ingenuity of a most fertile mind was put in requisition. Although means were promptly, but cautiously, taken to see that she did not squander her large pecuniary resources, Dunscomb early saw that they were uncalled for. Few persons were better qualified to look after their money than was this unfortunate lady, in the midst of the dire visitation that intellectually reduced her below the level of most around her. On this head her sagacity was of proof; though her hand was not closed in the grip of a miser. Accustomed, from childhood, to a liberal expenditure, she was willing still to use the means that an inscrutable Providence had so liberally placed in her way, her largesses and her charities continuing the same as ever. Down to the present moment the fund-holder, the owner of town property, the mortgagee, and the trader is allowed to enjoy his own, without any direct interference of the demagogue with his rights; but how much longer this exception is to last, is known only to the Being who directs the destinies of nations; or, at least, not to any who are now on earth, surrounded equally by the infirmities and ignorance of the present state.

But Mildred was, and is yet, permitted to exercise her rights over her own property, though care is had to see that no undue advantage is taken of her sex, years, and ignorance. Beyond this her control was not disputed, and she was suffered to manage her own affairs. She set about the matter of a divorce with the whole energy of her nature, and the cunning of her malady. Timms was again summoned to her service, unknown to Dunscomb, who would never have winked at the measures that were taken, though so much in accordance with 'the ways of the hour.'

Provided with proper credentials, this managing agent sought an interview with Mons. de Larochefort, a worn-out debauchee of some rank, who, sooth to say, had faults even graver than that of taking snuff. Notwithstanding the great personal attractions of Mildred, the motive for marrying her had been money: as is usually the case in a very great proportion of the connections of the Old World, among persons of condition. Love is to succeed, and not to precede, matrimony. Mildred had been taught that lesson, and grievously had she been disappointed. The snuff got into her eyes. Mons. de Larochefort – Mons. le Vicomte as he had been, and was still determined to be, and in all probability will be, in spite of all the French 'republican simplicity' that was ever summoned to a nation's rescue – Mons. le Vicomte was directly approached by Timms, and a proposal made that he should put himself in a condition to be divorced, for a stipulated price. Notwithstanding the opinion of the learned Attorney-General of this great state, of the European aristocracy, and who is so every way qualified to give such an opinion, *ex officio* as it might be, Mons. de Larocheforte declined lending himself to so vile a proposition, Frenchman and noble as he was. Nor did the husband believe that the discreditable proposal came from his wife. He compelled Timms to admit as much, under a menace of losing his case. That worthy was puzzled at this result, for he had made the proposal on his 'own hook,' as he afterwards explained the matter to Williams, in the fullest confidence of 'republican simplicity,' and was astonished at meeting with the self-respect of a gentleman, if with no very elevated principles in a nobleman! It was accordingly necessary to have recourse to some other mode of proceeding.

Luckily for the views of Timms and his fair client, one can scarcely go amiss in this country, when a divorce is desired. Although a few of the older states remain reasonably inflexible on this subject, in some respects *unreasonably* so, indeed, they are generally surrounded by communities that are more indulgent. By means of some *hocus pocus* of the law, that we pretend not to explain, the names of Gabriel Jules Vincent Jean Baptiste de Larocheforte, and Mildred de Larocheforte, were just beginning to steal on the dawn of the newspapers, in a case that, ere long, might blaze in the meridian of gossip.

Dunscomb frowned and reproached, but it was too late to recede. He has told Mildred, and he has told Timms, that nuptial knots tied in one community, cannot be so readily unloosed in another, as many imagine; and that there must, at least, be good faith – the *animus revertendi* – in the change of residence that usually precedes the application. But money is very powerful, and smooths a thousand difficulties. No one could predict the termination; and, as the Vicomte, though only to be approached in a more delicate way than that adopted by Timms, was as tired of the connection as his wife, and was very anxious to obtain a larger share of the fortune than the 'cup-and-saucer' law will give him, it was by no means improbable that the end of the affair would be a *quasi* divorce, that would at least enable each party to take his or her own course, without fear of molestation from the other.

In the mean time, Millington was married very shortly after the trial. The engagement had not been long, but the parties had known each other intimately for years. The bridegroom, in one sense, was the head of his family, though by no means possessed of its largest fortune. In this character, it devolved on him to care for the interests of his fair relative. Although as much opposed as Dunscomb to the course she was taking, he did not shrink from his duties as a relative; and it is understood that his house is Mildred's home when in town. Rattletrap opened its hospitable doors to the unfortunate woman, whenever she chose to visit the place; and Timbully has also claims on her time and presence.

Dunscomb announced his intention to retire from practice at the end of a twelvemonth, the morning that Michael and Sarah were married. In the intervening time, John Wilmeter and his new nephew were received as partners, and the worthy bachelor is now sedulously but silently transferring as respectable and profitable a list of clients, as any man in the courts can claim. His own advice is promised, at all times, to his old friends; and, as not a soul has objected, and the young men bid fair, there is every reason to hope that useful and profitable labour will keep both out of mischief.

CHAPTER XXX

Some curate has penn'd this invective,
And you have studied it.

MASSINGER.

The day set apart for the nuptials of John Wilmeter and Anna Updyke finally arrived. The ceremony was to take place in a little church that had stood, time out of mind, in the immediate neighbourhood of Timbully. This church was colonial in its origin, and, while so much around it has undergone vital changes, there stands that little temple, reared in honour of God, in its simplicity, unpretending yet solid and durable architecture, resembling, in all these particulars, the faith it was erected to sustain. Among the other ways of the hour that are worthy of our notice, the church itself has sustained many rude shock of late – shocks from within as well as from without. The Father of Lies has been roving through its flocks with renewed malice, damaging the shepherds, perhaps, quite as much as the sheep, and doing things hitherto unheard of in the brief annals of American Ecclesiastical History. Although we deeply regret this state of things, we feel no alarm. The hand which first reared this moral fabric will be certain to protect it as far as that protection shall be for its good. It already effected a great reform. The trumpet is no longer blown in Zion in our own honour; to boast of the effects of a particular discipline; to announce the consequences of order, and of the orders; or, in short, to proclaim a superiority that belongs only to the Head of all the churches, let them be farther from, or nearer to, what are considered distinctive principles. What the church is now enduring the country itself most sadly wants, – a lesson in humility; a distrust of self, a greater dependence on that wisdom which comes, not from the voices of the people, not from the ballot-boxes, not from the halls of senates, from heroes, god-likes, or stereotyped opinions, but from above, the throne of the Most High.

In one of those little temples reared by our fathers in the days of the monarchy, when, in truth, greater republican simplicity really reigned among us, in a thousand things, than reigns to-day, the bridal party from

Timbully was assembled at an early hour of the morning. The company was not large, though it necessarily included most of the nearest relatives of the bride and groom. Dunscomb was there, as were Millington and his wife; Dr and Mrs McBrain, of course, and two or three other relations on the side of the bride's father, besides Mildred. It was to be a private wedding, a thing that is fast getting to be forgotten. Extravagance and parade have taken such deep root among us that young people scarce consider themselves legally united unless there are six bride's maids, one, in particular, to 'pull off the glove;' as many attendants of the other sex, and some three or four hundred friends in the evening, to bow and curtsy before the young couple, utter a few words of nonsense, and go their way to bow and curtsy somewhere else.

There was nothing of this at Timbully, on that wedding-day. Dunscomb and his nephew drove over from Rattletrap, early in the morning, even while the dew was glittering on the meadows, and Millington and his wife met them at a cross-road, less than a mile from McBrain's country-house. The place of rendezvous was at the church itself, and thither the several vehicles directed their way. Dunscomb was just in time to hand Mildred from her very complete travelling-carriage, of which the horses were in a foam, having been driven hard all the way from town. Last of all, appeared Stephen Hoof, driving the respectable-looking Rockaway of Mrs McBrain – we were on the point of writing his 'master,' but there are no longer any 'masters' in New York. Stephen, himself, who had not a spark of pride, except in his horses, and who was really much attached to the person he served, always spoke of the doctor as his 'boss.' Jack Wilmeter, somewhat of a wag, had perplexed the honest coachman, on a certain occasion, by telling him that 'boss' was the Latin for 'ox,' and that it was beneath his dignity to be using Pill and Pole-us (Bolus) to drag about 'oxen.' But Stephen recovered from this shock in due time, and has gone on ever since, calling his master 'boss.' We suppose this touch of 'republican simplicity' will maintain its ground along with the other sacred principles that certain persons hold on to so tightly that they suffer others, of real importance, to slip through their fingers.

Stephen was proud of his office that day. He liked his new mistress – there are no bossesses – and he particularly liked Miss Anna. His horses were used a good deal more than formerly, it is true; but this he rather liked too, having lived under the *régimes* of the two first Mrs McBrains. He was doubly satisfied because his team came in fresh, without having a hair turned, while that of *Madam*, as all the domestics now called Mildred, were white with foam. Stephen took no account of the difference in the distance, as he conceived that a careful coachman would have had his 'boss' up early enough to get over the ground in due season, without all this haste. Little did he understand the bosses that his brother-whip had to humour. She paid high, and had things her own way.

Anna thought Stephen had never driven so fast as he did that morning. The doctor handed her from the carriage, leading her and his wife directly up to the altar. Here the party was met by John and his uncle, the latter of whom facetiously styled himself the 'groomsman.' It is a ceremony much more easily done than undone – great as the facilities for the last are getting to be. In about five minutes, John Wilmeter and Anna Updyke were pronounced to be 'one flesh.' In five minutes more, Jack had his sweet, smiling, happy, tearful bride, in his own light vehicle, and was trotting away towards a pretty little place in Westchester, that he owns, and which was all ready to receive the young couple. The ponies seemed to understand their duty, and soon carried the bride and bridegroom out of sight.

'Them's awful trotters, them nags of Mr Jack Wilmington's,' said Stephen, as the double phaeton whirled away from the church door, 'and if Miss Anny doesn't disapprove on 'em, afore long, I'm no judge of a team. I'm glad, however, the young gentleman has married into our family, for he does like a hoss, and the gentleman that likes a hoss, commonly likes his vife.'

His remark was overheard by Dunscomb though intended only for the ears of the counsellor's coachman. It drew an answer, as might have been foreseen.

'I'm glad you approve of the connexion, Stephen,' said the counsellor, in his good-natured way. 'It is a great satisfaction to know that my nephew goes among friends.'

'Fri'nds, sir! Admirers is a better tarm. I'm a downright admirer of Mr Jack, he's sich tastes; always with his dog, or his gun, or his hoss, in the country; and I dares to say, with his books in town.'

'Not just all that, Stephen; I wish it were so; but truth compels me to own that the young rogue thinks quite as much of balls and suppers, and tailors, and the opera, as he does of Coke upon Lyttleton, or Blackstone and Kent.'

'Vell, that's wrong,' answered Stephen, 'and I'll uphold no man in vot's wrong, so long as I can do better. I know'd both them racers, having heard tell on 'em at the time they vos run, and I've heard good judges say, that timed the hosses, that Kent come in neck and neck, if justice had been done. Mr Jack will rectify, and come to see the truth afore long – mattermony will do that much for him. It's a great help to the seekers arter truth, is mattermony, sir!'

'That is the reason you have so much of it at Timbully, I suppose,' returned Dunscomb, nodding familiarly towards his friend the doctor, who had heard all that was said. 'If matrimony rectifies in this way, you must be three times right at home, Stephen.'

'Yes, sir,' answered the coachman, nodding his head in reply; 'and when a body does better and better, as often as he tries, there's no great harm in trying. Mr Jack vill come round in time.'

'I dare say he will, Stephen, when he has sown all his wild oats; though the dog pretends to like the code, and what is more, has the impudence to say he understands it.'

'Yes, sir, all wrong, I dares to say. But Miss Anna will set him right, as a righter young lady never sat on the back seat of a coach. I wish, now we're on the subject, 'Squire Dunscomb, to hear your ra'al opinion about them vild oats; vether they be a true thing, or merely a fancy consarning some vegetable that looks like the true feed. I've often heard of sich things, but never seed any.'

'Nor will you, Stephen, until the doctor turns short round, and renews his youth. Then, indeed, you may see some of the grain growing beneath your feet. It is doctor's food.'

'Meshy, and good for the grinders of old hosses, I dares to say.'

'Something of the sort. It's the harvest that age reaps from the broad-cast of youth. But we are keeping Mrs McBrain waiting. Stephen will take one less back with him than he brought, my dear lady.'

'I trust not. Mr McBrain has given me reason to hope for the pleasure of your company. Your nephew has carried off my daughter; the least you can do is to come and console me.'

'What is then to become of that dear, but unfortunate young lady?' glancing towards Mildred.

'She goes with her relatives, the Millingtons. Next week, we are all to meet at Rattletrap, you know.'

The next week the meeting took place as appointed.

'Here I am,' cried Dunscomb, 'truly and finally a bachelor, again. Now for the reign of misrule, negligence, and bad housekeeping. Sarah has left me; and John has left me; and Rattletrap will soon become the chosen seat of discomfort and cynicism.'

'Never the last, I should think,' answered Madame de Larocheforte, gaily, 'as long as you are its master. But why should you dwell alone here, in your declining years – why may I not come and be your housekeeper.'

'The offer is tempting, coming, as it does, from one who cannot keep house for herself. But you think of returning to Europe, I believe?'

'Never – or not so long as my own country is so indulgent to us women!'

'Why, yes; you are right enough in that, Mildred. This is woman's paradise, in a certain sense, truly; though much less attention is paid to their weakness and wants, by the affluent, than in other lands. In every Christian country but this, I believe, a wife may be compelled to do her duty. Here she is free as the air she breathes, so long as she has a care not to offend in one essential. No, you are right to remain at home, in your circumstances; that is to say, if you still insist on your mistaken independence; a condition in which nature never intended your sex to exist.'

'And yourself, sir! Did not nature as much intend that you should marry, as another?'

'It did,' answered Dunscomb, solemnly; 'and I would have discharged the obligation had it been in my power. You well know why I have never been a husband – the happy parent of a happy family.'

Mildred's eyes swam with tears. She had heard the history of her grandmother's caprice, and had justly appreciated the wrongs of Dunscomb. This it was not difficult for her to do, in the case of third parties, even while so obtuse on the subject of her own duties. She took the hand of her companion, by a stealthy and unexpected movement, and raised it still more unexpectedly to her lips. Dunscomb started; turned his quick glance on her face, where he read all her contrition and regrets. It was by these sudden exhibitions of right feeling and correct judgment that Madame de Larocheforte was able to maintain her position. The proofs of insanity were so limited in the range of its influence, occurred so rarely, now she was surrounded by those who really took an interest in her, and this not for the sake of her money, but for her own sake, that her feelings had become softened, and she no longer regarded men and women as beings placed near her, to prey on her means and to persecute her. By thus giving her affections scope, her mind was gradually getting to be easier, and her physical existence improved. McBrain was of opinion that, with care, and with due attention to avoid excitement and distasteful subjects, her reason might again be seated on its throne, and bring all the faculties of her mind in subjection to it.

At length the time for the visit of the young people arrived. Anxious to see happy faces assembled around him, Dunscomb had got Mildred, the McBrains, and the Millingtons, at Rattletrap, to do honour to the bride and groom. Good Mrs Gott had not been overlooked, and by an accident, Timms drove in at the gate, just as the whole party, including Jack and his blooming wife, were setting down to a late breakfast. The counsellor welcomed his man of all work, for habit renders us less fastidious in our associations than most of us imagine.

Timms was very complimentary to both of the young couples, and in a slight degree witty, agreeably to his own mode of regarding the offspring of that effort of the imagination.

'What do you think of Williams's getting married, 'Squire Dunscomb?' the attorney asked. 'There's a man for matrimony! He regards women and niggers as inferior beings.'

'Pray how do *you* regard them, Timms? The women only, I suppose?'

'Oh! dear, no, 'squire; as far as possible from that! I reverence the ladies, without whom our state in this life would be——'

'Single – I suppose you wish to say. Yes, that is a very sensible remark of yours – without women we should certainly all get to be old bachelors, in time. But, Timms, it is proper that I should be frank with you. Mildred de Larocheforte may manage to get a divorce, by means of some of the quirks of the law; but were she to be proclaimed single, by sound of trumpet, she would never marry *you*.'

'You are sharp on me this morning, sir; no one but the lady herself can say *that*.'

'There you are mistaken. I *know* it, and am ready to give my reasons for what I say.'

'I should be pleased to hear them, sir – always respect your reasoning powers, though I think no man can say whom a lady will or will not marry.'

'In the first place, she does not like you. That is one sufficient reason, Timms——'

'Her dislike may be overcome, sir.'

'Her tastes are very refined. She dislikes her present husband principally because he takes snuff.'

'I should have thought she might have discovered her feelings on that subject before she went so far.'

'Not as they manage matters in Europe. There, the suitor is not permitted to kiss his intended, as so often happens among ourselves, I fancy; and she had no opportunity of ascertaining how unpleasant snuff is. You chew and smoke, and she will endure neither.'

'I'll forswear both, rather than not be agreeable to dear Mary Monson.'

'Ah! my poor Timms, I see you are deeper in this affair than I had supposed. But I shall turn you over to Mrs Gott, who has promised to have an explanation with you, and who, I believe, will speak by authority.'

Timms was not a little surprised to see his old master very unceremoniously leave him, and the sheriff's wife occupy his place.

"Squire Timms,' the latter commenced, without a moment's hesitation, 'we live in a very strange world, it must be admitted. Gott says as much as this, and Gott is commonly right. He always maintained he never should be called on to hang Mary Monson.'

'Mr Gott is a very prudent man, but he would do well to take more care of his keys.'

'I have not been able to find out how that was done! Mary laughs when I ask her, and says it was witchcraft; I sometimes think it *must* have been something of the sort.'

'It was money, Mrs Gott, which kept Goodwin concealed to the last moment, and brought about half of all that happened.'

'You knew that Peter Goodwin was alive, and hid up at Mrs Horton's?'

'I was as much surprised, when he entered the court, as any one there. My client managed it all for herself. She, and her gold.'

'Well, you have the credit of it, Timms, let me tell you, and many in the county think it was very well done. I am your friend, and ever have been. You stood by Gott like a man, at his election, and I honour you for it. So I am about to give you a great proof of my friendship. Give up all thoughts of Mary Monson; she'll never have you.'

'What reasons have you for saying this?'

'In the first place, she is married already.'

'She may get a divorce. Besides her present husband is not a citizen. If I go to the senate, I intend to introduce a bill to prevent any but citizens getting married. If foreigners want wives, let them be naturalized!'

'You talk like a simpleton! Another reason why you should not think of Mary Monson is that you are unsuited to be her husband.'

'In what particular, I beg leave to ask?'

'Oh! in several. You are both too sharp, and would quarrel about your wit, in the very first month,' returned Mrs Gott, laughing. 'Take my advice, Timms, and cast your eyes on some Duke's county young woman, who has a natur' more like your own.'

Timms growled out a dissent to this very rational proposition, but the discussion was carried on for some time longer. The woman made an impression at last, and when the attorney left the house, it was with greatly lessened hopes for the future, and with greatly lessened zeal on the subject of the divorce.

It was singular, perhaps, that Mrs Gott had not detected the great secret of Mary Monson's insanity. So many persons are going up and down the country, who are mad on particular subjects, and sane on most others, that it is not surprising the intelligence and blandishments of a woman like Mildred should throw dust into the eyes of one as simple-minded as Mrs Gott. With the world at large, indeed, the *équivoque* was kept up, and while many thought the lady very queer, only a few suspected the truth. It may be fortunate for most of us that writs of lunacy are not taken out against us; few men, or women, being under the control of a good, healthful reason at all times, and on all subjects.

In one particular, Madame de Larocheforte was singularly situated. She was surrounded, in her ordinary associations, with newly married persons, who were each and all strenuously resolved to regard the relation in the most favourable point of view! Perhaps there is nothing on earth that so nearly resembles the pure happiness of the blessed, as the felicity that succeeds the entire union of two hearts that are wrapped up in each other. Such persons live principally for themselves, regarding the world at large as little more than their abiding place. The affinity of feeling, the community of thought, the steadily increasing confidence, which, in the end, almost incorporates the moral existence of two into one, are so many new and precious ties, that it is not wonderful the novices believe they are transplanted to a new and ethereal state of being. Such was in a measure, the condition of those with whom Mildred was now called on to associate most intimately. It is true, that the state of the doctor and his wife might be characterized as only happy, while those of the young people amounted to absolute felicity. Mildred had experienced none of the last, and very little of the first, on the occasion of her own marriage, which had been entered into more as a contract of reason, than a union of love. She saw how much she had missed, and profound was the grief it occasioned her.

'You seem very happy,' she remarked one day to Anna, as they were again threading the pretty little wood at Rattletrap – 'more than that – delighted would be a better word.'

'Jack is very kind to me, and the only complaint I have to make of him is, that he is more fond of me than I deserve. I tell him I tremble lest our happiness may not last!'

'Enjoy it while you may. It is so rare to find married persons who are so completely devoted to each other, that it is a pleasant sight to look upon. I never knew any of this, Anna.'

'I regret to hear it, dear mamma – it must be that you began wrong. There should be a strong attachment before the nuptial benediction is pronounced; then, with good hearts, and good principles, I should think almost any woman might be content with her fate.'

'It may be so,' returned Mildred, with a profound sigh; 'I suppose it *must* be so. We are created by God, to fulfil these kind offices to each other, and to love our husbands; and there must be something very wrong when different results follow. For myself, I ought never to have married at all. My spirit is too independent for matrimony.'

Anna was silent; for, possibly, she might have read 'headstrong' for 'independent.' The most truly independent thinkers are those who are willing to regard all sides of a subject, and are not particularly wedded to one. Mildred was acute enough to see that the beautiful young bride did not exactly like the allusion she had made to her new character.

'You do not agree with me?' she demanded quickly, bending forward to look into her companion's eyes.

'How can I, mamma Mildred! As I think no one, man or woman, should have a spirit that disqualifies her for the duties imposed by nature, which is merely the law of our great Creator, how can I agree to your notion of so much independence. We are not intended for all this independence, but have been placed here to do honour to God, and to try to render each other happy. I wish – but I am too bold, for one so young and inexperienced.'

'Speak freely, dear. I listen with pleasure – not to say with curiosity.'

'I am afraid, dear mamma, that the great guide of human conduct is not as much studied in France, as it should be. That teaches us the great lesson of humility. Without humility we are nothing – cannot be Christians – cannot love our neighbours as ourselves – cannot even love God, as it is our duty, as we ought to do.'

'This is very strange, Anna, coming from one of your age! Is it common for American girls to reason and feel in this way?'

'Perhaps not, though I hope more so than is commonly supposed. You will remember what a mother it is my good fortune to possess. But, since you really wish me to be frank with you, let me finish what I have to say. I suppose you know, Mildred, how much more you have to contend with than most of your sex?'

'Mons. de Larocheforte, you mean?'

'Not at all,' returned Mrs John Wilmeter, slightly smiling. 'I put all thought of contention with a husband out of the question. You know I have not been married long enough for that, and I could almost hope that the first day of such a scene might be the last of my life! John would cease to love me, if I quarrelled with him.'

'You will be an extraordinary pair, my dear, if scenes, as you call them, do not occasionally occur between you.'

'I do not expect faultlessness in Jack; and, as for myself, I know that I have very many motes to get rid of, and which I trust may, in a measure, be done. But let us return to the case of a woman, young, well-educated, handsome, rich to superfluity, and intellectual.'

'All of which are very good things, my child,' observed Mad. de Larocheforte, with a smile so covert as to be scarcely seen, though it betrayed to her companion the consciousness of her making the application intended – 'what next?'

'Wilful, a lover of power, and what she called independent.'

'Good and bad together. The two first, very bad, I acknowledge; the last, very good.'

'What do you understand by independence? If it mean a certain disposition to examine and decide for ourselves, under all the obligations of duty, then it is a good thing, a *very* good thing, as you say; but if it merely mean a disposition to do as one pleases, to say what one likes, and to behave as one may at the moment fancy, then it strikes me as a very bad thing. This independence, half the time, is only pride and obstinacy, dear mamma!'

'Well, what if it is? Men are proud and obstinate, too; and they must be fought with their own weapons.'

'It is easy to make smart speeches, but, by the difficulties I meet with in endeavouring to conquer my own heart, I know it is very hard to do right. I know I am a very young monitress——'

'Never mind that. Your youth gives piquancy to your instructions. I like to hear you.'

'Well, I will finish what I had to say. I have ever found that the best assistant, or it might be more reverent to say, the best mode of subduing error, was to comport ourselves with humility. Ah! my dear mamma, if you could understand how very strong the humble get to be in time, you would throw aside your cherished independence, and rely on other means to secure your happiness!'

Perhaps Mildred was as much struck with the circumstances under which this rebuke or admonition was given as with the advice itself. It had an effect, however, and Dunscomb coming in aid of his niece, this singular woman was gradually drawn from the exaggerated notions she had ever entertained of herself and her rights to the contemplation of her duties, as they are exercised in humility.

If there were no other evidence of the divine origin of the rules of conduct taught by the Redeemer than the profound knowledge of the human heart, that is so closely connected with the great lessons in humility everywhere given in his teachings, we conceive it would be sufficient in itself to establish their claim to our reverence. If men could be made to feel how strong they become in admitting their weaknesses; how clearly they perceive truth, when conscious of gazing at its form amidst the fogs of error; and how wise we may become by the consciousness of ignorance, more than half of the great battle in morals would be gained.

Humility was, indeed, a hard lesson for Mildred Millington to study. Her whole life had been in direct opposition to its precepts, and the great failing of her mind had a strong leaning to a love of power. Nevertheless, there is a still, searching process of correcting, so interwoven with the law of the New Testament, as to be irresistible when brought to aid us, in the manner prescribed by its own theory. No one knew this better than Dunscomb; and he so directed the reading, thoughts and feelings of his interesting charge, as to produce an early and a very sensible change on her character. The tendency to insanity is still there, and probably will ever remain; for it is not so much the consequence of any physical derangement as of organization; but it already promises to be so far controlled, as to leave its unhappy subject, generally rational, and, for most of her time, reasonably satisfied.

Dunscomb had several interviews with the vicomte – no–vicomte – whom he found a much more agreeable person than he had been prepared to meet, though certainly addicted to snuff. He was made acquainted with the mental hallucinations of his wife as well as with the fact of their being hereditary, when a great change came over the spirit of his dream! He had married to perpetuate the family de Larocheforte, but he had no fancy for a race of madmen. Dunscomb found him very reasonable, in consequence, and an arrangement was soon made, under the advice of this able counsellor, by means of which Mildred virtually became her own mistress. M. de Larocheforte accepted an ample provision from the estate, and willingly returned to Europe, a part of the world that is much more agreeable, usually, to men of his class than our own 'happy country.' His absence has proved a great assistance to those who have assumed the care of Mildred's mental state. As all the schemes for a divorce have been discontinued, – schemes that could have led to no strictly legal consequence, – and her husband has left the country, the mind of Mildred has become calmer, and the means have been found to bring her almost completely within the control of her reason.

We have very little to say of the other characters. Timms is still himself. He boasts of the fees he got in the great Mary Monson case. His prospects for the state Senate are far from bad, and should he succeed, we shall expect to see him whining about 'republican simplicity,' abusing 'aristocracy,' which in his secret heart, means a clean shirt, clean nails, anti-tobacco-chewing and anti-blowing-the-nose-with-the-fingers, and aiding anti-rentism. He is scamp enough for anything.

Williams is actually married, and, in reply to Timms's accounts of the fees, he intimates that Peter Goodwin's ghost would not have appeared, had *he* not 'been choked off.' It ought to be strange that these two men like to boast of their rascality; but it is in obedience to a law of our nature. Their tongues merely echo their thoughts.

The McBrains seem very happy. If the wife be an 'old man's darling,' it is not as a young woman. Dunscomb still calls her 'widow,' on occasions, but nothing can interrupt the harmony of the friends. It is founded on mutual esteem and respect.

Michael and Sarah promise well. In that family, there is already a boy, to its great-uncle's delight. The parents exult in this gift, and both are grateful.

We care little for Jack Wilmeter, though a very good fellow in the main. Anna loves him, however, and that gives him an interest in our eyes, he might not otherwise enjoy. His charming wife is losing her superfluous enthusiasm in the realities of life, but she seems to gain in womanly tenderness and warmth of healthful feeling, precisely in the degree in which she loses the useless tenant of her imagination.